The World and the Netherlands

The World and the Netherlands

*A Global History
from a Dutch Perspective*

*Edited by
Marjolein 't Hart, Manon van der Heijden
and Karel Davids*

BLOOMSBURY ACADEMIC
LONDON • NEW YORK • OXFORD • NEW DELHI • SYDNEY

BLOOMSBURY ACADEMIC
Bloomsbury Publishing Plc
50 Bedford Square, London, WC1B 3DP, UK
1385 Broadway, New York, NY 10018, USA
29 Earlsfort Terrace, Dublin 2, Ireland

BLOOMSBURY, BLOOMSBURY ACADEMIC and the Diana logo are trademarks of
Bloomsbury Publishing Plc

First published in Great Britain 2023

Copyright © Marjolein 't Hart, Manon van der Heijden and Karel Davids, 2023

Marjolein 't Hart, Manon van der Heijden and Karel Davids have asserted their right under the Copyright, Designs and Patents Act, 1988, to be identified as Editor of this work.

Translated by Vivien Collingwood. English language translation © Vivien Collingwood, 2023.

Cover image: Dutch East India Company in Amsterdam showing warehouses and shipyard. Hand-colored woodcut. (© Alamy Stock Photo)

The publisher gratefully acknowledges the support of the Dutch Foundation for Literature.

Nederlands letterenfonds
dutch foundation for literature

All rights reserved. No part of this publication may be reproduced or transmitted in any form or by any means, electronic or mechanical, including photocopying, recording, or any information storage or retrieval system, without prior permission in writing from the publishers.

Bloomsbury Publishing Plc does not have any control over, or responsibility for, any third-party websites referred to or in this book. All internet addresses given in this book were correct at the time of going to press. The author and publisher regret any inconvenience caused if addresses have changed or sites have ceased to exist, but can accept no responsibility for any such changes.

Every effort has been made to trace copyright holders and to obtain their permissions for the use of copyright material. The publisher apologizes for any errors or omissions and would be grateful if notified of any corrections that should be incorporated in future reprints or editions of this book.

A catalogue record for this book is available from the British Library.

A catalog record for this book is available from the Library of Congress.

ISBN: HB: 978-1-3501-9193-8
PB: 978-1-3501-9192-1
ePDF: 978-1-3501-9194-5
eBook: 978-1-3501-9195-2

Typeset by Deanta Global Publishing Services, Chennai, India
Printed and bound in Great Britain

To find out more about our authors and books visit www.bloomsbury.com and sign up for our newsletters.

CONTENTS

List of text boxes, maps, tables, charts, and figures viii

About the authors xiii

Preface xv

Introduction 1
0.1 *'How ordinary people lived the big changes'* 2
0.2 *Basic problems* 3
0.3 *Changes, phasing and demarcation in time and space* 5
0.4 *The structure of the book* 9

PART I
Before the Great Divergence, *c.* 1000–*c.* 1800

1   Introduction to Part I 13
1.1 *Population development and the natural environment* 13
1.2 *Long-distance connections* 16
1.3 *The three basic problems: Contours of change* 23

2   Growth and economic development before the Great Divergence 25
     KAREL DAVIDS

2.1 *Economic development in the world* 26
2.2 *The rise of the Dutch economy* 43
2.3 *Labour relations and income distribution* 52
2.4 *Industrialization and the Great Divergence* 56
     Summary 65

3   The struggle for power: Sociopolitical developments 67
    MARJOLEIN 'T HART

3.1 *International political relations and state formation* 68
3.2 *State formation in the Netherlands* 78
3.3 *Participation and political culture* 88
3.4 *Overseas colonization and the Atlantic revolutions* 96
    Summary 106

4   The tension between the community and the individual: Social-cultural developments 108
    MANON VAN DER HEIJDEN

4.1 *Patterns of marriage and family formation* 109
4.2 *Social order, social care and disciplining* 118
4.3 *A changing world view and the growth of the private sphere* 132
    Summary 143

5   Conclusion to Part I 145

PART II
After the Great Divergence, *c.* 1800–present day

6   Introduction to Part II 153

6.1 *Population development and the natural environment* 153
6.2 *Long-distance connections* 155
6.3 *The three basic problems: Contours of change* 160

7   Expansion, stagnation and globalization: Economic developments 163
    JEROEN TOUWEN

7.1 *Industrialization and the growth in world trade before the First World War* 164
7.2 *Conflict and stagnation, 1914–1945* 178
7.3 *Institutional renewal and economic growth after 1945* 184
7.4 *Changing priorities and new players, 1973–2010* 195
    Summary 205

8   State formation, democratization and social care: Sociopolitical developments 207
    LEO LUCASSEN

8.1 *Nation states, social engineering and international cooperation* 208
8.2 *Democratization and citizenship* 222
8.3 *Social policy and the rise of the welfare state* 230
    Summary 247

9   New opportunities, values and norms: Sociocultural developments 248
    LEX HEERMA VAN VOSS

9.1 *Demographic changes and the risks of existence* 249
9.2 *Social order and social mobility* 260
9.3 *Disciplining and counter-movements* 277
9.4 *Lifestyles, worldviews and the Netherlands as a 'model country'* 285
    Summary 295

10 Conclusion to Part II 297

Recommended literature 303

Index 310

LIST OF TEXT BOXES, MAPS, TABLES, CHARTS, AND FIGURES

Text box 2.1	Guilds in the world 40
Text box 2.2	The VOC in Asia 51
Text box 2.3	The abolition of the slave trade and slavery 54
Text box 3.1	The European state system, based on the sovereignty of nation states 77
Text box 3.2	Repertoires of collective action 81
Text box 3.3	The Financial Revolution 84
Text box 3.4	Economic, social and cultural capital 90
Text box 3.5	Habermas's theory of the public sphere 95
Text box 3.6	Colonialism and environmental awareness 97
Text box 3.7	Three phases in the colonization from Europe 98
Text box 3.8	The Patriot Movement, 1785–87 105
Text box 4.1	Risks of existence in the pre-industrial period 112
Text box 4.2	Neighbourhood organizations 116
Text box 4.3	Peace and reconciliation 124
Text box 4.4	Charivari, social control from below 127
Text box 4.5	The transition from family economy to family consumer economy 130
Text box 7.1	Latin America, stunted growth 169
Text box 7.2	Gerschenkron and catch-up growth 170
Text box 7.3	The Gold Standard 175
Text box 7.4	Keynesians and monetarists 183
Text box 7.5	Exchange rates after the Gold Standard 185
Text box 7.6	Economic growth and the environmental problem 188
Text box 7.7	Milestones in European cooperation 194
Text box 8.1	Direct and indirect rule 209
Text box 8.2	Types of nationalism 212
Text box 8.3	The origins of the European Union 214
Text box 8.4	The North exploits the South, 1815–30 217
Text box 8.5	Political system and protest. The environmental movement 232
Text box 8.6	Modernity and modernization 244

LIST OF TEXT BOXES, MAPS, TABLES, CHARTS, AND FIGURES

Text box 9.1	Natural disasters and the fragility of life	252
Text box 9.2	Unemployment in the economic crises of 1931, 1982 and 2009	257
Text box 9.3	Immigrants in the Netherlands after the Second World War	258
Text box 9.4	Racism, a tenacious nineteenth-century doctrine	281
Text box 9.5	The generation of the 1960s	286
Text box 9.6	Science and society in the nineteenth and twentieth centuries	294

Map 0.1	Map of the Netherlands, c. 2020	xviii
Map 1.1	Long-distance trade networks in the thirteenth century by the historical sociologist Janet Abu-Lughod	18
Map 2.1	China in the late Qing Empire	31
Map 2.2	The Atlantic World in the Early Modern period	61
Map 3.1	Towns in Europe, early sixteenth century	75
Map 3.2	The Dutch Republic, in *c.* 1650	86
Map 5.1	The most important towns in Europe, early nineteenth century	146
Map 6.1	The British world empire in *c.* 1900	158

Table 1.1	Estimated Population Trends in Different Parts of the World, 1000–1800	14
Table 1.2	Estimated Population Trends in Various European Countries, 1300–1800	14
Table 1.3	Urbanization in Various European Countries, 1300–1800	15
Table 1.4	Estimated Growth in Intercontinental Overseas Trade to and from Europe, 1500–1900	20
Table 1.5	The African Slave Trade, 1500–1900	21
Table 1.6	Cross-border Migration by Europeans, 1500–1850	21
Table 2.1	Average Harvest Yield per Seed for Sowing in Europe, 1300–1800	32
Table 2.2	Corvée Labour and Wage Labour on Rural Estates in Korczyn (Poland), 1533–1660	34
Table 2.3	The Occupational Structure of Holland/the Netherlands by Sector, in Percentages, Compared to Several Other European Countries, 1500–1800	44
Table 2.4	Estimated Income per Capita of the Population in the Netherlands, Compared with Several Other European Countries, 1500–1820	44
Table 2.5	Overseas Imports to the Netherlands, Great Britain and France, *c.* 1770	47
Table 2.6	Development of Imports to the Netherlands from Asia and the Western Hemisphere by Value, 1640–1780	48
Table 2.7	Estimated Value of Capital Holdings in Holland, in Millions of Guilders, 1650 and 1790	52
Table 2.8	Taxonomy of Labour Relations	53
Table 2.9	Real Daily Wages of Unskilled Construction Workers in European Towns, 1500–1850	56

Table 2.10	Real Daily Wages of Unskilled Labourers in India and the Yangzi Delta (China), Compared with Southern England, 1550–1850 58
Table 2.11	Estimate of Average Annual Growth in Income per Capita in England, 1700–1870 63
Table 2.12	Cost of Spinning a Pound of Raw Cotton Yarn, in 1784 Prices, England, 1760–1830 63
Table 3.1	Revolutionary Situations in the Netherlands, 1500–1800 91
Table 4.1	Average Age of Marriage of Women in Western Europe, Late Eighteenth Century 109
Table 4.2	Life Expectancy in Western Europe and East Asia until the Nineteenth Century 111
Table 4.3	Heads of Households in Leiden, and Poverty, 1622 117
Table 4.4	Social Stratification of the Population of Saxony, 1550 and 1750 119
Table 4.5	Estimated Production of Manuscripts and Printed Books in Europe, 1000–1800 138
Table 6.1	Population Trends in Europe and Different Parts of the World, 1700–2000 154
Table 6.2	Estimated Growth in Intercontinental Overseas Trade to and from Europe, 1700–1992 156
Table 6.3	Foreign Investment as a Percentage of Total World Production, 1870–1995 156
Table 7.1	Gross Domestic Product per Capita, 1820–2010 165
Table 7.2	Total Length of Railway Track per Country, 1850–1910 166
Table 7.3	World Energy Consumption, 1800–1990 189
Table 7.4	Economic Growth in North-western Europe, 1890–1992 191
Table 8.1	Central Government Spending in the Netherlands in 1850, 1900 and 1960 218
Table 8.2	Collective Expenditure by the Dutch State, as Percentage of GDP, 1815–2020 218
Table 8.3	Municipal Expenditure in Guilders per Capita of the Population in the Netherlands, 1862–1907 218
Table 8.4	Introduction of Universal Suffrage in Western Countries, 1840–1920 222
Table 8.5	Number of Strikes in the Netherlands by Decade, 1851–1940 225
Table 8.6	Introduction of Social Legislation in Various Countries, 1890–1965 235
Table 8.7	Typology of Police Services in European Countries 241
Table 9.1	Population Development in the Netherlands, Belgium and Germany, 1800–2000 253
Table 9.2	Immigrants and Their Descendants in the Netherlands, 1972–2020 260
Table 9.3	Employment by Sector in the Netherlands, Great Britain, the United States, Finland and Indonesia, 1800–2000 261
Table 9.4	Male Working Population of the Netherlands, 1899–1992 263

Table 9.5	Income Inequality in the Netherlands and the United States, 1800–2019 265
Table 9.6	Percentage of 20- to 24-year-olds in Higher Education, 1910–2005 273
Table 9.7	Women in the Labour Market in Europe and the United States, 1850–2019 276
Table 9.8	Number of Prisoners per 100,000 Inhabitants in Several European Countries, 1950–2018 279
Table 9.9	Percentage of Extramarital Births in Several European Countries, 1870–2019 287
Table 9.10	Legalization of Pressing Ethical Issues in a Number of Countries, 1920–2020 289
Table 9.11	Ownership of Consumer Durables in Industrialized Countries per 1,000 Inhabitants, 1937–2010 291
Table 9.12	Faith and Churchgoing in Different Countries, 1947–2014 293
Chart 2.1	The subsistence crisis in Amiens, 1693–4 27
Chart 3.1	The rise of towns in Central Europe, 1150–1950 73
Chart 7.1	The development of unemployment in the Netherlands and its most important trading partners, 1929–39 180
Chart 7.2	Growth in GDP and employment in the Netherlands, 1970–2013 198
Chart 7.3	GDP for several emerging economies, 1950–2018 201
Chart 7.4	Four periods of economic growth, 1900–2000 204
Chart 9.1	Stages in the Demographic Transition 250
Chart 9.2	Birth and mortality rates in the Netherlands (per thousand), 1804–2019 253
Chart 9.3	Migration to and from the Netherlands (per thousand) 1866–2018 256
Chart 9.4	Percentage of unemployment in the Netherlands during the crises of 1931, 1982 and 2009 256
Chart 9.5	Share of the total population of inhabitants born outside the Netherlands, 1600–2010 259
Chart 9.6	The Kuznets curve 264
Chart 9.7	Social origins of members of the Dutch House of Representatives, 1849–1967 266
Chart 9.8	Share of white-collar jobs in the working population, Germany and the Netherlands, 1850–1986 270
Figure 0.1	The relationships between the three basic problems in history 4
Figure 0.2	The relationships between the three basic problems in history and mental constructions 4
Figure 2.1	The pillar of the Holy Trinity in Olomouc (Czech Republic), erected to commemorate the end of a plague in 1715 28

Figure 2.2	Amsterdam price-list from January 1686, showing goods prices by type and/or origin 42
Figure 2.3	Ribbon mill depicted on the stamp of the Haarlem-based businessman Cornelis van den Brie, eighteenth century 49
Figure 3.1	*Riddarhuset* in Stockholm, Nobility Chamber of the Swedish Parliament, seventeenth century 70
Figure 3.2	Rioters plunder the house belonging to the tax collector on the Singel canal in Amsterdam, 1748 82
Figure 3.3	Fort Galle, Dutch East India settlement on the South-Western coast of Sri Lanka 100
Figure 4.1	Portrait of the *Dordtse Vierling* (quadruplets, including Elizabeth who died directly after birth), 1621 115
Figure 4.2	A granary with a fence and veranda in a Chinese village at the time of the Song dynasty 122
Figure 4.3	Rasp house (prison for young male criminals) in Amsterdam in the seventeenth century 129
Figure 4.4	Caricature of wig fashions in England in the late eighteenth century 141
Figure 7.1	Political cartoon on the power of Standard Oil from 1904 172
Figure 7.2	Kindleberger's spiral 182
Figure 7.3	The Mount Washington Hotel in Bretton Woods, New Hampshire 186
Figure 8.1	Dutch East Indies Army on patrol, *c.* 1935 220
Figure 8.2	Dutch poster on suffrage and pension legislation, early twentieth century 242
Figure 8.3	The Anti-Revolutionary Party as the champion of church, state, family and law, 1929 245
Figure 9.1	Advertisement poster from the 1920s 269
Figure 9.2	Women's labour in agriculture, 1898 274
Figure 9.3	Campaigning poster against alcohol abuse, 1932 280
Figure 9.4	Provos promoting the 'White bike' bicycle-sharing scheme, 1966 283

ABOUT THE AUTHORS

Karel Davids is Professor Emeritus of Economic and Social History at the Vrije Universiteit Amsterdam. His research interests are global history, maritime history and the history of knowledge, in particular the history of early modern technology. His publications in English include *The Rise and Decline of Dutch Technological Leadership. Technology, Economy and Culture in the Netherlands, 1350-1800* (2008), *Religion, Technology, and the Great and Little Divergences: China and Europe compared, c.700-1800* (2013), *Global Ocean of Knowledge, 1660-1860. Globalization and Maritime Knowledge in the Atlantic World* (2020) and (co-edited with Jan Lucassen) *A Miracle Mirrored. The Dutch Republic in European Perspective* (1995). See also https:// https://research.vu.nl/en/persons/ca-davids.

Marjolein 't Hart is Professor Emeritus of the History of State Formation in a Global Context at the Vrije Universiteit Amsterdam and research fellow at Huygens Institute for the History of the Netherlands (Amsterdam). Her research focuses on the history of and resistance to political power formation, war and economics, environmental history, urban networks and the role of money. 't Hart is the author of, among others, *The Making of a Bourgeois State. War, Politics and Finance during the Dutch Revolt* (1993) and *The Dutch Wars of Independence. Warfare and Commerce in the Netherlands, 1570–1680* (2014), and the co-author of *Globalization, Environmental Change, and Social History* (2010). See also https://research.vu.nl/en/persons/marjolein-t-hart.

Lex Heerma van Voss is research fellow at the International Institute of Social History in Amsterdam and Professor Emeritus of the History of Social Security at Utrecht University. He conducts research on the international comparative history of occupations in the period between 1600 and 2000, and on the North Sea coasts. He is the author of *De doodsklok van den goeden ouden tijd. De achturendag in de jaren twintig* (1994) and co-editor of two volumes *Wereldgeschiedenis van Nederland* (2018, 2022), *The Ashgate Companion to the history of Textile Workers, 1650–2000* (2010) and *Selling Sex in the City, Prostitution in World Cities, 1600 to the Present* (2017). See also https://iisg.amsterdam/en/about/staff/lex-heerma-van-voss.

Manon van der Heijden is Professor of Urban History at Leiden University. She specializes in the field of social history in the Early Modern period. She is the author of *Civic Duty. Public Services in the Early Modern Low Countries* (2012), *Women and Crime in Early Modern Holland* (2016) and co-editor of *The Uses of Justice in Global Perspective, 1600-1900* (2019) and *Women's Criminality in Europe, 1600-1914* (2020). See also https://www.universiteitleiden.nl/en/staffmembers/manon-van-der-heijden.

Leo Lucassen is Director of the International Institute of Social History in Amsterdam and Professor of Global Labour and Migration History at Leiden University. He specializes in migration history, urban history and sociopolitical developments in modern states. Among his publications are: *The Immigrant Threat. The Integration of Old and New Migrants in Western Europe since 1850* (2005); co-editor of *Globalising Migration History. The Eurasian Experience (16th-21st Centuries)* (2014); co-editor of *The Encyclopedia of Migration and Minorities in Europe. From the 17th Century to the Present* (2011); and co-editor of *Borders and Mobility Control in and between Empires and Nation-States* (2022). See also https://iisg.amsterdam/nl/about/staff/leo-lucassen.

Jeroen Touwen is Associate Professor of Economic and Social History at Leiden University. He wrote his doctoral thesis on the economic history of colonial Indonesia, and is now researching the economic history of the Netherlands in international comparative perspective. His publications include: *Extremes in the Archipelago. Trade and Economic Development in the Outer Islands of Indonesia, 1900–1942* (2001) and *Coordination in Transition. The Netherlands and the World Economy, 1950–2010* (2014). See also https://www.universiteitleiden.nl/en/staffmembers/jeroen-touwen.

Preface

Several years ago, we conceived a plan to write a new textbook on social and economic history. The aim was to produce a book that would give university and college students, as well as other interested readers, a concise, up-to-date overview of the current state of knowledge in this field. We would pay the requisite attention to Dutch history, of course, but always in relation to developments in other parts of the world, both within Europe and beyond, while embedded in academic theory. We bear in mind the wise words of the American baseball star 'Yogi' Berra: 'In theory there is no difference between theory and practice. In practice there is.' Drawing on the latest research, the textbook would cover a long period: a thousand years, no less. After all, when viewed from the perspective of global history and current Dutch historiography, the developments that took place before 1500 are just as important as those that occurred after 1500 or 1750. The new textbook would also reveal as many connections as possible between economic, social, political and cultural-mental developments.

The result of our enterprise, which began in 2007, is this book: *The World and the Netherlands: A Global History from a Dutch Perspective*. As the reader will immediately see from the table of contents, the book consists of two parts, each containing three chapters, an introduction and a conclusion. The first part covers the period from *c.* 1000 CE until what is known as the 'Great Divergence' between Europe and Asia in *c.* 1800. The second part covers the period between the Great Divergence and the early twenty-first century. The structure of the book is explained in the general introduction. In each chapter, in addition to the running text – which is supported by tables, charts, maps and figures – the reader will find several text boxes that highlight particular topics in more detail. These can be read in relation to the surrounding text or separately. The book concludes with a list of recommended literature and an index. There is also a supporting website (https://www.bloomsburyonlineresources.com/the-world-and-the-netherlands), where readers will find a glossary, questions about the material, files that delve into major debates and issues in the field, and an extended bibliography for each chapter.

The book is the outcome of a collaborative process between six authors, each of whom was responsible for one of the main chapters. Karel Davids wrote Chapter 2, Marjolein 't Hart Chapter 3, Manon van der Heijden Chapter 4, Jeroen Touwen Chapter 7, Leo Lucassen Chapter 8 and Lex Heerma van Voss Chapter 9. The introduction and Chapters 1, 5, 6 and 10 were written by Karel Davids and Marjolein 't Hart. Marjolein, Manon and Karel were responsible for the coordination and final editing of the book.

While writing the book, the authors frequently discussed and commented on each other's chapters. We also received helpful and inspiring feedback from the following participants in a workshop held at Columbia University, New York, in June 2010, where we presented our ideas for this textbook: Julia Adams, Carolyn Arena, Laura Cruz, Philip Gorski, Evan Haefeli, Martha Howell, Ira Katznelson, Wim Klooster, Richard Lachmann, Anne McCants, Steven Pincus, Ariel Rubin, Margaret Schotte, Pamela Smith, Carl Strikwerda, Wayne te Brake and Carl Wennerlind. In addition, helpful suggestions came from numerous colleagues, among whom are Ariadne Schmidt, Marlou Schrover and Anton Schuurman. All chapters received a thorough update for the English edition.

We are also grateful for the enthusiasm and expertise of the Bloomsbury team that made the publication of *The World and the Netherlands* possible, with Rhodri Mogford and Laura Reeves in Editorial, Emma Tranter in Production, and Joseph Kreuser and Wei Ming Kam in Marketing. In the first, and Dutch edition, we received inestimable support from Eva Wijenbergh, Juliette Geers, Aranka van der Borgh, Geert van der Meulen and other staff at Uitgeverij Boom. Vivienne Collingwood did an excellent job in translating the text into English. Her kind, proactive attitude helped us solve numerous problems regarding terminology.

On behalf of the authors,
Marjolein 't Hart, Manon van der Heijden and Karel Davids
August 2022

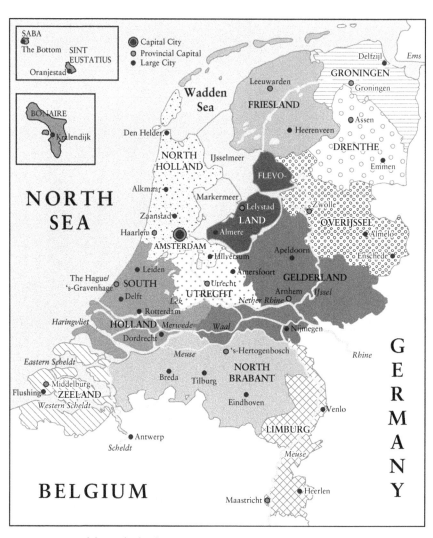

MAP 0.1 *Map of the Netherlands, c. 2020.*
Source: Wikimedia Commons, public domain.

Introduction

This is a textbook on economic and social history that examines the connections between developments in the world and the Netherlands between *c.* 1000 CE and the early twenty-first century. It is a new type of textbook; we aim to go beyond the old national frameworks, present Dutch history in the context of global history and take account of recent historiography.

Since the end of the Cold War (1989), the rapid expansion of the European Union and increasing globalization – as shown by the explosive growth of international capital flows, the breathtaking rise of the Internet and the phenomenal spread of mobile phone technologies, for example – it has seemed harder to achieve a clear view of the world. The 'state of the world' can no longer be summed up on a Sunday-afternoon radio talk show, as it used to be. As the connections with the outside world become denser and more complex, there is a growing need in the Netherlands and in other countries to profile ourselves more as groups, regions or nations. Increasing unpredictability has been met with loud calls for the protection of people's 'identities'.

Historiography, by contrast, has shown the opposite trend. More and more historians are moving away from the relatively closed circle of national historiography and towards the more open, spacious sphere of what is now known as 'global history', 'world history' or 'transnational history', where the traditional dividing lines between nations, epochs and sub-disciplines are gradually fading. Likewise, historians who focus on the history of a single country in a single period are increasingly examining the interconnections between their 'own' research field and the outside world, and paying more attention to comparisons.

The changes that have occurred in the world and in the Netherlands, and the relations between them, are the focus of this book. We are guided by the following questions: What are the similarities or differences between developments in the Netherlands and other countries, to what extent has Dutch history been influenced by other countries, and how far has the Netherlands influenced developments elsewhere? At certain points, the history of the Netherlands diverged remarkably from developments in the West and the rest of the world, and at times the Netherlands clearly influenced what happened in other parts of the globe. But we shall also see that the Netherlands often took paths that had been taken by other countries, too. Connections and comparisons such as these will be traced over the following chapters.

0.1
'How ordinary people lived the big changes'

In this book, we approach developments in the world and the Netherlands from the perspective of economic and social history. To quote the American historian and sociologist Charles Tilly, the objective of this approach is to describe and analyse 'how ordinary people lived the big changes'. We will therefore consider both major, fundamental changes in history, and the ways in which ordinary people experienced and reacted to them. What exactly did large-scale changes such as industrialization, globalization or the rise and fall of states involve, and why did they happen? How did these changes affect the lives of ordinary people? How did people try to respond to these developments, and how did they attempt to shape them? These are the questions that drive economic and social historians. When answering them, they tend to focus on the *collective* aspects of human existence: they examine how people form groups (or are grouped), how they act collectively, their shared experiences and opinions, how groups of people differ (or want to differ) from one another and how they enter into conflicts or make agreements with other groups. Groups can be formed on the basis of all kinds of criteria: well-being, lifestyle, power, occupation, generation, religion, sex, origin and so forth; and combinations of criteria are also possible.

A further characteristic of the economic and social historian's approach to the past is the attention paid to both the long and the short term. Economic and social history does not focus primarily on a particular event or period, but on developments. The duration of these developments can range from a few years to a number of decades or even several centuries, meaning that the traditional dividing lines between periods (the Middle Ages, the modern age, the post-war period) become less significant. Taking a long-term perspective is not only important because changes often occur very gradually, but also because events that might appear to have happened very rapidly, such as revolutions, may have roots that stretch far back into the past, and because something that started to happen a very long time ago may still resonate today. Urbanization in the Late Middle Ages and the Early Modern period, the growth of long-distance trade and the division between the Northern and the Southern Low Countries all have left their mark on present-day Dutch society.

Economic and social historians take a problem-oriented approach. They focus on specific, clearly defined historical problems that they attempt to solve in a systematic way. This is often done by using a combination of description, analysis and comparison, making frequent use of quantitative data and insights and methods from related disciplines, including sociology, economics, anthropology, geography and political science. A work of economic and social history – such as this textbook – will usually contain descriptive sections as well as tables, charts and theoretical argumentation based on social-scientific concepts. In this way, economic and social historians work at the interface between the humanities and the social and behavioural sciences.

0.2
Basic problems

Like many other textbooks on social and economic history, this book takes a problem-oriented approach. We describe and analyse the developments in the Netherlands and the rest of the world with reference to several basic problems. These are the general problems encountered by human societies; problems that people have wrestled with over the ages, regardless of time or place. These basic problems can be summarized under the headings 'income', 'power' and 'risks', and each covers a number of aspects.

a. *Income:* the problem of acquiring and distributing income. This covers questions such as: How is the economy structured? How many goods and services are produced? How is this linked to technological developments? How is wealth distributed? How could we describe the patterns of consumption? Which groups influence the acquisition and distribution of income, and in what ways?

b. *Power:* the problem of forming and distributing power. This includes questions such as: How is access to power regulated? Which groups are excluded from this? Which groups influence the degree and forms of disciplining and social control? Which groups determine frameworks of social cohesion? How does state formation work?

c. *Risks of existence:* the problem of the fragility of existence. Here we address questions such as: How are people, individually or collectively, able to manage or limit the risks of existence (illness, disability, old age, mortality, unemployment, poverty, disasters, war, etc.)? What measures can they take, or which institutions or organizations can they form to do this? To what extent are access to and the quality of facilities equal for all kinds of groups?

These three basic problems are linked, of course, because there are interchanges between them. Political power can magnify the risks of existence, for example, as in the case of war; but the government can also ensure that risks are managed more effectively or reduced, and economic growth can increase the scope for taking social measures to fight sickness and unemployment, and so forth. The interactions between these influences are shown in the following diagram (Figure 0.1).

This diagram is incomplete, however. When dealing with any problem, people's actions are shaped by their customs, traditions, ideas, convictions or beliefs. These, in turn, are shaped by their options with regard to the distribution of income and power, and the nature and extent of the risks of

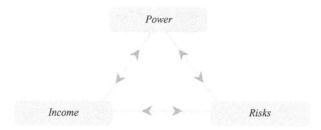

FIGURE 0.1 *The relationships between the three basic problems in history.*
© *Karel Davids and Marjolein 't Hart.*

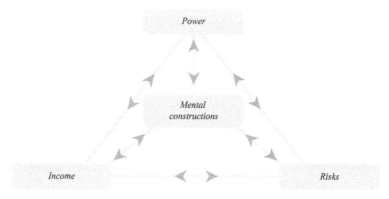

FIGURE 0.2 *The relationships between the three basic problems in history and mental constructions.*
© *Karel Davids and Marjolein 't Hart.*

existence. At the same time, ideas and beliefs also shape the development of wealth, power relations or social arrangements, institutions and organizations. These actions are guided by what we shall describe in this book as 'mental constructions'. In Figure 0.2 they form a separate component. As shown in the diagram, mental constructions both shape the three problem fields and are in turn influenced by the circumstances in these problem fields.

It is no accident that mental constructions lie at the heart of the diagram. Views on identity, justice or honourable behaviour, for example, cannot be separated into economic, sociocultural or sociopolitical spheres. Likewise, the economy only functions thanks to the existence of specific norms and values, such as confidence in the currency, opinions on what constitutes a fair wage or consumer preferences for certain products or services: e-books rather than paper books, designer suits rather than ready-to-wear clothing, eating out rather than microwave dinners. Moreover, mental constructions function as a connecting link: if the distribution of income is perceived as being unfair, this can have an effect on power relations and motivate people to act within sociocultural networks. The same views (e.g. in the religious sphere) can regulate access to power and institutions providing social support. A world view that presents the Netherlands as part of 'the' West or as belonging to 'the' Calvinist stronghold has far-reaching consequences for all kinds of areas, not least the political-military field. The fact that mental constructions have been placed at the heart of Figure 0.2 does not mean that they form the most important element of this book, but we shall return to them frequently in the description and analysis.

0.3
Changes, phasing and demarcation in time and space

The basic problems of income, power and risks are a constant in human society, but they can be tackled in different ways. The solutions to these problems can change over time as a result of long-term, fundamental processes, such as population growth, urbanization, increasing long-distance migration, industrialization, growth in international trade, democratization, religious reform, rationalization, state formation and nation-building, imperialism or European unification.

Researchers usually classify major changes in recent centuries under the heading of 'modernization'. Until recently, 'modernization theory' had many proponents. This theory asserts that the transformation of a 'traditional' society into an industrialized society always follows a standard pattern; that this standard pattern consists of a complex of mutually dependent changes in the demographic, economic, institutional, social and cultural spheres; and that the outcome of the transformation is roughly the same in all highly developed countries. These days, few still hold this view. Although today's societies are still regularly described as 'modern' (and the period between 1500 and 1800 is commonly referred to as 'Early Modern'), 'modernization' as an overarching concept has become obsolete in scholarship. That is because it is overly suggestive of a one-dimensional, linear course of development; as though everything used to be traditional and under developed, and that all societies will eventually reach the same 'endpoint'.

Historical research shows, though, that societies in the past were *different*, above all else, and that the path to today's societies could (and can) be taken in different ways, with different consequences for different social groups. Outcomes can vary by region. Modern societies in Western Europe may be different from those in the United States, Russia, Japan or China, but it is not possible to say which is the most 'modern'. In any case, Western European societies can no longer be seen as a general yardstick. It is better to conceive of modernity as a programme of core values pursued by certain groups, than as a description of a historical situation or historical process. These core values include 'economic growth', 'equality', 'individual freedom', 'self-determination', 'emancipation', 'mobility', or 'primacy of reason', for example, but the emphasis of the programme can differ by group, time or place. 'Modernity' is thus a plural, programmatic concept, and it is in that sense that it will be used in this book.

Another general concept that frequently appears in this book is that of 'globalization'. Globalization refers to the expansion and intensification of relationships between people on a global scale. In addition to economic facets, these relationships also have cultural, social, political or ecological aspects. Globalization need not mean that everywhere in the world increasingly resembles everywhere else; as well as homogenization or convergence, there are also trends towards divergence. Indeed, divergence can occur precisely because countries are becoming more closely intertwined: industrialization in the metropole, for example, may go hand in hand with de-industrialization in the colonies. Although globalization is therefore a rather amorphous concept, it is nevertheless a useful tool for describing certain large-scale changes that have occurred over the past millennium.

The timing, nature, causes and consequences of globalization between 1000 CE and the present day are the subject of a lively debate between historians and social scientists. Aspects of this debate will be addressed later in this book. Here it is sufficient to say that globalization, like modernization, has not followed a single, fixed pattern. Globalization did not begin in the late twentieth century, but much earlier, and the expansion and intensification of global connections took place in waves, with various ups and downs. Before the sixteenth century, in any case, Europe occupied a decentralized, even rather peripheral, place in the web of global connections; and within Europe, the Northern Netherlands played only a marginal role until the Late Middle Ages. Until that time, the most important interchanges in the world were situated in China and the Islamic world. Within Europe between 1200 and 1500, the economic centres were located in Northern and Central Italy, Southern Germany/Rhineland, Flanders/Northern France, Catalonia and the Hanseatic cities along the Baltic Sea.

From the late fifteenth century, various movements emerged that would radically change this pattern. A process of transoceanic expansion began from the Iberian Peninsula, aided by Italian knowledge and capital, leading to new connections with Africa, the Americas and Asia. Within Europe from the late sixteenth century, the economic centre of gravity shifted from the Mediterranean towards the Atlantic coast and the North Sea region, giving North-western Europe a head start in productivity and income. This development is also known as the 'Little Divergence'; 'little' in comparison to the 'Great Divergence.' In the eighteenth century, Britain emerged as a new economic centre that, as the cradle of the Industrial Revolution, contributed to the sharply growing gap in wealth that emerged between North-western Europe and Asia after 1800: the Great Divergence.

Like globalization, the concept of the Great Divergence – which was introduced by the sinologist Kenneth Pomeranz – is also subject to debate. Historians disagree about precisely when and to what extent levels of prosperity in Europe and Asia began to diverge. The arguments in this debate will be discussed later in this book, but what we can say for sure is that the Great Divergence was 'great' because of its large-scale, global consequences. From *c.* 1800, a growing gap emerged between the industrialized part of the world, namely Western Europe, North America and later also Australia and Japan, and the less prosperous part, namely Asia, Africa, and large parts of South and Central America. For many years, this latter group was also known as the 'Third World', in contrast to the 'First World' (the capitalist West) and the 'Second World' (communist Europe and Asia). In addition, from *c.* 1800, globalization speeded up in comparison to previous centuries. Since then, global connections have expanded and intensified considerably. It is no accident that the stock market crash of 1929 and the credit crisis of 2008 are described as '*global* crises', and that we refer to the First and Second *World* Wars. International migration expanded and 'Americanization' became a worldwide phenomenon.

The Great Divergence thus marks a clear turning point in world history, with economic as well as political and sociocultural aspects. It was not an abrupt transition; its causes can be traced back to the preceding centuries. In the late eighteenth century and early nineteenth century, however, more and more people noticed that the parameters in the problem fields of income, power and risks were changing. History is often written as a path-dependent process, in which the course of later developments is largely dependent on specific events or choices made in a more-or-less distant past. The period between 1750 and 1850 was a remarkably 'open' period in history, with many opportunities to branch off from previously followed paths and to choose from a range of new ones. The decisions made at that time and the paths that were followed would determine global economic, political and sociocultural relations for many years to come. In this textbook, we will therefore use the 'mega-event' of the Great Divergence as the key dividing line to phase global changes.

This book will discuss the relationship between developments in the Netherlands and these global changes. In view of the main question formulated earlier, more specifically, we describe and analyse the extent to which, the ways in which and when the Netherlands was a 'plaything' or a 'key player' (or one of the key players) in the Great Divergence and the Little Divergence. Was the Netherlands a trendsetter or a trend-follower? We shall see that the phasing of certain developments in the Netherlands sometimes differed from that in other countries.

The period covered by this book runs from *c.* 1000 CE to the beginning of the twenty-first century. The choice of end point requires little explanation. Tracing the course of events through to the present helps to deepen our understanding of the background to the current situation in the Netherlands and the world. We decided to begin our account in *c*. 1000 CE, for it was only then that a large part of the area that is now called 'the Netherlands' was brought under cultivation and populated. The changes that were set in motion at that time would leave their mark on social developments for centuries. On a global scale, too, radical changes took place around 1000 CE. In the Chinese Empire under the Song dynasty and in the Islamic world, from the Middle East to Southern Spain, an economic and cultural dynamic developed with effects that would penetrate far into the rest of Asia and Europe.

In the previous paragraph, 'the Netherlands' was formulated somewhat cautiously, and not without reason. The Netherlands is a historical construction, and emerged gradually as a political unit. The current borders of Dutch territory were not drawn until after 1830. There is a large overlap with what used to be the Republic of the United Netherlands, but prior to this, the areas that now constitute the Netherlands were formally part of composite dynastic states (such as Bavaria, Burgundy or the Spanish Hapsburg empire), including territories that now belong to other states in Europe or beyond (such as Belgium, France, Germany, Spain and Italy). In addition, from the early seventeenth century the Dutch ruled various regions in Asia, Africa and the Americas that are nowadays almost all independent states or form part of independent states, such as Indonesia, India, Sri Lanka, South Africa, Ghana, Brazil, Suriname, Guyana and the United States. Indeed, the 'Kingdom of the Netherlands', to which the Netherlands belongs, still stretches across the Western Hemisphere; its neighbours not only include Belgium and Germany, but also Venezuela and a French territory in the Caribbean.

Writing about the Netherlands, the Dutch and Dutch history thus inevitably involves making certain geographical choices. How narrowly or how broadly should we interpret these concepts? We opted for a pragmatic approach. The 'Dutch' to whom we refer are the people who live in the geographical area that today forms the state of the Netherlands on the European continent. Thus, this textbook is not about the Low Countries as a whole, nor does it offer a complete history of the Dutch global empire. We do describe and analyse links between the Netherlands and other areas within and beyond Europe, of course, and we also compare developments in the Netherlands with those in other countries within and beyond Europe. In addition, we often refer to the Southern Netherlands (which largely overlaps with modern-day Belgium) and to overseas territories with which the Dutch have long maintained intensive ties (such as Indonesia).

'The world' is likewise interpreted in a pragmatic way. Some chapters, mainly the economic ones, virtually cover the entire world, but the sociopolitical and sociocultural chapters tend to be limited to those areas with which the Netherlands had the most ties, such as North-western Europe and the United States. We frequently look to China for comparison, not because it offers a model for the 'rest of the world', but because of the availability of thorough economic and socio-historical research.

0.4
The structure of the book

This book is structured both chronologically and thematically. The main division is chronological: Part I concerns the period before the Great Divergence, and Part II concerns the period afterwards. The first part begins in *c.* 1000 CE and runs to around 1800, while the second part begins in *c.* 1800 and runs until the beginning of the twenty-first century. In order to understand some of the developments properly, it is occasionally necessary to deviate from these time periods. For example, we sometimes need to look beyond 1800, or to begin earlier than the year 1000 or 1800. Moreover, on several occasions, we see that the timing of certain changes in the Netherlands was not identical to that in other countries. Sometimes an economic, political or cultural change began earlier, sometimes later.

The changes in the world and in the Netherlands, and the relationship between them, had different layers or aspects. In this book, we have allowed for this complexity as far as possible. We address a broad spectrum of layers and aspects of historical reality: geography and the environment, economics and demography, state formation and empires, politics and ideology, social relations and mental constructions. In addition, we always consider the connections between these historical layers and aspects. In each part of the book they are grouped thematically under headings: economic, sociopolitical and sociocultural developments. Each part opens with a chapter on economic developments, not because we believe that these are all-determining, but because we think that the major changes in the world and the Netherlands can best be explained if we begin with this aspect.

Each chapter tackles the different basic problems (income, power, risks of existence), focusing on a single basic problem each time. To make a distinction that is commonly used in the social sciences, in some chapters we consider developments primarily from a structure-oriented perspective, in other chapters mainly from a more actor-oriented angle, or from a combination of the two. When taking a structure-oriented perspective, the emphasis is on large-scale, more anonymous, processes. When following an actor-oriented angle, we take greater account of the influence of people – with their feelings, convictions, ideas and decisions, both collectively and at the individual level. The chapters are thus structured as follows:

>In the chapters on economic developments, the emphasis is on the basic problem of income, and we mainly follow a structure-oriented approach. These are the chapters that pay most attention to globalization, because economic phenomena often go beyond political borders. Attention is also paid to developments and decision-making at the national level.

>In the chapters on sociopolitical developments and state formation, the emphasis is on the problem of power, and we take both a structural perspective and an actor-oriented approach. The international context for developments in the Netherlands is mainly Europe, specifically North-western Europe. The national level is the most important unit of comparison.

>In the chapters on sociocultural developments, we focus on the basic problem of risks of existence, and mainly take an actor-oriented approach. In doing so, we cover arrangements, institutions and organizations, such as marriage, justice, guilds, unions and ecclesiastical bodies, and pay considerable attention to differences, similarities and relationships between certain groups (such as estates, classes, men/women, heterosexuals/homosexuals, natives/migrants). Mental constructions play a key role. Here, too, the international context is largely North-western Europe.

The reader will note that in each part, some topics, such as the standard of living, poor relief or migration, are addressed in more than one chapter. That is logical, because these themes can be approached from several perspectives. It is also the case that certain topics that in the first part are discussed primarily in the chapter on sociocultural developments, such as poor relief, are addressed in the second part in the chapter on sociopolitical developments. This reflects the changing role of the state after 1800, something that is addressed at length in Part II.

In the introductions to each part, we first describe population developments, the environment and long-distance connections between different parts of the world, and sketch the contours of the major economic, sociopolitical and sociocultural changes. In the conclusions to Parts I and II, we discuss the extent of the differences between societies, we look at the relationships between them, as summarized in Figure 0.2, and we consider how far the Netherlands was a 'plaything' of or 'key player' in global change.

PART I

Before the Great Divergence, *c.* 1000–*c.* 1800

1

Introduction to Part I

Prior to the Great Divergence, the world was constantly in flux, as it is today, but the changes occurred at a different pace. Before we look in more detail at the economic, sociopolitical and sociocultural changes that took place between 1000 CE and the late eighteenth century, in this introduction we first sketch out the contours of this world that was both similar to and different from ours. How many people lived on earth at that time, and where did they live? What changes occurred in the natural surroundings in which they lived? To what extent and how were different parts of the world connected? How can we describe the overall changes that occurred in relation to income, power and risks? These questions are addressed in the following sections.

1.1
Population development and the natural environment

Prior to 1800, censuses were rarely held. For this reason, the figures for population size in this period are almost invariably based on estimates. It is estimated that the total population of the world grew from *c*. 260 million people in 1000 to *c*. 950 million people in around 1800. Of the total world population at this time, around one-half to two-thirds lived in Asia, and one-sixth to one-fifth in Europe. Europe had fewer inhabitants than China, Africa or the Indian subcontinent, but more than America (Table 1.1).

Within Europe, the most populous areas were France, Italy, Spain, Germany, Austria/Hungary and Russia. In the late eighteenth century, England and Scotland (united from 1707) joined this leading group. In terms of population size, the Netherlands and the Southern Netherlands (roughly present-day Belgium) were among the smaller European countries, and in the same category as Switzerland, Portugal, Ireland, Poland and Scandinavia (Table 1.2).

TABLE 1.1 *Estimated Population Trends in Different Parts of the World, in Millions, 1000–1800*

	Europe (excl. Russia)	**Africa**	**India Pakistan Bangladesh**	**China**	**America**
1000	30		40	59	
1200	49		69	115	
1300	79		100	96	
1350	54				
1500	70	87	95	103	42
1600	91		145	160	
1700	102	107	175	150	12
1800	154	102	180	330	24

Source: Malanima, *Pre-modern European economy*, 4, 7, 10.

TABLE 1.2 *Estimated Population Trends in Various European Countries, in Millions, 1300–1800*

	1300	*1400*	*1500*	*1600*	*1700*	*1800*
France	16.0	12.0	15.0	18.5	21.5	29.0
Italy	12.5	8.0	9.0	13.3	13.5	18.1
Spain	5.5	4.5	5.0	6.8	7.4	10.5
Germany	13.0	8.0	11.0	16.2	14.1	24.5
Austria + Hungary	10.0	9.0	11.5	12.8	15.5	24.3
(European) Russia	15.0	11.0	15.0	16.0	13.0	35.0
England + Scotland	5.5	3.4	4.3	5.4	6.6	10.9
Southern Netherlands	1.4	1.2	1.3	1.3	1.9	2.9
The Netherlands	0.8	0.6	0.9	1.5	1.9	2.1

Source: Malanima, *Pre-modern European economy*, 9.

Around 1000 CE, the great majority of the world's population lived in rural areas. Urbanization had yet to advance in most parts of the world.

Even in the areas that were most urbanized at that time, the Middle East and China, it is estimated that no more than 5 per cent of the total population lived in towns. One of the largest centres was Baghdad, with around 500,000 inhabitants. In *c.* 1200, more than one million people lived in Hangzhou, China.

Rural life continued to be the norm in the following centuries, although urbanization did increase slightly in certain parts of the world, mainly in Europe. While the share of the Chinese population who lived in towns of 10,000 or more inhabitants was yet to exceed 4 per cent in the eighteenth century, in Europe (excluding Russia) this figure was 8–9 per cent, and in Japan, 12 per cent. In 1800, there were six cities in the world with more than 500,000 inhabitants; three of them were in Asia (Beijing, Canton and Edo (Tokyo)), and three in Europe (Constantinople (Istanbul), Paris and London). Strikingly, as we can see from Table 1.3, the pattern of urbanization from the Late Middle Ages onwards differed somewhat from that of the total population. The leading group did not include France, Germany and Russia, but Italy, Spain, the Southern Netherlands and – after 1500, in any case – the Netherlands. They were joined by England and Scotland in the eighteenth century.

TABLE 1.3 *Urbanization in Various European Countries, 1300–1800: Percentage of Total Population Living in Towns with 10,000 or More Inhabitants (estimated)*

	1300	*1400*	*1500*	*1600*	*1700*	*1800*
France	5.2	4.7	5.0	6.3	8.7	8.9
Italy *North and Central*	18.0	12.4	16.4	14.4	13.0	14.2
Italy *South*	9.4	3.3	12.7	18.6	16.1	21.0
Spain	12.1	10.2	11.4	14.5	9.6	14.7
Germany	3.4	4.1	4.1	4.4	5.4	6.1
Austria + Hungary	0.6	0.5	0.8	1.6	1.7	3.2
(European) Russia	2.1	2.3	2.0	2.4	2.1	3.6
England	4.0	2.5	2.3	6.0	13.2	22.3
Scotland			2.3	1.5	5.3	23.9
Southern Netherlands	18.8	17.4	21.7	18.6	21.3	16.6
The Netherlands			17.8	29.5	32.5	28.6

Source: Malanima, *Pre-modern European economy*, 246; De Vries, *European urbanization*, 39.

The percentage of town-dwellers depended on agricultural productivity to a large extent. This, in turn, was closely linked to the climate. Climate research has shown that the average temperature on earth, at least in the Northern Hemisphere, fluctuated substantially over the longer term. The period between *c.* 1000 and the late thirteenth century was a time of rising temperatures, and agricultural production increased as a result. This was the period when Europe's population grew most rapidly (see Table 1.1). For this reason, most towns in Europe date from that time. This was followed by a prolonged fall in the average temperature, which reached its low-point between *c.* 1570 and 1730. This 'Little Ice Age' did not come to an end until the nineteenth century. Since then, average temperatures have shown an upward trend again.

Not only was Europe's growing population absorbed by new towns from the twelfth century, but there was also a wave of large-scale colonization from the West to the far less densely populated area to the east of the Elbe. The farmer-colonists there enjoyed a high degree of freedom. Urbanization and the large-scale migration to the East were accompanied by an erosion of feudalism. The population growth during this period put pressure on feudal power relations, which consisted of mutual agreements between lord and vassal (the vassal was allowed the use of certain estates in exchange for political and military support). It proved to be more efficient for landowners to employ agricultural labourers when they were needed than to maintain a manorial system with serfs. From the late fifteenth century, though, the opposite development occurred in Europe to the east of the Elbe (see Chapters 2 and 4).

The Little Ice Age had different consequences for each continent. In the moderate zones in Europe, China and North America, it meant a greater frequency of harsh winters, cold springs and wet summers. This led to a fall in agricultural production and poorer harvests, which could in turn lead to an explosion in food prices and rising mortality. In the mid-fourteenth century, the outbreak of the Black Death was accompanied by an enormous fall in the population in almost every part of Eurasia. In West Africa, by contrast, the consequences of the changing climate were much more positive. Average rainfall there in the summer months was higher in 1500–1800 than in the centuries before or after. As a result, the boundary between the savannah and the desert shifted northwards, leaving a much larger region that could be used for agriculture.

1.2
Long-distance connections

Between 1000 and 1800, regular contact arose between different parts of the world. In some periods, the connections expanded rapidly and became more intensive; in others, contact stagnated. There were phases of acceleration between roughly 1000–1300 and 1500–1650. Long-distance connections could take different forms. Some of these were commercial or military-political in nature, but they could also cover social, cultural and ecological aspects: people migrated, knowledge and information were exchanged, and plants, animals and pathogens were transported from one region to another.

Europe played a minor role in the first acceleration phase. The driving forces came from the Middle East and Central and East Asia. The commercial expansion in the Islamic world and China under the Song dynasty (960–1279), followed by the explosive rise of the Mongols, who under Genghis Khan (1162–1227) built an empire in the thirteenth century that stretched from China and India to Ukraine and Iraq, resulted in a huge expansion in the network of long-distance connections (on the Mongol Empire, see network III on Map 1.1). Cities such as Cairo, Tabriz (Iran), Bukhara, Samarkand (Central Asia), Cambay (Gujarat), Calicut (Southern India), Malacca and Zaiton (China) were the most important interchanges in this network, supporting a heavy flow of people, goods and knowledge. European trading centres such as Venice, Genoa and Bruges lay on the periphery of this universe (see Map 1.1).

By contrast, the second acceleration phase, which began in the late fifteenth century, was led by Europe, which itself grew into a key region. Boosted by Italian knowledge and capital, a process of overseas expansion began from the Iberian Peninsula, establishing all kinds of new connections across the world. Not only was a new regular connection established between Europe and Asia around the Cape of Good Hope, but for the first time there was also regular traffic across the Atlantic Ocean between Europe, Africa and America, plus a route was opened up across the Pacific between America and China, via Acapulco and Manila. When a Portuguese crew led by Fernão de Magalhães sailed around the world between 1519 and 1522, this was not an isolated event: it marked the beginning of a new era. Thereafter, the English, Dutch and French joined the Spanish and the Portuguese, taking part in overseas intercontinental trade on an increasingly large scale.

According to some researchers, the 'birth' of globalization can be dated to Columbus's arrival in America. Others make the case for 1571, the year when a permanent connection across the Pacific Ocean was established, and silver from Spanish American mines began to flow directly to China. In any case, the large-scale extraction of precious metal from Peru and Mexico had all kinds of repercussions for global economic, demographic and ecological development. Due to the expansion of long-distance trade, the continents became increasingly interwoven in an ever-closer web. For example, the silver that the Spaniards extracted from America was converted into Spanish *reals*, many of which were transported to the East by the Dutch East India

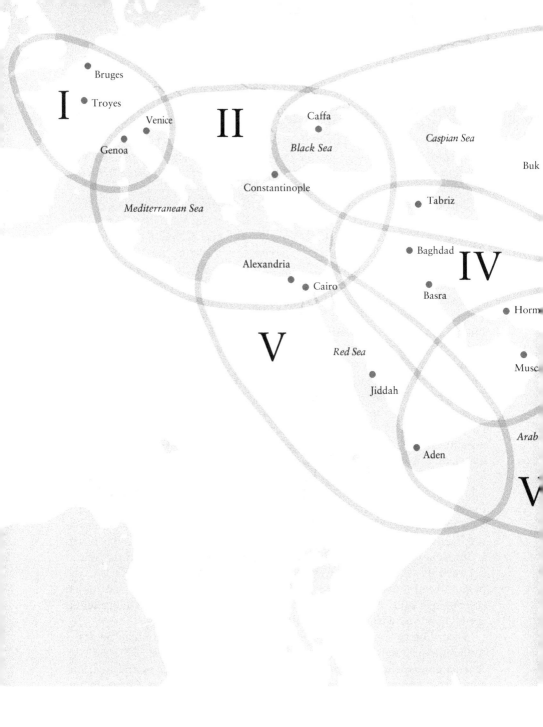

MAP 1.1 Long-distance trade networks in the thirteenth century, by the historical sociologist Janet Abu-Lughod. She identifies eight 'circuits': I A small, peripheral circuit that she calls the 'European sub-system', which maintained contact with other circuits via the Italians; II A Mediterranean trade network that linked Europe with Arabian and Mongolian merchants; III The network of the Mongolian Empire under Genghis Khan; IV A network around the

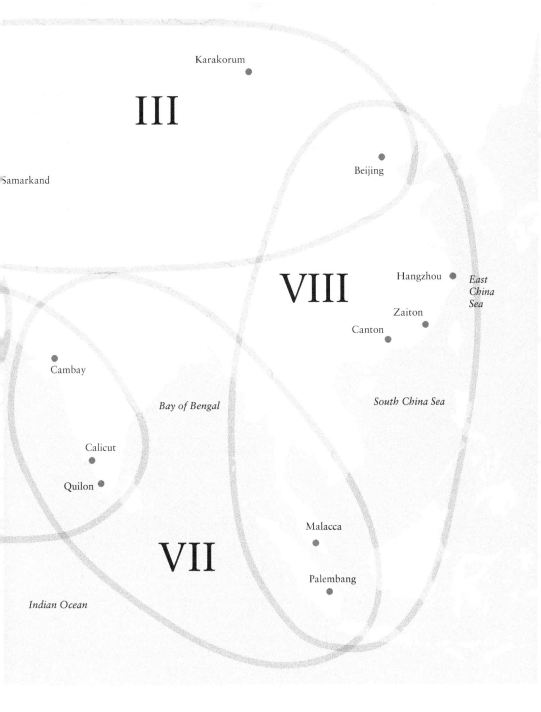

Persian Gulf; V A circuit around the Red Sea, dominated by the Egyptians; VI A South Asian circuit in the western Indian Ocean; VII A South Asian circuit in the eastern Indian Ocean and, finally, VIII The trade network of the Chinese Empire.
Source: Abu-Lughod, *Before European Hegemony*, 34. Designed by René van der Vooren.

Company (VOC). At the same time, the new colonial settlements disrupted the ecological structure of American societies.

Other historians have argued that we cannot refer to globalization before international commodities markets were integrated. In practice, there were large divergences in price levels in different parts of the world before 1800. These historians therefore argue that globalization got underway only in the nineteenth century.

Many social historians, however, emphasize that globalization should not be seen as a strictly economic phenomenon. Globalization could take different forms, which could be cultural, religious, social or political. Although the intercontinental overseas trade to and from Europe before 1800 did not grow as fast as it later would (see Table 1.4), the spread of Christianity and Islam was already having a major impact on numerous distant societies. In addition, the nature of consumer culture in Europe had changed significantly in the eighteenth century, due to the importation of Asian and American products such as tea, coffee, porcelain and tobacco. In that sense, we can also refer to 'globalization' before 1800.

TABLE 1.4 *Estimated Growth in Intercontinental Overseas Trade to and from Europe, 1500–1900*

	Average annual growth, in %
1500–1599	1.26
1600–1699	0.66
1700–1799	1.26
1820–1899	3.85

Source: O'Rourke en Williamson, 'After Columbus', table 1.

Although Europeans rarely ventured into the African interior before the nineteenth century, the consequences of the new developments were no less tangible for that continent. The establishment of direct trade routes between Western Europe and the Far East around the Cape put pressure on the earnings of the caravan trade. It also indirectly affected the tax income of the Ottoman Empire, which had dominated both the Middle East and the whole coast of North Africa since the sixteenth century. What is more, sub-Saharan Africa was severely impacted by a rapid expansion of the slave trade. In addition to the existing trade in slaves from East Africa to the Middle East, the sixteenth century saw the rise of the transatlantic slave trade, which mainly focused on the west coast. The transatlantic slave trade became even larger than that in the Indian Ocean (Table 1.5). The Portuguese had the greatest share in this slave trade: 46 per cent. England accounted for 28 per cent, France for 13 per cent and the Netherlands and Spain for slightly less than 5 per cent each.

TABLE 1.5 *The African Slave Trade, 1500–1900. Number of Transported Enslaved People*

	From Africa across the Atlantic Ocean	*From Africa to Middle East*
1500–1900		4,300,000
Before 1600	325,000	
1601–1700	1,900,000	
1701–1800	6,700,000	
1801–c. 1870	2,600,000	

Source: Held et al., *Global transformations*, 293.

For Europeans, globalization was also expressed in greater mobility. A growing number of Europeans left their familiar neighbourhoods to migrate to large towns, sail the seas, serve in the army, temporarily work in another region or settle permanently elsewhere on the European continent or in a colony overseas. In doing so, they left their own communities behind. Expressed as a percentage of the total European population – the migration ratio – the share of this physically and culturally mobile group rose considerably, especially in the seventeenth and nineteenth centuries, as shown by Table 1.6.

TABLE 1.6 *Cross-border Migration by Europeans, 1500–1850*

	Migration ratio, in %
1501–1550	12.9
1551–1600	14.8
1601–1650	19.9
1651–1700	18.5
1701–1750	17.7
1751–1800	17.2
1801–1850	22.7

Source: Lucassen and Lucassen, 'Mobility transition revisited', table 1.1.

The expansion and intensification of long-distance connections had other cultural effects, too. From the twelfth century, for example, Christian scholars in Southern Spain came into contact with the rich heritage of Greek writings on nature, which had been disseminated in Arabic translation from the heart of the Abbasid Empire in Baghdad across the whole Islamic world. Once translated into Latin, these Greek texts, including works by Aristotle and Ptolemy, had a major influence on the development of science in Europe. The Mongol expansion in the thirteenth century established durable connections that made it much easier for Europeans to gather knowledge about China. Long-distance connections allowed religions to expand to other parts of the world. Via trade networks, Islam spread deep into Africa and Central and Southeast Asia. European overseas expansion from the sixteenth century made an important contribution to the worldwide dissemination of Christianity. Partly under the protection of the Spanish and Portuguese governments, Christian missionaries made deep inroads into America and Asia. The growing links between different parts of the world left traces in material culture, too. Eighteenth-century Africa saw a fashion for brightly coloured cotton textiles, for example, which were imported from India and later from England. Europeans in their droves developed a taste for tea, coffee, cocoa and sugar from Asia and America.

Plants, animals and pathogens followed in people's wake. From the eighth century onwards, the trade networks around the Indian Ocean brought crops and fruits such as sugar cane, apricots, mangos and citrus fruit from Southern and Eastern Asia to the Mediterranean. From the sixteenth century onwards, crops such as maize, peanuts and potatoes spread from America to Eurasia, leading to significant growth in the population. China profited above all from the American sweet potato. After 1500, European conquerors brought horses, grain and a whole series of other products to America. The Portuguese introduced American maize to West Africa.

The plague, which claimed the lives of one in three people in Europe in the mid-fourteenth century, reached these regions via the intensively used Central Asian trade routes. The consequences of European expansion from 1492 were catastrophic for the native population of America. The indigenous population is thought to have plummeted by around 90 per cent after Columbus's arrival. Bloody wars of conquest and forced labour in the mines led to rising mortality, but it was mainly diseases such as smallpox, measles and influenza that claimed numerous victims. This even led to the complete depopulation of some Caribbean islands within a few decades, providing colonialists with 'empty' areas in which to establish plantations.

1.3
The three basic problems: Contours of change

The changes in income level that occurred before the nineteenth century were not as spectacular as those that occurred afterwards. During this period, societies in which income per capita rose over a long period were the exception, not the rule. They included China under the Song dynasty, Italy and Flanders in the High Middle Ages, and the Netherlands during the so-called 'Golden Age'. In Chapter 2, we look at how historians and social scientists analyse the possibilities and limits of economic development, and how they explain the occurrence of a prolonged increase in prosperity in certain regions during certain periods. In doing so, we explain the background to the development in the Netherlands in detail. The Industrial Revolution, which began in England in the late eighteenth century, facilitated a stronger and more prolonged rise in income levels. Thanks to industrialization, Europe would temporarily overtake the rest of the world in terms of prosperity. Within and beyond Europe, the distribution of income also developed in diverse ways. Free wage labour increased in some places, but in large parts of the world (including many European colonies), systems of forced labour expanded; and these provided little or no freely available income for those who did the work.

In the meantime, the formation and distribution of power underwent radical changes. As we shall see in Chapter 3, this was more the case for Europe than for other parts of the world. States were formed, new types of state arose, state systems developed and some states extended their power far overseas. Mutual rivalry and warfare were the driving forces behind these processes. The internal structure of states also changed, due to the centralization and bureaucratization of state financing, for example. Ordinary people were barely able to make their voices heard, aside from rising up in revolt, but a kind of 'public sphere' where free speech was possible would develop in some societies.

For most people in the world around 1800 there had been no or little reduction in the risks of existence that had affected people for the eight hundred years previously. The chances of becoming sick, disabled, poor or unemployed, or falling victim to war or natural disaster had not lessened. As we shall see in Chapter 4, however, the social order and the way people viewed the world had changed in the meantime. The majority of the population still lived in the countryside, but due to the erosion of feudal power structures, communal bonds had disappeared and people had more freedom to determine where they worked, travelled and lived.

In Western Europe in particular, this led to a more individualized world with the nuclear family at its heart. Who was responsible for mitigating risks also changed, as the government gradually took over more and more facilities. The authority of the church declined as a result, a trend that was further reinforced by the rise of reason and experimentation as aids for understanding the world.

2

Growth and economic development before the Great Divergence

KAREL DAVIDS

Continuous growth in income per capita is a relatively recent phenomenon. It was little more than two centuries ago that, initially in a small part of the world, economic growth began to increase more rapidly and in such a way that this accelerated growth assumed an almost permanent character. Although economies in the past, in both Asia and Europe, had experienced periods of prosperity like that enjoyed by the seventeenth-century Netherlands, such heydays rarely lasted more than a hundred years. The great majority of the world's population lived in the countryside, worked in agriculture and took only a fraction of their production to the market. Most people's lives were determined by a precarious balance between the size of the population and the means of livelihood. The agricultural production capacity of one's region, on which technology had little impact as of yet, placed narrow limits on opportunities for economic growth. Continuous economic growth, which until recently was generally equated with 'modern' economic growth, dates from the Industrial Revolution, which began in Great Britain in the late eighteenth century. A growing wealth gap emerged between the 'West' and other parts of the world. This growing gap is now often called the 'Great Divergence'.

These basic data on global economic history form the starting point for this chapter. The discussion will be guided by the following four questions:

1. To what extent was economic development possible prior to the mid-nineteenth century? What were the limits to economic development?
2. How can we explain the fact that the Netherlands was the leading economy in Europe for some time? What internal or external factors lay at the root of this?

3. What did these changes mean for people's lives? To what extent did different groups share the costs and benefits of economic development, stagnation or contraction?
4. How can the 'Great Divergence' between the 'West' and other parts of the world be explained? Did it begin with the Industrial Revolution? Why did the Industrial Revolution take place in the West, and why was it led by Great Britain in particular?

2.1
Economic development in the world

To what extent was economic development possible prior to the mid-nineteenth century? Economists and economic historians use different approaches or models to answer this question. The most important of these can be described as the Malthusian, Marxist, Smithian and institutional models. Each focuses on a different combination of factors, namely population and means of livelihood, class conflict and modes of production, commercialization and specialization, and institutions, respectively. In this section, we draw on the aforementioned approaches to discuss the different combinations of factors.

POPULATION AND MEANS OF LIVELIHOOD The Malthusian approach is named after the English preacher and political economist, Thomas Robert Malthus (1766–1834). In a series of publications beginning with *An essay on the Principle of Population* (1798) and ending with *A Summary View of the Principle of Population* (1830), Malthus argued that there is an inherent tension between a population's natural tendency to grow and the limited capacity of agriculture to feed an increasing number of people. If population growth were to continue spontaneously, food shortages would be become so severe over time that the population would be depleted by famine, disease and falling birth rates. Malthus called this hard brake on population growth the 'positive check'. He also identified a different path, though, whereby the gap between population size and the capacity of the means of livelihood could be reduced or abolished, which he called the 'preventive check'. A rise in the age of marriage, a fall in the frequency of marriage and limiting births could curb growth before a peak in mortality occurred. Once the population size had fallen to a level that was lower than the capacity of the means of livelihood, growth could start again. Malthus assumed that these principles of population development were always valid, because he believed that people were unable to increase the yield from agriculture over time.

Since then, historians have developed and applied his model in order to understand the economic development of pre-industrial societies over the longer term. We can get a more refined picture of the relationship between population development and agricultural production if we consider the regional level and/or shorter periods. Chart 2.1 shows what happened when food prices rose sharply after poor harvests and less grain was available: mortality rose rapidly, because a considerable proportion of the population no longer had enough to eat, given the high prices, and the birth rate fell. 'Subsistence crises' such as these, in which mortality suddenly spiked, occurred in France and other European countries a number of times until the early nineteenth century. After this, such phenomena became rare in this part of the world. One of the last European subsistence crises was the Great Famine in Ireland between 1845 and 1850.

The rise or fall in the frequency of poor harvests and famines was partly related to the changing climate, which was discussed in Chapter 1. It was also related to the way in which state and society functioned. In China, the opposite development took place. Subsistence crises, which had rarely occurred before 1800, became a recurrent phenomenon in the late nineteenth and early twentieth centuries, because the system of food provision and distribution deteriorated as the empire's governance problems intensified.

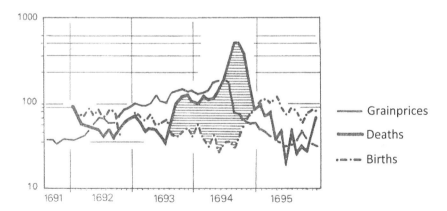

CHART 2.1 *The subsistence crisis in Amiens, 1693–4. The chart uses a semi-logarithmic scale. Changes of an equal size (e.g. a twofold increase) are shown by equal distances on the y axis. The dashed area shows the abnormal number of excess deaths.*
Source: Dupâquier, *Histoire de la population française*, 208.

FIGURE 2.1 *The pillar of the Holy Trinity in Olomouc (Czech Republic), erected to commemorate the end of a plague epidemic in 1716.*
© Henryk T. Kaiser/Rex Features/Hollandse Hoogte.

In practice, the relationship between food prices, population development and agricultural production was often more complex, because price development was also dependent on factors other than changes in the scale of production or population size. In Europe, the growth in the quantity of money as a result of silver imports from Spanish America and currency manipulations contributed to what was then unprecedented inflation, later called the 'price revolution', which lasted from the early sixteenth century until the mid-seventeenth century. Disruption to the food supply due to war could also drive food prices even higher.

Moreover, the population could adapt to agricultural capacity in ways other than abnormally high mortality. After all, as well as the positive check, there was the preventive check: regulating the population by means of changes in the age of marriage, the frequency of marriage or the birth rate. Social and cultural factors played a key role in this. In Chapter 4, we look at how the preventive check worked in practice and the different forms it could assume.

It should be added that food shortages were not the only potential reason for a spike in mortality. Epidemic disease, further aggravated by wars that spread sicknesses more rapidly, was also responsible for many casualties. Between the mid-fourteenth and early eighteenth centuries, the European population was decimated time and again by plague epidemics. The 'Black Death', which reached Europe in 1346 via the Central Asian trade routes, was the first in a long series. As late as 1720, 'plague columns' in honour of the Virgin Mary or the Holy Trinity were erected in Central European cities to commemorate the end of yet another outbreak (see Figure 2.1). In the Ottoman Empire, the disease would recur many times before the mid-nineteenth century.

There were also frequent epidemics and wars in China. The fall in the population from *c.* 115 million people in around 1200 to 65 million in 1393 is partly attributed to plague epidemics, especially around 1350, and partly to the succession of Mongol invasions after 1227, and the expulsion of the Yuan by the Ming dynasty 140 years later. Outbreaks of plague and other mass epidemics repeatedly occurred until the end of the Qing dynasty in 1911.

Population growth could also be slowed by emigration. People could migrate to a town, a different region or even a different continent. In China, for example, the population's centre of gravity gradually shifted towards the south-east. Whereas in *c.* 750, only 40 per cent of all Chinese lived south of the Huai River, by *c.* 1100 this share had risen to almost three-quarters. Within Europe from the twelfth century, a protracted colonization movement began towards the region east of the Elbe. Similar migratory movements occurred in the British Isles and the

Iberian Peninsula. Between 1500 and 1800, another 100,000 Europeans – mainly Spanish – migrated to America.

Finally, agricultural production was not entirely static. Agricultural yields could be boosted by expanding the acreage under cultivation. Reclaiming wasteland and lakes, embanking salt marshes, irrigating arid soils: all of these methods were used to increase the amount of land on which to grow food. Another way to boost yields was to use the existing acreage more productively. One measure that is often used to compare agricultural productivity across regions and periods is the 'seed-sowing factor'; that is, the amount of seed used for sowing versus the crop yield. The higher the seed-sowing factor, the greater the share of the harvest that remained for consumption. Table 2.1 shows that the seed-sowing factor for crops such as wheat, rye and barley varied considerably between different European regions and over time. In North-western Europe (England, Belgium and the Netherlands), agricultural yields rose sharply, especially after 1700, whereas they practically stagnated in Central and Eastern Europe.

There were also variations in agricultural yields in China. Whereas the crop yield in Northern China, where wheat and sorghum were the main crops, grew little in the eighteenth century, the rice yield increased in the paddy-fields of Southern China and the Yangzi Delta in the same period (see Map 2.1). The rise in land productivity was facilitated by innovations such as more intensive manuring, the reduction of farrow and the increased cultivation of feed crops such as tubers, clover and alfalfa. Improving water management by constructing irrigation systems or reinforcing dykes, which took place in Southern China, the Yangzi Delta and on the North Sea coasts, could also improve yields. New crops such as potatoes and maize, which were introduced from the New World to Europe and China from the sixteenth century, also contributed to a rise in productivity in the long term.

Moreover, a particular region's population was not always completely dependent for its food supply on the production capacity of agriculture in the immediate surroundings, or on fortuitous harvests. Food could also be imported from elsewhere, and food reserves functioned as a buffer in leaner times. In this way, some regions were less troubled than others by problems with grain production as a consequence of the changing climate.

MAP 2.1 *China in the late Qing Empire. For centuries, the Yangtze Delta (Jiangnan) was one of the most fertile and wealthiest regions in the world.*
Source: Richards, *Unending Frontier,* 116. Designed by René van der Vooren.

Important regions in China, such as the lower reaches of the Yangzi and the coastal region in the south-east, were net importers of food in the mid-eighteenth century. Large towns in the Early Modern period, such as Beijing, Edo (Tokyo), Istanbul, Madrid, Amsterdam or London, could only continue to flourish because they were constantly supplied with food from distant regions. Sometimes supplies were organized in the form of a tribute system under state auspices, as happened in Beijing or Edo. Istanbul could be sure of supplies because peasants in the Romanian provinces were obliged to deliver a specified quantity of grain each year, at fixed prices determined by the state. In Amsterdam, which imported a lot of grain from the Baltic region, the food supply was left entirely to the market.

Stockpiling was a means to absorb the unpredictability of the harvest and stabilize grain prices. In China, an extensive system of granaries had functioned for centuries, reaching a high level of efficiency in the eighteenth century. In Europe, it was common for grain storage to be left to the municipal authorities (see Chapter 4). Before 1700, European states mainly used price regulation to influence the supply of grain. The more the power of central government expanded in the eighteenth century in Europe, the more this stimulated the free trade in grain.

TABLE 2.1 *Average Harvest Yield per Seed for Sowing in Europe, by Zone, 1300–1800*

	England, Northern and Southern Netherlands	**France, Spain, Italy**	**Germany, Switzerland, Scandinavia**	**Russia, Poland, Czech Republic, Slovakia, Hungary**
1300–49	3.8	4.8		
1400–49	4.6	4.9		
1500–49	7.4	6.7	4.0	3.9
1550–99	7.3		4.4	4.5
1600–49	6.7		4.5	4.0
1650–99	9.3	6.2	4.1	3.8
1700–49		6.3	4.1	3.5
1750–99	10.1	7.0	5.1	4.7

Source: Slicher van Bath, 'Agrarische produktiviteit', 162.

CLASS CONFLICTS AND MODES OF PRODUCTION Like Malthusians, Marxist historians assume that pre-nineteenth-century agricultural productivity was generally low, and that there was generally little growth in the agricultural sector. They have a different theory as to why this was the case, however. Inspired by the work of the German philosopher and economist Karl Marx (1818–83), they argue that the explanation for the stagnation should be sought in the organization of the production and distribution of the produce. The crux of the problem lay, in their view, in the nature of the relations of production. By this, they meant the relations between those who owned the means of production – all of the means used to produce goods and services – and those who supplied the labour. These groups formed classes with different economic interests. The relations of production varied according to the dominant modes of production; that is, the structure of the economic organization and the legal system, the form of the state, culture and the religious beliefs that accompanied this.

Marxists describe the mode of production that existed in most of Europe in the Middle Ages as 'feudal'. A typical characteristic of the feudal mode of production was that production mostly took place in relatively small units (family farms), and that part of the yield of these farms was relinquished coercively to a group of landowners who themselves were not, or only indirectly, involved in agrarian production. Medievalists describe a combination of serfdom, landlordship, manorial system and banal domains (the *ban* was a judicial system). Serfs were subordinate to lords, landowners who exercised jurisdiction over a certain domain (manor), part of which they utilized themselves.

Marxist Robert Brenner, who was the fiercest critic of the Malthusian vision, argued that economic development was almost impossible so long as the feudal ownership structure continued to exist in the countryside. This structure precluded growth in practice: farmers did not invest in the innovations that could have boosted productivity, because a large part of the yield went to the lord; and the landowners did not invest so long as they could collect their income coercively from the peasants. The continuation of the feudal structure was not determined by economic factors, but by the power relations between landowners and peasants. Change could only take place through conflict between these classes. Class conflict did not occur everywhere in the same way, however, and did not always have the same outcomes. These variations, according to Brenner, can explain why different parts of Europe took different economic paths in the Late Middle Ages.

Brenner argued that violent class conflict erupted when the long-term decline in agricultural prices in the late fourteenth and early fifteenth century, as a result of the shrinking population, also put pressure on landowners' incomes. In England, where landowners – more than on the continent – were still utilizing their domains themselves, the landlords succeeded in drastically reducing the land ownership of small peasants and organizing production in larger units managed by tenant farmers, who produced for the market. This form of agrarian capitalism, which formed the key to long-term economic growth, failed to get off the ground in France. In that country, the main source of income for landowners until the late eighteenth century consisted of the taxes that were collected from peasants, by virtue of their rights as banal lords or landed proprietors. Small-scale production by family farms continued to exist.

According to Brenner, the class struggle also explains the extreme curtailment of freedom in Europe east of the Elbe from the second half of the fifteenth century. Together with the growing power of the state (see Chapter 3), landowners in this region curtailed the freedoms that peasants had gained during the colonization movement in previous centuries. Any resistance from the rural population was ruthlessly suppressed. Landowners imposed heavy taxes on peasants and forced them to spend an increasing part of their time working for the lord (corvée labour). Free wage labour declined, while the domain of the lords expanded. The landowners reaped the benefits of these growing burdens by selling a considerable share of the production in the market. Table 2.2 shows this development on Polish estates between *c*. 1530 and 1660.

The approach taken by Brenner and kindred spirits gave an exceptional boost to social-historical research, but historical reality nevertheless proved more complex than the Marxists had thought. There was hardly any violent class struggle in the English countryside. Violent confrontations, such as the Peasants' Revolt of 1381, were rare. Small, independent farms were able to manage well until long into the seventeenth century. Moreover, large-scale production units were not the only way in which 'agrarian capitalism' could emerge, as shown by the development of the Low Countries (see further herein). Change or stagnation in the countryside also turned out to be related to the role played by the towns, the urban citizenry and institutional factors other than property relations. These factors, which received less attention in Brenner's account, will be covered in the following sections on the Smithian and institutional approaches.

TABLE 2.2 *Corvée Labour and Wage Labour on Rural Estates in Korczyn (Poland), in Percentages of Number of Working Days, 1533–1660*

	1533/1538	1564/1572	1600/1616	1660
Wage labour	35	19	15	5
Corvée: transport	65	53	40	33
Corvée: agricultural work		28	45	62
Total	100	100	100	100

Source: Kriedte, *Spätfeudalismus und Handelskapital*, 89.

COMMERCIALIZATION AND THE DIVISION OF LABOUR The core element of the Smithian approach – named after the Scottish philosopher and economist Adam Smith (1723–90) – is the development of trade. The growth of prosperity, Smith argued in his principal work *The Wealth of Nations* (1776), mainly results from an increasing division of labour, which in turn is 'the necessary, though very slow and gradual consequence' of the general human tendency to barter and exchange. The division of labour is dependent on the size of the market. The more the market expands, the more opportunities for prosperity there are, due to the division of labour. The more specialized labour becomes, the higher productivity can rise, thanks to specialization and the improvement of skills. This is paired with gradual technical innovation. Smithians argue that if this path is taken, a certain level of economic growth is also possible in pre-industrial societies.

The expansion of the towns and the emergence of markets, greater agricultural specialization and the increasing use of money and credit are all indications of commercialization and growing specialization. Towns could grow and flourish thanks to the division of labour. Town-dwellers were fed with food that was produced in the agrarian sector, and transported to towns by means of a system of levies or free trade. Towns, in turn, provided a wide range of goods and services for the immediate surroundings and more distant regions, from common artisanal products and luxury items to trade-related services (such as markets), education, the administration of justice and medical care. There was more occupational differentiation within the towns than outside them.

The dissemination of markets is also an indicator of commercialization, whether they were markets for products or markets for factors of production (land, labour, capital). The former tended to emerge before the latter, and they were usually more visible because they were generally held at fixed times (once a week or once a year, for example), in particular places. Towards the mid-fourteenth century, for instance, there were no fewer than 1,500 weekly markets in English towns and villages, a thousand of which appeared after 1200. The quantity of products that were traded at these markets rose sharply, along with the share of traded goods in total production. It is estimated that in 1330, the majority of the wool and a third of the total amount of grain produced in England were taken to market. In some parts of China, the number of markets doubled or tripled between the sixteenth and eighteenth centuries. Separate markets arose for rice, cotton and silk.

Moreover, extensive long-distance trade networks developed both within Asia, Europe and North-east Africa, and between the continents. Within Europe in the twelfth and thirteenth centuries, for example, clusters of annual markets emerged in Champagne, Flanders, Southern England, the Lower Rhine region and Schonen (South-western Sweden), which became meeting-points for traders from different regions. Around 1350, merchants' associations from the North Sea and Baltic regions began to establish a long-term overarching alliance to protect their interests, known as the Hanseatic League. By the Late Middle Ages, it eventually covered around 200 towns, arching from the Low Countries via Northern Germany and Scandinavia to the Baltic coast. From the eleventh century, the Genoese, Pisans and Venetians established colonies and trading posts in the Levant, Black Sea region and North-western Europe, from which they could maintain contact with Central Asia and the Hanseatic League. Jewish merchant communities in Europe and North Africa operated in the Mediterranean and the Indian Ocean. Persians, Gujarati and Chinese were active around the Indian Ocean and in Central Asia, and Armenians traded both in Asia and in Europe.

Commercialization and specialization not only occurred in towns, as mentioned earlier; these processes also took place in the countryside. American economic historian Jan de Vries has shown that when a population grows and opportunities for trade emerge, a rural society will normally follow one of two paths. He describes the first as the 'peasant model'. In this model, agrarian householders focus more on self-sufficiency than on production for the market. They respond to population growth by dividing existing plots of land into smaller units, and start to work the land more and more intensively. Agricultural work is combined with non-agrarian activities, such as spinning and weaving. The majority of the population stays in the countryside, and the exchange of products between urban and rural areas remains modest. In much of Europe and Asia until far into the nineteenth century, the peasant model was the most common pattern. The second path that a rural society could follow is known as the 'specialization model'. In this case, agrarian households make maximal use of the opportunities offered by the market. They specialize and start to operate in a more commercial way. They keep their property intact, give up non-agrarian tasks and specialize in producing products – dairy, meat, vegetables, fruit or raw materials for industry, such as hops, hemp, flax, madder or rapeseed – which can be sold at nearby or more distant markets. In exchange, they obtain goods and services at the market that they do not (or no longer) produce themselves. Those living in the countryside who can no longer find agricultural work seek their living in non-agrarian activities, such as construction, transport or craft, or migrate to the town. Exchange between towns and rural areas increases. In the Early Modern era, this specialization model was followed in the countryside in the west of the Low Countries, Southern England and Northern France. In other words, Smithian developments also occurred outside the towns in these regions.

In a certain sense, the peasant model and the specialization model represent extremes; in practice, paths can be taken that lie between the two. One very common middle course was that of 'proto-industrialization'. The term 'proto-industrialization' (also known as cottage industry, rural industry or the putting-out system) is generally used to refer to a system of production in which industrial products are made in households with the aid of simple machinery (such as the spinning wheel or the loom) and then sold beyond the local market. This form of production took place in scattered, small-scale units and was mainly located in the countryside. Financing and organization – especially the buying and supply of commodities and the transport and sales of products – were normally in the hands of urban merchants. Textile production was the most important proto-industrial activity. As well as spinning and weaving flax, wool or cotton, proto-industrial labourers also worked wood, leather or metal, for example to make pins or nails. In the Early Modern period, proto-industrialization fanned out across many regions in Europe and Asia, including Yorkshire, Flanders, Northern France, the Eastern Netherlands, Saxony, Switzerland, Southern India and the Yangzi Valley. Participating in cottage industry could provide a supplementary source of income for specialized farmers. In addition, the system also functioned as an alternative to specialization for peasants who, due to the poor quality of their land or the small size of their property, had few opportunities to increase the productivity of their farms (especially in sandy or mountainous regions).

With regard to the final indicator of commercialization and specialization – the increasing use of money and credit – China was initially the leader. In the eleventh century, the quantity of money there multiplied by more than ten times. In 1024, China was the first state in the world to bring paper money into circulation. Although this monetary system was abandoned again before 1400, the use of money and credit remained widely dispersed. For example, the granting of credit played an essential role in silk and cotton production in the late imperial period.

In imitation of methods that had developed in the Islamic world, there was also an expansion in the use of money and credit in Europe in the Middle Ages and Early Modern period. Italian cities, which had extensive contact with Islamic trade networks, were the frontrunners in this regard, with other regions following on their heels. In the late eleventh century, it is estimated that there was no more than £30,000 of coins in circulation in the whole of England. At the beginning of the thirteenth century, this amount had risen to £200,000, and a century later, £1,700,000. The quantity of money grew much more rapidly than the population or prices. The total quantity of money also grew as a result of the granting of credit in the form of loans, advances and exchanges. In Holland, the level of interest on long-term loans fell from almost 30 per cent in the late twelfth century to 10 per cent in around 1250, and 5–6 per cent in the fifteenth century. Such a fall in the interest level was relatively common across Western Europe. Beyond Europe, it was only Japan that experienced a similar development; there, the level of interest fell in the eighteenth century from around 13 to 8 per cent.

Various key developments (the growth of towns, the emergence of markets, agricultural specialization, the growth of money and credit) thus indicate that commercialization and the division of labour increased in Asia and Europe between *c.* 1000 and 1800. How far did commercialization and specialization extend into the economy and society as a whole? Some researchers argue that these processes went so far in Early Modern Europe that they constituted 'merchant capitalism'. In this form of capitalism, the merchant, not the industrialist, was the dominant figure. Merchants possessed the most capital, and they were the ones who determined how it was used. Capital mainly had a 'floating' character; it consisted largely of reserves, advances and loans, rather than machinery or buildings. Merchants strove to make a profit in the market by controlling the supply of commodities and the sale of products. They played little role in production itself. Merchant capitalists did gain control over productive activities in urban or rural areas (via proto-industry), but they did not change the production process itself. The example of China shows that a market economy in which the demanding and supplying parties exchanged goods and services at mutually agreed prices could also function in the absence of 'merchant capitalism'. From the Song dynasty onwards, China certainly had a market economy. Merchants played an important role in the economic exchange. Nevertheless, terms such as 'merchant capitalism' or 'capitalism' are rarely used in the Chinese case, because the government regulated large parts of the economy.

In *The Modern World-system* (1974), historical sociologist Immanuel Wallerstein argued that commercialization and specialization had particularly radical effects in the world from the fifteenth century onwards. From that time, according to him, a 'world economy' emerged from Europe that could be described as 'capitalist'. In his vision, the essence of capitalism lay not in a certain mode of production, but in the production of goods for sale in the market. In his theory, Wallerstein argued that (1) the connections between different parts of the world increasingly assumed the form of an economic system from the fifteenth century, (2) that this system was clearly hierarchical, (3) it was capitalist in nature (initially with primacy in the sphere of trade), (4) the system affected its composite parts (in the sphere of labour relations, property relations, production systems and the degree of centralization) and (5) its geographical heart lay in North-western Europe for centuries. With regard to all of these points, he maintained, the capitalist world economy represented something new compared to previous economic relations. Moreover, according to Wallerstein, the scope of the capitalist world economy was much greater than that of any other system. Its communication lines spanned the entire globe. This world economy also included the plantations in America and the Caribbean, where sugar, tobacco and other commodities were cultivated for the European market using the labour of enslaved people. These areas formed the periphery, from which the core in North-western Europe drew part of its prosperity.

Wallerstein's world-system theory has sparked much debate since the 1970s. Historians have questioned, for example, whether the 'capitalist world economy' was really subjugated to single 'system' after 1500, and whether Europe before 1800 really occupied such a central position in the world.

INSTITUTIONS Finally, the institutional approach mainly focuses on the framework for economic development. The key idea is that differences in economic performance can be explained by differences in institutional context. The concept of the 'institution' thus lies at the heart of this approach. By institution is meant a system of rules, norms, beliefs and organizations that together ensure regularity in behaviour, including social behaviour. Institutions can take the form of informal customs and arrangements, or formal regulations and complex structures. Markets can also be seen as institutions. Institutions emerge through interactions between groups or individuals – often on rational grounds – but over time they often acquire a gravity and dynamic of their own, which can elude the control of individual actors. They can emerge from below, through voluntary agreements, or be imposed from above, for example by a sovereign or a state. Institutions can vary significantly over time and place. These variations are linked to differences in culture and state formation, which will be covered in more detail in the following two chapters.

From the perspective of economic development, a particularly important role is played by institutions relating to the cost of transactions; that is, the costs incurred when goods or services are transferred from one party to another. Transaction costs include both the costs associated with measuring the value of goods or services that are exchanged (information) and the costs associated with protecting property rights and ensuring compliance with agreements. Informing, protecting and enforcing do not happen automatically; they carry costs. The size of these costs is partly dependent on the state of technology, and partly on the nature of institutions. As argued by one of the founders of the institutional approach, economic historian Douglass North, this takes us to the heart of why institutions are so important for explaining differences in economic development: as institutions become more effective, transaction costs fall and economic growth can occur.

Researchers have applied this approach at different scale levels. For example, a comparison of two groups of merchants in the Mediterranean between 1050 and 1350 – Jewish traders from North Africa (Maghribis) and Christian merchants from Genoa – brought interesting institutional differences to light. The Maghribis were attached to the community, the Genoese were more individualistic. The Maghribis opted for informal agreements and solutions to conflicts, the Genoese preferred formal, written contracts and legal sanctions for wrongdoers and swindlers. The Maghribis formed individual enterprises, while the Genoese established family businesses with longer life spans, for which the members were collectively liable.

TEXT BOX 2.1 GUILDS IN THE WORLD

European guilds were permanent, local, government-recognized organizations of people working in the same trade or the same branch of business, which had the primary goal of defending their exclusive right to practise that trade against outsiders. They were mainly located in towns. Guilds emerged in the eleventh century and were not abolished in many countries (including the Netherlands) until the early nineteenth century. As well as supervising the training of fellow craftsmen and the quality of production, they frequently played social roles, too, such as supporting destitute members. Before the Reformation, the guild system was closely interwoven with religious life; many guilds had their own altar at a church, for example. In some parts of Europe, such as Italy and Flanders, guilds also participated in the town government for many years.

Much recent historical work has cast the guilds in a much more positive light than traditional historiography. They are often no longer seen as bastions of conservatism and a brake on technological progress, but rather as institutions that could have a positive effect on economic development, thanks, among other things, to their contribution to the formation of 'human capital'.

Guilds or guild-like organizations (in the sense of more-or-less independent associations of fellow workers who represented communal interests) were not exclusively found in Europe. For centuries, they also existed in the Middle East, China, Japan and parts of Latin America. They did not disappear from Turkey until 1924, or in China until the founding of the People's Republic in 1949. One difference, compared to Europe, was that the growth of the guild system in many of these countries began later, and in their attempts to gain control over the labour market, guilds in Asian towns usually had to compete with various kinds of organizations, such as associations of fellow believers or of people with the same ethnic or geographical background.

We can also make out institutional variations at the level of an economy or society as a whole, which can explain differences in economic development. From around the eleventh century, Europe saw the emergence of increasing numbers of communal, non-kinship-based institutions, such as 'sworn communities' (associations of free citizens), trade guilds and craft guilds. These institutions protected property rights and stimulated market exchange by guaranteeing the quality of training and products. In this way, they helped to lower transaction costs. This category of institution also included associations of users of communal land (commons, marks), which spread in Western Europe during this period. In 1273, for example, the king of Castile brought together the owners of sheep herds in a national organization, the Mesta, which in exchange for contributing to the treasury was given complete control over the use of grazing land in much of Spain. The Mesta not only gave an enormous boost to wool production, but it would also play a central role in Spain's economic and political order for centuries.

Institutional stagnation may also explain why economic development in the Middle East increasingly trailed behind that in Europe from the Middle Ages onwards. The Islamic law of succession, which determined that estates had to be divided between various relatives and kin, hindered the accumulation of capital. The absence of the concept of a 'corporation' in Islamic law impeded the formation of large, sustainable enterprises. Only in the late nineteenth century would the legal system gradually be reformed in line with the Western model.

Moreover, in the Early Modern period, more and more European states followed the example of Venice and Florence by creating a system of patents for inventions, protecting the ownership of new discoveries in such a way that both the inventors themselves and society could benefit. This institution would provide a favourable framework for technological innovation. From the seventeenth century, the Netherlands and England were at the forefront of developing institutions that provided information for entrepreneurs (exchanges, price-lists; see Figure 2.2) and protected those who lent money to the government. After all, if creditors could be sure that the government would meet its obligations, they would be more willing to lend money; and the more easily the government could obtain money, the stronger the government apparatus would become – which would ultimately benefit the entrepreneurs again.

If we compare China and Europe in the Early Modern period, we can also identify striking differences: although China had a much more developed system for assuring food provision, which was partly managed by the state (see Chapter 4), it lacked the financial institutions and organizational forms that facilitated the rise of merchant capitalism in Europe. A rather highly developed capital market arose in various places in Europe in the Early Modern period, with interest rates of 3–5 per cent, serving both businesses and governments. The interest on loans in China was much higher than in Europe at the end of the eighteenth century. When it came to the provision and protection of capital, the institutional framework in the Chinese Empire was less efficient.

Cours van Koopmanschappen tot Amsterdam. Den 26 January

ANNO 1686.

Met Consent van de EE. Groot-Achtb. Heeren Burgermeesteren.

No. 1. Peper en Specerÿen/bÿ 't ℔ in Banco.

Swarte Peper		₰ 14	
Witte Peper		₰ 25, 2, 6	
Nagelen st. 75	Nooten	st. 60	
Nagel-poejer		st.	
Foely of Macis		₰ 19, 2 ₰	
Caneel Lange st. 30 a 80 Korte		st. 32 a 42	

No. 2. Boom-Olÿ bÿ 't Vat van 717 meng.

Genuaes ℓ 54 a 75	Poulie	ℓ 55	
Sivilse ℓ	Malleg.	ℓ	
Majorckse ℓ	Portug.	ℓ 50	

No. 3. Suÿkeren bÿ 't ℔. contant. oct.

Candy Broodsuyker	₰ 16
Poeyer-brooden	₰ 15 a 15, 2
Nette Rafinaden	₰ 12
Nette Melissen	₰ 10, 4 a 6
Lompen	₰ 9, 4 a 6 p.
Witte Candy	₰ 20, 21 a 23
Bruyne Candy	₰ 11, 6 p. 2 12
Gestooren Poejer	₰ 9, 4 a 11, 2 p.
Brasilse witte poejer	₰ 8, 2 p. 10, 4
Pan-goet	₰
Rouwe Barbados	₰ 4, 6 a 5, 4 p.
Caribes en Surinaamse	₰ 4, 6 a 5, 4 p.
Mascavados, met 18 m. rabat.	₰ 7 a 7, 6 p.
Panneelen met 18 m. rabat.	₰ 4, 6 a 5
Suyker Syroop de 100 ℔	₰ 20, 6 a 21

No. 4. Saffraen en Cruidenierÿen / bÿ 't ℔.

Gattinois Saffraen	₰ 32
Montaban en la Roche	₰ 24 a 28
Oranje	₰ 20 a 22
Engels ₰ Arragons	₰ 6 a 12
Geconfijte Gember	₰ 20 a 23
Natte Succaden	₰ 10 a 12
Genees Greyn	₰ 8
Nagelhout	st. 19 a 20

No. 5. Cruidenierÿen / bÿ de 100 ℔.

A Mand. lang ₰ 44 a 45	Valence	₰ 31 a 32	
Provence ₰ 23, 10 a 24	Barbar.	₰ 23 a 24	
Anys Alic. ₰ 21 a 22	Roomse	₰ 20 a 21	
Veneetse ₰	Malthes.	₰ 14 a 15	
Turckse ₰ 9 a 10	Maagd.	₰ 17 a 18	
Cappers ₰ 23 a 24	Comyn	₰ 17, 10 a 18	
Corenten N. ₰ 16	Oudt ₰ 10 a 11		
Gember Wit ₰ 10 a 13	Blauw ₰ 11		
Pruym. lang ₰ 15 a 15, 6	Ronde	₰ 20 a 22	
Rosijn lang N. ₰ 13, 10 a 14	Oudt	₰ 10 a 12	
Rijs Milaens ₰ 31, 6 a 32	Root-c. ₰ 33, 6 a 34		
Bracke ₰ 30 a 32	Styfzel ₰ 10 a 10, 15		
Vygen Nieu ₰ 8 a 8, 10	Oude ₰		
Zeep Alicant. ₰ 21 a 21, 10	Marsil. ₰ 18, 10 a 19		

No. 10. Drogerÿen / bÿ de 100 ℔.

Bitter Amandelen	₰ 17 a 20
Cassia fistula	₰ 15 a 25
Sap van Soethout	₰ 35 a 42
Irias ₰ 22, 10 Labdanum	₰ 23
Veneerse Terpentyn	₰ 35 a 36

Drogerÿen bÿ het ℔.

Benzoin ℔ st. 14, 48	Boras ger.	st. 18	
Cacauw st. 7 a 8	Cam. ger.	st. 42	
Cardem. min st. 28 a 36	Card. major	st. 26	
Cassia lign. st. 33	Coculus	st. 7 a 8	
Collapisc. st. 22 a 32	Colloquin.	st. 10 a 11	
Cubeben st. 10	Galanga	st. 13	
Gum Drag. st. 14 a 15	Jalappa	st. 17 a 18	
Manna st. 38: 44: 54	Mastix	st. 20	
Mexioc. in st. 8 a 9	Mirrha	st. 13 a 14	
Olibanum st. 8: 10: 14	Lange Pep.	st. 6 a 7	
Quiks. banco st. 36	Rhabar.	₰ 4, 5, 7	
Rad. China st. 24, 40, 90	Salarmon	st. 10 a 12	
Salsaparilla st. 25 a 46	Scamon.	₰ 4. 6. 9	
Sedoar st. 12	Seneblad.	st. 10, 16, 20	
Severslaet st. 17 a 20	Turbith	st. 42 a 44	

Drogerÿen / bÿ d'Once.

Amberg. ₰ 60 a 66 d. Noir	₰ 34 a 44
Beso. Ori. ₰ 10 a 14 Occident,	st. 42 a 54
Civet oprecht Amsterdams	₰ 12
Musc. tonq. ₰ 12 a 14 Bengael.	₰ 8 a 9
dito buyten blasen	₰ 12 a 20
Stamp-paerlen, Orient.	₰ 10
dito Occidentael	st. 15: 28: 48

No. 11. Vlas en Hennep / 't schip ₰ van 300 ℔.

Reyn-heyligh Vlas	₰ 53 a 54
Coninxb. Paternoster	
Rijgs Paternoster	₰ 45 a 46
Hekelts Letous	₰ 34 a 35
Pruysch	
Ezens of Rozeys	₰ 36 a 37
Memels	₰ 40 a 45
Driebant oud ₰ 35 a 36 Nieuw	₰ 24 a 25
Rijgsche Reyn Hennep	₰ 26 a 27
Coninxb. en Nerfs Reyn	₰ 26 a 26, 10
Rijghsche Pas	₰ 18 a 19
Coninxb. en Nerfsche Pas	₰ 16 a 16, 10
Muscovische Hennep	₰ 18 a 20 a 24
Courlants en Memelts	₰ 18 a 19
Hollants gewas, de 100 ℔	₰ 6, 10 a 7
Touwerck van Reyn Hennip	₰ 33, 10 a 34
van Moscovische Hennip	₰ 28 a 29
Cabel-garen van Reyn Hennip	₰ 32
van Mosc. of Inlands Hennip	₰ 24, 10 a 25
Zeyl-garen de 100 ℔	₰ 20 a 21

No. 12. Pot-asch / met 18 M. Rab.

2.2
The rise of the Dutch economy

One part of the world that enjoyed above-average economic development before the nineteenth century was the Netherlands. For many years, the Netherlands had a higher level of economic growth and a higher standard of living than any other country in Europe. According to economic historians Jan de Vries and Ad van der Woude, it was the first country with an economy that can be described as 'modern'. By this, they mean a national economy with the following characteristics: (1) the presence of markets for goods and factors of production (land, labour and capital) that are relatively open and accessible; (2) a level of agrarian productivity that is high enough to maintain a social and occupational structure that can serve as the basis for a complex division of labour; (3) the presence of a government that pursues policies to protect property rights, freedom of contract and freedom of movement, and pays attention to the material conditions in which citizens live; and (4) levels of technological development and social organization that facilitate sustainable economic development and that can support a material culture of sufficient diversity to maintain market-oriented consumer behaviour. Thus, such an economy need not experience constant economic growth, but it does have certain structural characteristics that can be described as 'modern'.

Economic growth in the Netherlands began before the period known as the 'Golden Age' (c. 1580–1680), but historians still disagree on when exactly it started. In the fifteenth century? The fourteenth century? Or even earlier? What we know for sure is that Holland, in any case, underwent such fundamental changes before 1500 that its sixteenth-century economic structure deviated markedly from the normal pattern in pre-industrial societies: most people did not work in agriculture, as was the norm, but in industry and in the service sector (see Table 2.3).

From the late sixteenth century, growth accelerated rapidly, taking place across a broad front. All sectors – from agriculture and fishing to industry and international services – contributed to this growth, which continued until the third quarter of the seventeenth century. According to current available estimates, after c. 1675 there was first a stagnation and then a slight fall in income per capita. Economic historian Jan Luiten van Zanden has shown that until c. 1800, the level of prosperity was probably higher than in any other European country, including England, which experienced steady economic growth from the seventeenth century onwards (see Table 2.4). In other words, the 'Golden Age' did not end with a dramatic decline, but with a soft landing.

◄ FIGURE 2.2 *Amsterdam price-list from January 1686, showing goods prices by type and/or origin.*
© *Netherlands Economic History Archive Amsterdam, Special Collections; photo: Karel Davids.*

TABLE 2.3 *The Occupational Structure of Holland/the Netherlands by Sector, in Percentages, Compared to Several Other European Countries, 1500–1800*

		Agriculture and fishing	Industry	Services
1514	Holland	39	38	22
1675	The Netherlands	38		
1700	Great Britain	61	19	20
1750	The Netherlands	41	32	27
	Great Britain	53	24	23
1800	The Netherlands	43	26	31
	Great Britain	36	30	34
	Germany	62	21	17

Sources: De Vries en Van der Woude, *The first modern economy*; Van Zanden, 'Taking the measure'.

TABLE 2.4 *Estimated Income per Capita of the Population in the Netherlands, Compared with Several Other European Countries, 1500–1820 (index number Great Britain 1820 = 100)*

	1500	1570	1700	1750	1820
The Netherlands	58	58	94	94	92
Southern Netherlands	46	55	55	61	62
Great Britain	43	43-45	69	84	100
Italy	67	65	57	61	53
Spain	43-48	43-48	39-44	40-41	48

Source: Van Zanden, *The long road*, 241.

The growth that occurred from the Late Middle Ages can be explained on the basis of the interplay between external impulses and internal changes.

In the fourteenth and fifteenth centuries, the area today known as 'the Netherlands' was increasingly drawn into larger trade networks established by merchants from Flanders, the Hanseatic region, Southern Germany, Italy, France and the Iberian Peninsula. There was growing demand from the Baltic and the Southern Netherlands for products from Holland and Zeeland, such as fish, textiles, beer and peat, and for shipping services from the provinces providing international and regional cargo transport. Migrants from other parts of Europe also contributed to economic development, even before the major migration movement from the Southern Netherlands, which began after 1570.

Although external impulses such as these were also present in other regions, they did not have the same effects as in the Netherlands. To a considerable degree, the remarkable economic development was facilitated by endogenous conditions and incentives. In this sense, the Netherlands followed a path that deviated in some respects from the pattern in most other European regions. This becomes clear when we consider the Dutch case in the light of the aforementioned general models.

First, the Netherlands does not fit into the pure Malthusian model, which focuses on the relationship between the population and means of livelihood. Unlike in France and other European countries, the Netherlands (at least, the west of the country) was relatively quick to escape the limits of agricultural production capacity at home. Food imports, commercialization and urbanization reached high levels at a relatively early stage.

The internal boost that launched these developments was the result of changes in the physical environment. The peatlands inwards from the coast, which had been reclaimed from the ninth century onwards, initially supported agriculture and animal husbandry. On higher-lying parts of Holland rye, barley and flax were cultivated, for example. Over time, though, soil densification and the shrinkage and oxidation of peat layers resulted in settling, and the ground level was lowered. People responded to the sinking ground level by increasingly intervening in the management of water systems, from dredging ditches and constructing quays and locks to building dykes and windmills driven by horse-power or wind-power. Although these proved to be useful solutions to the constant drainage problem, they could not prevent large parts of the land in the Western Netherlands from becoming unsuitable for arable farming. This point was reached in the second half of the fourteenth century. Those living in rural areas had little choice but to focus on animal husbandry, seek work outside the agricultural sector or move to the towns. The Western Netherlands was no longer able to feed itself. As a consequence, more and more grain was imported from Northern France and the Baltic region. A significant share of the available labour in rural Holland was devoted to market-oriented, non-agrarian activities, such as spinning and weaving, brewing, brick-making, lime-burning, shipbuilding, fishing, cargo transport, dyke-building and peat-digging. There was also a sharp rise in urbanization. While it is estimated that just 14 per cent of the population of Holland lived in towns in 1300, this had risen to 23 per cent in 1348, 33 per cent in 1400 and 45 per cent in 1514.

The deviation from the Malthusian model is related to a second unique characteristic that became manifest in the west of the Netherlands. The agrarian householders there did not focus on achieving self-sufficiency but turned to the market at an earlier stage than in many other places in Europe. This market orientation was already evident in the fifteenth century. From the late sixteenth century, it was accompanied by increasing specialization. Farmers abandoned the non-agricultural activities that had still provided a considerable share of their income around 1500. Instead, they focused on animal husbandry, horticulture or cultivating crops for industry, such as flax, hemp or rapeseed. They also invested in improving the quality of their land, buildings, equipment and livestock, and gained increasing know-how in their specialization, allowing them to boost the productivity of their business. Thus, in these regions the specialization model, not the peasant model, was the rule.

The transition to the specialization model was partly facilitated by the unique institutional environment and the prevailing ownership relations. Institutions that were commonly found in Medieval Europe, such as serfdom, the manorial system and banal domains, also featured in the west of the Netherlands. Traces of them have been found in the oldest inhabited parts of Holland, namely the coastal regions and along the major rivers, where most of the property owned by noble lords, religious houses and charitable institutions was located. But the power of 'standard' institutions such as these declined considerably when, on the initiative of the counts of Holland and the bishops of Utrecht, the great reclamation of the peatlands began. The farmers who settled in this new area from the eleventh century were free of all kinds of servile or feudal obligations from the outset. After this, such obligations gradually disappeared on 'older' land, too. Of the cultivated land in Holland around the mid-sixteenth century, just 5–10 per cent was owned by the nobility, and 10 per cent was owned by religious or charitable institutions. Town-dwellers owned 20–30 per cent, and the rest belonged to farmers. Many farmers owned much of the land they worked themselves.

The purchase of land in the countryside by town-dwellers did not mean, though, that the latter intervened extensively in its use. Other measures taken by towns, such as the prohibition of industrial activities in the countryside (*buitenneringen*) or the obligation to use municipal markets, put few obstacles in the farmers' way in practice. The fierce inter-town rivalry, the power of the sovereign and resistance from the countryside itself meant that no single town in the Western Netherlands was able to dominate its surroundings in the way that Italian city-states could. Farmers in Holland were thus largely free to take their own path, unhindered by feudal lords or dominant towns. In this way, flourishing markets for both factors of production (land, labour and capital) and products had already emerged in the countryside of Holland in the Late Middle Ages. When the circumstances were auspicious, agrarian households opted for specialization.

Thus, in many respects the foundations for the Dutch 'Golden Age' were laid long before the sixteenth century. The Habsburg Netherlands was still a unified whole prior to the Revolt, with Holland and Zeeland forming part of the core area, along with Flanders and Brabant. Around the mid-sixteenth century, a certain degree of labour specialization had emerged in this highly urbanized and commercialized core area, with the North functioning as the heart of the maritime industry and the South as the centre of industry. In terms of capital, trade expertise and breadth of contacts by, however, the South was superior to the North. The top of the economic hierarchy lay not in Amsterdam, but in Antwerp. The Revolt, the subsequent constitutional separation of the Habsburg provinces and the migration of largely Protestant merchants and craftsmen from the South to the North ensured that the Northern Netherlands ('the Dutch Republic') became a separate economic unit with particularly high growth potential.

A wave of innovations followed in the late sixteenth century, ensuring that the Republic experienced substantial economic growth until around 1675, and it also continued to enjoy a rather high level of prosperity during the subsequent period of stagnation. This growth took place in various sectors. In the primary sector, although the herring industry had passed its peak by *c.* 1620, the whaling industry experienced a robust expansion in the seventeenth century. In the secondary sector (industry), existing branches of industry such as ship building, beer-brewing, the production of woollen cloth and linen-weaving lost vitality towards the late seventeenth century. They were replaced by a whole series of new 'leaders', including calico printing, the silk industry, fustian production, tobacco-processing, pipe-making, pottery-manufacturing, the paper industry, distilleries, sugar-refining and the chemical industry, which provided much employment and ensured extensive and often high-quality production. The secondary sector as a whole did not begin to contract until after 1740.

After 1580, the services sector acquired a larger scale and more diverse character. Following in the footsteps of the Spanish and the Portuguese, the Dutch expanded their network of trade and shipping connections to Asia and the Western Hemisphere. Although, unlike in Great Britain and France, intercontinental trade and shipping in the Republic were always much less important than trade within Europe and the Mediterranean (see Table 2.5), both imports from Asia and imports from the Atlantic region experienced striking growth between *c.* 1680 and 1770 (see Table 2.6; this does not show the trade of the Dutch East India Company within Asia and the extensive Dutch slave trade in the Atlantic region). After 1680, the emphasis of the imports from Asia shifted from spices to coffee, tea, sugar, silk, porcelain and cotton fabrics. Imports from the Western Hemisphere largely consisted of coffee, sugar, tobacco and cocoa, all of which were produced with the labour of enslaved people. From Africa, Dutch traders imported substantial

TABLE 2.5 *Overseas Imports to the Netherlands, Great Britain and France, by Value in Millions of Guilders, c. 1770*

Origin	The Netherlands	Great Britain	France
Western Hemisphere	15.7	58.1	74.1
Asia	20.0	24.5	9.6
Europa and Mediterranean	107.3	80.4	90.8
Total	143.0	153.0	174.5

Source: De Vries, 'Connecting Europe and Asia', 92 and 93.

TABLE 2.6 *Development of Imports to the Netherlands from Asia and the Western Hemisphere by Value, 1640–1780 (index number 1770–1779 = 100)*

	Asia	Western hemisphere
1640–9	39	20
1680–9	52	9
1700–9	69	19
1720–9	93	25
1740–9	80	45
1760–9	107	80
1770–9	100	100

Source: De Vries, 'The Dutch Atlantic economies', 19.

amounts of gold, ivory and gum. A strong growth in financial services occurred from the 1740s onwards. It was easy for plantation owners and foreign governments to raise loans on Amsterdam's capital market. The contribution of slave-based activities to the Dutch economy significantly increased in the eighteenth century, reaching an estimated 5.2 per cent of the gross domestic product (GDP) in 1770, and even 10.36 per cent of the GDP of Holland, the richest province in the Dutch Republic.

After 1580, the economic expansion was partly facilitated by the more intensified use of factors of production. First, the amount of capital expanded, partly as a result of the migration of merchants from the South. More raw materials were also available, thanks to growing trade. Peat and wind-power delivered much of the extra energy needed for industry. Later, increasing use was made of imported coal. Furthermore, the amount of land under cultivation expanded as a result of land reclamation and impoldering. Nor did the relatively small size of the Dutch Republic's population act as a bottleneck; the growing need for temporary labour in the countryside, in industry and on the ships was met, to a considerable extent, by the flow of migrant workers from other regions of North-western Europe, especially Scandinavia and Germany. It is estimated that in the seventeenth century, half of all paid work in the Dutch Republic was performed by economic migrants, a higher share than in any other European country.

Moreover, technological innovations in almost every sector of the economy contributed to the rise in productivity. A good example is the man-powered ribbon mill (*lintmolen*), which allowed many more ribbons to be made at the same time (Figure 2.3). Another example is the large-scale use of wind-power in industry. Hundreds of industrial windmills

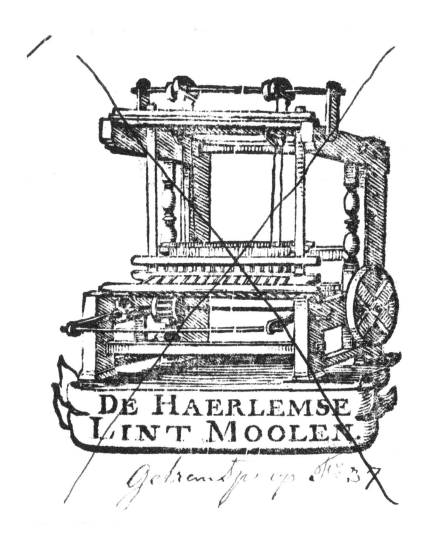

FIGURE 2.3 *Ribbon mill depicted on the stamp of the Haarlem-based businessman Cornelis van den Brie, eighteenth century. This is one of the few surviving images of the machine. The cross through the image was made by a clerk in the eighteenth century.*
© *Atlas North Holland Archives, Haarlem. Photo: Karel Davids.*

such as these were operating in the Zaanstreek region *c.* 1700. Until long into the eighteenth century, the rest of Europe viewed the Netherlands as a technological paradise. Finally, the growth in productivity was accompanied by a rising level of education. After 1600, literacy rates among Dutch men and women were higher than in other European countries, and the same is likely to have been true for numeracy (Chapter 4). An extensive system of vocational training created an even larger pool of human capital. This vocational training was partly embedded in the guild system, which saw its greatest expansion during the 'Golden Age'.

In addition to the more intensive use of factors of production and technological innovations, institutional developments also played a key role. New organizational forms emerged in trade and shipping, such as the joint-stock company, which allowed capital to be tied up for longer periods. This organizational form was used for the first time by companies that were granted exclusive rights by the States General to sail to Asia and the south and west of the Atlantic Ocean, accompanied by a delegation of sovereign rights, such as the right to wage war and conclude treaties; namely, the Dutch East India Company (Verenigde Oostindische Compagnie or VOC, founded in 1602) and the Dutch West India Company (West-Indische Compagnie or WIC, founded in 1621). Shares in the VOC and the WIC were traded on the stock exchange. In the first decades of the seventeenth century, the patent system for inventions was used more intensively in the Dutch Republic than in any other European country. The reason why Amsterdam remained a leading centre of world trade until long into the eighteenth century was not because of its position as a concrete staple market for goods (which was relatively limited), but because of its role as an information interchange. Amsterdam was the ideal place in which to gather, exchange and analyse information. It was where all kinds of correspondence networks came together, and people from every part of the world met at the stock exchange, the notary's office, in bookshops or at the VOC headquarters (the Oost-Indisch Huis). In other words, when it came to information, Amsterdam had the lowest transaction costs. Moreover, the government of the Dutch Republic was renowned for protecting the rights of investors and traders.

A period of stagnation began in the late seventeenth century, lasting until *c.* 1820. Various reasons can be identified for this. To start with, conditions deteriorated in the export markets. Due to protectionism and increasing competition from other up-and-coming European economies (England, France, Prussia, Sweden, Denmark and Russia), Dutch entrepreneurs found it increasingly hard to sell their goods and services abroad. In addition, after 1713 the Dutch Republic was less able, politically and militarily, to defend its economic interests adequately, labour costs in the west of the Netherlands were relatively high (partly as a result of the rather high tax burden) and the capacity for technological innovation declined. This meant that entrepreneurs were unable to offset the high labour costs and shrinking

TEXT BOX 2.2 THE VOC IN ASIA

Prior to the arrival of the Europeans in Asia, there were already complex trade networks in the Indian Ocean and Chinese Sea. Important hubs in these maritime networks included Aden, Hormuz (at the entrance to the Persian Gulf), Gujarat and Calicut (on the western coast of India), Malacca, and Canton and Zaiton (in China). In the sixteenth and seventeenth centuries, the Portuguese, Dutch and English took over some of these key positions and founded some new trading posts, too, such as Goa and Batavia. However, no single European state or trading company succeeded in gaining complete control over the Asian trade networks. In general, the Europeans had to adapt to existing patterns.

The power of the VOC was likewise limited in practice. Although the States General gave the company the exclusive right in 1602 to transport goods overseas from Asia to the Netherlands, and it used brute force to obtain an almost complete monopoly on the sale of mace, cloves and nutmeg from the Moluccas and cinnamon from Ceylon, it was not the only company to transport products from Asia to Europe. Aside from the few regions where the company exercised political and military power for shorter or longer periods (South Africa, the Indonesian Archipelago, Ceylon and the southern coast of India), the VOC behaved more like a 'merchant' than a 'ruler'.

However, the Company had a significant impact on slavery and the slave trade in Asia. The estimated number of enslaved people in VOC territories rose from about 8,000 in 1625 to more than 75,000 in the second half of the eighteenth century. By 1780, one in four people in Batavia were enslaved, and one in two in VOC settlements in Cochin. Recent estimates put the total number of enslaved people brought to VOC settlements in Asia between 1625 and 1800 at 660,000 (minimum) to 1,135,000 (maximum). This exceeded the numbers brought to Dutch settlements in the Atlantic, which are now estimated at 495,000 (minimum) to 850,000 (maximum). Although the Company's own share in the Asian slave trade was relatively limited, hundreds of thousands of enslaved people were carried by VOC employees as private traders.

The commercial success of the VOC lay primarily in its capacity to finance the purchasing of Asian products for the European market largely from profitable transactions within Asia. In this way, the company used silver and copper from Japan to purchase Indian textiles or pepper from Sumatra; Japanese copper, in turn, was paid for by selling silk from Bengal. This successful formula lost its power in the eighteenth century, however. Increasing competition from other European companies and private traders from England ('country traders'), as well as rising military costs in Asia caused by the growing conflict with native leaders, left the VOC with spiralling financial problems; a predicament that would eventually prove fatal in 1799.

TABLE 2.7 *Estimated Value of Capital Holdings in Holland, in Millions of Guilders, 1650 and 1790*

	1650	**1790**
Real estate	180	480
Merchant fleet	20	22
Stocks	200	200
Government debt	130	360
Foreign loans	—	650
Total	530	1712

Source: Van Zanden, 'Economic growth', 23.

export markets by boosting productivity, developing new products, and thereby opening up new markets. Despite this, the features of the 'modern' economy described earlier remained intact during this period of stagnation. Moreover, in the early nineteenth century, the Netherlands could still boast of a large reserve of physical and financial capital (Table 2.7) and a multitude of colonial possessions in the world beyond Europe.

2.3
Labour relations and income distribution

Economic development means that a society enjoys a rising level of income. Stagnation and shrinkage, on the other hand, mean that the level of income remains the same or declines. But how are the costs and benefits distributed? To what extent do different groups share the costs and benefits of economic development, stagnation or shrinkage? In order to answer this question, we need to consider labour relations and the distribution of income. Who were the workers? How was the work organized? How was the output of work distributed? In practice there were many variants, which in turn depended on power relations in society and the arrangements for mitigating the risks of human existence. A recently designed taxonomy is set out in Table 2.8.

This taxonomy can be read as follows. Every society includes some people who do not work: they are too young, too old or too unwell, they are unable to find work, or they can afford not to work (such as people of private means; column 1). Of those who do work, some work in reciprocal relationships (e.g. within a household or community, such as a religious institution; column 2); others supply labour in the form of an unpaid tribute (forced labourers,

TABLE 2.8 *Taxonomy of Labour Relations*

Non-workers	*Workers: type of relation*			
			Commodified labour	
	Reciprocal	*Tribute labour*	*In market*	*In non-market institution*
Too old/too young/too disabled to work	Within a household	Forced labour	Wage labour	Wage labour
Unable to find work	Within a community	Indentured labour	Self-employed work	
No need to work		Servitude/ Serfdom	Employership	
		Slavery		

Source: Based on IISG, A Global Collaboratory on the History of Labour Relations in the Period 1500–2000.

conscripts, servile labour/serfs, slaves; column 3); and yet others supply labour as a 'commodity', whether as free wage-labourers, self-employed workers or employers (column 4), or as the paid employees of a non-market institution (such as a public enterprise or a church employer; column 5). Thus, in the case of commodified labour, people are remunerated for their work.

How societies in the past dealt with non-workers is discussed in Chapter 4. When we consider those who did work, in most societies until the nineteenth century, the three main types of labour (reciprocal labour, tribute labour and commodified labour) existed alongside one another. Free wage labour could exist alongside forced labour, serfdom, slavery and unpaid services in a household or religious institution. Free labour, where the level of wages is subject to market forces, did not become the standard pattern prior to 1800.

Over time, though, the dissemination of different kinds of labour did undergo several important changes. Slavery, which had disappeared in practice in Europe around 1000 CE, returned at the end of the fourteenth century and was subsequently exported overseas, too. Within Europe, the differences became greater from the fifteenth century onwards. In the region to the west of the Elbe, the size of the commodified labour category grew in relative terms. By contrast, in the area to the east of the Elbe and in European colonies overseas, the category of tribute labour grew. Serfdom assumed extreme forms in Central and Eastern Europe. The further east one went, the less freedom there was. Russian serfs in the eighteenth century could be sold, pawned, exchanged and gambled away. The 'second serfdom' (the 'first serfdom' refers to serfdom in Western Europe in the Middle Ages) affected tens of millions of people. On the eve of the emancipation in 1861,

> **TEXT BOX 2.3 THE ABOLITION OF THE SLAVE TRADE AND SLAVERY**
>
> From the late eighteenth century, the slave trade and slavery increasingly became a subject of debate in Europe and the United States. Leading critics included evangelical Christians (such as Quakers, Baptists and Methodists) and Enlightenment thinkers. The debate was dominated by principled, non-economic arguments. Critics described the slave trade and slavery as immoral, and as contrary to the principle of equality between people.
>
> The first important success was achieved in 1794, when the National Convention in Paris abolished the slave trade and slavery in French colonies (a measure that would be reversed by Napoleon eight years later). Of even greater significance was the change in Great Britain, which traditionally had a large stake in the slave trade. Parliament initially banned the trading of slaves by British subjects in 1807, after which the British Navy began to act against the trading of slaves by subjects of other nations. The United States banned the importation of slaves from 1808. The Netherlands, France, Spain, Denmark and other countries introduced similar bans on the importation of slaves in their colonies in the early nineteenth century. The slave trade would continue illegally for many years. It is estimated that another two million slaves were transported from Africa to America after 1815.
>
> With the prohibition on slavery in the Atlantic region, Great Britain again set a good example: slavery in the British colonies was abolished in 1833. France and Denmark followed in 1848, the United States (after a devastating civil war) and the Netherlands in 1863, Spain in 1886 and Brazil in 1888. The Arabian slave trade in Africa would continue to exist for longer than the Atlantic slave trade. The Ottoman Empire began to take action against slavery and the slave trade only after the revolution of 1908 brought a group of reformers ('Young Turks') to power.

the tsar's empire alone was home to more than fifty million peasants who were the 'property' of the state or private landowners. Serfdom was less common in the Ottoman Empire, but much tribute labour was supplied in the form of duties for the state or for tax farmers, or as slave labour. Slaves served in the army and in various sectors of the economy. In China, Japan and Vietnam, by contrast, slavery had all but disappeared in the eighteenth century.

The British colonies in America were initially populated to a large degree – probably as much as 60 per cent – by unfree labourers from Europe. Eight out of ten of them were men. For a period of four or five years, these labourers were contractually almost entirely at the mercy of the employers who had paid for their passage; they were only released once they had worked for free for a certain period. This system of indentured labour continued to exist until the early nineteenth century. English convicts were also sent to America. After the American declaration of independence, Australia became the new destination. In the eighteenth century, however, the largest category of unfree labourers on the other side of the Atlantic Ocean consisted of enslaved people who were shipped from Africa. Virtually all of the many plantations that were established in North America, the West Indies and South America to produce sugar, tobacco, cotton, coffee or cocoa for the world market were worked by Black slaves.

The Netherlands occupied a rather exceptional place in this spectrum of labour relations in two respects. The market for commodified labour developed relatively early (in the Late Middle Ages), and from the seventeenth century a significant part of the economy was dependent on the use of migrant labour. But the presence of a labour market did not mean that everyone could negotiate it with equal ease, or that everyone had access to it. In the course of the seventeenth century, there was increasing segmentation in the labour market between people with permanent or regular work (such as municipal employees) and a 'pool' of temporary labourers, mainly migrant workers. It became increasingly difficult for people who did not belong to the public church – such as Catholics and Jews – to join a guild, especially in the Eastern and Southern Netherlands. Opportunities for women in the labour market remained limited, although they were better than in many other European countries (see Chapter 4).

Differences in economic development were accompanied by differences in wealth between and within societies. One well-known measure for establishing the latter is the standard of living. In societies where wage labour plays more than a marginal role, the standard of living is often measured on the basis of the development of real wages. Real wages are calculated by adapting nominal wages to changes in the price level of the most important consumer goods.

Real wages thus tell us how much bread, clothing, food and so forth a wage labourer could buy with what they were paid for their work. For towns and regions, the real wages of certain occupational groups (especially construction workers) can be reconstructed over a long period. Table 2.9 gives an overview for European towns between 1500 and 1850.

The differences in the standard of living between wage labourers in North-western Europe on the one hand and Southern and Central Europe on the other, which emerged after the great plague epidemics of the fourteenth century, became even greater over time. Within the most developed regions of Europe, income inequality also declined for a while, as the population loss as a result of the Black Death made labour scarcer compared to land. It rose again when demographic growth resumed, however, and the commercial and landed elites strengthened their position.

Nevertheless, wage labourers in North-western Europe, especially in the Netherlands and England, probably had more to spend in the long run,

TABLE 2.9 *Real Daily Wages of Unskilled Construction Workers in European Towns, 1500–1850 (index number London 1500–1649 = 100)*

	1500–1649	*1650–99*	*1700–49*	*1750–99*	*1800–49*
North-western Europe					
London	100	96	110	99	98
Amsterdam	97	98	107	98	79
Antwerp	98	88	92	88	82
Paris	62	60	56	51	65
Southern Europe	71	52	61	42	30
Central Europe	74	66	58	55	48

Source: De Vries, *Industrious Revolution*, 83.

because the number of days worked per year rose and the sum of earnings per household grew. In the Netherlands, there was a striking increase in hours worked after the Revolt. Under the influence of the Reformed Church, the number of free days (especially church holidays) was sharply curtailed. The number of hours worked rose on average from *c.* 3,100 hours per year to *c.* 3,700 in the mid-seventeenth century. In England, too, people began to work increasingly long hours: after the Reformation, in the second quarter of the sixteenth century, the number of days worked rose from 200 to 250 per year, and between 1750 and 1830 it increased further to no fewer than 300 days per year. By then, the real annual incomes of English workers finally exceeded the level reached after the Black Death.

Household disposable income also rose, because more family members, including women and children, spent part of their time working and brought money in. In turn, the growth in income that resulted from this extra work facilitated an increase in demand for consumer goods. This development is described by Jan de Vries as the 'industrious revolution', which preceded the Industrial Revolution, and accelerated the latter substantially.

2.4
Industrialization and the Great Divergence

In the long term, the difference in wealth levels also became evident between Europe (and former European colonies in America), on the one hand, and Asia, on the other. Throughout most of history, Asia, particularly China, undoubtedly had a higher level of economic development than Europe. Around 1500, Asia's share in total global production amounted to around 65 per cent, while that of Western Europe was just 18 per cent. Asia also had a much larger population (see Chapter 1). For centuries, the productivity of wet rice cultivation had overshadowed anything achieved in European agriculture. Moreover, until the late eighteenth century, Europe was more interested in products from Asia than vice versa. Other than precious metals, Europeans had little to offer in return for spices, silk, tea, porcelain or cotton textiles. Much of the silver that was mined in America would eventually end up in China and India.

Nevertheless, at a certain point, a gap in prosperity levels emerged between the two parts of the world; this is known as the Great Divergence. There is debate among economic historians as to when the divergence began and the factors that explain the growing gap. According to some researchers, the origins of the Great Divergence can be traced back long before the eighteenth century, whereas others argue that the gap emerged only around 1800. The latter mainly explain this with reference to the Industrial Revolution, while the former cite a combination of factors with a much longer history, which in some respects hark back to the Early Middle Ages.

A tentative comparison of real wage levels appears to suggest that the paths did indeed diverge before 1800. Table 2.10 shows a comparison of the real daily wages of unskilled labourers in relatively highly developed regions of Europe, China and India. In order to compare the levels, the table shows how much grain (wheat or rice) or silver a labourer's wages would buy; the latter measure allows for a greater variety of consumer goods than grain alone. According to the first measure, the levels across the three regions were relatively equal until the early eighteenth century, but then they diverged sharply. According to the second measure, a significant gulf emerged even earlier, which widened further from the eighteenth century onwards. In the Ottoman Empire, too, real wages were much lower than in North-western Europe.

Moreover, a recent estimate of income per capita shows that on the whole, the levels for China and Western Europe were roughly equal until the seventeenth century, and diverged sharply after 1700. The most developed areas of Western Europe (Southern England and the Netherlands) achieved a higher level of income in the eighteenth century than the most developed region of China (the Yangzi Delta). Whereas urbanization increased rapidly in those regions of North-western Europe, it hardly grew in China. Although at the end of the eighteenth century there were more people living in towns in China than in any other part of the world, in absolute terms, the density of the urban population in North-western Europe was greater at that time in relative terms. The shift from agrarian to non-agrarian economic activities was also more advanced there than in any region in China.

The Great Divergence therefore partly began *before* the Industrial Revolution. Before the mid-eighteenth century, the differences in prosperity

TABLE 2.10 *Real Daily Wages of Unskilled Labourers in India and the Yangzi Delta (China), Compared with Southern England, 1550–1850*

	Wage in India, expressed as percentage of wage in Southern England		*Wage in Yangzi Delta, expressed as percentage of wage in Southern England*	
	Calculated in quantity of grain	*Calculated in quantity of silver*	*Calculated in quantity of grain*	*Calculated in quantity of silver*
1550–99	83	21		
1600–49	95	27		
1550–1649			87	39
1650–99	80	25		
1700–49	40	21		
1750–99	33	14		
1800–49	29	12		
1750–1849			38	15

Source: Broadberry and Gupta, 'The early modern Great Divergence', 17 and 19.

between North-western Europe and the most developed regions in China and India were already gradually widening, and this growing discrepancy in Eurasia was accompanied by increasing differences *within* Europe. From the late eighteenth century there was an acceleration, in which Great Britain set the tone as the pioneer of the Industrial Revolution.

In institutional terms, there were already clear differences between Western Europe – that is to say, Europe west of the Trieste- St Petersburg line – and other parts of Eurasia before the mid-fourteenth century. The typical family was the nuclear family: a father, a mother, some children and at the most a few live-in servants. Family relations were less complex, extensive and strong than elsewhere in Eurasia (see more on this in Chapter 4). This meant that families could make more autonomous decisions about how to respond to changes in the outside world, such as the growth of markets. More so than in other regions, it was common for transactional agreements to be recorded in written contracts, rather than in merely informal, personal agreements. In much of Europe, markets were already quite efficient by the Late Middle Ages. In the case of the capital and labour markets, this can be deduced from the relatively low level of interest – mentioned earlier – and the relatively low skill premium. The skill premium is the difference between the remuneration of a skilled worker and that of an unskilled worker.

From c. 1350, the skill premium began to fall sharply throughout Europe, indicating that a relatively large supply of skilled workers was available. In North-western Europe and Central Europe, the premium subsequently continued to fluctuate around this new, low level for centuries. A similarly sharp fall did not occur elsewhere in Eurasia. Again, the fact that the 'extra' remuneration for skilled work in these regions of Europe remained relatively low was partly related to the level of willingness of government institutions and people themselves to invest in education. Levels of literacy and numeracy were already quite high in this region in the Early Modern period. The formation of human capital was relatively advanced.

When it comes to institutions and commercialization, Great Britain and the Dutch Republic stand out on two more points. Around 1700, individual ownership rights were protected in the Netherlands more effectively than anywhere else in Europe. Moreover, Great Britain and the Republic were in the vanguard of the industrious revolution (see p. 56); family members worked particularly hard, household disposable income rose and demand for consumer goods grew.

Why did Great Britain, of all countries, eventually surge ahead? As in the Low Countries, agricultural productivity rose gradually in England from the Late Middle Ages (Table 2.1). This raised the Malthusian ceiling for agrarian production. The growth in productivity was partly the result of gradual technological improvements, such as better drainage, more fertilization, more selection of suitable seeds and more cultivation of the nitrogen-fixing legumes (beans, peas, clover) that boosted productivity. None of these changes was spectacular in itself, but together they had a considerable impact. The improvements were introduced by commercially operating farmers, who hired agricultural labourers to do the actual work in the fields.

The developments in Great Britain also differed from those in the Netherlands. English agriculture was much more focused on grain production. The yield rose so sharply that between c. 1700 and c. 1770, the country was able to export grain on a large scale, including to the Dutch Republic. Moreover, the nature of the 'agrarian capitalism' that emerged in Southern England was unlike that in the west of the Netherlands. After all, an essential characteristic of this capitalism was that production was organized in large units, as mentioned earlier in the 'Brenner debate'. Most commercially operating farmers leased land from noble landowners with large estates. Land ownership in England was much more concentrated than in the Republic. This tendency towards concentrating land in the hands of a relatively small group of families continued, sometimes more rapidly and sometimes more slowly, from the Late Middle Ages until the late eighteenth century. An acceleration took place from c. 1540, when the property of the Catholic Church was taken over and sold as a result of the Reformation. A second acceleration took place in the eighteenth century, when the enclosure movement reached its peak. This movement involved the partitioning and fencing-off of open and/or common land with the approval of parliament; an institution that was, rather unsurprisingly, dominated by landowners.

Not only did rising agricultural productivity facilitate a further expansion of the towns, but it also resulted, together with the industrious revolution, in broad sections of the population having an increasing amount of disposable income. From the late seventeenth century, growing income led, in turn, to rising demand for industrial products and products from the services sector (such as education, postal services, theatrical productions, cafe entertainment or lectures on 'experimental physics'). The demand for industrial products focused on a wide range of items, some of which were imported, but many of which were also increasingly manufactured in Great Britain itself. This boosted a wide range of urban and rural industries, ranging from wool-weaving, the cotton industry, silk-weaving and hat-making to construction, the paper industry, printing, clockmaking, instrument-making, pottery-manufacturing, metalworking, tobacco-processing and sugar-refining. The technical knowledge needed for this was originally gleaned from abroad to a large extent, especially from the Dutch Republic and – via Huguenot immigrants – from France, but later it was increasingly developed in England itself. This is shown by the rise in the number of patent applications after 1700. When industry grew, so did transport and domestic trade. A boom in the construction of canals and toll roads led to a drastic improvement in the quality of essential infrastructure in the eighteenth century. A further consequence of the expansion of towns and the growth of the non-agrarian sector was a sharp rise in the demand for energy. This led to the increasing use of water-power and the intensification of coal production.

The growing demand for industrial products and services, however, cannot be attributed to internal economic factors alone. From the late seventeenth century onwards, the British economy also received a powerful boost from the expansion of foreign trade. Industry experienced strong growth in the export of goods to America and West Africa, and the import of commodities from overseas colonies. In fact, in the eighteenth century, the Atlantic trade was more significant for Great Britain than the trade with Asia. This is illustrated by Table 2.5, which shows imports around 1770. Nigerian historian Joseph Inikori has shown that Africans played a crucial role in the Atlantic connection. Africans made a key contribution to trade growth as buyers of British goods, suppliers of commodities such as rubber and palm oil, and slaves on American and West Indian plantations, which gave British consumers cheap access to sugar, tobacco and coffee (see Map 2.2). According to a recent estimate, the contribution of the transatlantic slave trade and all activities in the plantation economy amounted to about 11 per cent of British GDP by 1800.

MAP 2.2 *The Atlantic world in the Early Modern period, showing the most important sailing routes of the Spanish treasure fleets, the slave trade and British trade.*
Source: Elliott, *Empires of the Atlantic World*, 50. Designed by René van der Vooren.

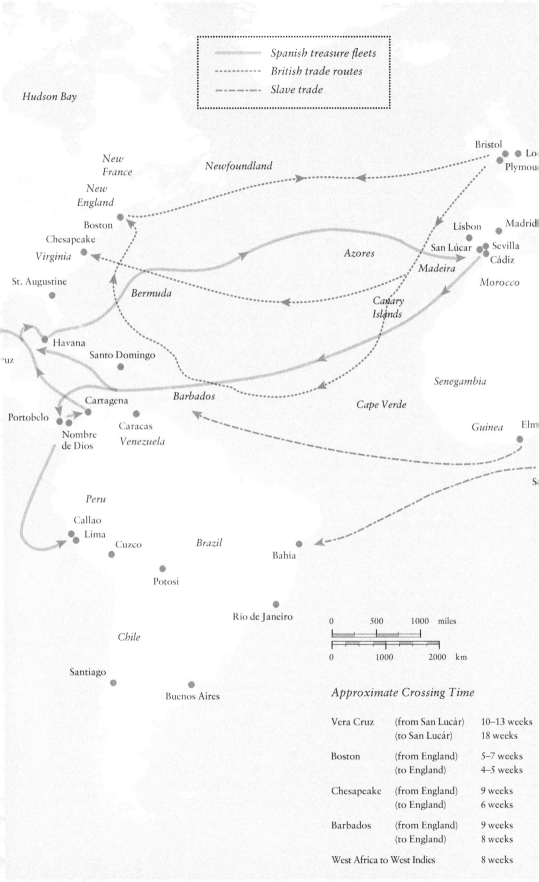

The expansion of foreign trade was not purely related to increased competitiveness due to higher productivity or lower transaction costs. Much more so than their counterparts in the Dutch Republic, British industrialists, merchants and sea carriers enjoyed protection from the state. From *c.* 1650, England (or Great Britain, after the union with Scotland in 1707) developed an extensive system of prohibitions, levies and subsidies to protect its own trade, shipping and industry from foreign competition, and thereby to increase the income and power of the state. This system, which was also established later in France, Sweden, Prussia, Denmark, Russia and other European states, is known as 'mercantilism'. It could be maintained by force of arms if necessary.

On balance, however, economic growth in Great Britain between 1700 and 1780 was little higher than that in France. Moreover, at the end of the eighteenth century it was by no means evident that this growth would continue. Around 1780, Great Britain lost many colonies in America. From the 1770s, the grain surplus was transformed into a shortage; grain was imported once more, rather than exported. Real wages fell and poverty rose. Neither Adam Smith nor Thomas Malthus expected the economy to grow sustainably. In 1776, Smith thought that a 'stationary state' was the most that could be achieved; and in 1798, Malthus foresaw the 'constant pressure of distress on man from the difficulty of subsistence' as the most likely prospect. They did not see the 'industrial revolution' on the horizon.

The concept of the Industrial Revolution would not come into vogue until much later on. The first to describe industrialization in Great Britain in the late eighteenth and nineteenth centuries specifically in these terms was the historian Arnold Toynbee, in 1880. Not only did the concept take root, but in the hands of many historians it assumed a rather radical nature, with an emphasis on its abrupt and rigorous character. Between *c.* 1760 and 1830, a rapid, far-reaching transformation was said to have taken place in the British economy and society. The acceleration was thought to have been at its greatest between 1780 and 1800. The economic historian Walter Rostow used the catchy term 'take-off' to describe this process.

Most present-day historians would agree with their predecessors that the changes in Great Britain in the eighteenth and nineteenth centuries were radical enough to deserve the label 'revolution'. Viewed from a world historical perspective, a genuine transformation took place. We can speak of a revolution in various respects: in technological/business-organizational, macro-economic and social terms. From a technological/business-organizational point of view, the revolutionary aspect lay in the far-reaching mechanization of production with the aid of machines that were not driven by human or animal power, plus the concentration of labour (especially in factories), which led to the emergence of modern industry. Viewed from a macro-economic perspective, the Industrial Revolution was characterized by continuous growth in income per capita, which is normally described as 'modern economic growth'. From a social perspective, the revolution entailed a structural change in people's occupations: whereas the share of the primary sector fell sharply, those of the secondary and later the tertiary sectors expanded. Fewer and fewer people worked in agriculture.

Today's historians, however, believe that the revolution in Great Britain did not begin as suddenly or take place as rapidly as was previously thought. After all, at the point when modern industry emerged, the British economy had already been growing for some time. Moreover, the starting level for the revolution was higher than previous generations of historians assumed. The revolution built upon growth that was already established. Recent calculations have shown that there was no spectacular acceleration in the rate of growth in the late eighteenth century (Table 2.11). The great 'leap' in productivity and income per capita occurred only in the second quarter of the nineteenth century.

Cotton, iron, coal and steam engines played a key role in the initial phase of the revolution. The rise in productivity, thanks to technological and organizational innovations, first became clearly evident in the cotton industry. Table 2.12 shows that the costs of spinning raw cotton yarn were halved between 1760 and 1830. The cost-savings lay mainly in the labour factor; much less labour was needed to supply a pound of spun yarn. For

TABLE 2.11 *Estimate of Average Annual Growth in Income per Capita in England, 1700–1870*

	Average annual growth, in %
1700–1760	0.30
1760–1800	0.17
1800–1830	0.52
1830–1870	1.98

Source: De Vries, *Industrious revolution*, 86.

TABLE 2.12 *Cost of Spinning a Pound of Raw Cotton Yarn, in 1784 Prices, England, 1760–1830*

	Energy source	*Organizational framework*	*Year*	*Pence per pound*
Spinning wheel	Manpower	Cottage industry	1760	35.00
Spinning Jenny	Manpower	Cottage industry	1775	31.28
Arkwright's water frame	Water-power	Factory	1784	27.94
Crompton's mule	Steam	Factory	1830	18.22

Source: Allen, *The British Industrial Revolution*, 185.

finer yarns, even greater cost-savings were achieved. The same development then took place in cotton-weaving and other branches of the textiles industry.

The consequences of the technological innovations from the late eighteenth century onwards were more far-reaching than those of innovations in previous periods. This is explained by the fact that these innovations were accompanied by a shift in the basic sources of energy used in the economy and society as a whole. The economic historian E. A. Wrigley has described this change as the transition from an 'organic economy' to a 'mineral-based energy economy'. An organic economy is an economy that is largely dependent on the productivity of the land. The land is the source not only of food but also of commodities (such as flax, cotton, wool or hides) and energy (in the form of wood, peat or food for people and draught animals). In such an economy, people tap a 'flow' of energy, as it were, that is produced by the land. The available amount of energy per capita thus remains relatively limited. The ceiling of economic development is low, precisely as Malthus predicted. In a mineral-based energy economy, raw materials and energy are mined underground to a much greater extent, initially mainly in the form of iron ore or coal. That means that more land becomes available for growing food, and there is more tapping of raw materials and energy from a 'reserve' than from a flow. Although this reserve is not infinite, it is much larger than that which could be supplied by a 'flow'. The potential amount of energy per capita is therefore much greater than in an organic economy. Moreover, the conversion of coal heat into mechanical energy using a steam engine, for example, facilitates a higher degree of mechanization. As a result, the Malthusian ceiling of economic development could be broken. This is what happened in Great Britain when increasingly intensive use was made of coal and steam engines. The scale on which this transition took place can be deduced from the growth in the share of steam-power as a source of energy for mechanical installations: from 6 per cent in 1760, via 20 per cent in 1800 and 47 per cent in 1830, to 90 per cent in 1870. In 1890, all of the steam engines together supplied twenty-seven times more energy than they had in 1760.

Great Britain's leading role in the development and introduction of technological innovations can partly be explained with reference to the price ratio of factors of production. Compared to other countries in Europe and China, wages were relatively high and coal was relatively cheap. A further part of the explanation lies in the availability of skills and knowledge. There was a broad base of human capital present in various groups in British society. Moreover, more than in any other country, from *c.* 1700 intensive communication emerged between entrepreneurs, landowners, craftsmen and practitioners of 'experimental physics' (based on the Newtonian model), creating a favourable seedbed for the dissemination and growth of 'useful knowledge'. The development of the steam engine, leading to the perfected version in James Watt's patent application of 1769, is a striking example. The economic historian Joel Mokyr has described the growth of this intermediary sphere as the 'Industrial Enlightenment'. It forms the connecting link between the Scientific Revolution and the Industrial Revolution. With this 'Industrial Enlightenment', Great Britain was evidently ahead of France and the Netherlands.

Since the Industrial Revolution, the flow of technological innovations has never come to a halt, although there have been fluctuations in intensity. Continuous technological change has become an essential part of economic growth. From *c.* 1830, this flow of technological innovations led to a sharp rise in structural investment. More and more capital was poured into buildings, machines and means of transport and infrastructure, such as canals, railways, roads, bridges, pipes and cables. This brought about a change in the nature of capitalism itself: merchant capitalism made way for industrial capitalism. Some countries in Europe and America, including Belgium, France and the United States, began to imitate the British example before 1850. They, too, followed the path of the Industrial Revolution. This revolution would penetrate further and more deeply after the mid-nineteenth century. From that time, industrial capitalism could assume increasingly unbridled forms as, following Great Britain's lead, the limits on the operation of markets for goods and the factors of production were abandoned in one country after another. According to the ruling liberal ideology, it was best for the market to regulate itself. What this would mean for the economy and society will be discussed in Part II of this book.

Summary

To conclude this chapter, let us briefly summarize the answers to the four questions that were posed at the outset:

1. Until the mid-nineteenth century, the possibilities for economic growth were mainly limited by low agricultural productivity. Nevertheless, some growth could occur here and there thanks to commercialization, specialization and the development of efficient institutions.
2. For many years, the Netherlands could play a leading role in economic development in Europe as a result of a combination of suitable institutions, technological innovations, a relatively high level of education among the population, easy access to capital, raw materials and energy, and the presence of a large pool of migrant labour.
3. From the fifteenth century, there were considerable differences in the degree of freedom and the remuneration of labour. Unfree labour (serfdom, slavery, indentured labour) expanded in many places in

the world, and the standard of living of wage labourers in Northwestern Europe rose more than that of wage labourers in Southern and Central Europe, and in the most developed regions of India and China.

4. The origins of the Great Divergence can be traced back before the eighteenth century, but the gulf widened rapidly from around 1800. The explanation for this lies largely in differences in institutions, the degree of commercialization and the formation of human capital, which eventually resulted in the Industrial Revolution. In these respects, Great Britain was more developed than the Netherlands, France or the most advanced regions in Asia.

3

The struggle for power
Sociopolitical developments

MARJOLEIN 'T HART

Around 1500, Europe's seventy million inhabitants lived in around 200 more-or-less independent political entities: counties, duchies, dioceses, city states, a few kingdoms and several peasant republics. These countries and polities had an average area of 25,000 km², roughly the same size as modern-day Macedonia, and an average population of 350,000, smaller than the population of modern-day Luxembourg. Access to power in each of these political units was organized in very different ways. The nobility dominated in most cases, sometimes in coalition with the clergy; sometimes the municipal elite were in control and the peasants held power in a few cases. In the late nineteenth century, a very different picture had emerged: by then, Europe was divided into thirty states with an average land area of 160,000 km² and an average population of ten million. The political landscape was dominated by nation states, often ruled by a monarch or president. There was a dramatic fall in the mutual differences in governance; by now, almost every country had a centralized administration and was governed with the aid of an extensive bureaucracy.

State formation in Europe thus moved in the direction of a series of larger, sovereign territorial entities. In this respect, the continent differed from other parts of the world, where large and powerful empires had ruled or centuries, or, by contrast, political fragmentation had persisted. War was the driving force behind European state formation, and a fierce struggle for power also took place in the colonies. The Netherlands stood out from the rest: between the sixteenth and late eighteenth centuries, this country was a federal republic with considerable military and colonial power, while regional and local authorities continued to exercise significant influence.

In this chapter, we will consider the consequences that this had for access to and the distribution of power in the Netherlands, and how the Netherlands related to the rest of the political world. We will focus on the following questions:

1. Why was the process of state formation in Europe so different from that in the rest of the world, and how can we explain the unique position of the Netherlands (a Republic with considerable military power)?
2. To what extent did political and religious tolerance and democracy feature in the Republic, compared to the rest of Eurasia and America? How can this be explained in the Republic's case?
3. What role did the Netherlands play in the colonization process compared to other colonizing powers, and how can we explain the wave of revolutions in the Atlantic world?

3.1
International political relations and state formation

INTERNATIONAL POLITICAL SYSTEMS Much of Eurasia was dominated by three large, centralist empires, each of which formed the core of an international political system. We refer to an 'international political system' if a group of countries take account of one another in their foreign policy and follow certain conventions. As shown by the payment of tributes, almost the whole of East Asia recognized Chinese hegemony, and this group of countries therefore formed an international political system. A second centre of power, the Mughal Empire, was located on the Indian subcontinent. Although a Hindu culture initially emerged in this region, the local rulers gradually fell under the influence of the sultan of Delhi. After the conquest of the sultanate in 1526 by Babur, a descendant of Genghis Khan, the ruler was known as the Great Mughal. The third large international system at this time was that of the Arabic-Islamic network. It was led by the caliph, the secular leader of the faithful, but after the Ottomans (a Turkish people) came to power, the caliphate was ruled by Turkish sultans and combined with a powerful military-political regime. The Ottoman Empire expanded its influence up to the North-western coast of Africa and Iran, and also increased its power in the (former) Byzantine Empire, the Balkans and Mediterranean Africa.

Each of these three international political systems was led by a single ruler: the Chinese emperor, the Indian sultan or Great Mughal, and the Ottoman caliph/sultan. Each saw himself as a suzerain, the supreme leader, and most of the surrounding states in principle recognized his hegemonic power. Political opposition from regional rulers or countries in the region aimed not to abolish the hegemonic centre but to change or to take control of it. In the fourteenth century, for example, the Mongol ruler Kublai Khan took over the Chinese Empire and system, but left the existing political structures intact.

Beyond Eurasia, political fragmentation was the norm. States did sometimes develop, but there were no international political systems. In America, the Mayan Empire had been in decline since the ninth century. It was not until the fifteenth century that the Inca Empire arose in Peru, and the Aztecs gained increasing power in Mexico. As there was no mutual contact between the Incas and the Aztecs, however, they did not form an international system. In West Africa, Ghana developed into a powerful empire after the eighth century, but this region fell into the orbit of the Arabic-Islamic system in the eleventh century. East Africa saw the development of the Mwanamutapa Empire, but here, too, no international system emerged, as this was precluded by the arrival of the Portuguese.

Given the lack of a large, centralized empire in Europe, historians have asked whether there was in fact an international political system there in the Late Middle Ages. After all, political fragmentation was the norm. The Roman Empire, which had arisen in the same period as the Chinese Empire, had collapsed in the fifth century. Despite this, almost all European states and polities maintained contact with one another, based on certain conventions. First, the Catholic Church had direct or indirect political influence over various Christian communities and sometimes whole territories, thanks to the framework of religious communities and dioceses. This political and religious network linked different countries and regions. The church reached the height of its power in the eleventh and twelfth centuries. Second, feudal structures, with their systems of lieges and vassals, created a criss-crossing network of international relations. Many German regions, for example, were loosely united under the emperor/liege of the German Holy Roman Empire. Members of the European nobility also built up a political network with marriages between families. Third, Latin functioned as a lingua franca in all kinds of religious, governmental and educational institutions. This allowed European elites to communicate with one another and access the knowledge and traditions of the Roman Empire. In this way, Latin provided Europeans with a common cultural foundation. A fourth network consisted of the multiple trade relations between towns and merchants. These sometimes took the form of close international political cooperation, as in the case of the Hanseatic League. Thus, thanks to these four very different, but partly overlapping,

networks, Europe also had an international political system in the Late Middle Ages, which permitted the development of political diplomacy with shared norms and values.

There was some contact between the European system and other Eurasian systems, but it was overwhelmingly economic in nature. Although Europe was not dominated by a single powerful empire, the potential power base was large, because in Europe, as in China, India and the Middle East, a system of regular agriculture had existed for several centuries. In his book *Guns, Germs, and Steel*, the American evolutionary biologist Jared Diamond has argued that in this respect, the whole of Eurasia had much more potential for state formation than the other continents. Agriculture promoted the formation of political elites, and the East–West connections across the whole of Eurasia (see Map 1.1, network III) facilitated the exchange of seeds and technology, allowing agriculture to develop more effectively on this continent than anywhere else in the world. The fact that no European empire emerged between 1000 and 1800 was due to the many natural borders within Europe and the possibility of establishing centres of power in multiple regions. The situation in India was different, for example. The heart of the Mughal Empire lay in the extensive Indus-Ganges plain, and there was no comparable potential power base of that size anywhere else on the Indian subcontinent.

RULERS AND CITIES IN EUROPE European state formation was given a powerful boost by the favourable climate in the eleventh and twelfth centuries. Population growth was facilitated by agricultural innovations and the expansion of trade relations, including with the Middle East and the Far East. As there were multiple power bases, these new riches were not skimmed off by a single hegemonic centre, as in China, but could instead be exploited by local elites to the full. The result was a feudal system in which the vassal was dependent, to a certain degree, on the lord. The European version of lord–vassal relations emphasized service and reciprocity; both parties were free to enter into the feudal 'contract', although the lord was richer and more powerful in a socio-economic respect. In thirteenth-century Flanders, vassals even had a feudal right to rebel in the case of political misrule. By contrast, feudal relations in Russia, China, Japan, the Ottoman Empire and the Mughal Empire were more focused on a single ruler, who had much more power over his liegemen. With the coming of the Reformation, Europe became even more politically fragmented, as the Protestant churches eroded the political-religious networks of Catholic rulers.

◄ FIGURE 3.1 *Riddarhuset in Stockholm, seventeenth century. This was where the Swedish nobility gathered for meetings at the Riksdag, the Swedish parliament. Buildings such as these demonstrate the typical European ability to form a powerful opposition to a central ruler.*
© *Marjolein 't Hart.*

Political fragmentation had far-reaching consequences for the intensity of warfare in Europe. After all, each opposing group was able to obtain weapons and troops from a different quarter, and coalitions could form. The constant, fierce rivalry between many and disparate elites resulted in a long series of wars, accompanied by an arms race with ever-larger mercenary armies.

The German sociologist Norbert Elias discovered a mechanism within these fierce European rivalries that he described as the 'royal mechanism', whereby a somewhat stronger sovereign could profit by playing the others off against one another. In this way, the sovereign would gradually gain control over all means of violence in his territory (monopoly on violence) and all taxes (tax monopoly). As the income from the sovereign's land and goods was in itself insufficient to pay the mercenaries, the sovereign had to levy more and more taxes. The feudal system, whereby the vassal came to his lord's aid with his men, was no longer adequate. In the financial-historical literature, this is known as the transition from the 'domain state' to the 'tax state'.

This transition was accompanied by the rise of a new kind of bureaucracy, which was needed to collect taxes. In the Middle Ages, the sovereign had selected his officials from a limited number of families. This was described by the sociologist Max Weber as the patrimonial system, because government offices were handed down through patrimonies (paternal inheritance). But that changed: in the new bureaucracy, officials were increasingly given positions because they had certain competences, such as having studied law at university. Objective criteria such as these became increasingly important, according to Weber.

The transition did not occur at the same rate everywhere, nor was it always linear. Over the entire Early Modern period, all kinds of hybrid forms of patrimonial and bureaucratic authority emerged, as well as many hybrids of domain and tax states.

The royal mechanism, the rise of the tax state and the accompanying bureaucratization were also found outside Europe. European state formation differed from that in the rest of Eurasia, however, because autocratic power was strongly curtailed: in exchange for paying taxes, subjects demanded a say. They were able to do so because economic resources were distributed much more widely, thanks to the growth of agricultural productivity, urbanization and the trade networks that profited from the many waterways in Europe. The brake on autocracy came from the estates, the political representation of privileged groups: the (lower) nobility, the clergy and urban elites. Meetings of the estates kept a check on rulers who exceeded their 'contract' by appropriating too much power or by levying arbitrary taxes. As early as 1127, for example, the States of Flanders successfully resisted a count who had been imposed on them by France. In England, the king was likewise forced by his vassals to adopt the Magna Carta in 1215, which limited the power of the crown.

There were no comparable limitations of political power in China, India or the Ottoman Empire. For that reason, in those parts of Eurasia, there was no institutionalized resistance when the ruler rapidly needed resources in times of war. This resulted in arbitrary taxation, something that significantly increased the risks for merchants' vulnerable capital holdings. In Europe, by contrast, the owners of capital had a system to protect them from capricious sovereigns, namely the towns the representation of the estates. This was also one of the reasons why capitalism could only emerge in Europe; it was possible to amass financial resources outside the control of the royal centres of power.

In Europe, capital mainly accumulated in the towns. This meant that in the longer term, most resistance to arbitrary royal demands came from the towns, too. As we can see from Chart 3.1, the towns grew particularly rapidly in the thirteenth century. Money was an excellent weapon against the rulers, who needed funds to pay their mercenary armies. In exchange for money, the lord granted the towns municipal rights and privileges, which considerably increased their degree of independent governance (autonomy). The towns used this autonomy to protect their merchants and craftsmen: citizens enjoyed special status within the city walls, with exclusive rights and duties. The ruler could only levy taxes in that town in consultation with the municipal government.

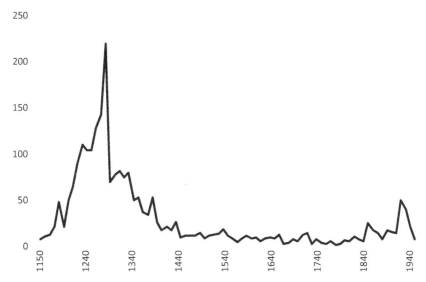

CHART 3.1 *The rise of towns in Central Europe, 1150–1950. The graph shows the number of new towns per decade. Towns flourished in the thirteenth century in particular, when the climate was favourable and agricultural yields rose due to technological improvements. The next such rise would not occur until the late nineteenth and early twentieth centuries.*
Source: W. Abel, *Geschichte der deutschen Landwirtschaft* (Stuttgart 1962), 46.

In the fourteenth century, a tradition arose in the Low Counties in which newly appointed rulers were obliged to recognize previously granted municipal privileges in a festive inauguration ceremony, known as the 'Joyous Entry'. In this way, some regions developed a constitutional system at an early stage; as early as 1356 in Brabant, where the Joyous Entry also applied to the entire province. The actions of the sovereign were thus limited by existing laws that had been enacted by his predecessors. Although the sovereign sometimes broke these laws at a later time, a political culture emerged in which subjects could increasingly fall back on former agreements or documents.

Constitutions such as these and autonomous towns were only really to be found in Europe. The rest of Eurasia had only the 'subjugated' city, a direct extension of the state. This meant that cities of over a million inhabitants, such as Beijing or Delhi, in fact had much less political power than small towns, such as Brielle or Purmerend, in the Dutch Republic. Delhi was even moved a few times in its history, simply because the Great Mughal desired to settle elsewhere. It is evident that the governors of these subjugated cities had no instruments to protect their inhabitants from arbitrary rule; it was much more difficult for them to resist an emperor, sultan or Great Mughal.

Until several decades ago, the literature on historical sociology underestimated the influence of towns and cities in the state formation process. The centralist, bureaucratic and autocratic form of the French state was taken as the standard European pattern. Many countries did not fit neatly into this pattern, however; the form of the Russian state was very different from that of the Dutch one, and France itself proved to be much less centralized and bureaucratized than previously assumed.

For this reason, in 1990 the American historical sociologist Charles Tilly developed a model that could explain the multiple variations in European state formation. As explained above, the sovereign was always forced to negotiate with representatives of the aristocracy, church and towns in order to find the money for war. In highly urbanized regions, this resulted in (1) a decentralized political system with (2) a light bureaucracy and (3) a high level of participation by local elites, participation that was largely borne by municipal governors with their own means of power: money. This participation thus led to (4) a bottom-up state formation process. Tilly called this the 'capital-intensive model'. By contrast, in vast rural territories with few towns and cities, (1) centralized states emerged with (2) autocratic bureaucracies, and (3) a high degree of aristocratic influence; and this led to (4) a top-down state formation process. This was described by Tilly as the 'coercion-intensive model'.

Various hybrid forms lay between the capital-intensive system and the coercive-intensive system. The Netherlands could be seen as a

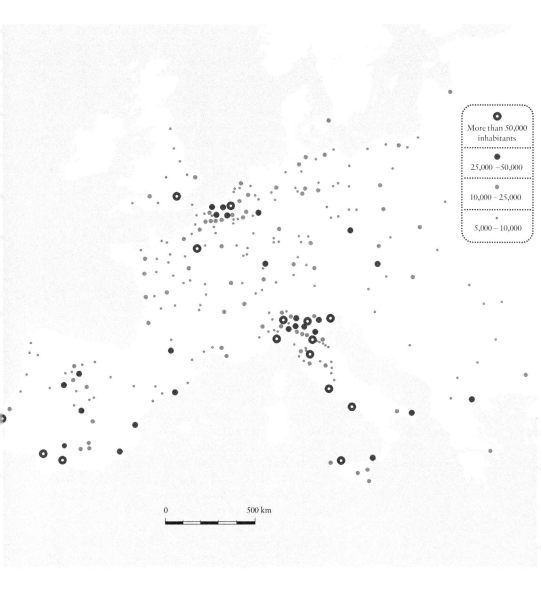

MAP 3.1 *Towns in Europe, early sixteenth century. Note the clear clusters of towns in Northern Italy and Flanders.*
Source: Pounds, *A historical geography of Europe*, 222. Designed by René van der Vooren.

prototype of the capital-intensive state form and Russia as a prototype of the coercion-intensive regime, with all kinds of variations in between. Over time, countries that were too dependent on the cities in times of war tended to over-emphasize the interests of local elites, and under-emphasize those of the central state; something that happened in the Netherlands. Coercion-intensive states, by contrast, experienced little resistance to promoting the interests of the central state and could act decisively in times of war, but they often faced the problem of being unable to generate enough money. Most of the state income had to come from taxes on land, but the multiple tax rises provoked peasant revolts that had to be suppressed, in turn, with the aid of the army. That, too, cost money – creating a vicious circle from which it was difficult for the tsar to escape.

England and France managed to combine the benefits of both models. Both countries had several larger cities that could gather financial resources efficiently, but they did not dominate the state formation process, because aristocratic networks provided a sufficient counterbalance. In these countries, it was thus possible to promote the national interest while still raise enough money for war. Tilly called this model the path of 'capitalized coercion': centralized control from above that was aided by sufficient capital (ready money).

The constant rivalry in Europe resulted in a dynamic that produced innovations in political representation (the States General in the Netherlands, Parliament in England), public finance (excise duties and long-term loans) and weapons technology and military tactics. By contrast, the drive to innovate stagnated in China and the Mughal Empire; mass military forces maintained authority in the regions. The tax system had to be kept as constant as possible in these countries, so as to avoid upsetting the social balance, and an efficient public loans system failed to get off the ground, too. These societies did innovate, of course, but political competition was less intense. Unlike in Europe, the potential of the new firearms technology was not tested in all kinds of ways in order to stay ahead of the opponent. For centuries, the defensive systems of China and the Mughal Empire were sufficient to keep the Europeans outside the walls. The Great Mughals of India preferred to pay protection money to the Dutch and the British than to equip their own warships to ward off attacks by other colonial powers. The disadvantage of this was that they failed to develop the expertise to equip ships with heavy cannon, expertise that eventually turned out to be key to the formation of colonial empires. In Europe, the political centre of gravity shifted from Southern Europe to the Atlantic coast: Spain, Portugal, France, the Netherlands and England, precisely the countries that had managed to equip seaworthy ships with heavy cannon. These countries would therefore play a leading role in the European expansion overseas (see the Section titled 'Overseas colonization and the Atlantic revolutions').

In Europe, there were attempts to rein in the many conflicts from time to time. The Peace of Augsburg in 1555, for example, established a key basis for curtailing warfare, with the famous slogan *cuius regio, eius religio* ('whose realm, his religion'). This started a trend that was set in a broader framework in the Peace of Westphalia (1648), which recognized the sovereignty of all states that signed the treaty. With this, the European international system underwent a fundamental change: the creation of the Westphalian system (see Text Box 3.1).

The Netherlands played a key role in the maintenance of the Westphalian system. Dutch statesmen, particularly Johan de Witt and Stadholder Willem III, were advocates of the Balance of Powers. If one of the European countries threatened to become too powerful, the others formed a coalition against it, often upon the initiative of the Dutch. The fact that two large-scale wars ended with the signing of a peace treaty on Dutch soil (the Nine Years' War: the Peace of Rijswijk 1697 and the War of the Spanish Succession: Peace of Utrecht 1713) is testament to the diplomatic mastery of the Dutch Republic. The Netherlands was thus an important player in European power politics. Although the French invasion of 1795 showed that the Balance of Powers did not always work, for the Netherlands, this was a strategy that prevented the country from being too easily overrun by another.

TEXT BOX 3.1 THE EUROPEAN STATE SYSTEM, BASED ON THE SOVEREIGNTY OF NATION STATES

After the Peace of Westphalia, the sovereignty of states was recognized throughout Europe; a concept that was unknown in other Eurasian international systems. The formulation of absolute sovereignty was a rejection of every claim by any hegemonic power. The Congress of Vienna (1814–15) and the Treaty of Versailles of 1919 were the logical outcomes of what is now known as the Westphalian state system. The same ideology would form the basis for the establishment of the League of Nations in 1919 and the United Nations in 1945. How the world looks today is largely a consequence of the dominance of the European international system. It was only with the founding of the European Union that this trend shifted in a direction in which the participating states would accept external interference in some areas again (see chapter 8).

3.2
State formation in the Netherlands

From the seventeenth century, advancing state formation in Europe increasingly encroached on the power of politically independent cities and towns. In the Netherlands, however, the towns would continue to exercise their considerable autonomy until the French invaded in 1795. This was the outcome of a sociopolitical legacy that harked back to medieval times.

THE MEDIEVAL LEGACY In the Middle Ages, the area covered by the modern-day Netherlands formed a loose, brittle whole that was of little significance in all kinds of respects (economic, political). It was not until the twelfth century that people began to reclaim land and the coastal areas on some scale. Utrecht, the centre of the diocese, was by far the largest town at that time. The development of other towns trailed far behind flourishing Flemish cities such as Ghent or Bruges. This is also shown by the formulation of municipal privileges, which often simply looked to the example of neighbouring towns in the South. The count's power was weak; weaker, in fact, than in the Southern Netherlands. Friesland did not even recognize a lord until 1498, and the Duchy of Gelderland remained an exceptionally turbulent and rebellious region until 1543. The lower aristocracy ruled the countryside, while religious houses provided an infrastructure for reclaiming land. The polder authorities had little influence in a political respect. Some proponents of the 'polder model' believe that we can find an age-old model for the consultative Dutch economy in the polders, but there is no evidence for this. Representation at estates meetings (later the Provincial States) by delegates from the towns and local nobility (and sometimes the clergy, such as in Utrecht) was initially borne mainly by the nobility. The polders were of minor political significance. From the fourteenth century, the more the towns in the Northern Netherlands expanded and trade increased, the more urban networks could exercise their power and a 'capital-intensive' model of state formation could get underway. Towns, not the polder authorities, played the driving role in this process.

The fourteenth century brought much unrest. The Black Death disrupted existing structures, and riots and war broke out in many parts of the Low Countries. One development of long-term significance, especially for the Southern Netherlands, was that artisans gained access to municipal power: after riots, various guilds were granted representation in the municipal government, which had always been dominated by an oligarchy of merchants and beer-brewers. Most towns in the Northern Netherlands lacked a large working class, meaning that the implications of this sociopolitical revolution were less far-reaching there, and the guilds would never gain as much political power as they had in Flanders or Brabant.

At the end of the turbulent fourteenth century, the powerful House of Burgundy gained a permanent footing in the Southern Netherlands. In 1433, Holland and Zeeland were also brought under Burgundian authority. The fact that the northern provinces alone were drawn into a process of intensive state formation at that time would be of fundamental importance in the later development of the Dutch Republic. As we shall see later, at the time of the Revolt, the provincial government of Holland and Zeeland was already much more efficient than those of regions such as Gelderland, Overijssel, Friesland or Groningen.

In the fifteenth century, the Netherlands underwent increasing centralization, based on the model of the French state. Duke Philip the Good transformed his court into a spectacle of power and splendour, and he introduced auditors to streamline taxation, and a common currency to facilitate mutual trade. In addition, the new high courts slowly but surely supplanted local customary law with the more universal Roman law. Many municipal privileges continued to exist unabated, however. Due to the frequent wars, meetings of provincial estate representatives were held increasingly often. In 1427, a supra-provincial representative organ was even established: the States General, with representatives from the provincial governments of the Low Countries. The Great Privilege that it formulated in 1477, after the death of Charles the Bold, was the first constitution for this region as a whole. From a global perspective, this was even one of the first ever documents of this nature.

In the early sixteenth century, the countries ruled by the Burgundians fell into the hands of the Spanish Habsburgs, dominated first by Emperor Charles V and then by his son, King Philip II of Spain. In one fell swoop, the Low Countries joined a global empire with relations stretching to America, Africa and Asia. Dutch merchants hardly suffered from this political unification. The strict royal coinage policy put limits on currency chaos and devaluation, and the spectacular growth of Antwerp stimulated trade in the Northern Netherlands. In addition, the expansion of trade links was accompanied by more export opportunities and safer trade routes. As the transaction costs of trade fell in this large empire (see Chapter 2), merchants were able to make profits more easily than they had done in the past.

FROM MOBILIZATION TO REVOLT Growing state power also had its disadvantages, however. Religious freedom came under pressure, as Charles V and Philip II attempted to establish a homogenous Catholic state religion in their territories. The more the Reformation spread, the stricter the anti-heresy policies became: between 1521 and 1550, the Inquisition sentenced thirteen inhabitants of the Low Countries to be burned at the stake each year, on average; in the period 1551–60, this rose to an average of 60 per year, and between 1561 and 1564, as many as 264.

The towns, by contrast, desired a climate in which foreign merchants from different religious backgrounds would not run the risk of being prosecuted. For this reason, they attempted to guard their legal and administrative independence. The provincial estates meetings still enjoyed significant power, in part thanks to the 'constitution' of 1477, and this layer of governance formed a buffer against the erosion of municipal autonomy.

The differences in religious politics intensified as socio-economic unrest grew. The Antwerp financial market received a bitter blow when the Spanish crown failed to meet its interest obligations upon its loans and went bankrupt in in 1557; the textile industry fell into decline, leading to rising unemployment; and grain imports stalled due to war in the Baltic region, followed by spiralling prices and hunger among the lower classes. All of these factors converged in the 1560s, intensifying the political and religious unrest. In 1566, a request (*Smeekschift*) from the lower nobility of the Netherlands to ease the religious policies went unanswered. This was followed by a rebellion, the iconoclastic fury, which left the entire political and religious regime reeling. Field preaching (open-air Protestant church services) drew huge crowds. The Spanish king sent Duke Alba as the new governor to restore order with an army, but his arrival had the effect of crystallizing the existing differences.

In this age of political-religious crisis and economic decline, there was no lack of motives for revolt; for many, Alba's 'Council of Blood' and tax policy were the straw that broke the camel's back. But revolutions do not only succeed because many people are critical of political policy. In addition to (1) motives and criticism, there is always a need for (2) a social structure that can mobilize the discontented masses, led by (3) a well-organized revolutionary minority that ultimately manages to (4) mobilize sufficient means to maintain the resistance.

The social structure that activated the discontented masses in the Netherlands lay in the autonomous towns. No lasting resistance emerged from the nobility. Prince William of Orange's attempt to march against Alba with an army, financed by his network of family and patronage, failed in 1568. It was much easier for a counterculture to arise in the towns, because discontent could spread via civic guards, guilds, church congregations and other organizations. There was also a broad 'repertoire' of urban rebellion in the Netherlands, which served as an example for the rebels (see Text Box 3.2).

TEXT BOX 3.2 REPERTOIRES OF COLLECTIVE ACTION

How people protest is not only dependent on existing social relations, but also on the previous history of conflict, for it is much easier to rebel if one has an example of a successful campaign. Charles Tilly called these examples 'repertoires of collective action'. One of the best-known forms of rebellion in the pre-industrial period was plunder. The aim of plunder was to destroy riches, not to steal them, as the term 'to plunder' is usually understood today (see also Figure 3.2). This is precisely what happened during the famous iconoclastic fury of 1566: people destroyed the things that symbolized the contested policy. Other well-known forms of rebellion included hunger or tax riots, which also followed a certain pattern of action.

Towns also had their patterns of revolt. In 1488, Maximilian of Austria (who would later become emperor of the German Holy Roman Empire) was held hostage by townsmen for a few months. It was not the first time that this happened; in 1325, Louis, Count of Flanders, had been held prisoner by the Bruges militia for six months. The desire for autonomy was dominant. The city of Ghent made several attempts to establish an independent municipal district: in 1379–85, in 1451–3, in 1537–40 and again in 1578–84, the final time as a Calvinist republic. The revolt by Brielle (1572) was a variant on these examples, and again provided other towns in the Netherlands with a model for rebelling against Alba and siding with William of Orange.

Early Modern labour conflicts were expressed in a different way: the workers went from one workplace to another, calling on servants to down tools, and then demonstratively left the town. After the Industrial Revolution, a new repertoire of resistance developed. Modern strikes emerged when big groups of wage labourers started working for large industrial companies. The twentieth century saw demonstrations, banners, similar clothing and caps: the same patterns always played out.

This is why the Revolt only gathered pace when one town after another sided with William of Orange. The regime found it difficult to contain the resistance from multiple centres: the town walls and defensive inundations alone provided powerful protection for the rebels. In Holland, the rebels first won Brielle for Orange, followed by Vlissingen and Enkhuizen and, soon afterwards, larger cities. A common pattern was for municipal governors to fear unrest among the lower classes, and lose faith in their own civic guard. They chose the path of least resistance and opened their gates to the rebels. Once enough municipal governors had made this step, it was a relatively simple matter to organize a

revolutionary meeting of the provincial Holland estates in Dordrecht in July 1572, at which William of Orange was elected stadholder. In this way, the rebels took control of a consolidated territory that covered a large part of Holland and Zeeland, with enough wealth and taxpaying residents to be able to fund an army; we shall consider this further below.

The Revolt therefore succeeded thanks to the intensified socio-economic and political-religious differences of the 1560s and the successful mobilization of the autonomous towns; but we have yet to address the third factor, that of the 'revolutionary organization', in sufficient detail. William of Orange was masterful at keeping the different rebellious elements together. His preference was for religious freedom for all, including the Catholics, who still formed the majority of the population. Despite William of Orange's powerful leadership, though, events would take a different course: the Calvinists would dominate the Revolt and the Catholics would subsequently be forbidden from publicly professing their faith. Thanks to their underground network of synods, the Calvinists were extremely well organized; in the rebel groups, they were the ones putting unremitting pressure on the Spanish.

Other religious groups were unable to form revolutionary organizations. The overly rigorous Inquisition had alienated Catholics in the Northern Netherlands from their church, and good leadership was lacking. The Lutherans did not play a driving role in the Revolt, either, for this movement was too elitist in the Low Countries. Although the Baptists were very radical, after the suppression of the Anabaptist Revolt in Münster in 1535 they forswore violence (whereupon they called themselves 'Mennonites' in the Netherlands, after their new leader, Menno Simons).

The Calvinists also maintained close links with fellow believers across the border; in the Southern Netherlands, of course, but also in important centres such as Geneva and Emden (in nearby Eastern Friesland), and with groups such as the Huguenots in France and radical Calvinists in England. This network provided ideas, troops and funds to the rebellious provinces. The Calvinists in the Northern Netherlands were also supported by the enormous stream of refugees from the south. Around 10 per cent of the population, no less, had left the Spanish-dominated provinces when the repression was stepped up there. Many were confirmed Calvinists, often even more radical than their fellow believers in the north. William of Orange became more and more involved in the Calvinist network, and was eventually forced to take this direction because he could not operate without them. Catholics therefore became second-class citizens in the Revolt, with fewer rights than the Calvinists.

Deep social differences, rapid mobilization via urban corporations and well-organized revolutionaries were not enough to make a revolution succeed, however; money was also needed to maintain the fight against the Spanish,

◀ FIGURE 3.2 *Rioters plunder the house belonging to the tax collector A.M. van Arssen, on the Singel canal in Amsterdam, 1748.*
© *Collection of Amsterdam City Archives / Rijksmuseum, Amsterdam.*

the most powerful army of its day. The medieval legacy of state formation in Holland and Zeeland would play a decisive role in this respect, for the rebels could rely on the administrative system with efficient taxation and a robust state loans apparatus that had developed under Charles V (see Text Box 3.3).

TEXT BOX 3.3 THE FINANCIAL REVOLUTION

Holland had a sophisticated tax system that was combined with a flexible financing system. Pay came from loans, not directly from taxation, which meant that soldiers never had to wait too long to be paid. War debts did mount up as a result, but as most taxes were on consumer goods (excises, comparable to present-day value added tax), incomes were sure and steady; the perfect basis for paying the interest on loans. The excises were collected by tax farmers, who were kept under close supervision; contracts were short (mostly for half a year) and the districts were small (a town or region). Tax leases were sold at public auction. The situation in a country such as France was very different. French tax farmers were large financiers, often noblemen, with contracts that spanned many years, covering several provinces and several excises. The same financiers often guaranteed large loans to the French state. The system was thus open to abuse. In the Dutch Republic, by contrast, the loans came from large numbers of small private investors.

The literature uses the term 'Financial Revolution' to describe the development of flexible public financing. The author who came up with this term was the British historian Peter Dickson, who studied innovations in the British polity after the Glorious Revolution of 1688. A new institution, the Bank of England (1694), replaced more expensive short-term public loans with cheaper public loans that spanned longer periods. The investing public had a high degree of confidence, because (1) having the bank in the background guaranteed good financial policy, and (2) there was an efficient tax system (with many excises and customs duties), which guaranteed the payment of interest.

These financial innovations supported British policy, as they allowed wars to be financed quickly and cheaply. According to the American historian James Tracy, however, the principles of this policy were developed in Holland in the sixteenth century, in the age of Charles V. Charles V needed money, which the towns provided. The towns guaranteed each other's loans, which boosted the confidence of the investing public, and new taxes on consumer goods ensured that there was sufficient income to pay the interest on time. It became less and less necessary to appeal to rich foreigners, and the common people of Holland also had an interest in the state loans. As a result, interest rates fell over time: a rate of just 2.5 per cent was charged in the eighteenth century, lower than in any other European state.

In order to mobilize as many resources as possible, a whole series of smaller towns, not just the large cities, were granted direct representation in the administration; eighteen in total. In this way, the Revolt reinforced the trend towards decentralization: more towns now had a political voice in the provincial government. The towns agreed to unprecedented tax rises in exchange for political power. The trade-based wealth of the coastal provinces also played a role, of course; riches that had largely been amassed under Charles V. For government leaders, though, the art was to tax this wealth in a balanced, regular way. Beyond Holland and Zeeland, the traditional tax freedoms enjoyed by the nobility and urban elites hindered the development of a flexible financial system. In those areas, the tax burden often fell disproportionately on the peasants, and they were unable to keep paying more taxes. Time and again, loans also proved to be of crucial importance in wartime, but a developed framework for long-term loans was a rarity in Early Modern Europe. Holland, though, had developed such a framework before the Revolt; it was a legacy of the Middle Ages. Until the late eighteenth century, the financing system of highly urbanized Holland functioned as the mainstay of the Republic; a classic example of capital-intensive state formation.

With the towns' major role in financing the state, the nobility were marginalized. Sovereign power came to lie in the provinces, not with the court. The stadholder served the Provincial States and was thus subordinated to this layer of governance, which was dominated by the towns. The provinces sent delegates to the States General, which represented the common interests of the Republic. The nobility continued to exercise influence at the highest level in committees and in the army. No new nobles were added, however, now that there was no longer a king who could grant titles. The nobility could access political power via a position in municipal government, not by expanding their landed property, as was the case in almost every other European country. The socio-economic basis of the nobility was also weakened by the military inundations after 1570; in that decade, as much as two-thirds of the countryside of Holland was under water. Tenants were unable to pay their leases for a period of six to ten years, which dealt an enormous financial blow to noble landowners.

WAR, ECONOMICS AND SOCIETY The Netherlands was unique in yet another respect during the Eighty Years' War: the war was accompanied by strikingly robust economic growth, as mentioned earlier in Chapter 2. This growth allowed the Republic to pursue a powerful military campaign, even though the Spanish could count on the annual flow of silver from America.

By contrast, most wars in the Early Modern period had disastrous economic effects. In many European garrisons, badly paid soldiers with their unpredictable behaviour caused great harm to the local economy. They often took what they needed from the population without recompense, or destroyed all kinds of property during mutinies and plunder. It made

a difference if the war was not fought on their own territory, as was the case for Holland after 1576, but that was not the only factor at play. The war was not waged on Spanish territory, either, but the Spanish economy nevertheless declined due to the heavy financial pressure of the war in the Low Countries.

The Dutch soldiers behaved in a rather disciplined fashion, however, because (1) they were paid regularly (thanks to the Financial Revolution; see Text Box 3.3) and (2) because of the tactical reforms introduced by William of Orange and Prince Maurits. The latter, in particular, ensured that the soldiers were drilled almost daily. The scale on which this was achieved was a novel phenomenon in Europe, and was much copied by other armies. There was also an effective compensation regulation in garrison towns for those who provided soldiers with accommodation (always voluntarily). Military companies boosted the demand for goods from local artisans and brewers. The army turned out to be a reliable client, not least because the soldiers were paid regularly, and this was also the reason why municipal governors often requested the extension of a garrison: garrisons had a beneficial economic effect. In almost all other countries, by contrast, municipal governments tried to keep soldiers beyond their walls. The ineffective payments system made it impossible to discipline the soldiers properly. Good regulations for accommodating the troops were also lacking: for this reason, this obligation was simply imposed on host families.

Due to the tight discipline, there were hardly any mutinies or looting in the Republic's territory. This strengthened the confidence of entrepreneurs and traders in the political system. Suppliers of the army and fleet benefitted to the full, and new fortifications brought employment for workers and contractors. The admiralty's shipyards gave a boost to shipbuilding, rope-making, sail-making and sawmills. Aside from this, though, the Golden Age was a Golden Age for the province of Holland in particular. Holland enjoyed an expanding series of economic opportunities, attracting workers, technological expertise and money. These flows were often to the detriment of other provinces, where the economy shrank. As the waging of war was so highly dependent on financing from Holland, this by no means threatened the outcome of the war; on the contrary, the war mainly benefitted Holland's interests and boosted its economy.

Military discipline meant that in no other state was civilian control over the military so effective as it was in the Dutch Republic. The decentralized form of the state left local elites deeply involved in affairs of war and peace, meaning that people were more willing to agree to tax rises. The people of Holland paid the most tax per capita of the whole world, many times more than Alba had ever dared to impose.

◀ MAP 3.2 *The Dutch Republic in c. 1650.*
Source: Designed by René van der Vooren.

In the seventeenth century, Dutch financial and military policy acted as a model for other countries. England, in particular, adopted several typically Dutch institutions in the area of public financing and army organization, which also boosted the development of Britain's empire around the world. The Netherlands was thus a key player in many respects, both in military organization and in war financing.

3.3
Participation and political culture

States were not only formed from above by wars or by elites; political culture was also determined by formal and informal opportunities for participation, revolts and riots.

POLITICAL PARTICIPATION The high degree of civilian control over the military, the important role played by local and provincial governors in political policy, and citizens' investment in the public debt made the Dutch Republic into a true 'civic' state. Despite this, though, access to power could not be described as democratic. The appointment of new members of the town council took place by means of co-optation. Representatives were elected from the town council to the provincial estates, and delegations from the provincial estates were then sent to the States General. In the sixteenth and early seventeenth centuries, newcomers still qualified for positions in municipal government, but in the course of the seventeenth century, such offices were increasingly shared by a small number of families. This process is known as 'oligarchization', a term coined by the German-Italian sociologist Robert Michels. Michels argued that all organizations (even if they are democratically elected) have a tendency over time to admit a limited group to their ruling structures. He called this phenomenon the 'iron law of oligarchy'. A different explanation was offered by the French sociologist Pierre Bourdieu, whose theory focused on networks. Town governors knew one another from all kinds of networks and therefore had a lot of 'social capital', with the result that only certain families obtained desirable political positions (see Text Box 3.4). In some towns, particularly in the east of the country, the guilds still had access to the municipal government. The 'iron law of oligarchy' also affected guild representation, however, and by the seventeenth century common artisans had hardly any access to municipal government in practice. In Holland during the Revolt, fear of the major influence of the civic guard led to the curtailing of the political powers of all corporations, including those of the guilds.

In a certain respect, eighteenth-century Great Britain was more democratic than the Republic; in that country, the Members of Parliament – a sovereign instrument alongside the monarch – were elected. But there, too, democracy was limited: there were nine hundred members of the

House of Commons and House of Lords for a population of nine million. Moreover, the Members of Parliament hailed almost exclusively from the high and low nobility, and there was a district system that disadvantaged some regions and groups, and a census franchise that excluded most citizens. In the Republic, power was held by 2000 regents out of a population of two million. Participation in governance was thus distributed more equally in the Republic, but the way in which the governors were chosen was less democratic than in Great Britain. We should add that the situation with regard to political participation was even worse in the rest of the world. In France, the last States General was convened in 1614, and the next would not convene until 1789. In Prussia, Elector Frederik Willem I sidelined the States altogether. Similar representative institutions were lacking in the Islamic Ottoman and Great Mughal empires, as well as in Russia and the Chinese Empire.

A more democratic element of Dutch political culture was the practice of submitting a *rekest* (petition) to the municipal government. Interest groups could use petitions to press for political initiatives. Although *rekests* were not always honoured, by any means, they did give citizens an opportunity to influence municipal decision-making. Not everyone was able to submit a petition, though; only burghers (people who were citizens of that specific city) could do so. This was one of the rights associated with being a burgher. Guild membership was open exclusively to burghers, for example. Many city residents were not burghers, but merely 'residents'. They either lacked the means to buy municipal citizenship or were unable to buy it, because they were excluded on the basis of their religious creed (see chapter 4).

REBELLION AND REVOLUTIONARY SITUATIONS When many people in the lower social classes disagreed with a policy, they often had little option but to rebel. Contrary to what is often assumed, revolts such as these were not irrational outbursts by 'the mob'. As we saw above, rebellions often followed certain patterns (see Text Box 3.2 on repertoires). In an article on the moral economy of the crowd, the British social historian E. P. Thompson argued that mass resistance from below was often legitimized on the basis of outrage at the government's actions. From a moral perspective, rulers could exercise power so long as they ensured a reasonable standard of living. Rising prices would not necessarily lead to unrest if some core products remained affordable, or if there was still a social safety net for the poor.

In the Netherlands, social unrest was often an expression of discord about taxes. As a rule, municipal governors had fewer problems with tax rises, because they themselves were hit less hard by the duties on consumer goods in a relative sense. In addition, most magistrates invested funds in government loans, meaning that they received a considerable share of their tax money back in the form of interest payments. In 1616 in Delft, a rise in the tax on grain provoked a riot, because the tax on wine – a luxury product – was lowered at the same time. It was the tax cut that was the problem: if there was such a great need for money, why did the rich have to pay less?

TEXT BOX 3.4 ECONOMIC, SOCIAL AND CULTURAL CAPITAL

In order to explain the high level of continuity within the elite (the same families repeatedly managing to obtain the top positions in society), in 1970 the French sociologist Pierre Bourdieu developed the concepts of economic, cultural and social capital. He later added another term, symbolic capital. The meaning of economic capital is the most obvious: it refers to material resources such as money, real estate, and ownership of the means of production. The second form of capital, cultural capital, is slightly less tangible. It refers to the knowledge and skills that someone acquires through education and experience. In a material respect, this could include a university degree, but it could also refer to books, instruments, artworks and suchlike. By social capital, Bourdieu meant the ability to participate in social networks (friends, clubs, associations). This capital consists almost exclusively of relations with others and rarely assumes a tangible form (aside from membership cards and so forth). We sometimes come across detailed source material on such relations: the powerful burgomaster of Amsterdam, Johan Huydecoper, kept a daily record of where he had been, whom he had met and to whom he had given special favours, allowing him to recall who owed him a favour in return. Symbolic capital, finally, is the least tangible form of all, and refers to the prestige derived from social recognition. To a certain degree, all of these forms of capital are exchangeable: if they are wealthy, people can study at the best universities and join the most exclusive clubs, where they will encounter people who may play a key role in their careers.

Thus, according to Bourdieu, social inequality is not a consequence of individual differences, but occurs because people from the upper classes want to control access to valuable resources (capital). This makes it difficult for people from the lower classes to penetrate higher social circles: whichever form of capital is used, the elite is nevertheless always able to take the best positions. This was also the case in the Dutch Republic, when it was difficult even for wealthier outsiders (Catholics, migrants) to penetrate this network, because the established families engaged in large-scale opportunity-hoarding (the hoarding of opportunities to earn money and exercise power). Thus, the term 'capital' does not refer to money alone; a better term would be 'resources'. A group with a high degree of social capital is one whose members possess many resources in order to undertake joint activities, formulate political demands, and support one another when necessary (see also Chapter 8 for the concept of 'social capital' developed by the political scientist Robert Putnam).

Most rebellions in the Netherlands, including tax riots, remained local in character, because a large part of the moral economy was regulated by local rulers. There were many tax riots in virtually every other country, but these were often on a much larger scale than in the Dutch Republic, because the central administration there played a much greater role in the moral economy.

Nevertheless, the Dutch Republic also faced revolutionary situations; periods of large-scale unrest during which it was unclear, for a time, who controlled the provincial government in Holland. Situations such as these arose when a political crisis at the highest level coincided with rioting by the discontented masses. People from different layers of society thus had very different motives for rebelling. Table 3.1 provides an overview of these revolutionary situations.

A number of times, such as in 1672, 1749 and 1787, discontent from below was channelled by a pro-Orange faction wanting to restore or strengthen the stadholder's power. The American social historian Wayne te Brake distinguished three parties involved in revolutionary situations: central state elites, local elites, and rebellious commoners. He identified three different outcomes: (1) local rulers joined the rebels and more or less turned against the sovereign (local consolidation); (2) the sovereign and local elites cooperated to suppress the lower classes (elite consolidation); or (3) the central sovereign formed an alliance with the rebels against local elites (territorial consolidation). Using his terminology, we could call the

TABLE 3.1 *Revolutionary Situations in the Netherlands, 1500–1800*

1566–81	*Iconoclastic fury*, followed by the Geuzen rebellion, the founding of the rebel army and independent States General, and renouncing of the King of Spain
1617–8	*Religious riots* and coup by orthodox Calvinists (incl. Prince Maurits) against moderates (incl. Van Oldenbarnevelt)
1650–3	*Failed coup* by Stadholder Willem II, followed by riots and First Stadholderless Period
1672–3	*Coups* by supporters of Orange in many towns, widespread unrest, end of First Stadholderless period
1703–6	*Defeat* of supporters of Orange in Gelderland *and* Overijssel, beginning of Second Stadholderless Period
1747–50	*Rebellion* by supporters of Orange in the United Provinces, end of Second Stadholderless Period
1785–7	*Revolution* by the Patriots, suppressed by the Prussian army
1795–1801	*Batavian Revolution*, encouraged by the French invasion

outcome of the situations in 1672, 1749 and 1787 'territorial consolidation': the strengthening of the national government led by the stadholder.

Local consolidation was even more common than territorial consolidation; however. In 1572, municipal rulers harnessed the rebelliousness of the lower classes to oppose the sovereign. In 1650, 1703 and 1785, municipal rulers preferred to maintain control over their rebellious citizens with the aid of the civil guard, and shunned intervention by the central army.

Elite consolidation was more common in other European countries than in the Netherlands. One example is France, where the state strengthened the coalition with the nobility and local rulers during many peasants' rebellions. Territorial consolidation prevailed in China. Although rebellious Chinese peasants were suppressed, state policy focused on pacifying the peasant class. Subservience was demanded from local elites, so that the peasants would have no cause to revolt.

URBAN ELITES AND POLITICAL CULTURE The power of the sovereign was weak in the Netherlands, but during the revolutionary situations of 1672, 1647 and 1787, the stadholder was able to strengthen his position by replacing politically hostile municipal governors with Orangists. Remarkably, though, this strategy only temporarily broke the existing oligarchic pattern. Within three years of the *wetsverzetting* (change of legislature) of 1749, for example, Amsterdam had again eluded the influence of the stadholder's court.

Given this pattern of almost unbroken rule by a limited number of oligarchical families, the Dutch state could be described as 'patrimonial'. When filling a political post, people looked at which family the candidate came from, not at whether they were really suitable. The American historical sociologist Julia Adams described the Dutch system of rule itself as 'familial', because it was dominated by the fathers of a series of powerful patrician families. Oligarchization also occurred in other countries on a large scale, but there the sovereign was able to shake up the elite balance of power from time to time and replace one oligarchy with another. In Great Britain, it was easy for the king to give concessions to new merchants, thereby replacing the existing charter of the British East India Company; in the Netherlands, by contrast, the Dutch East India Company remained an unchanging bastion of a small number of families. In France, the sale of offices on a large scale ensured renewal within the elite. In the eighteenth century, the king of Prussia broke the process of oligarchization by establishing a new, militarized bureaucracy. When it came to bureaucratization, China was far ahead of all of the European states: in that country, based on a schooling system, a bureaucracy had emerged that in the Early Middle Ages already resembled the nineteenth-century ideal type described by Weber.

It was a paradox: in finance and in the military, the Netherlands was considerably bureaucratized, as the officials who worked in these areas were selected mainly for their education and performance; but within the administrative elites in the towns and provinces, the Netherlands remained a country ruled on the basis of patrimony. This striking mix produced a unique political culture with both conservative and progressive elements. The progressive elements were not only present in the tax system and the army; in three other areas, too, Dutch political culture was exceptional in Early Modern Europe, namely: (1) the permanent separation of the church and state with (2) a high degree of religious tolerance and (3) a highly developed public 'sphere' in which numerous political opinions could be freely expressed.

After the Reformation, so-called 'established churches' arose across Europe, bringing ecclesiastical organization directly under the influence of the state. This happened in England under Henry VIII, for example; having broken with the pope, the king established an Anglican Church with a mix of Catholic and reformational principles. The king was also the head of the church. With the Counter-Reformation, established churches were also created in Catholic regions. German historians call this the *Konfessionalisierung:* the process in which local rulers gained far-reaching influence over the appointment of religious officials, leading to a significant increase in the sociopolitical power of the church and state in all areas of life.

In the Dutch Republic, however, the separation of church and state endured, despite pressure from the Calvinists. William of Orange had ensured that 'freedom of conscience' was included in the Dutch 'constitution', the Union of Utrecht of 1579. The Calvinist church became the privileged church, not the state church. Belonging to the Calvinist church was a precondition for holding public office, and the Calvinists were assigned the main church buildings. The government did not appoint church leaders, however, and did not prescribe what pastors had to preach. Other faiths were permitted to remain, so long as they did not practise too openly. The Catholics, in particular, were expected to worship in private.

Although the Calvinists had the most sociopolitical influence, there was no strict central administration in the ecclesiastical system, with its regional synods. This led to a wide range of degrees of religious tolerance in practice. Many Calvinists were far from tolerant. As there were different Calvinist factions, however, the sociopolitical impact differed. Jews who were not allowed to build a synagogue in one town moved to another, where this was permitted by the ruling Calvinist faction. Amsterdam, in particular, pursued a liberal policy, because it attracted merchants from different religious backgrounds. This cosmopolitan city was home to more non-Calvinist places of worship, including a very large synagogue, than Calvinist churches. There were also towns that were not tolerant at all, however, especially in Zeeland and the east of the Netherlands. But there, too, local rulers were prepared to allow dissenters to worship in private, if they paid a special tax.

In practice, this pragmatic freedom of religion attracted a large influx of religious refugees to the Dutch Republic, joining the great stream of economic migrants. Many European countries made the lives of dissenters particularly difficult from time to time. Jews and Moriscos (Muslims who had been forced to convert to Christianity) were persecuted in Spain, and Calvinist Huguenots were persecuted in France in the late seventeenth century. The intolerant climate in Britain provoked many British dissenters to emigrate to America, and there was no longer any religious freedom in most German states and towns after the *Konfessionalisierung*. One exception was eighteenth-century Prussia, where, influenced by the Enlightenment, the sovereign as an 'enlightened despot' propagated a high degree of religious freedom.

Strikingly enough, religious persecution was less of a problem beyond Europe. There was a high degree of freedom of conscience, including for Christians, in China and in the Ottoman Empire. The politicization of religion was a typically European phenomenon; it did not occur, or occurred less frequently, in non-European countries.

In addition to the high degree of religious tolerance and the absence of an established church, a further characteristic of the Republic was the lack of effective censorship. Censorship was especially strict in more autocratically governed countries, such as China, the Ottoman Empire, France and Prussia. Like all other countries in Eurasia, the Netherlands did have censorship; a right that belonged to the sovereign power, the provincial estates. It was not, or hardly, enforced centrally, however, but left to local government. In principle, there was no preventive censorship; as a rule, publications did not have to be passed by a censor beforehand, and if someone was not allowed to publish something in one town, it could often be published in another. This meant that the seventeenth-century Netherlands had an unprecedentedly lively culture of debate, conducted by societies, pamphlets and newspapers. Thanks to the unusually high density of publishers and printers in the Republic (in no other country was so much published), it was impossible to maintain central control over the printing press. In the seventeenth century, around 100,000 titles were printed in the Republic; in the eighteenth century, 200,000. Freedom of speech thus existed de facto, although this right was only formally enshrined in the Dutch constitution of 1798.

Freedom of speech plays an important role in the theory of the 'public sphere' developed by the German philosopher Jürgen Habermas. Debating matters of a political nature boosts the democratic character of a country (see Text Box 3.5). The Dutch culture of debate allowed space for all kinds of radical political opinions. Franciscus van den Enden (1602–74), for example, formulated the idea of popular sovereignty long before it was put forward by Rousseau, and Pieter Cornelis Plockhoy (*c.* 1625–*c.* 1694) tried out his egalitarian, social revolutionary ideals in the colony of New Netherland in America.

The Dutch were not the only ones to benefit from the public sphere in the Netherlands. French radicals also came to the Republic to publish their writings. In this way, the wide public sphere in the Republic boosted the Enlightenment, both in the Netherlands and beyond, and contributed significantly to the radical political ideas that would later be put into practice during the French Revolution.

One was thus able to think or publish all kinds of things in the Dutch Republic, but it remained virtually impossible to penetrate the structures of power from below. This combination (an extensive culture of debate but no access to power) created great revolutionary potential, as we shall see in the section in this chapter on the revolutions in the Atlantic world.

TEXT BOX 3.5 HABERMAS'S THEORY OF THE PUBLIC SPHERE

Habermas believed that the public sphere (Öffentlichkeit) played a key role in the development of a democratic order. He argued that the public sphere emerged in England in the late seventeenth century, when people were able to discuss matters of general interest freely and openly in coffee houses. For Habermas, an essential factor was the development of rational argumentation, with discussions held on the basis of mutual equality, on matters that might concern government policy but that were held by people who were outside the political sphere. Habermas's concept of the public sphere should be understood in a broad sense: it did not always need to involve somewhere as tangible as a coffee house or salon, but could emerge through the exchange of ideas in the press, on proviso that access to this 'sphere' was also free.

Historians have contributed to the debate about the public sphere in various ways. According to some, for example, there was also a public sphere in China and one in the Ottoman Empire. These claims tend to be based on the existence of religious organizations, guilds or local governments that allowed freedom of speech. But the public sphere is not about the freedom of speech alone; discussions in organizations such as these tended to concern very particular local interests and goals, not state policy. Moreover, these were not associations to which anyone could belong, in principle. In addition, in the case of China, there was no clear division between the state and elites, or between the state and society.

Habermas did not consider the case of the Netherlands when developing his theory. There are clear signs that a public sphere emerged in the Netherlands at an early stage; by the seventeenth century, in any case. As well as the many pamphlets and societies, another medium arose at that time: the newspaper. Initially, there were around 600 copies per paper, mainly filled with notices and containing little commentary. Around the mid-eighteenth century, however, four larger newspapers appeared that also published political opinions. The Oprechte Haerlemse Courant, the Amsterdamsche Courant, the Leydsche Courant and the 's Gravenhaegsche Courant had a combined print-run of around 20,000 copies, and these papers were also read outside their home localities. Assuming that every newspaper reached ten people, on average, this implied a reading public of around 200,000 people, around 10 per cent of the population, who mainly lived in the urbanized, western part of the Netherlands.

3.4
Overseas colonization and the Atlantic revolutions

EUROPEAN COLONIZATION AND GLOBALIZATION The broad culture of debate brought many opinions and perspectives, and the Netherlands was also exposed to increasing amounts of information from distant overseas territories. The civic elite in the coastal provinces played a decisive role in maintaining the colonial connections; other countries with colonies were always dominated by royal politics.

Through colonial enterprises, a large part of the world gradually became drawn into the European international system (see also Text Box 3.6). It is often asked why China, India and the Ottoman Empire did not establish such large-scale, long-term overseas expeditions. The answer is simple: the Europeans were driven by fierce, costly military competition. Any enterprise that could raise money was therefore of interest, and they were lured overseas by stories of unprecedented riches (gold, silk and jewels). In the rest of Eurasia, there was less military competition, financial resources were under stricter centralized control, and these regions were already home to great riches, or access to such wealth was regulated well via the regular Arabian trade networks that extended over the whole of eastern Eurasia (caravans, coastal trade). In addition, innovations in shipbuilding in the Atlantic ports of Europe gave an important boost to colonial enterprises. The new ships had enhanced sail-bearing capacity so that they could sail on the high seas, and a larger hold and stable trim, so that they could be equipped with heavy guns.

In the first centuries, colonialism was largely limited to the establishment of trading posts on the coast, but colonists gradually exercised more and more power in inland regions (see Text Box 3.7). Every colonizing nation traded in slaves. Although this trade also took place in Asia (and the VOC was involved), the greatest demand for slaves emerged in the eighteenth century from plantations in the Western Hemisphere. It was mainly Africa that supplied the workers in this phase of globalization.

Colonization itself was facilitated by territorial 'springboards': large countries that were already considerably centralized and bureaucratized, which greatly accelerated the penetration by the Europeans after they had been taken over. For Spain, the subjugation of the Aztecs (1521) and the Incas (1533) brought about an enormous territorial expansion in one go. A similar shock conquest took place in the eighteenth century when, after the Battle of Plassey (1757), Great Britain managed to overpower Bengal, which was followed by the takeover of the Mughal Empire. The British used India as a base to force the next springboard: China was unable to withstand the heavily armed British warships that sailed to Canton in 1841. Although China remained independent, after the Opium War the

TEXT BOX 3.6 COLONIALISM AND ENVIRONMENTAL AWARENESS

The colonization of overseas territories by the European powers was often accompanied by far-reaching environmental damage. In the first decades of the fifteenth century, some of the Canary Islands were almost completely covered with sugar plantations. A series of Caribbean islands met a similar fate in the sixteenth and seventeenth centuries. From 1667, for example, the plantations in Barbados could only function thanks to imports of wood and food from beyond the island. Deforestation encouraged erosion, the level of biodiversity fell and the climate changed: there was less rainfall. Europeans were not responsible for all of these problems; in some cases, deforestation had started before the arrival of large-scale plantations. But the scale of the exploitation by Europeans was certainly new, and in the nineteenth century the disastrous environmental effects were no longer limited to vulnerable, smaller tropical islands, but also affected far larger continental regions.

Richard Grove's *Green Imperialism: Colonial Expansion, Tropical Island Edens and the Origins of Environmentalism, 1600–1860*, published in 1996, sparked a debate among historians. Grove's thesis, in short, was that the colonization of what were mainly tropical islands created a sense of environmental awareness among colonizing powers. The environmental impact of colonization rapidly became manifest on these islands, sometimes within one or two generations. Ecocide, the destruction of species and/or of whole ecosystems, was already a topos in the fifteenth and sixteenth centuries; Columbus had warned the Spanish that the deforestation of the Canary Islands might be repeated in the Caribbean. According to Grove, this sense of environmental awareness could not have arisen in Europe itself, where most environmental effects only became apparent after several generations. As early as the eighteenth century in Ile de France (Mauritius), Pierre Poivre implemented a series of laws to counter the deforestation of the island. Not long afterwards, this example was copied on the British islands of St. Helena, Tobago and St. Vincent. One problem was that measures such as these were often unsuccessful: there was significant resistance from local plantation owners and entrepreneurs, and the plans were sabotaged. Grove nevertheless traces the emergence of a lobby of environmentally aware colonial policymakers in the early nineteenth century.

His book brought nuance to the 'dark' side of colonialism and imperialism, by emphasizing its 'green' side. According to other authors, though, we can also identify other potential founders of environmental awareness. Early Modern European rulers were also concerned with domain and forest management,. In the eighteenth century, Germans, in particular, were aware of the threat of Holznot, the depletion of timber reserves due to far-reaching deforestation. It thus happened remarkably often that nineteenth-century colonial administrators employed German foresters, who introduced a sustainable element to the policy on Java, for example.

> **TEXT BOX 3.7 THREE PHASES IN THE COLONIZATION FROM EUROPE**
>
> In general terms, we can identify three phases of colonization from Europe:
>
> 1. 1500–1700 The phase of the trading posts, determined by the presence of heavily armed ocean-going ships. The emphasis was on trade. European influence was limited to the coastal areas, on the whole, with the exception of Central and South America.
> 2. 1700–1850 The phase of the plantations, when the Europeans began to exploit territories inland. Mass plantations were cultivated and the slave trade, which went hand in hand with the plantations, accelerated rapidly. Despite this, most Europeans still experienced large problems when expanding their power inland. Only Great Britain was able to break through in India, meaning that Asia became more closely involved with Europe in this phase.
> 3. 1850–1950 The imperialist phase, when colonists successfully established themselves in the interior, supported by the rise of steamships and the construction of canals and railways. Now governed by Western elites, the colonies were closely linked to the metropole. In this phase, Europeans procured commodities from their colonies on a large scale.
>
> This process of globalization was supported by infrastructural innovations, such as the development of large ocean-going ships, the improvement of marine measuring instruments and, in the nineteenth century, the new communication forms of the industrial era (steamships, steam trains, the telegraph, aeroplanes). Steamships allowed colonists to penetrate deep into the African continent by sailing up the Senegal, the Congo and the Nile. In the final phase, every continent came under the influence of the European international system.

emperor was forced to allow the establishment of Western trading posts in the empire. Large amounts of capital now lay beyond the emperor's control for the first time.

From the early seventeenth century, the many European wars became global in scope, as the fighting extended to the colonies. The Netherlands pursued an unusually aggressive strategy from an early stage. Cornelis Matelief's fleet, for example, which sailed to the East in 1605, was explicitly tasked with destroying the Portuguese possessions; only in second place was it tasked with establishing VOC trading posts. Owing to the lucrative spice trade, the Dutch focused on gaining central positions in the East, supported by forts that were strong enough to resist attacks from other European colonists. The construction of Dutch fortifications on the Moluccan Islands cost as much as 1.7 million guilders; an enormous sum, considering that the VOC's original capital amounted to just 6 million guilders.

Although the European colonial powers resembled one another in their quests for overseas wealth, they took different approaches. We can roughly distinguish three models: (1) a dynastic imperial model, (2) a commercial model and (3) a national model.

Spain was typical of the dynastic imperial model. The Spanish monarchs viewed the country's overseas territories as direct extensions of their global empire. In imitation of their earlier fight against the Muslims, the Catholic religion and the Castilian language and legislation were also imposed on the colonized territories. The viceroys encouraged the arrival of Spanish colonists. Indigenous elites were integrated by allowing them to marry Spaniards.

The commercial model was represented by the Netherlands, and also, initially, by Portugal. Driven by the interests of merchants in overseas trade, this model was characterized by the establishment of fortified trading posts. There was a tendency to enter into contracts with indigenous rulers to supply goods. If European settlers came, they were often not compatriots. The settlements had a high degree of autonomy, much more so than in the dynastic imperial model. In contrast to the latter model, too, there was little integration with the indigenous population.

The Netherlands took the commercial model one step further than Portugal, by explicitly breaking with colonial missionary policy. Colonial religious policies were limited to the Dutch communities in the trading posts. In the Netherlands, companies were granted trade monopolies; the VOC had a monopoly on trade in Asia, for example, and the WIC on trade in America and West Africa. Like the settlements themselves, these companies also enjoyed a high degree of autonomy. Another difference between Dutch and Portuguese policy was that most of the costs of Dutch overseas settlements were covered not by the metropole, but by income from the region. In a relatively short period of time, the VOC succeeded in assuming crucial positions in East Asian regional trade (see chapter 2, Text Box 2.2). This brought in sufficient profits to support the Company locally. This, in turn, shortened the communication lines considerably and increased the battle-readiness of the colonists. Other colonists, including the Portuguese, tended to focus on their own trade, shipping goods to the metropole and then receiving the resources from the metropole for further trade. This was much less efficient than the Dutch model.

Great Britain and France implemented a national colonization model, in which the settlements were mainly populated by the British and French themselves. Integration with the indigenous population was limited, as with the Dutch model. The colonies maintained a high level of internal

FIGURE 3.3 *Fort Galle on the south-western coast of Sri Lanka. The fort was captured from the Portuguese in 1640, and expanded under the VOC into an important base for the Dutch commercial trading empire. After the English takeover in 1796, the fort was adapted several times in line with new military developments.*
© *Photo: Lodewijk Wagenaar.*

autonomy, but when it came to foreign policy and trade, the colonists had to follow the interests and guidelines of the metropole. British colonists, for example, were only allowed to export the products of their plantations to the metropole, and slave ships always had to put in at the ports of British colonies first. Moreover, the British state maintained many rights relating to the levying of tax. As in the commercial model, there were trade monopolies, such as the British East India Company and the French Compagnie des Indes, but these were under much tighter state control than in the Netherlands. The colonists also received significant support from the central state. The powerful British Navy intervened around the world to support the East India Company, whereas the VOC continued to bear all the costs of colonial warfare in the East. The English did imitate Dutch economic policies, though: local colonial proceeds were fed back into local colonial investments.

These different colonization models reflected political and military strategy in Europe: Spain pursued dynastic power and empire in Europe, Portugal and the Netherlands mainly wanted to protect their international trading positions, and Great Britain and France were powerful proto-national states. When it came to the commercial colonization model, the VOC was clearly a global game-changer, and brought about a process of globalization à la Wallerstein (see Chapter 2). It was not until the nineteenth century that the differences between the colonization models became blurred.

DUTCH COLONISTS AND THE INDIGENOUS POPULATION Dutch influence on colonial society was largely indirect until c. 1830. The VOC tended to enter into trading contracts with native rulers. Existing feudal relations were reinforced in the process: the contracts gave rulers the means to consolidate their position. The influence of the VOC was by no means negligible as a result. With the so-called Amphioen Society, the Dutch also controlled a large part of the eighteenth-century opium trade in the Far East. At that time, opium was often used as a means of payment in trade.

In some colonies, the Dutch presence had far-reaching consequences for the indigenous population, especially in the Banda Islands, the Cape and Suriname. In the Banda Islands (southern Moluccas), the usual VOC politics got out of hand. There was no strict hierarchical structure in the local population, meaning that the locals did not respect the agreements made between local chiefs and Jan Pietersz. Coen – the governor general of the VOC in the East Indies – regarding the supply of precious mace and nutmeg. Instead, they continued to supply the spices to the English, as the latter paid better. Coen saw this as a breach of contract, however, and sent a large-scale expedition to punish the islanders in 1621. Thousands of Bandanese perished, either as a result of executions or by fleeing to uninhabited areas, where they subsequently died of hunger after the VOC forbade food imports; the small group that remained was deported. Nowadays, this is known as genocide. On a now almost-depopulated island, the plantation owners had to cultivate the necessary spices using slave labour. It would be decades before the old level of production returned.

South Africa was a real Dutch settler colony (farming settlements, including beyond the trading post). The staging post at the Cape for VOC ships sailing to the East, which was established by Jan van Riebeeck in 1652, had to be economically self-sufficient. The VOC delivered the slaves, and employees of the VOC started farming businesses. This put pressure on the way of life of the native Khoikhoi, herdsmen with whom the Dutch initially had good trading relations. Around 1700, the Khoikhoi were only able to survive if they subjugated themselves to the Dutch. The conflicts with the indigenous population accelerated rapidly in the eighteenth century, when the 'Trekboeren' (migrant farmers) began to settle further and further inland.

After the arrival of the Dutch, Suriname was dominated by a plantation economy. The native Indian population retreated from the coastal regions; the WIC supplied the African slaves needed to work on the plantations. This marked the beginning of an era of pure slash-and-burn agriculture, which continued long into the twentieth century: as soon as the soil was exhausted, another plantation was begun, or a new crop, or mining had to tap new resources. This short-sighted environmental vision was also reflected in the attitude towards slaves. Eighteenth-century eyewitnesses described the plantation owners on Suriname (not all of whom were Dutch, by far; there were also many Portuguese Jews, French and English) as unusually cruel. A significant population of *marrons* ('maroons', runaway slaves) emerged, estimated at around 3,000 in *c.* 1750. As these *marrons* threatened the plantations and could not be subjugated with regular army force, the regime made peace with several groups.

THE REVOLUTIONS IN THE ATLANTIC WORLD Colonial relations gave rise to tensions that would transform the existing political relations in Europe and America in a wave of Atlantic revolutions. As we have already seen, the administrators of the British colonies had a high degree of autonomy. The East Coast of North America was home to many dissenters, who felt they had enjoyed too little freedom in Great Britain to practise their faith. The colonists also attracted fellow believers from other European countries. With the lack of a central state power in the new location, a society arose with a high degree of religious tolerance; more so, even, than in the Netherlands. There was an unusual degree of freedom in the public sphere, thanks to the high level of literacy and the circulation of newspapers, as well as a lack of effective censorship. Fundamental rights were part of British political culture and, unlike in the Netherlands, the colonists were familiar with a system of suffrage. When Great Britain started to pursue a more centralist policy in the eighteenth century, this specific mix of a free public sphere and democratic traditions proved to have immense revolutionary potential.

The colonists, after all, had to follow the British state's lead in relation to international trade and foreign policy. The debt burden of the Seven Years' War (1756–63), which was also fought on the American continent, shattered the peaceful relationship between metropole and colonies. The attempts by the British administration to force the colonists to shoulder part of the burden resulted, in other things, in the imposition of new import duties on tea. At the same time, in the political sphere, budding nationalism emerged in Great Britain. This reduced the colonists to being second-class citizens, thus sharpening the divisions. Thanks to the high level of solidarity in the American dissenter communities, a large group of colonists managed to mobilize under the slogan 'no taxation without representation', leading to a large-scale protest in 1764. The perceived injustice that the British, with their new nationalistic sentiments, had excluded them boosted ideas about natural rights and the rights of man; after all, such rights had not been granted by the British, but were inherent to all humanity. What made the American Revolution different from all of the preceding revolutionary upheavals was the wording of its constitution, which began: 'We the People'. With this, sovereignty was vested in 'the people' for the first time in history. This was followed, in 1789, by a president voted for by a public system of suffrage; yet another novelty.

In standard historical accounts, explanations of the French Revolution rarely consider the colonial connection. Its causes are usually sought in the 'French Enlightenment' and tensions in French society. Yet the colonial connection is undeniable; it is clear that the American War of Independence provided the French revolutionaries with a model, or, to use a different term, a 'repertoire'. Enlightenment philosophers had discussed the inalienable rights of man, of course, but this was but one of many existing philosophical movements. It is necessary to explain why this movement in particular became dominant. The Americans demonstrated the immense propaganda potential of a radically formulated constitution. The French people were now seen as the bearer of sovereignty, too.

A further parallel can be identified in the background to the revolution. The French war efforts to support the American colonists resulted in an unbearably high level of state debt. Attempts to reform the tax system resulted in large-scale resistance from the nobility, who were unwilling to relinquish their tax privileges; the break between the king and the nobility (a break in the 'elite consolidation') became a fact. In the power vacuum that followed, the French king convened the States General in 1789, for the first time since 1614. This gave the revolutionaries from the Third Estate, the citizenry, who could mobilize rapidly thanks to the corporative structure of society, an opportunity to formulate an alternative political system. The slogan 'no taxation without representation' would prove particularly appropriate for the situation in Europe too.

In the wake of the French Revolution, another revolution broke out: the revolution in Haiti (1791–1804). This was the first revolution in the world in which Black slaves fought for independence from colonial rule. Inspired by the French Revolution's slogans of freedom and equality, Toussaint L'Ouverture, a former domestic slave who himself had slaves, managed to transform and broaden a fragmented slave rebellion in 1791 into a battle for political independence. Even the troops sent by Napoleon were unable to break the resistance. The rebels, one should add, were aided by yellow fever, which knocked out the majority of the French soldiers, but to which the slaves themselves were immune.

In turn, the Haitian Revolution proved to be a source of inspiration for other rebellions in the region. Aided by the military weakening of the metropole during the Napoleonic Wars, a series of revolutions occurred in Latin and Central America. The first revolutionary government, led by creoles, was formed in Venezuela, which declared its independence in 1811 (see also Chapter 8).

Even before the French Revolution broke out, the Americans had inspired another group of revolutionaries: the Dutch Patriot Movement (1785–7). The struggle for American independence was followed with great interest in the Republic, due to its similar political structure (federation) and common enemy (Great Britain). Great Britain's demand that the Dutch cease their financial support to the US resulted in the Fourth Anglo-Dutch War (1780–4), which went disastrously for the Republic. In the ensuing crisis of authority, a space opened up for new 'Atlantic revolutionary' ideas. For the first time, a political movement succeeded in breaking the existing oligarchy from below. The failure to sustain the revolution was linked to the decentralized political structure (see Text Box 3.8). In 1787, Stadholder Willem V managed to suppress the revolt only with the aid of Prussian troops.

The Patriots had laid the foundations for political reform, however. When the French revolutionary troops invaded in 1795, the second act took place, and thanks to the preliminary work of the Patriots, this was a 'velvet revolution'. The Revolutionary Club in Haarlem, for example, arranged for elections to be held, so that the municipal government had already been replaced before the French arrived. A national assembly was founded, based on the French model. The democratic experiment did not last for long, however; as early as 1798, there was a counter-coup by the 'moderates'. What was new, though, was that the National Government now took responsibility for all kinds of policy areas. It introduced a national taxation system, a general education act and state regulations on medicine, for example. From that time onwards, the country was divided into municipalities, all of which were officially equal. This brought an end to the power of autonomous town governments and locally defined municipal citizenship, and marked the arrival of the centralized state in the Netherlands.

TEXT BOX 3.8 THE PATRIOT MOVEMENT, 1785–7

In a country divided by corpora and municipal privileges, a pamphlet that was circulated anonymously in 1781, written by a nobleman from Overijssel, Johan Derk van der Capellen tot den Pol, addressed a very broad spectrum of groups in the Republic for the first time: 'the people'. In imitation of this pamphlet, the Patriots propounded the radical political ideal of equality and fraternity that would soon take root in the French Revolution as well. They attacked the ruling oligarchy that had governed the country so badly before and during the war with Great Britain.

The movement began in the middle classes, who mobilized via the many organizations in the towns, but it was also joined by lower-class groups. Intimidating citizen militias conducted drills in the streets. Purely political newspapers emerged for the first time, such as the *Politieke Kruyer* and the *Post van den Neder-Rhijn*, which were published weekly or even more frequently. The revolutionaries benefitted from the high degree of freedom in the public sphere; if Rotterdam banned a certain publication, for example, one merely had to walk to nearby Delfshaven to get hold of a copy. When the publisher and editor of *De Politieke Kruyer* was imprisoned in Amsterdam in 1785, the paper continued to be printed, while sympathizers held collections to pay his legal costs.

The Patriots' political tactics were hindered, however, by the federalist structure of the Republic. Each town and then each province had to be conquered from the inside, via complicated administrative layers. This was a slow process, and gave Willem V an opportunity to seek support from his in-laws in Prussia. Unlike France, the Netherlands lacked a political institution such as the Assemblée Nationale, which aided the formation of nationwide political opinion.

THE RISE OF NATIONALISM The process of globalization that had been set in motion by colonial enterprises thus had all kinds of political consequences for Europe. It would be incorrect to seek the causes of the French Revolution in European developments alone. Even nationalism, which is often studied solely in relation to European state formation, acquired its contours during the wave of Atlantic revolutions. When Europeans started to build national identities in the second half of the eighteenth century, the European colonists suddenly became aware of their inferior status within the colonial relationship, especially in the British and Spanish colonies.

Until 1800, nations and states could coexist, but in the nineteenth century the ideal was increasingly for these boundaries to coincide. A nation is a form of collective identity (alongside other collective identities, such as gender, class, ethnic background, resident of a town or region, youth and old-age pensioner). The British anthropologist Benedict Anderson has called nations 'imagined communities', 'imagined' because it would be impossible for all of a nation's inhabitants to be acquainted with every other inhabitant; the national community exists exclusively in people's minds. Nationalists located 'the people' on a continuum with the past, emphasizing the times when the country had acted in a united fashion, but 'forgetting' periods marked by a divergence of opinion (see also Chapter 8).

Nationalist feeling had existed prior to the rise of the nation state, including in the Dutch Republic. The States General sometimes held national days of prayer to commemorate the same event in the churches. The annuals known as the *Nieuwe Nederlandsche Jaarboeken,* which were published from 1748, recorded news from across the Republic. From around 1750, the concept of the *vaderland* (native country) came up more and more frequently in language use, and societies such as the Maatschappij tot Nut van 't Algemeen ('the society for public welfare') were committed to the reform of the nation.

With the French Revolution, nationalist sentiment became even more intense. One important impetus for this feeling was the *levée en masse* of 1792: massive general conscription for all able-bodied, unmarried men aged between 18 and 25. The sovereignty of kings also disappeared: the revolutions emphasized the sovereignty of the people. The question of who the people were, though, was not always easy to answer. The Congress of Vienna in 1815 made international agreements about which states had the right to exist. For the Netherlands, this gave a certain raison d'etre to the continuation of the recently installed monarchy (1813), whereby Luxembourg and Belgium became part of the new Netherlands. The rise of Dutch nationalism was hindered by the past, however. The Revolt against Spain and the Calvinist religion could no longer function as binding elements, as they had done in the age of the Republic. After all, Belgians and Catholics did not share the same memories and feelings as the people of Holland and Protestants.

We should add that nationalist ideas fitted perfectly into the European international structure, with its famous Westphalian state system that had emphasized the sovereignty of each state, and were unknown to the Ottomans, Great Mughals and Chinese, where the ideal of a multi-ethnic state still prevailed. Although a few multi-ethnic states continued to exist in Europe (Austria-Hungary, Russia), the nation state became the standard model.

Summary

To conclude, let us return to the questions that we asked in the introduction:

1. The course of the state formation process in Europe was so different from that in the rest of Eurasia because the means of power were dispersed, and because the geographical situation

created opportunities for founding power bases in different regions. The meetings of the estates and the towns functioned as a natural brake on autocratic states. Beyond Eurasia, political fragmentation continued to prevail, because agriculture and trade were much less developed there. The unique position of the Netherlands (a republic with considerable military power) can be explained with reference to the medieval legacy, whereby Holland acquired an extremely efficient form of governance, creating a base for the flexible financing of war. The towns enjoyed decisive political influence and troops were effective and well disciplined, meaning that the presence of soldiers did not disrupt Holland's economic development, but actually promoted it.

2. Compared to the rest of Europe, there was a high degree of political freedom and religious tolerance in the Dutch Republic, despite the absence of an established church, and a high level of municipal autonomy, which facilitated de facto freedom of speech. There was also religious tolerance in China and the Ottoman Empire, however, and the North American British colonies had an even larger public sphere than the Netherlands. The democratic electoral system in the Netherlands was none too developed (in contrast to Britain), but access to power was reserved for a small elite in most European countries up to 1800.

3. The Netherlands reinforced the process of globalization by engaging in successful colonization, mainly based on commercial interests in the Far East. Other countries followed dynastic or national models. The national model of colonization pursued by the British gave the initial impetus to the American Revolution, which in turn shaped a political repertoire that proved invaluable to European revolutionaries. The Atlantic revolutions set in motion an internationalization of norms and values, particularly the concepts of freedom and equality. The Netherlands encountered these transatlantic revolutionary ideas at a very early stage, as expressed in the Patriot Movement in 1785.

4

The tension between the community and the individual
Social-cultural developments

MANON VAN DER HEIJDEN

Between 1000 and 1800, there was a shift in Western Europe in the relationship between the community and the individual. Whereas family and community ties had initially played a major role in shaping individuals' actions and decisions in relation to work, family and religion, in the course of the pre-industrial period individual preferences became more important. According to the German sociologist Max Weber (1864–1920), this process was accompanied by increasing rationalization: people began to act more consciously by weighing up ends and means, while action based on habit, emotion or belief became less important. This shift from communal to individualistic thinking was expressed in all kinds of social areas, from politics to the economy and culture.

Different paths were followed in other parts of the world. In East Asia, family and community ties remained more important than individuals' personal preferences. State, religion and population were strongly integrated in this part of the world, while in Europe, the state, church, aristocracy and citizens were competing forces. This had far-reaching consequences for the ways in which people attempted to mitigate the risks of existence.

In this chapter, we will describe and compare sociocultural developments in different parts of the world, particularly in Western Europe and China, in the period before 1800. We focus on the following three questions:

1. What were the patterns in demographic behaviour: which differences or similarities can be identified in the development of

marriage, family formation and marital fertility, and in the ways in which people handled disease and death?
2. Which changes occurred in the social order and the relations between the community and the individual, how can these be explained and what implications did these have for the way in which people dealt with the risks of existence? Did the Netherlands occupy a unique position in this regard, and if so, how can this be explained?
3. How did people's visions of the world, the individual and society change, and how can these changes be explained? Did the Netherlands follow a different path in this respect?

4.1
Patterns of marriage and family formation

The Malthusian model, which was discussed in Chapter 2, distinguishes between two ways of bringing the size of a population into balance with the available means of livelihood. Malthus called these the 'preventive check' (before famine breaks out) and the 'positive check' (the famine itself). These checks did not work in the same way in all societies. Historians have shown that in this respect, there were several striking differences within Eurasia.

The Norwegian historical demographer, John Hajnal, has shown that the age of marriage in Western Europe (west of the St Petersburg-Trieste line) was higher than elsewhere in the world. Women often married when they were over twenty-five, and men married even later (see Table 4.1). A large proportion of women and men remained unmarried; it was

TABLE 4.1 *Average Age of Marriage of Women (upon First Marriage) in Western Europe, Late Eighteenth Century*

	Average age upon first marriage
The Netherlands	26.5
Belgium	24.9
France	25.3
Germany	26.6
Great Britain	25.2
Scandinavia	26.1

Source: Clark, A farewell to alms, 76.

not uncommon for 15 per cent of the population, or even more, to be 'permanent celibates'. The relatively late age of marriage and the rather high percentage of unmarried people put a brake on population growth. The age of marriage was so high because young couples started their independent households (neolocality), and did not live with their families. This was possible only if a couple had sufficient income. The 'European Marriage Pattern', as Hajnal called it, thus worked as a preventive check. It is not entirely clear when this pattern first emerged, but it existed in the fourteenth century, in any case.

People tended to get married earlier in Asia. Around 1800, women in China married aged nineteen, on average, and men at the age of twenty-one. Few women – just 1 per cent – remained unmarried. The share of unmarried men was 16 per cent. Marriage fertility in East Asia was lower than in Western Europe, however. Around 1800, a married woman would have five children, on average, between her 20th and 45th years. The equivalent in Northern Europe at the time was eight. In both the lower and the upper social classes, married Chinese woman stopped having children at the age of thirty-four, on average; in Europe, this generally happened only when a woman turned forty. Although the preventive checks in China and Europe were thus different in nature, the effects were similar. In both societies, population growth was controlled by a limit on the number of births. There was yet another parallel: in both European and Chinese society, extended breastfeeding functioned as a way to reduce the number of births.

In China, there was yet another method to reduce population pressure: the practice of infanticide (killing children soon after birth). Infanticide occurred on a limited scale in European countries, but in China it was not uncommon for parents to kill their newborn child if she was a girl. Around 1800 in the northernmost Chinese province of Liaoning, around 20–25 per cent of girls died in this way. The practice of infanticide also explains why so many more men than women remained unmarried; there was a surplus of men.

Life expectancy at birth in Western Europe and East Asia varied little between the fourteenth and nineteenth centuries, as shown in Table 4.2. In both cases, the figure fluctuated at around twenty-five and thirty-five years. This pattern was also followed in the Netherlands. The low life expectancy was strongly influenced by death just after birth or in early childhood. In England between 1580 and 1800, 18 per cent of children died in their first year, while only 69 per cent of children reached the age of fifteen. Around 1800, the life expectancies of twenty-year-olds in China, Japan and England were similar: they could expect to live another 35–38 years, on average. In the seventeenth century, more than 15 per cent of English men who made a will died aged seventy or older. The greatest risks of death were thus concentrated in the first twenty years of life.

The risk of death was higher in urban areas than in the countryside (see Table 4.2 for London and Beijing). Mortality rates in European towns before 1800 were so high that urban growth was always the result of immigration,

TABLE 4.2 *Life Expectancy in Western Europe and East Asia until the Nineteenth Century*

	Life expectancy at birth
Western Europe	
Germany before 1800	35
England 1550–99	38
England 1650–99	35
France before 1750	25
France 1750–99	28-30
England 1750–99	38
London 1750–99	23
East Asia	
China (Anhui) 1300–1880	28
China (Beijing) 1644–1739	26
China (Liaoning) 1792–1867	26-35
Japan, countryside 1776–1815	33

Sources: Clark, *A farewell to alms*, 94; Wong, *China transformed*, 28.

mainly from the countryside. In London between 1580 and 1650, there were just 0.87 births for each death. Without migration, the population would have fallen by half a per cent per year. In the second half of the eighteenth century, average life expectancy in London was just twenty-three years. People in pre-industrial towns often lived in high-density housing with few sanitary facilities such as clean water, sewerage or a regular refuse-collection service. As a result, diseases such as plague, typhus, dysentery and smallpox could spread rapidly. There was also a greater risk of fires in towns and cities.

The high level of mortality in the pre-industrial era was characteristic of the whole of Eurasia. In the Netherlands, too, the mortality level remained high even after the disappearance of the plague after *c.* 1670, due to the arrival of dysentery and smallpox; at the end of the eighteenth century, almost 10 per cent of the Dutch population died of these diseases. Until the eighteenth century, there were few methods for fighting infectious diseases. People used herbs, potions, salves or magic and sorcery to ward off illness. There were also more official forms of medicine. In China, medicine in the pre-industrial period was based on the balance between the opposing forces of *yin* (feminine) and *yang* (masculine). The usual way to cure disease was to restore the balance through the use of acupuncture. In Europe, medicine was based on Galen's theory of the humours from the second century, which sought the causes of illnesses in an imbalance in the body's humours (black bile, yellow bile, phlegm and blood). The standard remedy was to regulate the humours by means of blood-letting, vomiting, sneezing and laxation. Critical study of Galen's work by Andreas Vesalius (1514–64) led to more knowledge about the anatomy of the human body, meaning that bone fractures could be treated more successfully, for example. It was not until the nineteenth century that chemists and physicians such as Louis Pasteur and Robert Koch discovered that diseases and infections were caused by bacteria, and there was growing awareness that hygiene could reduce mortality rates. In addition, the vague and unclear descriptions of diseases in medical treatises were gradually replaced by detailed cause-of-death statistics. A more quantitative approach improved people's understanding of the typical course of disease outbreaks and the determinants and circumstances of particular diseases.

TEXT BOX 4.1 RISKS OF EXISTENCE IN THE PRE-INDUSTRIAL PERIOD

The risks of existence in the pre-industrial period were closely linked to the demographic cycles. In both the towns and in rural areas, the high risk of mortality affected all social groups, regardless of origin or income. We can identify four types of risks:

Death Most couples had a large number of children, but a significant number of them died shortly after birth. Many people remained alone after their partner died, while old age also brought risks. A forty-five-year-old woman, for example, had probably experienced the death of her parents, the majority of her brothers and sisters, and often more than half of her own children in her lifetime, and by that age she was usually a widow, too.

Illness Due to illness, accidents or disability, people risked becoming unemployed, losing income and incurring high costs due to nursing and recovery. Plague, dysentery, smallpox and leprosy were common illnesses, while patchy medical knowledge increased the likelihood of disability and poor recovery after an accident.

Lack of work On the whole, small self-employed workers and wage labourers were at the greatest risk of temporary or long-term unemployment, because their work often consisted of seasonal labour or small, separate jobs. In times of economic decline, shopkeepers, craftsmen and wage labourers faced a high risk of sharply rising prices for basic necessities.

Disasters War, storms, floods, fires and cattle plagues damaged property and were often accompanied by famine, unemployment and the spread of disease. There were frequent fires, especially in towns and cities, destroying houses, shops and possessions.

Improved nutrition could also prevent excess mortality. One example is the spread of the consumption of potatoes in Europe in the eighteenth century, which helped to remedy vitamin C deficiency. The standard European diet was based on milk, porridge, beer and sometimes fish or meat. It supplied calories, but offered little variety. In China, the diet included rice, fish, vegetables and tea, and sometimes meat, too; people's diets were therefore more varied. The arrival of sweet potatoes from America in China (see Chapter 2) gave a considerable boost to the general calorific value of the Chinese diet.

RELATIONS WITHIN THE FAMILY The development of the European Marriage Pattern (EMP) was linked to changes in marriage and inheritance law, which developed from the eleventh century onwards under the influence of the Catholic Church. In Christian societies, there was a growing conviction that reciprocal consent on the part of the man and the woman should form the basis of marriage. A marriage could thus take place without the interference of the parents or family members. Arranged marriages at a young age were more the exception than the rule. This was true for the lower and middle classes, at any rate; arranged marriage remained extremely important for the elite.

Furthermore, European inheritance law allowed not only men but also women to inherit; women were often able to own property and assets, too, even if they were married. Christianity played a major role in this development, too. From the eleventh century, the Catholic Church attempted to expand its worldly possessions by curtailing the power of people's relations and boosting the power of individuals to dispose freely of their inheritance. This meant that people, often encouraged by positive expectations of life after death, were able to leave their goods to the church without having to fear opposition from their relatives. In this way, the church unintentionally contributed to the emancipation of the individual and the rise of an individualistic outlook on life.

European marriage and inheritance law encouraged both men and women to participate in the labour process, leading to the growth of the labour market. After all, flexible labour and individual choices went hand in hand with commercialization, wage labour and labour migration. The fragmentation of traditional feudal power relations further advanced this process. The Black Death of 1348 was an extra catalyst, because the scarcity of labour created opportunities for both men and women in the labour market.

The question is whether individualization and more flexible labour relations also led to changes to relations within the family. Were people able to choose their marriage partners freely in the pre-industrial era? Were the relations between family members affectionate and loving? Was the position of children actually any different from that after 1800? Historians have debated such questions at length.

Historians of the family, such as Philippe Ariès, Lawrence Stone and Edward Shorter, believed that there was little affection between spouses, parents and children in the pre-industrial period in Western Europe. This vision was based on a number of assumptions. First, it was assumed that the model of the 'extended family' prevailed throughout Europe: families in which parents, grandparents and children, and possibly servants, all lived in one household. Second, it was assumed that until *c.* 1800 there was a high degree of inequality between men and women: patriarchal relations were thought to have prevailed in Europe (as they did in other parts of the world). A third point concerned the choice of marriage partner: people could not choose freely, it was thought, but the choice was instead made by parents and relations. Fourth, these historians of family life assumed that economic interests formed the basis of marriage and family relations: families were production units composed of parents and children. The purpose of marriage was to reproduce and to secure the family property.

An important fifth reason for these more business-like or economic family relations lay, according to the aforementioned historians, in the high risk of death in the period before 1800. High rates of child mortality were thought to have led to parents to become less attached to their children and to their showing little care, affection and love as a result. Children were viewed as young adults who had to join the production process as soon as possible. There were many remarriages, too, because many people lost their partner early in life due to illness, war, shipwreck or childbirth, meaning that the relationship between spouses is unlikely to have been affectionate or loving.

Other historians have added nuance to this picture in recent decades. Research by a number of historical demographers at Cambridge University (England) has shown that most families in North-western Europe did not live in extended families, but in nuclear families: a father and a mother with several children and, at most, some live-in servants. The negative picture of family relations in the pre-industrial age has also been revised. Diaries, letters and travel journals show that the relations between spouses and those between parents and children were usually affectionate in Western Europe before 1800. Parents certainly mourned the death of their children, even if most children died young (see Figure 4.1).

When it came to choosing a marriage partner, there were differences between social groups. The nobility, wealthy citizens and farmers had an interest in pursuing an arranged marriage: after all, it was necessary to secure their land and assets. In the Netherlands, urban regents used marriage in an attempt to safeguard their political and economic interests, but members of the lower social classes had more freedom to choose their partners. There were also differences between urban and rural areas. Family ties were tighter in the countryside, and land ownership made arranged marriages the more obvious choice. Individualization among young people was greatest in Western European towns and cities. Unlike elsewhere in the world, it was very common for adolescents to go and work outside the parental home, and this freedom brought them into contact with more marriage candidates.

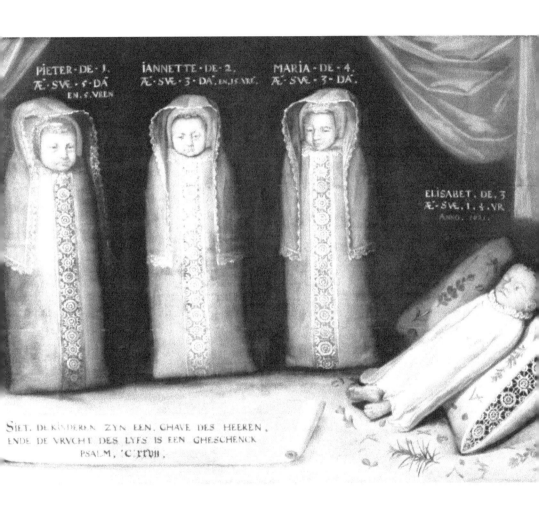

FIGURE 4.1 *Portrait of the Dordtse vierling (quadruplets from Dordrecht), painted by an unknown artist shortly after their birth on 9 June 1621. Elisabeth, who died immediately after birth, lies by her siblings in a shroud.*
© *Dordrechts Museum, Dordrecht (on loan from the Noordbrabants Museum's-Hertogenbosch; public domain).*

> **TEXT BOX 4.2 NEIGHBOURHOOD ORGANIZATIONS**
>
> One typical feature of Western Europe was that of the neighbourhood organizations that emerged in the Late Middle Ages, often known as *gebuurten* or *buurtschappen* in Dutch towns. The nature of these organizations varied by region and town, from informal reciprocal assistance to formal organizations with powers. Not all towns had such organizations, but where they did exist, they played a role in social control. 'Neighbourhood masters' (*buurtmeesters*; the father of the painter Rembrandt was one such master) mediated in conflicts and acted as intermediaries between the government and individuals. They also registered newcomers to the neighbourhood and kept track of who moved where. Finally, the organizations helped people in times of need, by providing financial aid or assistance in the event of accidents or funerals. The organizations also helped to organize celebrations on the occasion of marriages and births.
>
> In this way, they played a key role in mutual care and strengthened social cohesion. They are illustrative of the way in which citizens and churches in Early Modern societies held responsibilities that would be assumed by central government in the modern age. With the rise of the nation state, they would lose their role.

Compared to other countries in Western Europe, the relations between men and women in the Low Countries were remarkably free. The factors mentioned earlier in relation to the European Marriage Pattern (marriage law, inheritance law and free labour relations) were particularly applicable in the Dutch context. After the Reformation, the emancipation of the individual, which had begun in Europe in the eleventh century, was reinforced further in Protestant areas. From the mid-sixteenth century, it was possible to get a divorce in Scotland, the Netherlands and Protestant regions of Germany, and this right was also introduced in England in a limited form.

Related to this, the legal and economic position of Dutch and Belgian women was also relatively strong compared to that in other countries. They were able to trade independently and enter into financial agreements. In the seventeenth and eighteenth centuries, 70 per cent of the fish stalls and 20–60 per cent of the vegetable stalls in Leiden's markets were run by women. Female labour participation was high; it was not for nothing that travellers and immigrants were astonished at the independent position and domineering manner of women in the Republic.

The individualization of labour and family relations in Western Europe also had implications for mitigating the risks of existence. Not everyone could rely on family in hard times, and people became more dependent on support from the church and government. Table 4.3 shows that widows,

TABLE 4.3 *Heads of Households in Leiden, and Poverty, 1622*

Head of household		Households (N)	Households (%)	Of which poor (%)
Man	*Married*	3085	72.8	19.2
	Unmarried, widower	246	5.8	12.6
Woman	*Unmarried*	288	6.8	17.4
	Widow	539	12.7	25.4
Other/unknown		77	1.8	6.5
Total		4235	100	19.3

Source: Schmidt, 'Survival strategies of widows', 269.

who headed 13 per cent of households in Leiden, had a particularly tough time; as many of a quarter of them lived in poverty. In the Netherlands and Sweden, the average share of widows at that time was around 15 per cent. In England it was 13 per cent, a share that rose to almost a quarter of households in the larger towns and cities. It was not always easy to find a new marriage partner. In Italy, in particular, women often lived alone after the death of their spouse; in the eighteenth century, just 17 per cent of all women who had become widows before turning 34 remarried.

While the emphasis of family relations in Europe began to shift from the community to the individual, in China, marriage remained a contract between two families. In practice, marriage was focused on two objectives: the continuation of the paternal family name and securing care for the parents. Chinese women were unable to claim an inheritance in this patriarchal system (a system determined by paternal authority). In a system of parental authority, there was no need to wait for economic independence before getting married. Young couples did not choose freely, after all, and when they married, they usually lived with their spouse's parents. As a result, there was no nuclear family in China; the composition of households was much more complex. As in Western Europe, lower-class households in China consisted of around five people. In the middle and upper classes, however, it was common for children, children by marriage, uncles and aunts, grandparents and other family members to live in a single household together. A single household sometimes consisted of more than fifty people. Even in smaller households, though, broad family ties, established via the so-called clans, were much more important than in Western Europe. The individual thus enjoyed less personal freedom in the Chinese marriage culture, but on the other hand, individuals could rely on more protection from parents and other relations in difficult times.

4.2
Social order, social care and disciplining

The increasing individualization of labour and family relations in Western Europe was accompanied by a changing social order. A considerable share of the population moved from the countryside to the city, leading to the rise of a separate community that was not tied to the land, but dependent on wage labour: the proletariat. In Eastern Europe, however, the opposite development took place: the group of serfs who provided unfree labour grew rapidly. This limited the freedom of movement of the peasantry, a group that had enjoyed a high degree of freedom in the previous era of colonization (see Chapter 2).

Unlike in Europe, such clear social divisions did not develop in pre-industrial China, because the state exerted more influence over society. The aristocratic elite class was decimated in China in the tenth century, leaving a nobility that was directly dependent on the imperial family. According to American sinologist and historian Bin Wong, under the Ming (1368–1644) and Qing (1644–1912) dynasties, beliefs about the ideal social order were reproduced in local elites via the family and extended family, with the male head of the family playing a key role. This had the moral aim of supporting the peasant class, because the power of the state was ultimately determined by the well-being of the peasantry. In Europe, the elites were engaged in a fierce struggle for power, and were not in a position to promote a unified ideal. In China, there were no independent and competing political entities (nobility, church, urban corporations) that were separate from the state. Nor was there any concept of urban citizenship in China, which in Europe became a political power factor to rival the state from the Late Middle Ages onward. In China, citizens could form brotherhoods or other types of associations for mutual support, but these organizations had no political influence (see also Chapter 3).

In Europe, the rising middle classes were usually able to provide more of a counterweight to the power of the king and the nobility. Commercialization and labour specialization led to growing social diversity among the population, and thereby an opportunity to ascend or descend the social ladder. As such, there were significant differences between countries and regions.

In France, the classes remained relatively closed. The country was overwhelmingly agrarian, with almost 90 per cent living in rural areas. The peasant population paid the most tax: 12–15 per cent of their income to the state, plus an additional variable portion of feudal taxes to noble landowners. Under Louis XIV (1638–1715), the Sun King, there was a significant expansion of centralized state power via an extensive bureaucracy, in which the aristocracy, in exchange for supporting the king, received lucrative posts at court, in the legal system and in the military and fiscal apparatus. The mutual dependency between the king and the aristocracy was reinforced further by the sale of a considerable share of the state offices.

In Germany east of the Elbe, the landed nobility – the so-called *Junkers* – gained a lot of power from the fifteenth century. These were originally the nobles who had led the *Ostsiedlung* (colonization from the West). Increasing urbanization in Western Europe led to growing demand for grain. By forcing the peasants to grow more and more grain on their land and reselling the grain to traders (mainly from Holland), the landed nobility saw a sharp rise in their income and social status. The peasant class became poorer, and the percentage of smallholders rose considerably. This process was clearly evident in Saxony, which formed part of the Elbe basin. In 1550, smallholders had made up less than 5 per cent of the population of Saxony, but 200 years later, this share had risen to more than 30 per cent. At the same time, the towns were becoming home to increasing numbers of urban-dwellers who had no rights as burghers (see Table 4.4).

In England and the Northern Netherlands, the traditional dominance of the aristocracy was broken by agricultural commercialization and the rise of a relatively large middle class in the towns. There were many noble landowners in England, too, but as a class they had fewer privileges than the nobility in Eastern Europe, and they actually promoted the commercialization of agriculture (see Chapter 2). The Dutch aristocracy had even less power, due to the land reclamations of the Middle Ages, and the decentralized governance and predominance of urban elites in the Early Modern period (see Chapter 3). Both in England and in the Netherlands,

TABLE 4.4 *Social Stratification of the Population of Saxony in Numbers and Percentages, 1550 and 1750*

	1550		1750	
	Number	%	**Number**	%
Citizens	116,000	26.7	200,000	19.7
Other city-dwellers	22,000	5.1	166,000	16.3
Farmers	215,000	49.5	250,000	24.6
Smallholders	20,000	4.6	310,000	30.4
Other villagers	55,000	6	82,000	8.1
Clergymen	3,500	0.9	4,500	0.4
Nobility	2,400	0.6	5,500	0.5
	434,000	100.0	1,018,000	100.0

Source: Kriedte, *Spätfeudalismus und Handelskapital*, 72.

there were few differences between the city and countryside; there was an exceptionally high degree of political and economic integration between the two.

As a result of the urbanized culture in the Netherlands, opportunities for social advancement mainly arose in the towns. The occupational guilds, which grew in number and diversity, were an excellent means for citizens to strengthen their economic position. Social historians Piet Lourens and Jan Lucassen have calculated that in the period between 1560 and 1670 alone, as many guilds were founded as in the four preceding centuries. Women, too, sometimes had access to the guilds.

Guilds were an instrument for citizens to form their identity, through rituals, eating and drinking together and establishing the rules surrounding the occupational group. According to the social historian Maarten Prak, this gave rise to a corporative culture, one that was particularly pronounced in the Netherlands. It had a very diverse social structure, because every corporation was unique. No corporation was identical to another; each town had its own typical drapers' guild regulations and so forth. In addition to guilds, civic militias and neighbourhood organizations (see Text Box 4.2) organized processions and festivities that gave citizens a sense of social cohesion. Many guilds also developed forms of social security, so they could support their members in the case of disability, sickness or death. Corporatism was supported by the middle classes, craftsmen and shopkeepers. Corporations were not an exclusively urban phenomenon; there were also guilds in the countryside. The universal structure of the Christian church strengthened the formation of the civic community even further. Every new resident of a town was able to join a local parish. The situation was different in China, where ancestor worship meant that the link with one's place of origin remained much stronger. Chinese urban brotherhoods and associations were therefore organized on the basis of kin and ethnic relations.

The great increase in the number of guilds reflects the growth of the labour market and, accompanying this, growing employment opportunities for wage labourers. As we saw in Chapter 2, wage labourers in North-western Europe in the pre-industrial era were better off in terms of income than wage labourers elsewhere in Europe. But although opportunities for work increased, the distribution of wealth within Holland became more unequal. Not everyone saw their real wages rise; some were only able to earn more by working harder, together with the rest of their family. After all, social diversity did not only mean more opportunities to advance socially; there was also a greater chance of slipping down the social ladder.

To start with, guilds were only accessible to citizens. Citizenship rights were acquired at birth or purchased, but not everyone could afford the fee. Moreover, not everyone was allowed to become a citizen. Jews were almost always excluded, and the children of Catholic or Baptists did not always automatically inherit citizenship rights from their parents in the Republic. The rules differed per town, though. In Amsterdam, Jews could gain the status of burgher, although there were certain limits. In the east of the Netherlands, discrimination against non-Calvinists was much stronger than in the west of the country. When it came to the bottom of society, those who had no citizenship rights were often only able to become casual labourers or porters.

Thus, socio-economic differences grew in practice, both in the Netherlands and in England. Private capital holdings in Holland multiplied from around 40 guilders per capita in 1500, to 650 guilders in 1650, and to 2,150 guilders in 1790. The greatest share of the growing wealth, however, increasingly flowed towards a small group of regents, merchants and people of independent means. This is illustrated by the concentration of property ownership in Amsterdam: in 1500, 5 per cent of all owners owned 27 per cent of the total value of housing; by 1732, this figure had risen to 40 per cent.

POVERTY AND SOCIAL CARE The fundamentally different relations between the state and the population in China and Europe were also reflected in the arrangement of social care. The precarious balance between the food supply and the population frequently led to price hikes and increasing poverty. During a period of economic depression in Westphalia, the poorest group of taxpayers (day labourers and servants) rose from 29 per cent in 1580 to 39 per cent in 1594. In the English county of Kent in 1590, some of the self-employed artisans who had previously contributed to the poor tax were forced to appeal for municipal poor relief themselves. Although the population mechanisms and the consequences of crises affected the whole of Eurasia, the nature of the provisions for temporary or long-term aid in the two regions was very different.

In China, the state organized aid in the case of a famine. Public officials imported food, which was stored for use in times of crisis. Under the Qing dynasty, the system of granaries became even more efficient. The state established a grain-price information system and encouraged local communities to store grain for the relief of the poor, too. Wealthier households were expected to support the poor in times of crisis with cheap grain and loans. Moreover, the Confucian ideal of social order (see below) encouraged the support of impoverished clan or family members.

In Europe, there were no state granaries; the urban government alone was involved in storing grain. Similar measures were taken in the Northern Netherlands, too; both small and large towns built warehouses to store grain for the poor (*stadskoren*). The governors of English towns in the sixteenth and seventeenth centuries registered the granaries of private individuals and appointed administrators to monitor bread prices and bakeries. Dutch urban administrators also set maximum prices for bread. These measures were desperately needed in Western Europe from the mid-sixteenth century, due to growing specialization in the countryside and urbanization, which made large groups dependent on grain that had to be imported from elsewhere.

FIGURE 4.2 *A granary with a fence and veranda, in a Chinese village at the time of the Song dynasty. From the Keng Chih Thu, a series of illustrations and poems about the agriculture of Lou Shou (c. 1150).*
© *Public domain.*

The organization of poor relief in the pre-industrial period was typical of the relationship between government and citizens in Europe. Responsibility lay mainly with local ecclesiastical and municipal institutions. In village communities and for the permanent residents of towns, family members also provided support and aid in times of illness, poverty or unemployment, but such support was not, or hardly, available for the masses of urban migrants. The latter were much more reliant on the town's institutional network.

An infrastructure of facilities emerged within towns, in which corporations such as guilds and neighbourhood associations, and wealthy citizens joined the church and city in providing all kinds of social assistance. In commercial centres in Mediterranean regions, fraternities and church orders had established hospitals, orphanages and homes for the elderly as early as the fourteenth century. In *c.* 1300, Toulouse already had twelve hospitals, Zaragoza had eleven and León had nine. Municipal parishes played a major role in the care of orphans, the sick, the elderly or the disabled. During the Late Middle Ages and Early Modern period, more and more care was organized by civic officials, who used excises (taxes on consumer goods), loans, gifts from wealthy citizens or lotteries to finance the facilities. For example, the city government of Leiden organized a lottery in 1596, for which 28,000 people registered. The proceeds – a sum of 58,000 guilders – were used to convert a religious house into a shelter for plague victims, the mentally ill and the elderly.

After the Reformation, ecclesiastical poor relief continued to exist in Protestant regions, but it was more tightly coordinated by the towns and more centralized at the municipal level. In the German regions, it was increasingly subsumed under the process of *Konfessionalisierung*, the sociopolitical integration of municipal governance and the local church (Chapter 3). The Northern Netherlands was an exception in this tendency towards centralized municipal support. Instead, there was a further fragmentation of care in this region. This was because the Calvinist church became a public church, not a state church, after the Revolt of 1572 (see Chapter 3). As a privileged church, it received more financial support and freedom to develop activities than other churches, but Remonstrants, Catholics, Baptists, Lutherans and Jews also had care arrangements for their own communities. Various kind of private charity also continued to exist, and neighbourhood associations and guilds provided support in emergencies (see also Text Box 4.2). The contributions from guilds, among other things, served to mitigate the risks faced by guild members.

As more rural areas commercialized, the towns had to absorb a growing influx of migrants and the needy. Between around 1580 and 1650, it is likely that 10–25 per cent of the European population had to call on social care outside the family circle at some point or another. This was the case for 11 per cent of the population of Warwick in 1580, for example, 16 per cent of Toledo in 1573 and 25 per cent of Trier in 1623. During an agricultural crisis, such as that in the late eighteenth century, the share of inhabitants seeking aid rose to 30 per cent in Hamburg and 40 per cent in Montpellier.

Did Europe's fragmented system of social care work effectively before 1800? On this point, the Dutch sociologist Abram de Swaan referred to the so-called free-rider problem: How was it possible to pay for poor relief in the towns if only a small share of the population paid, yet any poverty-stricken outsider could in principle migrate to that town? According to him, the poor would gravitate to the places with the best provisions, meaning that the system would no longer be able to cope with the demand for relief during economic crises. Historical research has shown that this was not the case, however. To start with, most poor people appear to have received support from the institutions with which they had special ties (Jews were supported by Jewish organizations, Lutherans by Lutheran organizations, Baptist by Baptists and so forth). The relief organized by urban governments was only for those who fell outside all of the other categories of charity. The shelters were financed with funds from municipal taxes. These funds were also used as subsidies if a particular aid organization did not have sufficient resources from its own private charity. Due to the high degree of municipal autonomy, town governors were able to administer and use the resources in the ways they considered best; it was always possible to adjust the policy. Municipal agencies also provided cheap grain when needed.

TEXT BOX 4.3 PEACE AND RECONCILIATION

One important aspect of the ancient Germanic law that was maintained in Medieval Europe was the so-called reconciliation procedure (*zoenprocedure*). The interests of families and clans were the main focus of this form of justice, which was used to solve protracted disputes or feuds. Feuds could be caused by the theft of goods, violence against a member of the family, rape, or manslaughter and murder. With a reconciliation or 'kiss', the two parties would agree to keep the peace, by means of compensation or reparations for the damage.

From the Late Middle Ages, reconciliation in Europe was increasingly regulated by governments. This role was usually played by the towns, which gained more autonomy and developed their own judicial systems. Several aspects of the earlier procedure continued to exist, however. Most Early Modern towns were home to so-called justices of the peace, who were responsible for acting as intermediaries between disputing parties. In addition, crimes could often be bought off as soon as the two parties had been reconciled.

It should be added that poor relief was not as generous and warm-hearted as is sometimes thought. The welfare provided by various agencies was only intended to supplement insufficient income. The poor often survived through a combination of work, informal aid and formal assistance from municipal agencies. It was precisely because of the constant element of informal help (family, friends, neighbourhood) that people were unable to migrate randomly to any town.

Contemporaries did see the growing pressure on poor relief from the sixteenth century as a major problem, however. In 1531, Charles V issued a law for the Netherlands that forbade begging, and ordered the towns to merge the funds from the various institutions for the poor. England and Wales had regulations against tramping from the Late Middle Ages onwards, but it was not until the poor law enacted by Elizabeth I in 1601 that it was determined that poor relief should be funded by local taxation. In the sixteenth century, leading humanist scholars such as Thomas More, Erasmus and Juan Luis Vives argued for a stricter approach to beggars and the poor. They focused not on the motivation of the givers but on the attitude of the poor and sick themselves. Governments in Protestant countries therefore made an increasingly sharp distinction between the 'deserving' and 'undeserving' poor. The deserving poor had become impoverished through factors over which they had little control, such as war, the death of a spouse or illness. The undeserving poor were feckless and lacking in piety, and did not deserve aid, in their opinion. A solution was sought in forced labour and attempts to tackle loose morals.

From the late seventeenth century, with the stagnating economy and increasing pressure on municipal finances, marginal groups in the Netherlands were also increasingly excluded and segregated. The authorities issued various measures to target the poor and immigrants. The right to settle freely and access to poor relief were limited. Neighbourhood organizations made an increasingly strict distinction between their own residents and aliens, often on the orders of the local government. Religious exclusion also increased. Non-Calvinists received less support, and the number of subsidies from the municipal administration fell. This drove increasing numbers of faithful into the arms of the Calvinist church, which did have enough resources; Catholic poor relief organizations had to appeal more frequently to the 'klopjes', women who devoted their lives to pastoral care and charity. In difficult times, Catholics and members of other denominations outside the public church were thus much more dependent on their own family and friends than members of the Calvinist church.

Despite limitations such as these, the level of social care in the age of the Dutch Republic was unprecedentedly high. Economic historians Jan de Vries and Ad van de Woude estimate that around 3–4 per cent of national income was redistributed in this way to aid the bottom layers of society. On the positive side, it should also be noted that no Dutch region was afflicted by famine from the sixteenth century onwards, whereas such food crises continued to occur in France, for example, until long into the eighteenth century. The Dutch spent the most on poor relief per capita; it was not until the eighteenth century that the Republic would be overtaken by the British in this respect.

DISCIPLINING AND SOCIAL CONTROL Poor relief, disciplining and social control went hand in hand, one example being the aforementioned distinction between the 'deserving' and 'undeserving' poor. 'Disciplining' refers to the growing number of guidelines on how people should behave. 'Social control' describes how people's behaviour was monitored: conduct that was consistent with group norms was rewarded, and deviant behaviour was rejected or corrected. Expulsion and banning are the most radical forms of social control. Social control can be informal in nature, when people's behaviour is monitored from within their own social group. This is also known as social control 'from below'. Social control can also be formal and guided 'from above' by the authorities, such as religious institutions, municipal governments or central states.

Before 1500, most social control was informal and took place between individuals and within groups. People usually tried to solve legal disputes by making agreements between themselves (see Text Box 4.3). Ecclesiastical courts were occupied with matters of faith and marriage. The secular courts in towns mainly focused on property rights and questions of public order. After 1500, however, formal social control expanded across the whole of Europe: (1) by the church, (2) by the church and secular authorities together, or (3) by the secular authorities.

The first form of disciplining arose in Southern Europe, for example, where from the thirteenth century the Catholic Church developed an investigative method ('inquisition') to prosecute people who deviated from the rules of Catholic doctrine. The inquisition was a church court that carried out extensive and lengthy investigations into dissidents, such as the French Cathars, who were persecuted by crusaders as heretics between 1208 and 1250. Jews and marginal groups such as lepers also fell victim to such inquisitions.

After the Revolt, a form of non-governmental disciplining arose in the Northern Netherlands, too. The Calvinist church councils (consistories) that were formed in towns and villages used ecclesiastical discipline to call their members to account if they engaged in undesirable behaviour. As a punishment, they were (temporarily) banned from taking Holy Communion, or their behaviour was made public by the pastor, sometimes mentioning them by name and surname. Urban governments used legislation and the courts to discipline people, but this was separate from the aforementioned social control.

From the late fifteenth century, religious disciplining increasingly came about through cooperation between the ecclesiastical and secular authorities. In addition to the original inquisition, Spain, Portugal and Venice established an inquisition that was manned by priests, but under the control of the state. According to German historians, increasing cooperation between the religious and secular authorities to correct the moral and religious behaviour of the population went hand in hand with the *Konfessionalisierung*: in both Protestant and Catholic regions, governments acquired far-reaching powers to appoint public religious officials, meaning that the disciplining of citizens from above became stricter than before. This trend was weaker in the Netherlands, because local church organizations were responsible for disciplining. The ecclesiastical discipline practised by the Calvinists was the most influential, because it was organized most effectively. Other church communities, such as the Lutherans, adopted the practices of Calvinist discipline. In addition to ecclesiastical discipline, guilds and neighbourhood associations increasingly instructed their members on how to behave, and those who failed to follow the rules were fined.

TEXT BOX 4.4 CHARIVARI, SOCIAL CONTROL FROM BELOW

In Western Europe, norms and values were not only imparted by formal institutions, but there were also folk rituals, such as charivari, which coerced people into conforming to communal norms. This ritual was a way of making individuals' transgressive behaviour known to a community. The French term *charivari* refers to the ear-splitting noise that accompanied the ritual; in German regions, it was called *Katzenmusik*, in the Netherlands *ketelmuziek* and in England 'rough music'. In the North American colonies, the term *chivaree* was used, in imitation of the French.

How the ritual was performed varied by region: it could be a 'serenade' or a procession in which the accused was put on a dung cart, or similar. But it was nearly always a combination of serious reprimand and play. The behaviour that was mocked was almost invariably to do with marriage: an old man who was marrying a young woman, a man who let himself be beaten or dominated by his wife, or a couple who argued loudly. The corrections were intended to mock, but they could be accompanied by physical attacks.

The charivari is sometimes portrayed as a way of establishing male power over women, because the correction focused on forms of behaviour that deviated from existing male-female role patterns. It could be argued, though, that men who abused their patriarchal power were just as likely to be the object of ridicule.

Finally, a third form of disciplining arose, one that was practised by towns and states. The local and central authorities tackled the growing problem of poverty by expanding their legal powers via the extension of legislation and the administration of justice with regard to marginal groups (the poor, beggars, prostitutes and criminals). The inquisition procedure that had been developed by the church was subsequently used by the secular authorities in the secular courts, while the legal power of the churches was limited.

This was also accompanied by the establishment of new institutions. From the late sixteenth century, towns in North-western Europe established prisons, workhouses and houses of correction, based on the labour of those who had been sentenced. These were mostly local initiatives to control the moral behaviour of the population. Workhouses and reformatories were intended for criminals, but the distinction between criminals, the poor, the sick, the unemployed and beggars was blurred. From the sixteenth century, tramping and begging were banned, and licentious or immoral behaviour (drunkenness, adultery, premarital sex or living together) was punished increasingly frequently.

The first workhouses were established in England, such as in London in 1555 and Oxford in 1562. The Netherlands was quick to follow: the first workhouse was founded in Amsterdam in 1596 (Figure 4.3), there were more in Leiden and Leeuwarden two years later, and other towns followed in the early seventeenth century. Prisons were also established in Scandinavia, Germany, France and the Southern Netherlands at that time, usually as urbanization and the problem of poverty grew. In Italy, the first government-funded workhouse would be established only in the second half of the eighteenth century; in that country, social control remained in the hands of the Catholic Church for longer.

In their attempts to strengthen central authority, central governments also enacted legislation to regulate the behaviour of the poor and criminals, such as Charles V's aforementioned act of 1531. Social control by the state continued to be much weaker than municipal control, however. It was not until 1834 that the first centralized system emerged in Great Britain, the New Poor Law, in which local poor relief and workhouses were replaced with state-founded workhouses. In the Netherlands, too, poor relief was not centralized until the late nineteenth century (see Chapter 8). Growing control by the secular authorities did increasingly result in the literal expulsion of criminals from society, however. In Haarlem between 1611 and 1615, one-fifth of those arrested were sentenced to prison, and almost three quarters of them were expelled from the city for a specified period. The colonization of overseas territories gave rise to the possibility of expulsion from the country altogether, although this was rarely used in the Netherlands. In Great Britain, the deportation of convicted criminals to Australia became a common punishment from 1868.

FIGURE 4.3 *Rasp house in Amsterdam in the seventeenth century. This was a reformatory where young male criminals were locked up and had to rasp brazil wood. The powder was subsequently used to make textile dye.*
© *Melchior Fokkens, Beschrijvinge der wijdt-vermaarde Koop-stadt Amstelredam, 1662 (public domain).*

There are different visions of increasing disciplining by the secular authorities. The French philosopher and historian Michel Foucault related the development of the maintenance of law and order in Western Europe to the rise of the nation state. He argued that in the eighteenth century, schools, prisons, hospitals and factors increasingly formed a network of institutions that subjected the population of a society to the discipline of the state, a development that Foucault described as the 'great confinement'. Foucault thus saw increasing disciplining as a mechanism from above.

TEXT BOX 4.5 THE TRANSITION FROM FAMILY ECONOMY TO FAMILY CONSUMER ECONOMY

The long-term development of labour relations within families is often portrayed as a transition from a production unit to a consumption unit. In the pre-industrial period, the members of artisan families worked together in a single unit: the family economy. During industrialization, labour relations changed within families as wage labour began to dominate. In the phase of the nineteenth-century family wage economy, various family members still worked, but they might work outside as well as inside the home. Family relations changed further when, in the twentieth century, families mainly became consumer units, in which the man was the breadwinner and the woman cared for the household and children. Thus, in this modern family, women and children no longer worked for wages, and many of the family's activities took place in the private sphere. This phase is known as the family consumer economy.

There has been some criticism of this phasing. First, family members also worked outside the home for wages in the pre-industrial phase, including in England and the Netherlands, and this was true for women and children as well as men. Second, families also continued to work together after industrialization, for example in factories or peat-cutting. In addition to factory wages, other sources of income included cottage industry and craft. For many families, the ideal of one breadwinner per family (see Chapter 9) was unattainable for many years, because wages were too low. This meant that in most working-class families, many different family members worked to cover the cost of living. Finally, we can ask whether families did in fact play a key role as consumers much earlier than this. After all, they were important consumers of cheap textiles and other products from the seventeenth century onwards (see the industrious revolution, Chapter 2). The transition from the family economy to the consumer economy was thus less clear-cut than has been suggested.

The German sociologist Norbert Elias saw increasing disciplining partly as disciplining from above and partly from below. He drew a distinction between discipline imposed by the state, *Fremdzwang*, and that imposed by the people themselves, *Selbstzwang*. Growing state power in Europe led to the regulation of violence and a government monopoly on violence (see Chapter 3). An increasingly clear distinction was made between regulated violence, mainly to be used by the authorities and elites (only noblemen were allowed to carry swords, for example), and uncontrolled violence by citizens, which had to be suppressed. Rural elites appropriated certain rituals of violence, such as the duel between men for personal honour. Although duels were bloody and could have fatal results, this form of violence was managed and practised in accordance with strict rules. Violence was by no means unrestrained before the fifteenth century, but due to increasing disciplining, levels of violence fell in Western European societies during the pre-industrial era. The effect was particularly visible in the towns, where the authorities increasingly administered justice and disciplined the population. The level of violence fell less sharply in the countryside; until long into the nineteenth century, for example, conflicts in villages were often settled with ritual knife fights, and informal forms of control continued to exist there, too (see Text Box 4.4).

In addition to the pressure from above, Elias also identified a tendency to adapt from below. He argued that greater mutual dependency due to commercialization and labour specialization led people to control their behaviour and emotions to a greater degree. Growing social diversity blurred the behavioural norms of the different estates and classes. To maintain their position effectively in public contexts, people imposed self-discipline with regard to violence, sexuality and patterns of eating and drinking. According to Elias, at first it was mainly the noble elites at the French court who increasingly controlled their behaviour and emotions in this way, but the urban elites, middle classes and lower social classes later developed forms of self-control, too. The transfer of models of control took place via books of manners, such as Erasmus's etiquette book, which was published in 1530.

In recent years, historians have put much more emphasis on social control by local civic and ecclesiastical institutions. These models are largely based on Western European developments, however, and are not universally applicable. In China, for example, there was no comparable power struggle between the church and the state. The Ming and Qing dynasties propagated the Confucian conception of social order, with its emphasis on correct behaviour, justice and honesty. Ideally, every layer of the population, from the emperor to the peasants, had to conform. According to the teachings of Confucius, one had to control one's own behaviour before controlling others. Thus, there was self-discipline in China, too. Social control remained unrelentingly strong in the village communities.

During the Qing dynasty, 'charitable schools' were founded, which were intended to civilize the population in border areas and peripheral regions.

Like the granaries, both local elites and state officials took the initiative to found these schools. According to Confucian ideology, the two forms of charity complemented one another: together, the promotion of education and economic prosperity would form the basis for social harmony. An important distinction, however, lay in the target group. The granaries were intended for the whole population, whereas the schools focused on teaching Confucian morality and principles to marginal groups. In the eighteenth century, Chen Hongmou, a famous Chinese state official, founded 650 schools in the border region of Yunnan and delegated their leadership to the local elite.

4.3
A changing world view and the growth of the private sphere

Unlike in China, where familial and communal ties remained unrelentingly strong until the twentieth century, in Europe the division between the community and the individual grew over time. This was accompanied by the development of a different world view. As we have seen, there arose new visions of the social, political and moral order, which gave more space to individual reflection and personal preferences. Increasing weight was given to reason, too, in addition to or instead of belief and magical practices. A division arose between the private and public spheres, while personal identity (national, European or Christian) was demarcated more sharply as a result of knowledge of other indigenous peoples. These changes were linked, in part, to the accelerated phase of globalization that took place from the end of the fifteenth century, when Europeans increasingly came into contact with societies and cultures in other parts of the world.

BELIEF AND MAGIC The world view of the Middle Ages and Early Modern era was determined, to a great extent, by the doctrine and rituals of the church. The Catholic Church played a major role in the norms and practices that surrounded belief, inheritance law, marriage, sexuality, death and economic activity. The structure of the (Christian) ecclesiastical year regulated the rhythm of daily life, starting with the Sunday rest. Almost all festivities and holidays were linked to religious events, such as Lent, Easter, Christmas and saints' days.

Anthropologists and historians describe the religious views that are formalized by official institutions as the 'Great Tradition'; they are 'great' because they enjoy significant prestige. In addition to the formal calendar that was maintained by the ecclesiastical authorities, there was also a 'Little Tradition': informal belief in magic and sorcery, which were intended to ward off the hard reality of daily life, with its deaths, epidemics, failed harvests and natural disasters. The French historian Robert Muchembled characterized the magical world view in pre-industrial Europe as an 'animistic' view of the universe: not only were people thought to have souls or spirits, but also animals, plants and natural phenomena such as thunder, floods and epidemics. One important element of these magical representations was the belief in witches and sorcerers, who could cause disasters, bewitch people or animals to make them sick or infirm, and concoct potions or herbal salves to fight physical and mental illness.

The official doctrine of the Catholic Church was opposed to these magical practices. In the seventeenth century, Flemish priests complained that their parishioners would avoid them if they saw them in the morning, because of the superstitious belief that it was a bad omen if the first person you encountered in the morning was a priest. The church authorities also objected to the mixing of Christian belief with magic; for example, if the faithful used saints, the Eucharist or relics as magical remedies for sickness or failed harvests. In the view of the clergy, magical acts such as these were superstitions that fell outside the Christian faith. Protestants wanted to establish a faith that was as 'pure' as possible, one that focused on the relationship between God and man, not church rituals, whereby they also opposed the Catholic cult with its veneration of saints and relics.

From the sixteenth century, there was a gradual transition from a magical world view to a more rational one, whereby prophecies and magical rituals became less important, and increasing weight was given to reason and experimentation. The 'Great Tradition' of the major religions continued to exist for the time being. In Western countries, secularization would only really gather momentum at the end of the nineteenth century (see Chapter 9). The growing realization that people themselves could influence (some) situations did not immediately mean that people stopped believing in God. From the sixteenth century, however, a new world view did emerge that reduced the significance of magic and superstition. The English historian Keith Thomas has characterized this transformation as the 'decline of magic'.

The turning point in these mental changes was the persecution of witchcraft, which reached its zenith in Europe between 1450 and 1700. In this 250-year period, witch trials resulted in more than 100,000 convictions, 60,000 of which ended in execution. The belief in witches combined magical views with the official ecclesiastical position that witches were allies of the devil.

Historians have identified various causes of the witch persecutions. The rise of market-oriented labour and the growth of the proletariat led to increasing economic uncertainty for a growing number of people. In Central Europe, the witch persecutions tended to follow bad weather events such as hail, snowstorms or floods, which destroyed the harvest and threatened the well-being of the community. The transition from a collective village community with strong mutual ties, where people could rely on traditional forms of assistance, towards market-oriented communities where the ties were more business-like and more focused on individual interests, left many out in the cold. The sixteenth-century Reformation brought greater insecurity about the interpretation of belief and a stricter response to expressions of faith that were thought to threaten Christian doctrine, such as witchcraft. This economic, social and religious uncertainty is thought to have been expressed in the persecution of the most marginal groups in society: poor, mainly old women who lacked a regular income.

The causes of the witch persecutions should probably be sought in a combination of factors, as there were significant variations in the nature and intensity of the witch trials within Western Europe. In some regions, there were only trials against sorcery, whereas in other regions a real witch hunt emerged. The worst persecutions occurred in South-western Germany, where 3,229 so-called witches were put to death between 1561 and 1670. In Spain, Italy and Russia, there were far fewer executions. In England, the courts were mainly concerned with sorcery, not witchcraft. In the Netherlands, the scale of the witch persecutions remained relatively small. There were only three witch trials in Amsterdam, for example, and real persecutions only took place for a short period in Gelderland, Utrecht and Groningen.

In recent years, historians have shown that the witch trials were not so much the consequence of a changing world view, but that they actually contributed, in the longer term, to the rise of a more rational world view in which magic was pushed to the margins. Extreme witch persecutions are thought to have promoted a sceptical attitude to the belief in witches and the influence of the devil on human actions. Some of the elite lost faith in the fairness of the trials, with the result that other manners were devised to solve the problems surrounding magic and the devil: better procedures, rational argumentation that steered clear of extremes, and the introduction of a medical approach. In 1563, Johann de Weyer – a physician to the Duke of Cleves – argued that it would be wiser to give an old woman who was suspected of being in league with the devil better religious instruction or medical treatment, than to punish her.

In 1691, the Dutch pastor Balthasar Bekker went a step further, arguing in his *Betoverde Weereld* ('Bewitched world') that it was impossible for the devil to make people act in physical ways. This was because God had banished the devil and his demons to hell, meaning that biblical references to magic and witches were the work of impostors, frauds and illusionists. Bekker also thought that the cruelty and irrationality of the witch trials should be brought to an end. His book became an international bestseller and was translated into English, French and German, but it also provoked a fierce response from the Calvinist church, which banned the book for its denial of the existence of magic and witchcraft. Bekker was duly dismissed from his position as a pastor and banned from Holy Communion.

In the eighteenth century, the occasional witch trial occurred sporadically in Western Europe. The end of the witch persecutions marked the advent of a new, more rational world view, one that no longer gave credence to magical powers, sorcery and witch hunts. In the Netherlands, this changing world view was evident in the way that judges sentenced fortune-tellers, exorcists and magical healers: from the second half of the seventeenth century, such people were increasingly prosecuted as swindlers and charlatans, and no longer as sorcerers or soothsayers with special powers.

The scale of the European witch trials and the extreme treatment of those who were convicted were exceptional. In China, there were differences between official doctrine and popular belief, and the state undertook large campaigns against Buddhist monasteries and monks on more than one occasion, but there were no phenomena comparable to the large-scale witchcraft persecutions. The main religious traditions in China were Confucianism, Taoism and Buddhism, each with a corpus of classical writings, a group of masters who carried out rituals, and various cult and knowledge centres. Different movements or 'schools' developed within these Great Traditions. There were also popular beliefs, such as belief in local gods, the excommunication of angry spirits, burial rituals and the ancestor cult. The dividing line between the Great and Little Traditions was less stark than in Europe. Representatives of the Great Tradition sometimes acted as ritual masters in folk rituals. From the Tang dynasty (618–907) onwards, Confucianism was closely related to the governing elite, and knowledge of the Confucian classics was thus an important criterion for the exams held to select state officials. The state also permitted other religious traditions to some degree, including support for some Christians in the seventeenth century. Unlike Europe, China did not have an ecclesiastical hierarchy. The authority of the emperor, who had a 'mandate from heaven', superseded that of any ritual master.

RATIONALIZATION Between 1500 and 1700, in the period when the magical world view slowly receded, a Scientific Revolution took place in Western Europe. Through contact with the Arab and Byzantine world, where classical texts and commentaries on these texts were regularly published, Europe rediscovered works from Antiquity, such as the writings of Aristotle. This re-evaluation stimulated the acquisition of knowledge based on reason. One important step in rationalization concerned the development of mathematics, astronomy and physics, and the accumulation of knowledge to challenge the Christian conviction that the Earth, as God's creation, was the centre of the universe. In 1543, astronomical and medical works by the Polish astronomer Nicolaus Copernicus and the Flemish doctor and anatomist Andreas Vesalius were published, which no longer presented the Earth as the centre of the universe, and nature and the human body were represented in a realistic way.

This revolution in thinking developed further with new insights into the working of natural forces. The Italian natural philosopher and mathematician Galileo Galilei (1564–1642), provoked a revolution in astronomy when, based on regular observations with a telescope, he discovered that the universe was not as static as Aristotle had assumed. In the late seventeenth and early eighteenth centuries, the physics research by the Englishman Isaac Newton (1642–1727) and the Dutchman Christiaan Huygens (1629–95) produced insights on gravity and the development of theory on the nature of light. The establishment of learned societies, such as the Royal Society in London in 1660 and the Académie Royale des Sciences in Paris in 1666, promoted a scientific climate in which reason and experimentation formed the basis of knowledge. Critical, philological research on ancient texts by humanist scholars, such as Joseph Scaliger (1540–1609), gave rise to doubts about the dating of the age of the Earth, which had been derived from the Bible. In time, such criticism would also undermine the authority of the Bible itself.

With the growing infrastructure of knowledge and communication, the dissemination of information and new research methods increased significantly. In addition to universities and scientific societies, botanical gardens, anatomical theatres and observatories were founded. The Republic played a pioneering role in this process in many respects. For many years, Leiden University (founded in 1575), with its botanical garden, observatory and anatomical theatre, was one of Europe's leading centres of knowledge. The need for new knowledge and information was also expressed – mainly among the elites – in the collection of all kinds of objects and exotic artefacts (art, shells, animals and plants), which were exhibited in museums or cabinets of curiosity.

The growing trade links between different parts of the world after 1500 advanced not only the exploration of the world in an economic sense but also the discovery of new cultures, which made the Europeans conscious of their own identity and their place in the world. Increased contact with previously unknown regions and societies resulted in the rapid circulation of a new genre of books: 'discovery books' about America, Africa and Asia, such as the travel journal by the Italian Amerigo Vespucci, which was published in 1503–4, and that subsequently appeared in six languages and sixty editions. This described Indians from South America as 'naked savages' who lived in primitive conditions, were unable to read and write, worshipped idols and, in contrast to the Christian Europeans, had no sense of morality in relation to nakedness or sexuality. Such writings promoted a sense of cultural superiority in Europe. Although some scholars, such as the Spanish jurist Francisco de Vitoria, who taught at the University of Paris around 1510, questioned the justification of the slave trade, the growing economic and political supremacy of Europe led to an undervaluation of indigenous civilizations in Africa and America. The notion of an indigenous person as a fellow citizen was beyond the intellectual horizon of the average

European, who often persecuted Jews, Muslims, Protestants or Catholics in their own region. Thinking that Christian culture was superior, most white Europeans until the eighteenth century had no objection to the large-scale Atlantic slave trade and enslavement of African people (see Chapter 2 and Text Box 2.3). Only recently have historians begun to explore the presence of free and enslaved African migrants within Western European cities. The Dutch historian Mark Ponte has shown that there was a Black Afro-Atlantic community in Amsterdam in the mid-seventeenth century. This community consisted of sailors employed by the East India Company and the West India Company, and women who were presumably former enslaved servants. This feeling of superiority to foreigners was not exclusive to Europe. Under the Qing dynasty, the Chinese emperor was known as the 'lord over everything under the heavens'; non-Chinese peoples were seen as uncivilized groups, only some of whom were amenable to Sinification. Between 1680 and 1850, at least twelve million people were sent from various parts of China to colonize frontier areas and to civilize the people living there.

When it came to the development of new ideas, the culture of free speech in the Netherlands (see Chapter 3) provided a fertile seedbed for politics, science and philosophy. In recent decades, historians have increasingly shown how the Republic played a leading role in the emergence of the Enlightenment. Namely, in addition to the moderate Enlightenment, which was supported by an enlightened monarch and focused on rationalization and reform, the improvement of education, the encouragement of tolerance and combatting of superstition, there was also a Radical Enlightenment, which was dominated by liberal views on faith, freedom and democracy. As censorship in most countries did not allow the printing and publishing of more radical ideas, the Republic functioned as a linchpin in the development of the Radical Enlightenment. The most famous philosopher of the Radical Enlightenment was a Dutch Jew, Baruch Spinoza (1632–77). The Radical Enlightenment stimulated criticism of the existing moral and political order, culminating in a growing emphasis on the responsibility of the individual and the rights of man. In the late eighteenth century, these ideas were disseminated on a large scale by the wave of revolutions that swept the Atlantic world (see Chapter 3).

One important condition for the growth and dissemination of knowledge in Europe in the Early Modern period was the development of printing. Printing technology in the form of block printing already existed, namely in China and Korea, but it was labour-intensive and expensive, and therefore did not lead to strong growth in book production. Technology based on individual lead letters had much more potential. Despite this, technology in itself was not the only factor; also of major importance was the fact that the level of manuscript production was already very high in Europe, as can be seen from Table 4.5. This shows that there was enormous demand for books, mainly for cheap pamphlets that could be afforded by the lower

TABLE 4.5 *Estimated Production of Manuscripts and Printed Books in Europe, 1000–1800 (in Thousands)*

	Manuscripts	**Printed books**
1001–1100	212	
1101–1200	768	
1201–1300	1,762	
1301–1400	2,747	
1401–1500	4,999	
1454–1500		12,589
1501–50		79,017
1551–1600		138,427
1601–50		200,906
1651–1700		331,035
1701–50		355,073
1751–1800		628,801

Source: Van Zanden, *The Long Road*, 77; Van Zanden and Buringh, 'Charting the Rise of the West', 43.

classes. This demand spurred technological innovations. The Bible that was printed by Johann Gutenberg in Mainz in 1454–5 heralded a revolution: it was the first large book to be printed at an affordable price. After 1500, book production accelerated when new printing methods led to a sharp fall in prices. Book printers tended to establish themselves in urban areas; by the 1660s alone, the Dutch Republic had no fewer than 671 book printers and booksellers. More books were published per capita in the Republic in the second half of the eighteenth century than anywhere else: 488 per year per thousand residents, compared to an average of 122 per year across the whole of Europe.

At first, it was mainly the sons of the urban and noble elites who were able to profit from the new knowledge that was brought, via books and teaching, to Latin schools and universities in Italy, France, England and the Netherlands. Moreover, from the sixteenth century, the tradition of the 'Grand Tour' developed: an educational journey across Europe (with Italy as the high point), taken by young men from the aristocracy and the urban upper middle classes, who acquired knowledge of art and culture, politics, economics and the rule of law in different parts of Europe. In the seventeenth and eighteenth centuries, the tradition spread to England, France, the Netherlands, Germany, Denmark and Poland.

It would not be long before the new knowledge trickled down to the other social classes, however. The provision of educational facilities expanded and literacy rates increased. The ability to read and write was disseminated most widely in urbanized trade regions in Western Europe, such as Italy, Flanders, Holland and Southern England. By the sixteenth century, Italian towns were already providing free Sunday education for large numbers of children: in Milan, 12,000 children received schooling in this way; in Venice, 6,000 children. In the seventeenth century, literacy rates in Scotland and Scandinavia also rose rapidly; in 1616, an act in Scandinavia determined that every parish should have a school. The percentage of the adult population in Western Europe that was able to read and write was recently estimated to be 25 per cent in the seventeenth century and 31 per cent in the eighteenth century. In Holland, the level of literacy was relatively high: around 1700, three quarters of men and half of women in Amsterdam were able to read and write. In the eighteenth century, literacy rates rose rapidly, leading to what has been called the 'reading revolution' (see Table 4.5). As a result, increasing numbers of people, both men and women, began to read books. A new genre emerged: the novel. In the Netherlands, however, the reading revolution happened less through novels as such, as it did in England, and more through the incredibly large number of newspapers and other kinds of periodicals.

Fewer data are available for China, but here too, literacy rates undoubtedly increased long before the nineteenth century, and the reading culture spread. Under the Song dynasty (960–1279), there was an expansion of educational facilities and the production of written material. From the sixteenth century, education expanded, partly due to the development of the state examination system and the rise of commercial book production. Just as in Europe, there was an increase in scientific research in China, which mainly focused on astronomy, alchemy and medicine. In contrast to Europe, however, the Chinese acquisition of knowledge was not focused on debate and searching for natural laws (which called classical knowledge into question), but on consensus and the documentation of knowledge and information. In China, classical knowledge such as literature, philosophy and history continued to be the most highly regarded form of knowledge-gathering and knowledge transfer. European book production was also much more varied: according to a recent estimate, in the seventeenth century 3,750 new titles were published each year on the European market, compared to just 47 new titles per year in China.

INCREASING PRIVACY AND THE 'CONSUMER REVOLUTION' As explained earlier, until the Late Middle Ages the magical world view was shared by all layers of the European population. In the countryside, the community was closely involved in all kinds of personal matters relating to birth, marriage, work, sickness and death, and public spaces (churches, streets and squares) were shared by nobles, the clergy, the rich and the poor alike. The Early Modern period, however, saw the spread of a more individualistic and rational attitude to life. This led, particularly among the elites, to a need to distinguish oneself from popular culture.

The cultural historian Peter Burke described the 'Little Tradition' as the culture maintained by broad swathes of the population, whereas the 'Great Tradition' was the culture of a limited group: sovereigns, rulers, scholars and lawyers. The latter was great not in a quantitative sense, but in a qualitative sense, because it was more prestigious and official. The lower classes had hardly any access to this culture, whereas the Little Tradition could be accessed by almost everyone. The closed nature of the Great Tradition and the openness of the Little Tradition should be understood literally: the former took place in palaces, universities, patrician houses and courthouses, while the second was expressed in streets, fields, inns and barns. There was yet another distinction: the Little Tradition had a local character (in the village or the neighbourhood), whereas the Great Tradition was national or even European.

The growing gulf between public popular culture and official elite culture reflected an increasing need to manage and control one's own behaviour and that of others. Elias termed this change the 'civilizing process' that accompanied increasing *Fremdzwang* and *Selbstzwang* (see earlier). Municipal governments, church authorities and state elites stepped up control of behaviour that had previously been acceptable to both the elite and the people. There was increasing regulation of festivities, games, common drinking parties, funerals, guild processions, militias and all kinds of folk rituals. The growing awareness of time – due to the introduction of mechanical clocks from the fourteenth century, and the introduction of more regular working hours in industry from the eighteenth century – led to a stricter daily schedule, which was increasingly imposed on wage labourers, public officials and schoolchildren.

As distinct from popular culture, regents, landowners and monarchs developed more refined eating customs that initially remained unfamiliar to ordinary people. The dissemination of printing and the growing contact between European elites promoted the introduction of new manners from Italy, such as dancing, the manner of speaking, body language and posture. Etiquette books were reprinted multiple times in subsequent centuries, and were followed by new guides with even more prescriptive rules of conduct. In the highest circles, it was taboo to belch, sneeze or spit at table, while most food had to be eaten with cutlery. Some of the more elitist manners gradually trickled down to the lower classes. In order to teach his agricultural workers some table manners, for example, in 1608 the English landlord Thomas Coryate demonstrated the use of the fork at table.

FIGURE 4.4 *Caricature of wig fashions in England in the late eighteenth century: Miss Prattle consults Dr Double Fee about her impressive wig.*
© *Wellcome Library London, anonymous mezzotint (public domain).*

The withdrawal of the elite was accompanied by a growing need for privacy in general. Actions that people had been used to carrying out in public prior to 1500 were increasingly carried out in private. The tendency for individuals to shield themselves from public life was also expressed in the organization of the home, where separate rooms emerged for specific activities, such as the kitchen, dining room, reception room and separate rooms for sleeping and working. Soap, perfume and powder were used to combat bodily odours such as sweat, and disguise rotten teeth. In France and England, the use of powders in the eighteenth century became a true craze among upper-class men and women.

One visible expression of greater privacy was the development of forms of punishment. Until the mid-sixteenth century, it was common for criminals across Europe to be displayed, flogged, mutilated or executed in public. After this time, however, visible mutilation, such as putting-out eyes, chopping off hands or cutting off ears, became far less common, while branding was henceforth done on less visible parts of the body. In the final quarter of the eighteenth century, there was growing resistance to public executions and the display of the bodies of the executed.

The turn towards more individualization was also expressed in the way in which elites had themselves portrayed, and the increasing need to record personal experiences in diaries, biographies and travel journals. From the sixteenth century, these traditions became widespread in Italy, Germany and the Netherlands; painters such as Albrecht Dürer and Maarten van Heemskerck, for example, painted self-portraits, thereby emphasizing the importance of the individual.

Other characteristics of individualization included the enormous growth in and increasing diversity of consumer goods. As well as furnishing homes, much attention was paid to gardens, vehicles and clothing. Fashions in clothing and hairstyles increasingly became an expression of individual choice, especially in towns, allowing one to show that one was moving with the times. There was increasing interest in and circulation of wigs, colours, fabrics, dresses and trousers in the eighteenth century, and people's collars, sleeves and undergarments became more and more detailed. The development of consumption in Europe between *c.* 1650 and 1850 has been described by historians as the 'consumer revolution'. This revolution had the following characteristics: (1) a greater diversity and larger volume of consumption, (2) growth in the trade in consumer goods and (3) an increase in the number of shops in which these goods were sold and increasing specialization in retail trade. The rise of new consumer goods is illustrated by research on Dutch inventories; before 1700, for example, such inventories did not feature any tea or coffee sets; after 1750, however, drinking tea and coffee had evidently become a general custom. In the seventeenth and eighteenth centuries, the European diet was enriched by the introduction of spices, sugar and coffee from Asia and of chocolate, tomatoes and potatoes from South America. In *c.* 1800, English labourers also spent part of their wages on products such as sugar, spices and soap, which they had not or had hardly used a century beforehand.

After *c.* 1750, as well as tea and coffee sets, the average Dutch household also included sugar pots and drinking-chocolate dishes. The daily diet still consisted mainly of bread, supplemented with small quantities of meat, cheese and beer, but the taste was enhanced with sugar, pepper, salt and spices. One unique feature of the Dutch context was the widespread possession of paintings by various painters in all kinds of price classes, so that the ordinary man or woman in the town or the countryside often had a little painting on the wall, too. The great demand for paintings stimulated the development of a large group of master painters. In addition, after the mid-eighteenth century, most households also possessed various European and Asian fabrics and sheets, pottery and porcelain. The large-scale consumption of new goods stimulated the growth of shops. In the course of the eighteenth century, for example, 5–10 per cent of new members of the shopkeepers' guild in Antwerp were purveyors of tea and coffee. With products such as sugar, tea, coffee and cotton, globalization also reached the lower classes of the European population.

Summary

Finally, let us briefly summarize the answers to the questions that we posed at the outset:

1. In China and Western Europe, there were various preventive checks to population growth in the pre-industrial period. In Europe, people married late and a relatively large share of the population remained unmarried; in China, marital fertility was lower, and infanticide was practised. The differences in life expectancy between Western Europe and East Asia were small. One important difference lay in the marriage and inheritance laws, which became more individualistic under the influence of the Catholic Church. In China, meanwhile, the community and the patriarch continued to play a dominant role.

2. In Western Europe, the individualization of labour and family relations led to the growth of the proletariat and the rise of a civic community in towns. Familial and state protection against the risks of existence remained intact in China, while Europe saw the rise of urban and ecclesiastical agencies that provided a safety net. From around the sixteenth century, there was also a rise in the disciplining of marginal groups by European towns and states. Social care in the Netherlands continued to be highly decentralized, due to the high degree of urban autonomy and the corporative culture; the level of care was notably high compared to other European countries.

3. In Europe, belief and magical practices increasingly made way for reason and experimentation, supported by scientific networks, rising literacy rates and printing technology. The Netherlands occupied a unique place in this whole; the culture of free speech facilitated the rise of the Radical Enlightenment. Within Europe, there was an increasing sense among the elite that they were more civilized than the common people, a tendency that was accompanied by a growing desire for privacy. Increasing privacy and individualization contributed to a consumer culture that put increasing emphasis on personal preferences and a diversity of consumer goods.

5

Conclusion to Part I

In the preceding chapters, we saw how people sought solutions to the basic problems of income, power and risks in different parts of the world between 1000 and 1800. In this conclusion to Part I, we discuss when the Great Divergence and the Little Divergence began to emerge. We also analyse the interaction between the three basic problems with reference to Figure 0.2 on page 4, and we consider the extent to which Netherlands was a 'plaything' or a 'key player' in these developments.

Viewed as a whole, income per capita in East Asia and Western Europe remained roughly equal until 1800. However, the most developed parts of Western Europe (Southern England and the Netherlands) did achieve a higher level of income in the Early Modern period than the most developed region in China (the Yangzi Delta). Economically, then, we can already spot the origins of a divergence between the two outermost tips of Eurasia before 1800. An acceleration set in from the late eighteenth century onwards, with England, the pioneer of the Industrial Revolution, setting the pace. In addition to the increasing divergence in Eurasia, there were also increasing differences *within* Europe: a Little Divergence also occurred in the Early Modern period. In terms of income, wage labourers in North-western Europe were better off than wage labourers elsewhere in Europe, and agricultural productivity was greater. Remarkably, a kind of Little Divergence occurred in a political sense, too, as this region also had a relatively free public sphere in the eighteenth century.

When it came to power, it is striking that the empire continued to be the standard political unit between 1000 and 1800. However, in Europe numerous smaller types of states emerged: kingdoms, city-states and nation states. In this respect, there was already a significant divergence in the centuries before 1800. Europe was much more politically fragmented, and the centralization of the state apparatus happened slowly. Before the nineteenth century, no single Europe state managed to develop a governing apparatus that operated as rationally or was organized as uniformly as in China. Fiscal and military innovations did advance more quickly in Europe,

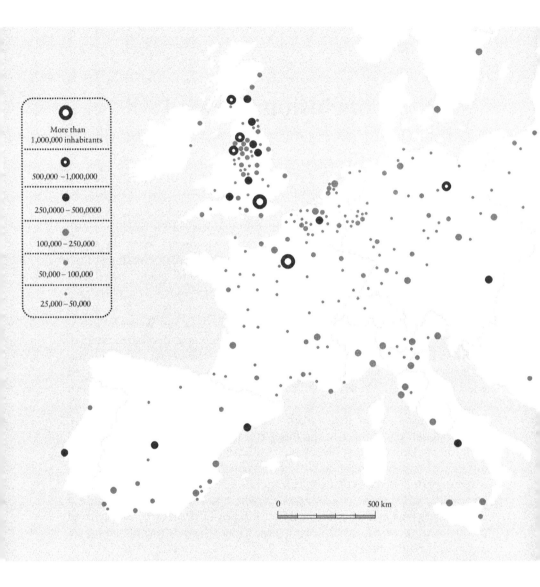

MAP 5.1 *The most important towns in Europe, early nineteenth century. Note the clear cluster of towns in North-western Europe: the Little Divergence was accompanied by rapid urbanization. If we compare this to Map 3.1 showing European towns in the sixteenth century, we see that the urbanized heart still lay in the Mediterranean region at that time.*
Source: Pounds, *A historical geography of Europe*, 325. Designed by René van der Vooren.

however. Another typical feature of Europe was that even in the larger state structures, towns and regions enjoyed a considerable degree of autonomy for many years, which allowed all kinds of groups in society, from aristocrats and the clergy to merchants and craftsmen, to entrench themselves behind impressive bulwarks of historically developed rights and privileges.

A Little Divergence took place within Europe: from the seventeenth century, a number of North-western European states broke new ground in war financing and the manner in which freedom of speech was facilitated. Remarkably enough, the timing of the political Little Divergence – in the seventeenth century – coincided with the economic one. As we can see from Map 5.1, these developments were accompanied by strong urbanization in North-western Europe.

The differences in state formation were reflected in the different ways in which societies dealt with the risks of existence. While in China the risk of failed harvests was absorbed by a state-supervised system of granaries, for example, in Europe it was mainly local governments, ecclesiastical institutions and civic organizations that were responsible for social provision. Nor did China experience a process of individualization that gradually eroded the role of the community. In Europe from the Reformation onwards, there was a Little Divergence in the sense that the secular government shouldered more responsibility for social care in Protestant regions than governments in regions that remained Catholic. From the Late Middle Ages, there was a growing difference between China and Europe in the way in which cultural elites interpreted order in the world and the place of humans within it. Unlike in China, Europe was increasingly dominated by the notion that the world worked on the basis of certain 'laws' that could be discovered through reason and experimentation, and that in this universe, man functioned as a self-contained, independent unit. People's mental constructions therefore increasingly diverged.

If we consider the interactions between the three problem fields and mental constructions, we see that the various developments in relation to income, power and risks clearly reinforced one another. Let us focus on several key points in the Dutch context. The relatively liberal views on marriage promoted the labour participation of both men and women, which stimulated economic growth. The extensive system of poor relief in the seventeenth century furthered the relatively high standard of living and indirectly boosted demand for consumer goods, which also had a beneficial economic effect. Disciplining by the ecclesiastical authorities promoted the enforcement of order, which coincided remarkably with the disciplining of the army. This resulted in a relatively peaceful and orderly situation in the Republic, ensuring that existing property relations remained intact and that transaction costs could remain low. The army maintained the territory's independence, which also allowed merchants to build up a strong basis for independent international trade relations, including the colonial campaigns. Municipal autonomy, which was maintained for a remarkably long period compared to almost all other countries in Europe, promoted the development of the guilds and facilitated tolerant policies, which attracted merchants to urban centres.

To what extent was the Netherlands a 'plaything' or a 'key player' in this pre-industrial world? Considering the long term, we can conclude that there was a shift in the Dutch position between these two extremes, but not in all respects simultaneously or to the same extent. In an economic and political sense, from the sixteenth century, the regions that would later form the Netherlands were highly dependent on external forces, such as the dynamics of the towns of Flanders and Brabant or the expansion of Burgundian and Hapsburg power. Despite being a second-rate player in this period, we can already make out the impulses at this time that would allow the Netherlands to forge its own path after the sixteenth century.

For example, the Netherlands managed to wrest itself from the purely Malthusian model at an early stage. Dutch farmers were not fixated on achieving self-sufficiency. When the land in large parts of the Western Netherlands became unsuitable for farming, country-dwellers turned their focus to dairy production or non-agrarian activities such as fishing or shipping. There was a marked rise in migration to the towns. Food imports, commercialization and urbanization thus reached high levels in the Netherlands at a relatively early stage. This development was also facilitated by the country's unique institutional environment and prevailing property relations. The institutions that existed throughout Medieval Europe, such as serfdom, the court system and banal domains, were also present in the Netherlands, but they became much less influential in the west of the country when the great reclamation of the peatlands began. Unhindered by feudal lords or domineering towns, farmers were largely free to go their own way. In a sociocultural respect, the transformation was evident, among other things, from the relatively independent position of women and the high level of education of the population. A relatively large amount was already invested in education and training in the Low Countries in the Late Middle Ages.

From the late sixteenth century, it was mainly in the economic, political and cultural arena that the Netherlands would grow into a 'key player' in Europe; a position that it would continue to hold, in many respects, long into the eighteenth century. The Republic played a leading role in agricultural productivity, industrial production, trade and shipping within and beyond Europe, technological innovations, capital provision, as a beacon for migrants, and in developing all kinds of effective organizational forms and institutions.

Politically, the Dutch Republic would prove to be a unique entity that deviated from the norm. Its decentralized structure hardly served as an ideal for state formation. From the late seventeenth century, though, the way in which the Republic financed warfare would provide a model for the financial-military system that played a crucial role in England's emergence as a global power, and thereby contributed to the Great Divergence. Moreover, the Netherlands played a prominent role in the development of an anti-hegemonic strategy in the emerging state system, first through its role in the realization of the Treaty of Westphalia, and later through its contribution to the coalition policy to maintain the balance of power in Europe. Both militarily and politically, the Republic exercised considerable weight in Europe for many years. The expansion of power overseas added an extra dimension to this.

The Netherlands was also distinguished by the emergence of a public sphere at a relatively early stage. There was already a remarkably robust culture of debate in the Netherlands in the second half of the seventeenth century, thanks in part to the decentralized state structure, the high level of education and the many religious refugees. This facilitated the development of rather radical ideas that, in the course of time, would have a massive impact in other European countries and the United States. The Netherlands was thereby at the forefront of the great transformation in world view that would distinguish Europe from the rest of the world.

For the Dutch, the period when the Great Divergence took place – roughly between 1750 and 1850 – was also a period when the old ways of doing things, which had played a decisive role for centuries, became increasingly inaccessible or even impossible, while new paths opened up. In economic terms, this was most evident in the shift of the world's financial centre from Amsterdam to London around 1780. Amsterdam's staple market was dealt a final blow during the Napoleonic period; although the Dutch would remain the richest people in the world (per capita) for a while, they would be overtaken by the British in *c.* 1820. In political terms, the urban oligarchy lost power, and traditional care arrangements made way for centralist institutions. The era of municipal citizens' privileges came to an end, to be replaced by a new age with a new conception of 'citizenship' that has applied to all residents of the Netherlands ever since. Until the end of the eighteenth century, the Netherlands was a key player in many respects. This was followed by a new century in which the Netherlands was largely a follower of trends.

PART II

After the Great Divergence, *c.* 1800–present day

6

Introduction to Part II

From the time of the Great Divergence, the pace of economic and demographic change accelerated. As not every country was able to keep up with the frontrunners, the differences between countries grew sharply, too. Before we consider the developments between *c.* 1800 and the present day in more detail, in this introduction, we again begin by sketching out the main contours. How large was the world's population in the nineteenth and twentieth centuries? What changes occurred in the natural surroundings in which they lived? To what extent and how were the different parts of the world connected to one another? How can we describe the major changes that occurred in relation to income, power and the risks of existence? These questions are addressed in the following sections.

6.1
Population development and the natural environment

On the whole, the data on population development in the nineteenth and twentieth centuries are more precise than those for the preceding period. That is because 1800 marks the birth of the 'statistical age' in many countries, which started to gather quantitative data systematically on all kinds of topics. Although the figures for the global population are still not entirely accurate, the overview in Table 6.1 probably comes close to the actual situation. While the world's population as a whole grew from around 950 million in 1800, via 1.6 billion in 1900, to 6 billion in the year 2000, there was also a shift in the balance between the regions. Europe's share of the global population increased from less than 20 per cent in 1800 to around a quarter in 1900, but would fall back to around 13 per cent a century later. In the twentieth century, the share of Asia, Africa and America would grow considerably.

Russia and Germany were by far the most populous countries in Europe after 1800. Great Britain, France and Italy remained some distance behind,

TABLE 6.1 *Population Trends in Europe and Different Parts of the World, in millions, 1700–2000*

	Europe (excl. Russia)	**Africa**	**India Pakistan Bangladesh**	**China**	**America**	**Oceania**
1700	102	107	175	150	12	3
1800	154	102	180	330	24	2
1900	295	138	290	415	165	6
2000	510	810	1327	1262	829	30

Sources: Christian, *Maps of time*, 344-345; Malanima, *Pre-modern European economy*, 7.

followed by Spain, Poland and Romania. The Netherlands underwent a remarkable development in the twentieth century, with its population increasing from around 5 million inhabitants in 1900, via 10 million in 1950, to 17 million in 2021. In doing so, the Netherlands clearly overtook countries such as Belgium, Sweden and Switzerland, which were previously roughly the same size.

In the early twenty-first century, around the half of the world's population lived in towns and cities, compared to less than 15 per cent in 1900. The pace and degree of urbanization differed greatly by region, however. While *c.* 1900, around 30–40 per cent of the population in Europe, the United States and Japan already lived in towns and cities, the figure for China, India, Latin America and Africa at that time was less than 10 per cent. Around 2000, the figure for Europe, the United States and Japan had risen to more than 75 per cent. Russia and Latin America experienced an enormous spurt in urbanization in the twentieth century: from 12 and 6 per cent respectively in 1900, to 66 per cent and over 70 per cent respectively in the 1990s. A similar acceleration occurred in China, India and Africa after the middle of the twentieth century. In fifty years, the share of the urban population rose from 10 to 15 per cent to more than 30 per cent.

The first country in the world to have more than half of its population living in towns and cities was Great Britain. This milestone was reached in 1850. Germany and Belgian crossed the threshold around forty years later, the United States around 1920, France and Japan in the 1930s, and Russia (then still the Soviet Union) in the 1960s. The Netherlands, which experienced a strong wave of urbanization in the nineteenth century, moved into this new category in the early twentieth century (the province of Holland had crossed the 50 per cent threshold back in the seventeenth century).

Towns and cities also continued to grow in size, and the centre of gravity of the population shifted over time. In *c.* 1900, there were only nine cities in the world with more than a million inhabitants. The largest cities were located in Europe, the United States and Japan: London (6.5 million), New York (4.2 million), Paris (3.3 million), Berlin (2.4 million) and Tokyo (1.5 million). In the late twentieth century, the number of cities with over a million inhabitants was more than 25 times greater. Some of these cities – including New York, Tokyo and Paris – expanded into conurbations with more than 10 million inhabitants. Today, the very largest and fastest-growing cities are to be found in Latin America, China, India and Africa: São Paulo, Mexico City, Shanghai, Beijing, Mumbai, Calcutta and Lagos. Compared to these, the Randstad, the largest conurbation in the Netherlands with over four million inhabitants, including Amsterdam, Rotterdam and The Hague, among others, is little more than a medium-sized urban concentration.

People's natural surroundings changed radically in the meantime. The surge in economic growth that began in the nineteenth century made unprecedented demands on natural resources. Initially, the damage to the natural environment was mainly visible in the pollution of the immediate surroundings. In wealthy countries in the late twentieth century, this form of environmental harm declined considerably again, thanks to technological innovations such as chimney filters, water purification and advanced waste-processing. The global economy, however, was increasingly characterized and governed by mass consumption. Over time, wealth became more and more dependent on the mass use of raw materials and fossil fuels. After 1970, people gradually became aware that reserves of raw materials and fuels were finite, especially after the publication of the Report for the Club of Rome in 1972. Deforestation and carbon emissions were found drastically to disrupt the global ecological balance.

Climate researchers concluded that the rise in the average temperature on earth in the nineteenth and twentieth centuries could not be attributed to normal natural processes alone, but had also been caused by human activity. Two hundred years of economic growth had left its traces in climate change. There was literally – as the environmental historian John McNeill put it – 'something new under the sun'.

6.2
Long-distance connections

After 1800, there was more intensive contact between societies in different parts of the world than there had been in preceding centuries. This was certainly true in an economic sense. One of the indicators for this was the development of intercontinental overseas trade to and from Europe. As we can see from Table 6.2, these trade flows grew much faster in the nineteenth and twentieth centuries than in the preceding period. Moreover, the economic historians O'Rourke and Jeffrey Williamson have shown that in the period 1850–1914, real wage levels in the countries around the Atlantic

TABLE 6.2 *Estimated Growth in Intercontinental Overseas Trade to and from Europe, 1700–1992*

	Average annual growth, in %
1700–99	1.26
1820–99	3.85
1900–92	3.65

Source: O'Rourke and Williamson, 'After Columbus', table 1.

TABLE 6.3 *Foreign Investment as a Percentage of Total World Production, 1870–1995*

	Percentage
1870	6.9
1900	18.6
1914	17.5
1930	8.4
1945	4.9
1960	6.4
1980	17.7
1995	56.8

Source: Crafts, 'Globalization and growth', 27.

Ocean increasingly converged, largely as a result of the enormous increase in overseas migration.

The advance of globalization also experienced the usual ups and downs in the nineteenth and twentieth centuries, however; it did not follow a continuous upwards trend. If we take the export of capital as our measure, expressed as a percentage of the total world production, we see striking fluctuations over time. Table 6.3 shows that globalization grew strongly until the First World War, then declined until the mid-twentieth century, and again showed considerable growth in the final quarter of the twentieth century, meaning that the 1914 level was reached again only at the end of the twentieth century.

Long-distance connections also expanded in social and cultural fields. In the second half of the nineteenth century, the migration ratio (the number of migrants per 1,000 people) for Europeans shot up from 22.7 to almost 31 per cent (see also Chapter 1, Table 1.6). After 1850, one of the most intensive periods of long-distance migration in history began. The historical literature has always focused on transatlantic migration. Between 1846 and 1940, a total of 55–58 million Europeans set off for the other side of the Atlantic Ocean. The United States alone attracted around 37 million European migrants during this period. Argentina, Brazil and Canada were also popular destinations. In addition, several million Europeans left for Australia and New Zealand. Migration from Europe to the colonies in Africa and Asia remained relatively limited in size.

The share of people from the Netherlands in the total flow of overseas migration before 1940 was relatively modest. In the nineteenth century, 140,000 Dutchmen and women emigrated to the United States, particularly in the 1860s, 1880s and 1890s, but the number of migrants after the Second World War was many times larger. Between 1946 and 1960, 464,000 Dutch left to build a new life overseas, 165,000 of whom left for Canada, 136,000 for Australia and 84,500 for the United States. From the 1960s onwards, the emigration surplus was transformed into an immigration surplus. Hundreds of thousands of migrants from overseas and the Mediterranean region settled in the Netherlands. A similar development took place in other European countries.

European overseas migration in the nineteenth and twentieth centuries was in fact less unique than recently thought. Asia experienced migration flows of a similar size to those of Europeans across the Atlantic Ocean. Adam McKeown has estimated, for example, that in the period between 1846 and 1940, around 48–52 million migrants moved from India and Southern China to Southeast Asia, and around 46–51 million people moved from North-eastern Asia (China) and Russia to Manchuria, Siberia and Central Asia. Yet the long-term effect of migration from Europe was much greater. In *c.* 1950, there were 250 million descendants of European emigrants living outside Europe, compared to 11 million descendants of Chinese emigrants living outside China and 4.6 million descendants of Indian emigrants living outside India.

Aside from the changing political conditions, the rise in the global flows of goods, capital and migrants was mainly facilitated by innovations in communication and transport. The extensive reaches of the vast British Empire (see Map 6.1) promoted these global connections. Globalization reached a provisional peak in *c.* 1890, steered by London as the world's financial heart.

Globalization stagnated from the First World War onwards. The large-scale military conflicts and the Depression of the 1930s disrupted British dominance and led to growing isolation between countries. The international network of the United States was yet to take over the British position. Globalization increased rapidly again from the 1950s, however, with the expansion of air travel and television, and in the 1990s with the emergence of the World Wide Web. With the United States as the most important world power, these kinds of technological innovations also contributed to the globalization of culture. In the twentieth century, news reports, music, films and branded goods circulated at a rapid rate from one part of the globe to another. The growth of organized tourism, which emerged on a modest scale in the mid-nineteenth century, exploded after 1950. Whereas *c.* 1950

MAP 6.1 *The British world empire in c. 1900 (shaded), with colonies, key naval bases and underwater telegraph cables. The map shows the political, military and economic aspects of Great Britain's powerful global network.*
Source: Held et al., *Global Transformations*, 42. Designed by René van der Vooren.

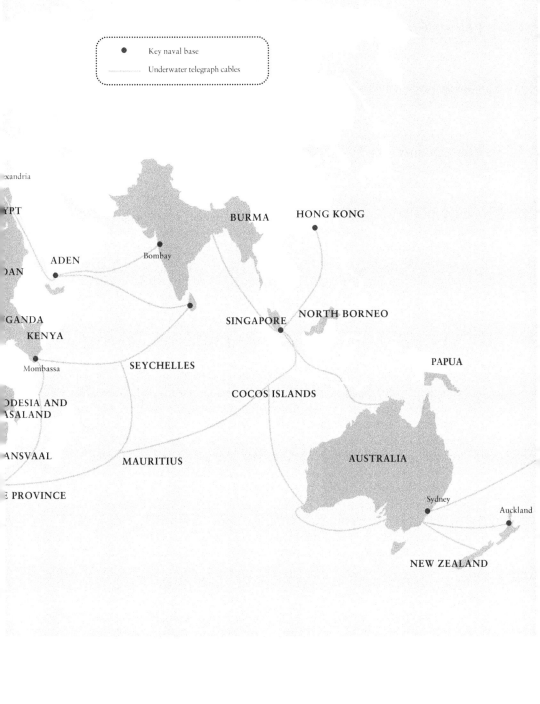

there had been only 25 million international tourists per year, in 1990 their number had grown to 454 million. The amount spent by these travellers rose disproportionately: from 2 to 255 billion dollars a year.

Plants and animals followed in the wake of people. For example, from the late eighteenth century, grapes, sheep and rabbits reached Australia and New Zealand, and the eucalyptus tree spread from Oceania across the rest of the world. After the arrival of the Europeans, the native inhabitants of Australia were afflicted by a similar disaster to that which had occurred a few centuries previously in America. From the moment that the first British colony was established in Botany Bay (close to present-day Sydney), the number of Aborigines fell dramatically: from 1.1 million in 1789 to 340,000 in 1860. The growth of long-distance connections after 1800 also meant that germs that left their local habitats could sometimes cause plagues of global proportions in no time at all. Particularly devastating examples of this effect of globalization were the cholera epidemics of the nineteenth century, the spread of Spanish flu shortly after the First World War, HIV-AIDS in the final quarter of the twentieth century and Covid-19 in the early 2020s.

6.3
The three basic problems: Contours of change

From the late eighteenth century, there was a true revolution in how the three basic problems facing human societies – the acquisition and distribution of income, the formation and distribution of power, and managing the fragility of existence – were tackled. Over time, this revolution would reach almost every part of the earth. In the initial phase in particular, Europe had a more powerful impact on global developments than ever before.

In an ever-growing part of the world, industrialization led to an almost constant rise in the income level. In the nineteenth century, modern industry spread from England to the European continent, the United States and Japan, and in the twentieth century to Latin America, South Africa, Oceania and a few countries on the Asian mainland. In Chapter 7, we will explain how the industrialization process took place in very different ways and at different rates. In Africa and some parts of Asia – referred to after the Second World War as the 'Third World' or 'developing countries' – the rise in prosperity took much longer, or failed to materialize altogether.

The Malthusian ceiling was broken, thanks to the use of fossil fuels and a wave of technological improvements. The economy was no longer based on a fragile balance between the size of the population and agricultural production. Cyclical fluctuations no longer originated in food prices but were determined by the dynamics of the industrial and financial sectors. As a result, millions of people in a large part of the world no longer had to worry about how to meet their primary needs. On the other hand, differences in the degree and rate of industrialization meant that income inequality *between* countries became much greater from the second quarter of the nineteenth century onwards. *Within* countries in the first phase of industrialization, income inequalities rose considerably. In Western industrial countries and countries in the communist bloc, they narrowed (temporarily) in the course of the twentieth century thanks to social democratic and socialist state policies.

The revolution in the economy was accompanied by a shift in the different categories of labour. Forced labour (slavery, hard labour, serfdom and suchlike) generally declined, with temporary exceptions such as in the Soviet Union and Nazi Germany. Commodified labour grew. Industrialized countries saw the emergence of a labour market in which salaries were determined by the demand for and supply of labour, and less by established structures or top-down regulation. At the same time, the number of unemployed increased sharply. One new phenomenon was the rise of the welfare state, which guaranteed that large groups in the population that did not earn any income from labour (such as the elderly and sick) were nevertheless assured of income.

From *c.* 1800, the state formation process also entered a new phase. By the end of the twentieth century, the new model of the state as a *nation* state, which first developed in Western Europe and was then adopted in other parts of the world, had become the standard model of territorial political organization. Another form of political organization that had served for many centuries as the 'normal' model, namely the *imperial* state – in which different ethnic groups fell under a single ruler – had its final heyday with the nineteenth-century European colonial expansion overseas (including the Dutch expansion), but imploded almost entirely in the 'short twentieth century' (1914–89). After the Second World War, a third, new form of political organization emerged in Europe: a voluntary, cooperative partnership between different nation states known as the European Union.

A fundamental shift in the distribution of power took place within these states, something that will be addressed in more depth in Chapter 8. The state centralized its power and developed a broader conception of its tasks and competencies. Power shifted from towns, churches, guilds and the nobility to national governments. Feudalism, serfdom and corporative structures were abolished or eroded. The bond between central government and citizens became more direct. Strongly inspired by Enlightenment ideals of reason and equality, people developed a broader conception of what the state could and should do.

It would be some time, however, before 'national citizens' had more say over these issues. In the nineteenth and twentieth centuries, democratization – in the sense of government by, of and for the people – first developed in the United States, Western Europe and the European settler colonies overseas (such as Canada or Australia), and subsequently spread to other parts of the world. On the whole, democracy flourished better in nation states than in empires, and proved to be more sustainable in countries with continuous economic growth than in countries with stagnating economies. The formation of voluntary organizations by citizens – also described as the growth of civil society – could strengthen the basis for democratization. In most Western countries, associations enjoyed their heyday between the mid-nineteenth century and the third quarter of the twentieth century.

In time, the expansion of state power, the increasing participation of the population and the growing influence of nationally organized interest groups also brought about a dramatic change in social policy. In answer to the growth of labour movements and/or influenced by major events such as the First World War and the Depression, most Western countries built up an extensive framework of social provisions to mitigate the risks of existence, under the charge of the state. This 'statification of welfare provision' led to both a temporary levelling-out of disposable incomes and an increased role for the government in the national economy.

Industrialization and political changes also led to changes in the social hierarchy, as we shall see in Chapter 9. A new entrepreneurial elite and a large industrial proletariat emerged, as did a new middle class of salaried workers. There was a gradual increase in social mobility, partly as a result of the expansion of education, but at the same time, wage labour left large parts of the population vulnerable to the ups and downs of the economic situation. The old 'estates' (nobility, clergy, town burghers) lost their significance as a dominant source of identity.

For many years, the transition to an industrial society was accompanied by growing disciplining. The aim of disciplining was to instil uniform, 'virtuous' values and behaviour in the population of the nation state. These attempts to form exemplary, well-behaved citizens were supported by the elites and the middle classes, as well as parts of the labour movement. This sometimes resulted in new, strict legislation, for example. on alcohol consumption and sexuality.

In the meantime, the composition of the population underwent a considerable transformation. This development was linked to the 'demographic transition' that occurred in most countries in the world, led by the Western industrial countries, in the nineteenth and twentieth centuries: a transition from a situation of high mortality rates and high birth rates to a pattern of low mortality rates and low birth rates. Life expectancy rose and the population became older, on average. A subsequent revolution occurred in the second half of the twentieth century, when the traditional ties between marriage, family formation and birth were severed. People increasingly lived together without getting married, and more and more marriages ended in divorce. The number of children conceived within marriage fell, and there was a relative increase in births outside marriage.

In the second half of the twentieth century, the world lost its euro-centric character. New powers, such as the United States and China, increasingly began to make the rules. The Great Divergence narrowed at the end of the twentieth century: China industrialized at a rapid rate, thereby closing much of the gap, and India also developed swiftly. Around the world, however, the inequality between industrialized countries and non-industrialized countries persisted, and European countries were still among the world's wealthiest.

7

Expansion, stagnation and globalization
Economic developments

JEROEN TOUWEN

After the Industrial Revolution in Great Britain, rapid economic growth took off in a number of Western countries. There was a continuous upwards trend in the growth in income per capita, despite cyclical fluctuations. This trend was particularly evident in Great Britain, the undisputed global economic power of the nineteenth century. Following the economist Simon Kuznets (1901–85), this development is known as 'modern economic growth'. Converted to its equivalent value in 1990 dollars, in 1820, national income per capita worldwide was 650 dollars a year; by 2000, it had risen to 6,000 dollars, nine times as much.

Industrializing countries achieved a much higher level of prosperity, and the difference in income with the rest of the world rose sharply. In economic terms, a growing gap emerged, known as the Great Divergence. In 1820, for example, income per capita ranged from almost 900 dollars in China to circa 1,600 dollars in Germany, 2,700 dollars in the United States and 3,000 dollars in the Netherlands. Between 900 and 2,700 is already a large difference (three times as much), but in 1970, income per capita in China was 1,400 dollars, while in the Netherlands it was 19,000 dollars and in the United States 24,000 dollars. The latter figure is no less than seventeen times as much as that for China (for the figures, see Table 7.1).

This chapter is about economic development in the world and the Netherlands in the nineteenth and twentieth centuries. We identify four periods: industrialization and growth in world trade until the First World

War, the decline and stagnation in economic growth between 1914 and 1945, the acceleration of growth between 1945 and 1973, and finally, the period from 1973 to the present day. The following questions will serve as a guide:

1. What were the most important driving forces of globalization? To what extent was there divergence or convergence between countries' economic development, and was there convergence towards a single, dominant type of economy?
2. How does the development of the European Union fit into the process of globalization?
3. How did the Dutch economy develop in comparison with other countries, and what was the legacy of its economic structure of the Early Modern period?

7.1
Industrialization and the growth in world trade before the First World War

INDUSTRIALIZATION AND ECONOMIC GROWTH 'Modern economic growth', as Kuznets defined it, implies a steady rise in income per capita. In most pre-industrial economies, economic growth was often accompanied by population growth: with some exceptions, income per capita did not or hardly rose. When a country became richer, this tended to be because more people were at work. They could work in a smarter way, divide tasks, specialize or cultivate larger plots of land, but it was ultimately the amount of labour that determined output. This changed with industrialization, because the productivity of individual employees rose thanks to technological and organization innovations, which we will address further herein.

Table 7.1 shows the economic growth that began in a number of countries in the nineteenth century. If we take purchasing power parity as our point of comparison (in other words, take account of price differences), the picture is as follows: in Great Britain, income per capita rose from 3,300 dollars in 1820 to 34,800 dollars in 2010; in the United States, from almost 2,700 dollars to more than 49,000 dollars; and in the Netherlands, from around 3,000 dollars to almost 44,000 dollars. In 1820, income per capita in China was 900 dollars and in Japan, 1,300 dollars. By 2010, this had risen to 9,600 dollars per capita in China and 35,000 dollars per capita in Japan.

TABLE 7.1 *Gross Domestic Product per Capita in Equivalents of 2011 Dollars, Based on Purchasing Power Parity, 1820-2018*

	Netherlands	Great Britain	Belgium	France	Germany	USA	China	Japan	World
1500	2,332	1,697	2,338	1,694	1,827		1,207		
1600	4,270	1,691	2,533	1,610	1,286		1,217	1,061	
1700	3,377	2,412	2,192	1,694	1,497		1,543	1,073	
1800	4,184	3,343			1,572	2,545	926	1,317	
1820	3,006	3,306	2,358	1,809	1,572	2,674	882	1,317	1,102
1850	3,779	4,332	2,944	2,546	2,276	3,632	858	1,436	1,225
1870	4,422	5,829	4,291	2,990	2,931	4,803	945	1,580	1,498
1900	5,306	7,594	5,947	4,584	4,758	8,038	972	2,123	2,212
1920	6,727	7,017	6,315	5,144	4,457	10,153		2,974	2,241
1930	8,931	8,673	7,936	7,224	6,333	10,695	1,012	3,334	
1940	7,701	10,928	7,272	6,443	8,612	12,005		4,882	3,133
1970	19,075	17,162	16,914	18,187	17,277	23,958	1,398	15,484	5,952
1980	23,438	20,612	23,060	23,537	22,497	29,611	1,930	21,404	7,233
1990	27,515	26,189	27,412	28,129	25,391	36,982	2,982	29,949	8,222
2000	37,900	31,946	33,720	33,410	33,367	45,886	4,730	33,211	9,915
2010	43,812	34,754	37,739	36,087	41,110	49,267	9,658	35,011	13,179
2018	47,474	38,058	39,756	38,516	46,178	55,335	13,102	38,674	15,212

Source: Maddison Project Database, version 2020.

These comparative figures have been converted to equivalent 2011 dollar values in order to offset the effect of inflation. The purchasing power parity method is used to convert national currencies into dollars, whereby differences in the price level between countries are neutralized by comparing the cost of a particular package of goods in each country. This allows us to compare the development in the prosperity level between countries.

After the Industrial Revolution gained momentum in Great Britain, most other European countries also started to industrialize in the nineteenth

TABLE 7.2 *Total Length of Railway Track per Country, Number of Miles, 1850–1910*

	1850	1870	1890	1910
United States	9,021	52,922	116,703	249,902
Great Britain	6,621	15,537	20,073	23,387
Germany	3,637	11,729	25,411	36,152
France	1,714	11,142	22,911	30,643
India		4,771	16,401	32,099
Japan			1,139	5,130
China			80	5,092

Source: O'Rourke and Williamson, *Globalization and History*, 34.

century. Technological knowledge was disseminated, and governments made attempts to speed up industrialization. On the European continent, Belgium was the second country after Britain to build a heavy industrial sector based on coal; the first modern textile industry on the continent emerged in Flanders. The two most important new industrial powers were the United States and Germany. This development is illustrated by the construction of railways, which formed a key link in industrialization (Table 7.2).

TWO NEW ECONOMIC GIANTS: THE UNITED STATES AND GERMANY In the nineteenth century, the United States was a frontier state, where colonists brought new territories in the West into cultivation at a rapid rate. American industrialization began around 1800, but it would accelerate after the Civil War (1861–5), when the northern states fought the South for the preservation of the Union and the abolition of slavery. The period of growth that followed is known as the Gilded Age (1877–1900). It was characterized by the rapid expansion of the railways, modern and extremely productive agriculture, and the emergence of a number of large and powerful enterprises. Successful businessmen and bankers in the United States amassed huge fortunes, with the result that we are still familiar with their names today. Sometimes known by the more derogatory term 'robber barons', due to their immense wealth, they included Andrew Carnegie, J.P. Morgan, John D. Rockefeller and Cornelius Vanderbilt. At least as important, though, was the emergence of an extensive, ethnically diverse working class, composed of migrants from numerous countries who made their living in America's modern industry.

Initially concentrated in traditional industries such as cotton and footwear, the centre of gravity of industrial activity gradually shifted to the electrical and chemical industries and machine-building. These branches of industry are typical of what has become known as the 'Second Industrial Revolution', a phase that most industrialized countries entered into in *c.* 1865 and that ended in the 1930s. The more these technologies advanced, the more labour and capital productivity (i.e. the quantity of goods produced by a unit of labour and a unit of capital) rose, meaning that production became cheaper. In this way, both the United States and Germany achieved a comparative advantage over Great Britain in the course of the Second Industrial Revolution.

America's rapid industrialization went hand in hand with a swift expansion of agriculture, aided by the cultivation of new territories in the West, which were taken from the Indians. Unlike in Latin America, the emergence of a class of small independent farmers and entrepreneurs was encouraged in the United States. The Homestead Act, signed by Abraham Lincoln in 1862, provided that applicants who worked a plot of land could take possession of it after five years. In 1873 the Timber Culture Act came into force, providing that anyone who planted trees on a quarter of a plot of land in certain arid regions could become the owner of that land. An enterprising immigrant to the United States could thus acquire land cheaply (that is to say, through their own labour alone). Salaries were also relatively high, and there was more political and religious freedom than in many countries in Europe or Latin America.

Improvements to the infrastructure transformed the United States into an important exporter of grain and industrial products. Thanks to the railways and the rise of steamships, goods could be transported to overseas destinations cheaply and quickly. Grain was not the only welcome export product; from 1870, after the invention of the deepfreeze, a lot of frozen beef was exported to Europe, too. Industrial and agricultural exports from the United States began to flood the world during this period. Exports from South America trailed significantly behind; see Text Box 7.1.

The other country that was propelled high in the world rankings by industrialization was Germany. For many years, Germany was a politically fragmented country with a large number of small states and entities, an inadequate infrastructure and a poor peasant class. As we saw in Chapter 2, the region east of the Elbe had a system of unfree labour, where the *Junkers* exploited smallholders. Although this cheap labour did facilitate some expansion of production, it was not accompanied by structural innovation. The territory to the west of the Elbe was mainly covered in small farms. In the early nineteenth century, this region experienced modest growth in agriculture. There was no modernization in agriculture, as there had been in Great Britain; there was hardly a consumer market and no investment in a burgeoning industry.

Despite this, some important changes did occur in the early nineteenth century. Napoleon's Continental System temporarily took the edge off competition with Britain, which stimulated German industry. In order to achieve greater economic unification, the *Zollverein* was established in 1834. Although this customs union did not initially cover the whole of Germany, its founding did mark the beginning of the end of economic fragmentation.

Between 1850 and 1870, economic growth picked up in Germany; and once industrialization was underway, it was almost unstoppable. We can distinguish two phases in this process. In the period between 1850 and 1870, industrialization was very similar to the previous development in Great Britain: a strong expansion of heavy industry, coal-mining and the railways, and, to a lesser extent, also the textile industry. After 1870, an extensive chemical and electrical industry and a modern steel industry developed in Germany, typical of the 'Second Industrial Revolution'. Thus, the two waves of industrialization followed one another rapidly in Germany, transforming this country into an economic superpower alongside the United States.

In the initial phase of industrialization, the construction of the railways was also of decisive importance in Germany (see Table 7.2). As in Great Britain, the construction of the railways stimulated demand for iron, machines and coal, but the emerging transport systems also brought regions into contact with one another, creating a much larger market: goods from remote areas could now be sold across the whole country, and the remote regions themselves were also opened up as export markets. The Ruhr, with its rich reserves of coal, formed the centre of this heavy industry. Steel had to be imported, until Germany's victory in the Franco-German war of 1870-1 led it to acquire Elzas-Lotharingen, which lay on large reserves of iron ore. In 1879, a procedure was invented to make high-quality steel from the phosphorus iron ore from these mines.

One key difference between industrialization in Germany and Britain was the contribution made by banking. In Great Britain, capital goods (machines, factories) tended to be purchased with the savings and profits of entrepreneurial industrial families. The British banks, which were themselves often family businesses, did provide short-term loans for the purchase of raw materials, but they were reluctant to make large-scale investments. British entrepreneurs therefore invested their own capital and reinvested the profits.

German banks were larger and more impersonal; they were not family businesses, but limited companies. These industrial investment banks lent large sums to large-scale businesses in heavy industry. German entrepreneurs could not gradually build up and reinvest their own capital, so they borrowed money for modern machines and installations from the banks.

TEXT BOX 7.1 LATIN AMERICA, STUNTED GROWTH

The United States grew into the world's strongest economy. Why did this not happen in the other part of the New World, South America? Compared to North America, Latin America was a rich and fertile region. Gold and silver were found in many places, including in Peru and Brazil. Contemporaries of the colonization in the seventeenth and eighteenth centuries expected more of this continent than of the dry prairies and extensive forests of North America. Despite this, Latin America trailed behind economically in the nineteenth century. The reason for this can be sought in political and economic institutions and in the nature of migration. The mentality of the colonists there was very different from that in the north: Spanish and Portuguese colonists came to get rich quickly and easily, and showed a different kind of entrepreneurial behaviour from the settlers in North America, who strove to establish their own farms. The Catholic Church also played a distinct role. The church tried to exclude dissenters or members of other faiths from society, and protected the established order. The large-scale organization of agriculture with haciendas promoted involuntary forms of labour and made the country less attractive to small-scale settlers.

By the end of the nineteenth century, Argentina had become the continent's success story. This country was the first to industrialize in South America, and although it did not develop as rapidly as North America, Argentine economic growth was strong, at an average of $c.$ 6.6 per cent between 1880 and 1913. However, Argentinian industry was a passenger, not a pioneer, of economic growth, because industry was driven by exports of agricultural products. The railways initially served to transport commodities and agricultural products (meat, grain) to the export harbours, not to open up the domestic market. Further industrialization barely got off the ground. Despite all this, Argentina flourished in this period. Spanish migrant workers were drawn to Buenos Aires, which was thought to rival Paris in terms of its fashions and nightlife. Argentinian economic development stagnated in the course of the twentieth century, and economic policy came under pressure from conflicting interest groups and inefficient government interventions. Other countries in Latin America developed some textile industries, including Brazil and Mexico (cotton, wool). Over time, however, the textiles produced there were largely superseded by cheaper textiles from other countries.

> **TEXT BOX 7.2 GERSCHENKRON AND CATCH-UP GROWTH**
>
> German industrialization can be described as rapid 'catch-up growth'. What exactly is meant by this? The term 'catch-up growth' was devised by the economic historian Alexander Gerschenkron (1904–78), and refers to the difference between imitating and inventing. Economic growth will develop differently when a country trails behind other countries that have already industrialized. Growth will be quicker, for example, factories will be larger and capital goods (machines and factories) will also play a greater role, because more advanced technology will be used. If the country's economy is also underdeveloped or backward, then credit banks and governments will play a more significant role, modernization in agriculture will play a less pioneering role in economic growth and the level of domestic consumption will come under pressure during the period of industrialization. These were indeed characteristics of the industrialization processes in Germany and Russia.

CONCENTRATION AND CONSOLIDATION IN THE BUSINESS WORLD Given the enormous size of the internal market, the large-scale investments in the United States led to the emergence of unprecedentedly large companies. This was also the case in Germany. Unlike in Great Britain, German companies were not directed by the owners themselves; in Germany the banks were the largest shareholders in industry, and thus co-owners of enterprises. These new companies were divided into different departments (such as production, sales, finance, development) and led by professional managers.

The business historian Alfred Chandler (1918–2007) emphasized the importance of management in large companies. He argued that a separate organizational structure developed in large companies, with senior managers, lower-level managers and specific management techniques, which allowed these companies to be more productive. Chandler unleashed a fierce debate among historians by arguing that companies could remain successful only if they transformed themselves into managerial firms, with investment from the stock change, not family capital or personal bank loans, and if professional managers took the helm. According to Chandler, traditional family firms were unable to make the necessary investments in production, distribution and management, especially in large-scale branches of industry, such as the chemical industry. Moreover, managers who were employed by a firm that they did not themselves own would be more willing to break with tradition and try to achieve profitable innovations. Business historians have shown, however, that there are examples of family firms in various countries (including the Netherlands) that did in fact continue to operate successfully, or that developed various kinds of intermediary forms to obtain capital without jeopardizing the family nature of the firm.

Innovation and rationalization benefitted when businesses continued to grow and achieved economies of scale. In 1910 in Germany, for example, the entire electrical industry was dominated by Siemens and the Allgemeine Electrizitäts Gesellschaft (AEG), and BASF and Bayer dominated the chemical industry. Many German businesses fixed prices or made agreements about the quantity of goods that would be produced.

Cartels also formed in the United States. Firms started to collaborate because upscaling was an extremely attractive prospect; after all, the domestic market was many times larger than in Europe, and this was further reinforced by urbanization. There was great demand among salaried workers in the towns and cities for consumer goods such as sewing machines, typewriters, cigarettes and foodstuffs such as frozen meat. Upscaling was also boosted by attempts to establish monopolies and thereby amass even greater wealth.

The first wave of mergers was fuelled by the expansion of the railway network. This allowed companies to form 'horizontal' combinations, whereby enterprises in a single industry (such as petroleum extraction) merged into larger entities. This form of cooperation was facilitated by the construction of the trust, whereby several companies were voluntarily placed under a holding company, which then divided up the market. The production process was subsequently uniformized and management centralized. This was how John D. Rockefeller's Standard Oil Company of New Jersey (see Figure 7.1), for example, and the United States Rubber Company emerged. The second wave, which took place between 1899 and 1904, consisted of a series of mergers in which smaller companies were taken over by larger ones, or companies merged voluntarily. This period saw the emergence of the US Steel Corporation and the American Tobacco Company, which managed to achieve a monopoly on cigarette sales in less than fifteen years. Consumers protested vociferously against these large monopolies. A coalition of politicians, journalists and lawyers fought for new anti-trust legislation, the most striking result of which was break-up of Standard Oil and American Tobacco in 1911.

GROWTH IN WORLD TRADE World trade underwent an unprecedented expansion between 1870 and 1914. The liberal ideas that emerged in many countries provided an ideological basis for the government's modest role in the economy. The government's role was merely to ensure order and security, while the invisible hand of the market would take care of efficient allocation and increasing prosperity. The 'night watchman state' may have been more of an ideal than reality, because governments did in fact intervene in the economy in practice. Free trade and international investments did rise sharply during this period, however. For this reason, we usually refer to these years as the era of *laissez faire*. The levels of trade and investment were especially high in the colonial empires.

Free trade nevertheless remained a fragile phenomenon: throughout the nineteenth century, it remained attractive for industrializing countries to protect their infant industries by levying import tariffs on foreign imports. In the United States, for example, tariffs remained strikingly high: the average import tariff on industrial products in the nineteenth century was around 40 per cent of the value. Dutch tariffs were extremely low by contrast, but it

FIGURE 7.1 *Political cartoon on the power of Standard Oil from 1904. This drawing by Udo J. Keppler portrays a Standard Oil storage tank as an octopus with its tentacles entwined around the steel, copper and shipbuilding industries, as well as the American Capitol and even the White House.*
© Wikimedia Commons (public domain).

was Great Britain that set the trend in the liberal era: this country opened up its market to foreign products to a remarkable degree in the second half of the nineteenth century. In the eighteenth century, Great Britain was still protecting its burgeoning industry with import levies; British cotton production was protected from competition from India, for example. There were also the Corn Laws, which regulated import tariffs on grain; these tariffs kept the domestic grain price high and protected the landowning elite, whose income was based on selling their tenants' agricultural products. The turning point in British policy came with the repeal of the Corn Laws in 1846. This led to a fall in grain prices, allowing the cost of wages in industry to come down. It can thus be seen as a victory by the industrial bourgeoisie over the landowning aristocracy. The openness of British economy was partly facilitated by Britain's dominance of the world market, and it went hand in hand with imperial policy: like other colonial nations, trade with the colonies formed a major part of Britain's foreign trade, and it was not in the country's interest to scale it back.

European expansion overseas accelerated in the final quarter of the nineteenth century, bringing large parts of Asia and almost the whole of Africa under colonial rule. Whereas earlier phases of colonization had involved setting up trading posts, the new wave involved exploiting colonies by establishing plantations and developing mining. This was accompanied by military oppression of the territories and growing administrative dominance. The European countries engaged in large-scale trade and processing of commodities from the colonies (tobacco, sugar, coffee, tea and later petroleum and rubber), and also improved the infrastructure of the colonized territories for this purpose. Western trading companies, banks and insurance companies were likewise established in the colonies. Imperialism formed the basis for great inequality between different parts of the world, which would largely persist after decolonization in the twentieth century.

THE AGRICULTURAL CRISIS IN THE LATE NINETEENTH CENTURY There was a protracted crisis in the agricultural sector between 1873 and 1895, highlighting the increasing globalization and the sector's fragility in the nineteenth-century industrialized global economy. Although the crisis barely affected industry, it led to a long-term fall in agricultural prices, putting farmers' incomes in Europe under considerable pressure. The most important cause was the increasing grain production across the world, particularly in the United States, Canada and Russia, and the sharp fall in international transport prices. American grain from the Midwest was transported by rail to the coast, whence it was carried by steamship to overseas destinations such as Liverpool in England, which functioned as a European transit port. The European market was flooded with cheap American grain as a result. The roots of the crisis lay in technological innovation: agricultural mechanization, the railways and steel steamships. In 1890–4, American grain in Liverpool cost just 61 per cent of what it had cost in 1870–4. During the same period, the cost of transporting goods from New York to Liverpool fell to 30 per cent of the previous level.

European countries responded to this in very different ways. Farmers everywhere pushed for import tariffs, but their appeals were not always heard. There were attempts in France and Germany to shield farmers with protectionist measures, but in Great Britain and the Netherlands, industrial and commercial interests weighed more heavily than agrarian ones.

In the Netherlands, the agrarian depression led not only to poverty in the countryside, but also to a restructuring of agriculture. In the early nineteenth century, Dutch agriculture was already more productive than in the surrounding countries. As a result of the crisis, specialization and efficiency increased: farmers in the coastal provinces switched from arable farming to horticulture, and the south and east focused on animal husbandry. These regions produced and exported milk, butter, pork and eggs. There was also greater efficiency thanks to new organizational forms: farmers set up production cooperatives (dairy factories), purchasing cooperatives (for artificial fertilizers and agricultural machinery, for example) and credit cooperatives (farm credit banks, following the example of the German Raiffeissenbank; see also Chapter 9).

European agriculture recovered after 1895, thanks to the rising standard of living, which boosted demand for dairy products, vegetables and fruit. Nevertheless, technological innovations and the slowing population growth meant that the threat of surplus remained.

THE CHANGING POSITION OF GREAT BRITAIN, 1875–1914 America replaced Great Britain as the global economic hegemon, but, remarkably enough, this did not become abundantly clear until after the First World War. This was because Great Britain remained the world's financial centre and the main supplier of international services, such as insurance and transport, which masked the relative decline in exports on the balance of payments.

The industrialization of other countries had major consequences for Great Britain. Growth in British industrial production slowed considerably in the face of international competition, and export markets were lost because newly industrializing countries protected their markets. During the entire period between 1811 and 1870, industrial production grew by 3.1 per cent per year, on average; in 1870-1913, this figure was just 1.6 per cent. The fragmentation of British industrial leadership was masked, however, by the expansion in world trade: Great Britain was both the world's greatest trading nation and the financial centre of world trade. Although Britain was earning less from exports, at the same time it was earning more income from transport, insurance, loans and overseas investments. British ships transported commodities, food and industrial products from around the world to Western Europe. Freightage could be kept low because British ships did not carry ballast, but coal – an important raw material in industrializing Europe. The British shipping industry flourished, cargo was insured by Lloyd's, and trade was financed by banks in the City of London. Due to Britain's trade supremacy and the Gold Standard (see Text Box 7.3), the pound was the leading international currency in this period.

TEXT BOX 7.3 THE GOLD STANDARD

The Gold Standard was a system of fixed exchange rates that functioned between the mid-nineteenth century and the 1930s. Every currency that participated in the system, such as the pound, the guilder and the dollar, was linked to a certain amount of gold, and this resulted in fixed exchange rates. The advantage of having fixed exchange rates is that there are no exchange rate fluctuations. This promotes international trade, because transaction costs are lowered (see Chapter 2). The drawback, though, is that countries must keep a careful eye on their balance of payments to prevent national gold reserves from flowing out of the country when imports exceed exports over a long period, thereby weakening the basis of their own currency. As a result of the internationalization of the economy, in the late nineteenth century countries gradually started to hold commonly used foreign currencies as reserves, too. The Gold Standard was suspended during the First World War, after which it was restored. It remained in place until 1931, when Great Britain devalued in order to stimulate exports, which had been hit heavily by the economic crisis, and other countries followed suit.

There is yet another reason why Great Britain trailed behind during this period. At that time, British entrepreneurs were less innovative than their contemporaries in countries such as the United States and Germany. Some historians refer to this as the 'dialectics of progress'. Once-modern factories were being overtaken by new industries. In Great Britain, there was less investment in new machines. Modern management in newly industrialized countries also resulted in innovation and increased productivity. By contrast, British industry mainly consisted of small-scale family businesses, which were often managed in an informal way by the owner-director. Cultural factors also played a role: the British education system put great emphasis on studying the classics, for example, whereas less status was attached to teaching practical and economic skills, such as engineering.

THE PARADOX OF LATE INDUSTRIALIZATION IN THE NETHERLANDS Around 1800, the Netherlands was a relatively prosperous country with a rich past. Compared to neighbouring countries, though, it also had to contend with a relative decline. Unlike Great Britain, the Netherlands did not yet have any burgeoning heavy industry. Nevertheless, the economy had a number of 'modern' features, such as a strong services sector and an extremely productive agricultural sector in the west of the country (see Table 2.3, Chapter 2). A period of growth began in the 1810s: investment increased and industry expanded. After 1830 these impulses disappeared, however, and it was again the 'traditional' activities relating to overseas trade (textiles, sugar, shipbuilding) that set the tone. It was not until after 1865 that a broad process of industrialization got going, and there was a real acceleration in economic growth. The country now saw the emergence of a modern industrial sector, as had previously happened in Great Britain, Belgium, Germany and the United States.

Why was the Netherlands so late to industrialize? For many years, this was explained with reference to the mentality of the Dutch, whose glorious past was believed to have left them passive and risk-averse. It was also argued that the Netherlands had fallen into a 'technological trap': although the path to technological development that the Netherlands had followed before 1800 had resulted in a high level of productivity, it was thought to provide few opportunities for further innovation. A technological system that was based on the use of peat, wind-power and canals was considered to have less capacity for growth than a system based on coal, steam-power and railways.

More recently, though, economic historians and historians of technology have come up with more convincing explanations. To start with, it should be noted that the Dutch economy did not trail behind those of its neighbours, but had a different profile: the Netherlands had a service-based economy and entrepreneurs were building on past prosperity. This left the country in a very different starting position from those countries that were overwhelmingly agrarian and less oriented towards international markets. Moreover, the Netherlands was also capable of technological innovations after 1800. This was partly achieved by improving traditional technologies (such as windmills), and partly through the selective adoption and creative use of new technologies from abroad (especially from Great Britain). In doing so, Dutch entrepreneurs showed a preference for small-scale production methods.

Three particular circumstances explain why the initiatives to build up modern industry in the first half of the nineteenth century subsequently failed: the institutional legacy of the Republic, the policies of King Willem I and the specific response of the small, open Dutch economy to trade liberalization after 1842.

Importantly, the institutional structure that was inherited from the Republic was characterized by the relatively powerful position of the cities. Due to the prosperity of that era, however, a certain degree of institutional rigidity had set in. The features that had been a trump card in the seventeenth century, namely strong dynamic and independent towns that formed an essential core of growth, proved to be a disadvantage in an era of nation state formation and integrated national economies. Industrialization benefitted from a nationally integrated economy with a larger export market, supported by collective provisions such as a good transport infrastructure. The entanglement of power and local interests in the Netherlands, however, held back the transformation to a national economy for many years. Groups of entrepreneurs, such as flour millers or brokers, opposed the reforms that were introduced by the state after 1800. Economic restructuring was also hindered by high taxes and a considerable public debt.

A second reason for the late industrialization of the Netherlands relates to the role of King Willem I, who reigned between 1815 and 1840. The policies of Willem I, nicknamed the 'merchant king', had good and bad aspects. He took a dynamic approach to economic development and experimented with various initiatives to boost growth: investing in infrastructure, such as canals and national roads, promoting industry, modernizing banking and trade, focusing on education and providing subsidies for the fishing industry. But he did not manage to win the support and trust of the financial elites of Holland, and he failed to create a favourable investment climate as a result. His fiscal policy, in particular, was inadequate; he left the government finances in chaos. The public debt rose from around 150 per cent of national income in 1815 to 250 per cent in the 1840s.

A third factor that explains late industrialization in the Netherlands is the response to trade liberalization after 1842. Liberal reformers came to power in the Netherlands in the 1840s; Thorbecke's Constitution of 1848 was a milestone in Dutch history. They put the government finances in order and abolished all kinds of import and export duties. Other countries likewise liberalized their trade policies between 1840 and 1870. As a result, there was initially a sharp rise in agricultural exports from the Netherlands. By contrast, Dutch industry, which was largely focused on the domestic market, was not equal to the competition from abroad. Moreover, high food prices after 1840 resulted in high wages and a low level of purchasing power.

THE IMPORTANCE OF THE EAST INDIES The colonial possessions were extremely important to the Netherlands; the wealthy and extensive Dutch East Indies made a particular contribution to the international standing of the Netherlands as a colonial great power. The economic significance of the Dutch East Indies was evident in all kinds of areas, including the trade in colonial commodities, as a stimulus for shipbuilding, as an export market for the textile industry, and for the role of the Netherlands as an international conveyor of goods. King Willem I's colonial policy was rather more successful than his industrial policy. The income from overseas territories ('colonial assets') increased during the century as a consequence of the Cultivation System (1830–70). This was set up by Johannes van den Bosch, the governor general of the Dutch East Indies between 1830 and 1834. In the Dutch East Indies, colonial products such as coffee, tea and sugar were bought from Javanese peasants at low prices and resold in Amsterdam for higher prices by the Netherlands Trading Society (Nederlandsche Handel-Maatschappij, founded in 1824). The resulting surplus was used to finance infrastructural investments in the Netherlands, among other things.

Following the abolition of the Cultivation System in 1870, private entrepreneurship flourished in the Dutch East Indies. After the end of the Aceh War in 1903, the Outer Islands (islands such as Sumatra, Borneo, Celebes and the Moluccas) were also opened up. These islands developed into important production areas for oil, rubber, tobacco, coffee and copra (coconut). The economic ties with the metropole loosened after the First World War. A great number of Dutchmen and women settled in the Dutch East Indies, pursued careers there and returned to the Netherlands with pensions, capital and dividends. The profits from Dutch agricultural and trade enterprises also flowed back, in part, to the mother country. Economist Jan Tinbergen has calculated that in 1938, income for the Dutch economy from the Dutch East Indies amounted to 14 per cent of national income.

The so-called Ethical Policy was launched in 1901, with the aim of increasing the prosperity of the indigenous population (see also Chapter 8). Although the Ethical Policy was not sufficient to absorb the consequences of growing population pressure on Java, the Netherlands did invest a lot of technological knowledge in the colony. For this reason, sociologist J. A. A. van Doorn called the Dutch East Indies a 'colonial project', with engineers who tried to modernize the country with irrigation technology and agricultural education. Compared to India, though, the number of university-educated Indonesians who entered the more senior ranks of the administration remained relatively small, something that would prove detrimental to the continuity of political and economic governance after the country became independent. Many Chinese were active in the indigenous sector of the economy. They worked as middlemen, transporters, financiers or importers, and kept in contact with mainland Southern China through family networks. Chinese traders stimulated the economy with credit and innovation, but they also reaped a considerable share of the profits. Historians thus refer to 'double colonial drainage': to the colonizing metropole and to China.

7.2
Conflict and stagnation, 1914–1945

WAR, REVOLUTION AND THE 'ROARING TWENTIES' Between 1914 and 1945, global economic development faltered. Economic growth slowed and world trade hardly expanded. This development was in stark contrast to the exuberant expansion of the period shortly before the First World War. In the industrializing economies, the years between 1895 and 1914 were dominated by the Second Industrial Revolution, with the rise of the electrical industry, machine-building and the chemical industry. The arrival of electricity in people's homes brought about a massive transformation. Electric lighting and the introduction of electric appliances made life much more comfortable. In the United States in 1899, just 3 per cent of households had electric lighting, but by 1929 this figure was 70 per cent. It was around this time that the car also made its entrance. It would go on to win a huge consumer market after the war, along with refrigerators and washing machines, for example.

Industry was slower to introduce new technology, because it took some time for existing capital goods to depreciate and be replaced. Electrically powered machines would not be used on a large scale until the second decade of the twentieth century, for example, even though electricity had been introduced around 1900. However, electricity would eventually give a great boost to productivity (production per hour or per worker, the key factor behind economic growth).

Technological innovation as a growth factor was strengthened, to a great extent, by international trade and international investment, which ensured that the new production capacity reached the market or developed in favourable locations. With the outbreak of the First World War in 1914, however, there was a sharp fall in global interconnectedness. The globalization of the world economy did not really get going again in the interwar period; in the 1920s, due to the aftermath of the war, and during the crisis of the 1930s, because many countries introduced protectionist policies.

Although the Netherlands remained neutral in the First World War, the war did have a major impact on the Dutch economy. The international economy was seriously disrupted by the war and trade relations fell into disarray. As with the agricultural depression in the late nineteenth century, though, which boosted specialization in agriculture and horticulture, the effects were not exclusively negative; the stagnation of imports led to a search for alternatives, which promoted the modernization of industry. There was increasing vertical integration of production (from raw material to end product), and companies were forced to collaborate more intensively. These years also saw increasing intervention by the Dutch government. Both developments advanced the emergence of the Dutch consultation economy, with a major role for collective bargaining.

Whereas the United States consolidated its economic dominance in this period, in a political respect it initially continued to pursue a policy of isolation; only in the Second World War would the United States prove willing to assume an international leadership role. The roaring twenties saw the development of a mass market for consumer goods in the United States. The American technological edge over Europe was reflected in the productivity figures; productivity per worker in 1935 was almost three times higher than that in Great Britain, for example. This was partly because more hours were worked, but production per hour in American industry was also more than twice as high.

As Western Europe recovered from the ravages of the First World War and had to contend with increasing dominance from the United States, in the 1920s a power bloc emerged in Eastern Europe and Central Asia that was based on very different economic principles. The October Revolution of 1917 brought the communists to power in Russia, led by Lenin (1870–1924). In 1922, the Union of Soviet Socialist Republics (USSR) was founded; led by the communists, this union would exist until 1991, and would form a key political and economic power bloc for half a century. Centrally planned economies were introduced by the communist regime, in which the state, not the market, determined what was to be produced. In this system, all industry and all banks were state-owned. A rapid period of industrialization took place from the early 1930s, mainly characterized by the building of a large heavy industrial sector to manufacture production goods. Five-year plans determined what had to be manufactured where. In the first five-year plan by Lenin's successor, Joseph Stalin (1879–1953), agriculture was reorganized on a massive scale into a system of state farms (*sovchoz*) and collective farms (*kolchoz*). This formed part of Stalin's plan to eradicate the class of free farmers, the kulaks.

THE WALL STREET CRASH OF 1929 AND THE GREAT DEPRESSION OF THE 1930S On Black Tuesday, 29 October 1929, share prices on Wall Street in New York plummeted by around 40 per cent, and many speculators who had borrowed to invest were made bankrupt in one fell swoop. Although the Wall Street Crash was but one of the causes of the crisis of the 1930s, it heralded the beginning of a decade of economic problems.

A deep economic crisis unfolded in the years that followed, one that spread rapidly across the whole world. As a result, the crisis of the 1930s, with its enormously high unemployment rates, was the deepest and most serious economic crisis of the twentieth century (see Chart 7.1). Consumer demand collapsed, meaning that many companies were no longer able to sell their products and went bankrupt. There was panic on the financial markets; investors tried to sell their shares, causing the prices to fall, savings balances evaporated, banks went bust and speculative investors went bankrupt.

In order to understand the origins of the crisis and how it developed, it is necessary to consider it from four different angles: (1) the imbalances in the international economy, (2) events in the real economy, (3) the policy responses to these events and (4) the monetary aspects of the crisis, which have formed an important focus of recent research.

1. The structural imbalances in the world economy were linked to the end of the First World War, which fundamentally disrupted international connections. By around 1925, however, confidence had returned. In that year, Great Britain returned to the Gold Standard (Text Box 7.3), but it had not yet accepted its new position in the world economy, and pegged the pound to gold at too high a value. This made British exports expensive compared

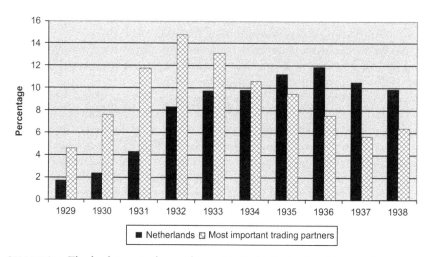

CHART 7.1 *The development of unemployment in the Netherlands and its most important trading partners (Germany, Great Britain and Belgium), 1929–39 (based on data from the ILO). An unweighted average has been calculated for the trading partners.*
Source: Van Zanden, *Een klein land*, 152.

to American exports. Another imbalance resulted from the payment of war debts by European countries to the United States, which brought about a flow of capital to America. Part of this money was lent out again by the United States to Germany, which had to pay massive reparations to the allies after the Treaty of Versailles (1919). These unbalanced capital flows had a detrimental effect when the crisis hit. After the Wall Street Crash, America called in its loans from Germany, which almost immediately put the German financial world under pressure. Another problem was that the market for consumer durables had become saturated, and farmers in the countryside had invested over-optimistically in mechanization, leaving many producers in difficulties.

2. The consequences of the American problems of 1929 for the real economies of other countries soon made themselves felt. American demand for import goods fell, setting off a chain reaction. Seeing their income from trade dry up, exporting industrialized countries responded with import tariffs and import quotas to protect their own industry from cheap foreign imports.

This led to a reduction in each other's export markets and trade opportunities. Protectionism rapidly brought world trade to a standstill. The collapse of exports led to bankruptcies, prompting a rise in unemployment around the world. In the absence of unemployment benefits, this immediately resulted in a drastic collapse in demand in domestic markets. Protectionism thus led to a downward spiral in world trade between 1929 and 1933, as the economic historian Charles Kindleberger has shown so clearly (see Figure 7.2).

3. The policy responses to the effects of the sharp fall in world trade also had an impact on the duration and depth of the crisis. Two patterns can be identified in the responses, both of which were linked to the Gold Standard. The first pattern was evident in Great Britain and the United States, which left the Gold Standard relatively quickly and devalued their currencies in 1931 and 1933, respectively. The lower exchange rate made their exports cheaper, meaning that industry could profit directly from the subsequent recovery. The Netherlands provides an example of the second type of policy response: it remained on the Gold Standard for many years, together with a number of other countries (France, Belgium, Poland, Italy and Switzerland). Together these countries formed the 'Gold bloc', in the hope that other countries would re-join after the crisis. Fixed exchange rates were good for international confidence and international prestige remained high as a result, not least because foreign holders of Dutch state bonds and equities were not negatively affected by depreciation. On the other hand, though, the guilder became an 'expensive' currency.

It was partly due to this policy decision that the crisis persisted in the Netherlands for a relatively long time. Dutch exports suffered heavily from the expensive currency between 1931 and 1936. With an 'adjustment policy', Prime Minister Hendrik Colijn attempted to reduce domestic production costs with low wages and low taxes, in the hope of keeping exports somewhat competitive despite the unfavourable exchange rate. This had the detrimental effect of eroding the population's purchasing power, and

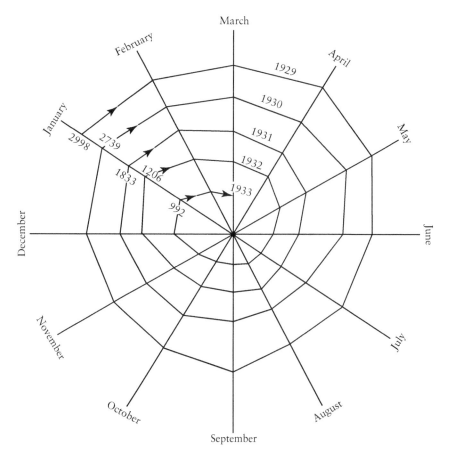

FIGURE 7.2 *Kindleberger's spiral, showing the monthly fall in imports of seventy-five countries in the period 1929–33, in millions of dollars.*
© *Wikimedia Commons (public domain).*

imports became expensive. The unemployed in particular bore the brunt of the crisis. The recovery would begin only in 1936, when the Gold Standard was eventually abandoned (see Chart 7.1).

A new economic approach was introduced during the 1930s, aimed at stimulating the demand side (Keynesianism; see Text Box 7.4). This entailed restarting the economic cycle with a spending boost from the government. In the United States, President Franklin Roosevelt's New Deal, which was introduced in 1933, provided (if unintentionally) a successful example of this approach.

4. The monetary aspects of the crisis should not be underestimated. After the Wall Street Crash, investors withdrew their money. As a result, the money supply fell and the recession increased, because there was not enough money as a medium of exchange. Some economists even argue that the strict and overly cautious monetary policy pursued by the Federal Reserve System (the American central bank, founded in 1913), in an attempt to preserve

confidence in the system, was a major cause of the crisis. In 1933, 11,000 of the 25,000 American banks went bust, and economic transactions were severely hampered by the lack of a medium of exchange.

TEXT BOX 7.4 KEYNESIANS AND MONETARISTS

After the 1930s, government policy in both the Netherlands and many other countries was influenced by the ideas of John Maynard Keynes (1883–1946). A brilliant and influential British economist, Keynes argued that the government should intervene counter-cyclically in the event of a recession. The business cycle is a wave movement in the economy with a period of around five to eleven years. Counter-cyclical policy dampens this wave movement, as government spending during a recession supports effective demand (total demand from consumers and investors in the macroeconomy).

Budget deficits were an almost permanent feature of post-1945 economic policy, because people's expectations of government rose constantly, especially in relation to social security. The welfare state even led to the emergence of so-called 'automatic stabilizers' that supported consumer demand and levelled out cyclical disruptions in a Keynesian manner. After all, benefits kept the purchasing power of the unemployed more or less level.

Keynesian policy focuses on achieving full employment as a means of keeping up demand (for consumer goods and services). Counter-cyclical fiscal policy does not offer any solutions for the structural problems in an economy, however, because these are problems on the supply side. The supply side consists of the sum of all enterprises in an economy; this determines the economy's production capacity. When it was found around 1980 that many countries' economic problems were of a structural, not a cyclical, nature, governments subordinated the policy goal of achieving full employment to attempts to improve the entrepreneurial climate.

Economists disagree on which monetary policy to pursue. In the era of the Gold Standard, it was thought necessary to monitor the money supply, because too much money would lead to inflation and inflation would make exports more expensive. In the period of Keynesian government policy (c. 1945–80), the dominant view was that a larger money supply would lead to an increase in the number of transactions in the economy. More money can keep consumption going; in that case, a little inflation is not a bad thing. By contrast, orthodox monetarists such as Milton Friedman (1912–2006) argued for a monetary policy that prioritized the fight against inflation, stating that the amount of money should not be allowed to grow too much. According to monetarists, the money supply can only grow without the threat of inflation if production capacity increases accordingly (this is structural economic growth). Whether or not there is unemployment is less of an issue for these economists.

7.3
Institutional renewal and economic growth after 1945

NEW INSTITUTIONS The Second World War marked a turning point in the twentieth century, both politically and economically. Political relations were radically transformed after the fascist regimes were beaten by the alliance of democratic and communist countries. The Cold War began, splitting the industrialized world into a capitalist bloc and a communist bloc. Decolonization gave rise to many new countries. India became independent in 1947, for example, and Malaysia in 1957. Indonesia became independent from the Netherlands after a struggle that lasted from 1945 to 1949. In 1954, Cambodia, Laos and Vietnam became independent from France, and after a conflict of more than seven years, Algeria also severed its colonial ties with France in 1962. Algeria was followed by other African countries. In 1955, at the initiative of India's first prime minister, Jawaharlal Nehru, a large number of former colonies joined a movement that refused to side with either the West or the communist world: the 'Non-Aligned Movement'.

Between 1945 and 1989, the Cold War set the tone for international relations. Although the Cold War was initially a response to the political aspirations of a new superpower, the Soviet Union, there were also economic aspects to the rivalry. Until the 1970s, the Soviet model formed a powerful alternative to capitalism. The centrally planned economy functioned effectively for many years, particularly in relation to the planned production of capital goods for industry, with the aim of making the state more prosperous.

Global economic relations also underwent fundamental changes after 1945. With the two world wars and the economic crisis of the 1930s in mind, the international community arrived at two fundamental insights. First, there was a realization that more international coordination was needed to safeguard global free trade. Second, it was concluded that government needed to play a greater role in absorbing economic fluctuations, and that people could not trust blindly in the invisible hand of the market economy.

In 1944, before the war had ended, representatives of forty-four allied countries met at a conference in Bretton Woods in New Hampshire, in the United States, to discuss these matters (see Figure 7.3). Based on the plans developed by the leading economists John Maynard Keynes and Harry Dexter White (1892-1948), politicians made agreements that would shape the post-war international economic order. These concerned coordination in three international policy areas: the exchange rate system (the Bretton Woods system and the IMF), economic growth (the World Bank) and trade (the GATT).

The Bretton Woods system introduced a new monetary system that was more flexible than the Gold Standard, but nevertheless provided international stability (see Text Box 7.5). The great advantage of the new system was that the internationally accepted dollar could now function as a reserve currency; whereas most gold was stored in bank vaults, dollars were suitable for new transactions, national and international. There were global fixed exchange rates until 1971, which was good for trade and investment, because transaction costs fell as a result (see Chapter 2).

Gradually, though, anchoring the system to the dollar led to difficulties. In the 1960s, President Lyndon Johnson (1963–9) increased government spending. His Great Society policy entailed the expansion of social services, with the aim of reducing poverty and racial inequality. At the same time, the Vietnam War caused an unanticipated rise in government spending. The lack of budgetary discipline put pressure on the dollar, and other countries increasingly opted for the fixed value of gold. Based on the fixed gold-dollar exchange rate, countries could request to redeem their dollars from the American gold reserves stored in Fort Knox. In order to prevent the United States from losing all its gold, President Richard Nixon (1969–74) banned gold exports on 1 August 1971. This brought an end to the Bretton Woods exchange rate system. It was replaced by a system of floating exchange rates, in which demand and supply determined the value of the currency in the money market. Restrictions on the international movement of capital were gradually removed, and as a consequence of innovations in communication technology, 'hot money' was moved round the world in large quantities in search of the highest return. As a result, the financial system became more vulnerable to crises.

TEXT BOX 7.5 EXCHANGE RATES AFTER THE GOLD STANDARD

After the Second World War, the Bretton Woods system was founded (1944–71). In this system, the various currencies were pegged to gold and the dollar, and there was international coordination of capital flows. The dollar had a fixed gold value ($35 per ounce). The International Monetary Fund (IMF) was founded so that countries could respond to temporary balance of payments deficits by borrowing money from the IMF.

After 1971, a global system of exchange rates was created around a floating dollar. Attempts to keep the value within a certain range failed, but some countries succeeded in pegging their currencies to the dollar for a long period. In Europe, the European Monetary System (EMS) was created in 1979. This system kept the European currencies within a certain margin (the Exchange Rate Mechanism) for some time. The system was the target of speculative attacks, but it enjoyed a new lease of life in 1999 as the basis for the euro.

FIGURE 7.3 *The Mount Washington Hotel in Bretton Woods, New Hampshire, where the Bretton Woods Conference was held in 1944.*
© *Wikimedia Commons (public domain).*

Bretton Woods also saw the creation of the General Agreement on Tariffs and Trade (GATT). The GATT was a platform of what was initially a small number of countries, which made agreements on lowering trade tariffs in order to prevent a return to the protectionism of the 1930s. It moved cautiously from consultation round to consultation round, based on two important principles: reciprocity and non-discrimination. Reciprocity meant that if a country decided to open its borders to, say, the import of cars from another country, neither this country nor others were allowed to levy important tariffs on imports of cars from the first country. Non-discrimination meant that agreements between two countries immediately also applied to all other countries that had joined the GATT. This was known as the 'most favoured nation principle', meaning that all member states benefitted equally. Thus, in practice, every treaty immediately went from being bilateral to being multilateral. Another aspect of non-discrimination was the 'principle of national treatment': countries were not permitted to set higher quality or safety requirements for foreign products than those for their own domestic products. This prevented non-tariff barriers from being used to thwart free trade.

The successive rounds of GATT talks between 1948 and 1995 ensured a steady fall in import tariffs on industrial products, contributing significantly to globalization. In 1995, during the Uruguay Round, the GATT was transformed into the World Trade Organization (WTO). Rather than a temporary organization with treaties that had to be extended every round, there was now a permanent organization with a small secretariat in Geneva, and an increasing number of countries joined the WTO. As a consequence, it became very difficult for the wealthier countries to protect their own industry from cheap imports from China or India, for example.

The GATT and the WTO focused on reducing trade barriers in industry, which mainly benefitted industrialized countries. When it came to agriculture, the European Union, Japan and the United States were still deeply protectionist. Many developing countries that depended on the export of commodities were still subject to high international tariffs. It was not until the Doha Round, which was launched in 2001, that the WTO attempted to make agreements on trade in agricultural products.

IDEAS ABOUT DEVELOPMENT COOPERATION Agreements on international economic cooperation were also made at Bretton Woods. The International Bank for Reconstruction and Development (IBRD), later renamed the World Bank, was founded in order to promote the post-war economic recovery and would play a major role in developing countries. This institution provided long-term loans to countries for investment in large-scale infrastructural and industrial projects.

Development economics could profit from the insights that were gained in relation to industrialization in Western countries. In 1960, W. W. Rostow had formulated a universal model of the industrialization process,

TEXT BOX 7.6 ECONOMIC GROWTH AND THE ENVIRONMENTAL PROBLEM

The scale of the economic growth that began in the nineteenth century was unprecedented. Due to the use of fossil fuels (see Table 7.3) and technological improvements, the Malthusian ceiling could be broken; millions of people in the industrialized part of the world now had fewer concerns about how to meet their primary needs (enough food, accommodation, clothing). But the surge in economic growth also resulted in increasing air pollution, particularly in regions where coal was the cheapest source of energy and where smelting works were established, such as Donetsk and Magnitogorsk in Russia, Katowice in Poland, the Ruhr in Germany, the British Midlands, the Osaka-Kobe region of Japan and the regions around Los Angeles and the Great Lakes in the United States. Until long into the twentieth century, these were the engines of economic growth.

Pollution did not remain limited to those regions, however. In the 1960s, a striking fall in fish stocks in rivers and lakes in Southern Sweden and Norway was found to have been caused by coal combustion in Britain ('acid rain'). This was the starting signal for similar studies around the world. Iceland and Portugal had been spared much of the pollution, because the prevailing wind in Europe comes from the West, meaning that pollution from Britain had hardly affected them. Areas with highly calcareous soil (such as in Greece) were less affected than, for example, the soil in Canada or Scandinavia, which was very vulnerable to acid rain. Acidification was caused by emissions of sulphur and nitrogen, and damaged the natural environment in a region stretching from Birmingham to Bratislava, where there were many cars and lots of coal combustion.

Air pollution also crossed national borders elsewhere in the world. The Canadian environment was harmed by the economic growth around the Great Lakes, and Japan likewise noticed that many of the emissions associated with growth in China and Southern Korea affected the Japanese islands. A division gradually emerged in the world between countries that were net exporters of air pollution, which were reluctant to sign international agreements (the United States, China and Great Britain), and countries such as Japan, Canada and the Scandinavian countries, which were net importers of pollution and wanted international measures to reduce polluting emissions. In the late twentieth century, air quality in the wealthier countries improved again, thanks to the use of filters and improved technology. It was around this time, however, that people began to discover the harmful effects of carbon emissions on the atmosphere (the 'greenhouse effect'), which are much more difficult to combat. In short, while the use of fossil fuels formed an essential precondition for industrialization, in the twenty-first century their abolition forms an equally essential precondition for stopping global warming and safeguarding the future of the planet.

TABLE 7.3 *World Energy Consumption, Calculated in Million Tons of Oil, 1800–2010*

	1800	*1900*	*1990*	*2010*
Total	400	1,900	30,000	43,000
Index (1900 = 100)	21	100	1,580	2,257

Source: McNeill, *Something new under the sun*, 15; US Energy Information Administration.

consisting of the five different phases that a country had to pass through to become a modern economy. For example, the World Bank was inspired by Rostow's model to use large investments to incite the take-off into self-sustained growth in developing countries (the phase in which industry gets going).

In the 1970s and 1980s, a later generation of development economists emphasized the unequal power relations between poor and rich countries. According to the structuralist school (also known as the Dependencia school), the former colonizing countries were preventing poor countries from reaching economic maturity, because rich countries benefitted from the cheap supply of commodities. Policy advisers argued for less dependence on the world market in response to this exploitation, also known as 'neocolonialism'. They advocated a policy of import substitution, in the hope that domestic industries would be able to manufacture goods that had previously been imported.

During the 1980s, when it proved that import substitution was no recipe for rapid economic development (because there was too little demand in the domestic market to make a business viable, among other things), attention again shifted to the international market. According to more recent insights, the characteristics of reliable economic institutions (such as rights of ownership and contract law; see also Chapter 2) and good governance (non-corrupt public administration) are essential preconditions for sustainable and sustained economic growth, in addition to issues such as education and infrastructure.

There has been much debate among historians as to whether Western expansion and the resulting colonization of non-Western countries were overwhelmingly detrimental to the former colonies, or whether colonization also had a beneficial impact on these countries. For example, the British in India invested heavily in infrastructure, but at the same time they hindered the development of the domestic textile industry. One recent addition to this debate is the thesis by Daron Acemoglu, Simon Johnson and James Robinson, who argue that a reversal of fortune took place in non-Western areas: economic growth in areas that had flourishing economies before the Europeans arrived was held back by the colonizers, while those that had been poor or underdeveloped actually benefitted from the arrival of the Europeans.

UNBRIDLED GROWTH IN THE WORLD ECONOMY, 1945–73 The Second World War did great damage to Western European economies, yet with hindsight, many were astonished at the speed of the subsequent economic recovery. In around five years, Western Europe was back to the level of income of the peak pre-war years.

The greatest impediment to European reconstruction was the lack of dollars. To allow industry and infrastructure to recover, it was essential to import goods from the greatest and most modern industrial power, and American food imports were also desirable until European agriculture recovered. The United States therefore developed the European Recovery Programme, better known as Marshall Aid, named after the American secretary of state George Marshall (1880–1959). The most important function of Marshall Aid was to provide loans and aid in dollars, so that imports could be financed without upsetting the balance of payments yet further. Between 1948 and 1951, the total aid amounted to more than 23 billion dollars in loans and donations. By then, the Eastern European countries formed part of the Soviet sphere of influence and were therefore unable to accept the help that was offered.

The Netherlands was one of the largest beneficiaries of Marshall Aid. The country received 821 million dollars as a gift in aid and 150 million dollars in loans, together coming to an average of around 5.7 per cent of the national income. The government used the funds to finance large infrastructural projects in cooperation with private companies, build homes in the devastated cities of Rotterdam and Arnhem, reclaim the flooded Walcheren region and pay off part of the public debt. The system thus had a double effect: companies had dollars and the government had more to spend. It solved the shortage of dollars (since there was much demand for American goods, and little yet to sell to the American buyer). Moreover, the system allowed for necessary public investment in infrastructure, supporting recovery from war damage.

Marshall Aid brought some relief to food shortages, but the economic recovery was in fact already in full swing. The support was not indispensable, in other words, although it gave a huge psychological boost. In addition to solving the balance of payments problems, Marshall Aid had two important immaterial effects. First, the Americans made it conditional on the Western European countries entering into a process of economic cooperation. This led in 1948 to the founding of the Organization for European Economic Cooperation (OEEC), later reorganized as the Organization for Economic Co-operation and Development (OECD); an important think tank for international economic policy, based in Paris and still in existence. Non-European countries, including the United States and Japan, also became members. Second, Marshall Aid resulted in an enormous expansion of American exports to Europe. Significantly, this paved the way for decades of technological transfer from the United

States. To a great extent, European economic growth in this period was a matter of catching up with the United States, and this process was given a head start by Marshall Aid. For example, Marshall Aid was used to finance educational visits to American companies.

The 'Golden Years' of 1950–73 were characterized by a strikingly high level of economic growth. Average annual growth in the gross domestic product (GDP) of Northern and Western European countries was 4.6 per cent in this period (corrected for inflation). This was exceptionally high compared to growth between 1913 and 1950, or between 1890 and 1913 (see Table 7.4).

The Dutch post-war recovery was faster than that of any other Western European country. In 1945, national income had fallen back to 1912 levels, yet it had already returned to the pre-war peak in 1947. It would be incorrect to suppose that the entire war had been a disaster for the economy. Until 1942, Dutch industry had been flooded with German orders. Along with hoarding by the population and government expansionism, this gave a huge boost to the economy. As a result, the Netherlands enjoyed an economic boom between May 1940 and the end of 1941, with almost full employment and a sharp drop in poverty. GDP rose in 1942 to 107 per cent compared to 1938, but then fell back to a meagre 86 per cent in 1944.

After the reconstruction, the Dutch government set its sights on industrialization, with robust growth in the chemicals and electrical engineering sectors. The share of the agricultural sector shrank further (see Chapter 9, Table 9.3). From the 1960s onwards, problems emerged in the mining, textiles and shipbuilding industries. By contrast, there was strong expansion in the services sector, especially in financial services. In the 1950s, the government used strict wage regulation (the 'guided wage policy') to limit

TABLE 7.4 *Economic Growth in North-western Europe, in Percentages per Year, 1890–1992*

	Growth in GDP in real terms	Population growth	Growth in GDP per capita	Growth per capita per hour worked
1890–1913	2.6	0.8	1.7	1.6
1913–1950	1.4	0.5	1.0	1.9
1950–1973	4.6	0.7	3.8	4.7
1973–1992	2.0	0.3	1.7	2.7

The table shows Belgium, Denmark, Great Britain, Finland, France, Italy, the Netherlands, Norway, Austria, West Germany, Sweden and Switzerland.
Source: Crafts and Toniolo, *Economic growth in Europe since 1945*, 2.

the wage rises that were expected with economic growth. This stimulated investment, boosted competitiveness and kept unemployment levels low. During the 1960s, however, wages started to rise substantially: on the one hand, due to the trade unions' demand that employees also benefit from the economic growth, and on the other hand, because employers were facing shortages in the labour market and were therefore prepared to pay higher salaries, particularly in profitable industries.

EUROPEAN INTEGRATION From the 1950s onwards, there was increasing economic and political cooperation within Europe. The Netherlands, which had by then embarked on a course of rapid industrial expansion, was actively involved in European integration from the outset. In hindsight, the loss of its colonial empire in the East in 1945–9 and 1962 was to some extent compensated by the new economic possibilities in Europe. The European Union developed economically into a very successful trading bloc. It had 28 member states by 2013, providing a counterweight to the power of the United States, China and Japan in a globalizing world economy (see Text Box 7.7 and Text Box 8.3).

Let us briefly reflect on the advantages of trading blocs. Aside from taking part in large multilateral negotiations, such as the GATT, it is often attractive for countries to conclude treaties with several neighbouring trading partners in order to promote mutual trade without exposing their own economy to the wider world. This results in trade blocs. The European Union is the best-known (and most successful) example, but there are dozens of such blocs around the world, including Mercosur in South America, ASEAN in Southeast Asia, and NAFTA (later USMCA) in North America. When a country opens its borders to trade with neighbouring countries, competition and upscaling lead to greater efficiency. In a globalizing economy, the trade bloc in question will be better equipped to compete on the world market. Viewed in this way, trade blocs not only put a brake on globalization (because they exclude the rest of the world), but they can also prepare the ground for further globalization.

The formation of the European trade bloc began with the founding of the European Coal and Steel Community (ECSC) by six countries: France, Germany, Italy and the Benelux (Belgium, Netherlands and Luxembourg had formed the Benelux customs union in 1944). After the European Community (EC) was founded with the Treaty of Rome in 1958, the aim was to create a common European market. But this aim would not be met until 1986, with the signing of the Single European Act by the then twelve members. The 1992 Maastricht Treaty intensified monetary cooperation by setting the objective of forming an economic and monetary union, as expressed by renaming the bloc the European Union. This meant making agreements to form a single currency. The Economic and Monetary Union (EMU) was established in 1999, locking together the currencies of the twelve member states, and the euro was introduced as the European currency in 2002.

A whole body of literature has arisen on the motives underlying this integration process. The political motive was that after two devastating wars, the countries of Europe wanted to achieve a long-lasting peace (especially between France and Germany). Cooperation would also help to strengthen Europe's negotiating position, for example in the GATT. In an economic respect, the EU brought expanded export opportunities for the member states and improved prospects for economic growth, thanks to the increase in productivity. The latter results from growing competition, economies of scale and transfer of technology. A report by the European Commission in 2003 estimated the advantages of the internal market between 1992 and 2002 to have been as follows: around 2.5 million extra jobs had been created, EU income had increased by 877 billion euros (5,700 euros per household) and there had been a sharp fall in customs-related bureaucracy.

Aside from opening up markets, an important element of European policy was to stimulate agricultural cooperation, in order to protect the large farming sector from the scrapping of tariff barriers. This was particularly important for France, where farmers made up nearly a quarter of the working population in the 1950s. The Netherlands still had a relatively large agrarian sector at that time, too (around one-sixth of total employment; see Table 9.3). The political objective of securing the national food supply was also a factor, so soon after the Second World War. Minimum prices were introduced for agricultural products, meaning that it paid to scale up and mechanize. The policy's success, on the one hand, led to its failure on the other: there was a massive rise in agricultural production, leading to a 'butter mountain' and a 'milk lake', funded by large subsidies. In some years, agricultural policy comprised 60 per cent of the total EU budget. Dutch farmers profited handsomely from the EU's agricultural policy. There was less focus on agriculture after 1990, when the priority shifted to improving infrastructure; in 2007, subsidies for improving road-building in the economically weaker member states took up around 30 per cent of the EU budget.

The unique characteristic of European cooperation is that countries voluntarily relinquish their authority in certain areas (see also Chapter 8). In an economic respect, the EU should be seen as a strong trading bloc, consisting of an internal market with no tariff barriers. This is the EU's greatest achievement: cooperation has led to increasing prosperity and higher productivity and competitiveness.

The Netherlands has the EU to thank for much of its growth in the post-war era. A relatively large share of Dutch exports (around 60 per cent) went to countries in Europe, while a larger share of imports came from non-European countries. After monetary unification, the Netherlands did relatively well out of the strong currency: this led to imports becoming cheaper, while exports – which mainly went to other member states, anyway – suffered little as a result.

> **TEXT BOX 7.7**
> **MILESTONES IN EUROPEAN COOPERATION**
>
> 1951 Treaty of Paris: founding of the ECSC at the initiative of Jean Monnet, the 'architect of European unification'.
>
> 1957 Treaty of Rome: founding of the European Economic Community (EEC), a common market.
>
> 1965 Merger Treaty: founding of the European Community (EC).
>
> 1986 Single European (Market) Act: improvement of the common market with the free movement of capital and labour.
>
> 1992 Maastricht Treaty: the EC becomes the EU. Intention to found an Economic and Monetary Union (EMU). Agreements on a maximum budget deficit of 3 per cent and maximum government debt of 60 per cent of gross domestic product (GDP).
>
> 1997 Treaty of Amsterdam, Euro Stability and Growth Pact.
>
> 1999 Exchange rates fixed between participants in the EMU.
>
> 2002 Introduction of the euro, the single European currency, by twelve countries: Belgium, Germany, Spain, France, Greece, Ireland, Italy, Luxembourg, the Netherlands, Austria, Portugal and Finland. Great Britain, Denmark and Sweden remain outside the eurozone.
>
> 2020 Great Britain withdraws from EU.

THE EXPANSION OF THE WELFARE STATE Another far-reaching social and economic change that occurred in Western countries after the Second World War was the establishment and development of the welfare state; that is to say, a system of social provision for all inhabitants of a democratically governed market economy, as distinct from a state in which all means of production are controlled by the state. In the 1950s and 1960s, most Western countries introduced social provisions to support the elderly, the sick, the disabled and the unemployed (see chapter 8). This system was closely related to economic developments. Social provisions were facilitated by economic growth, which led to higher tax revenues.

In the Netherlands (and also in Belgium, Germany and Sweden, for example), the nature of the relations between employers' and employees' organizations also played a positive role in the development of the welfare state. Employers' associations and trade unions regularly met in consultations on all kinds of socio-economic issues. These not only included negotiations on wages, but also on issues such as participation, benefits and the minimum wage. For example, national consultative bodies such as the Labour Foundation (STAR, founded in 1945) and the Social and Economic

Council (SER, founded in 1950) played a key role in the introduction of the guided wage policy in the 1950s.

There has been a fierce debate among economists about whether a generous welfare state hinders economic growth. When the government intervenes in the market by providing subsidies, this upsets the market equilibrium. The tax burden deters entrepreneurs from developing initiatives (after all, they are deprived of part of the proceeds). In the labour market, too, benefits are thought to remove the incentives for the unemployed or the sick to get back to work. On the other hand, the welfare state can also have positive economic effects in the form of a healthy and well-educated population, good collective provisions, fewer deep recessions, and clean and safe public space.

Not only did the benefits cost money, but the idea that the state should take responsibility for all kinds of issues led to a growing civil service. The development of social security, for example, prompted a huge expansion of central government. In the optimistic economic climate of the 'Golden Years', people accepted the idea of massive government spending. By around 1983, government expenditure in the Netherlands and Scandinavia had risen to more than 60 per cent of national income. The share in Great Britain was 47 per cent at that time, and 37 per cent in the United States (see Chapter 8).

7.4
Changing priorities and new players, 1973–2010

In the 1970s, the economic conditions worsened around the world. Inflation reared its head, world trade collapsed after fixed exchange rates were abandoned, and many countries faced high unemployment. In 1973, the oil-producing countries, united in the Organization of the Petroleum Exporting Countries (OPEC), caused the first oil crisis in response to America's support for Israel in the Yom Kippur War. The Arab countries raised the oil price by as much as 70 per cent, and cut monthly oil production by 5 per cent. They announced an embargo against the United States and several European countries, including the Netherlands. After the first oil crisis, trade and economic growth stagnated around the world, and the oil and commodities prices rose.

The European economies also faced a number of vulnerabilities that were now coming to light. Constantly rising wages meant rising labour costs for employers. In a number of countries, including the Netherlands, social benefits and civil service salaries (the government was now the country's largest employer) were linked to wages in the private sector, meaning that they rose automatically. Social security premiums also led to a rise in gross incomes. As labour costs were reflected in higher prices, this resulted in a wage-price spiral that was hard to break. At the same time, all kinds of rules were introduced in the 'Golden Years' that made the labour market inflexible, such as employment protection and measures to prevent temporary employment contracts. Combined with the external shocks in the world market, this resulted in a decade of stagnating economic growth, rising inflation and growing unemployment. This was known as 'stagflation'.

The Netherlands was able to weather the first oil crisis relatively well, because the government allowed expenditure to rise in line with Keynesian maxims, made it easier for consumers to obtain credit, and drew on natural gas revenues (particularly in order to pay for social security). After the second oil crisis in 1979, though, there was no room for manoeuvre left in the economy; unemployment had risen sharply, government expenditure was already extremely high, and the natural gas exports had pushed up the exchange rate of the guilder, making exports expensive (economists call this 'Dutch disease').

Income from natural gas supported generous social spending, but also formed an incentive to develop energy-intensive sectors in the economy, such as the chemical industry and horticulture (flowers, flower bulbs). For decades it provided industry with cheap electricity. The transformation of the Dutch coal mines into the chemical multinational DSM in 1965 was heavily subsidized with gas earnings. The energy-intensive character of the Dutch export sector enlarges the challenge to make the transition to a sustainable economy in the twenty-first century. The extraction of natural gas was concentrated in the province of Groningen and used to contribute several billions of euros to the treasury annually. However, it caused severe earthquakes in Groningen from 2003 onwards, damaging houses and farms. Social unrest led to the subsequent decision in 2020 to make an end to Dutch gas extraction.

THE 1980S AND 1990S: SUPPLY-SIDE POLICY AND RECOVERING ECONOMIC GROWTH In the early 1980s, Ronald Reagan (president of the United States, 1981–9) and Margaret Thatcher (prime minister of Great Britain, 1979–90) promoted an economic policy that revolved around recovery in the private sector. Embracing the free market, they focused on the supply side of the economy. Supply-side policy was accompanied by tax cuts, and also, in theory, lower government spending. In practice, though, the budget deficit rose sharply under Reagan. Ideologically, the rehabilitation of the private sector was accompanied by efforts to curtail the power of the trade unions. The key economic objective was now economic growth, not full employment and counter-cyclic Keynesian policy (see Text Box 7.4). In practice, this was translated into deep cuts in social provisions and, initially, rising unemployment.

Based on a stringent monetarist policy (see Text Box 7.4), central banks began to monitor the money supply in the economy more strictly in order to curb inflation. In the United States, the president of the Federal Reserve Board, Paul Volcker, intervened forcefully by raising the base rate (the rate paid by private banks to the central bank) to as much as 21 per cent in 1981. Although the so-called Volcker shock allowed the Federal Reserve to wrest control of inflation, it had the negative effect of contributing to the debt crisis in developing countries, because the latter suddenly had to pay much more interest on their considerable foreign debts. This transformed the dormant balance of payment deficits in developing countries into an acute problem. Cost-savings were made in the wealthy West by shifting industrial production to so-called 'low-wage economies', but this also brought massive redundancies and long-term unemployment in affected sectors in Western countries (such as shipbuilding and machine-building). Inventions in the field of ICT facilitated more efficient operational management and improved international communication. Viewed as a whole, worldwide investment and productivity rose during the 1980s, and there was strong growth in international trade, but this was achieved at the expense of the developing countries.

THE NETHERLANDS IN THE 1980S: AFTER THE WASSENAAR AGREEMENT
The governments led by Prime Minister Lubbers (1982–94) introduced supply-side policy in the Netherlands in the form of a moderate variant of Reaganomics and Thatcherism. This 'three-track policy' was a combination of government cuts, labour market policy and private sector incentives. The budget deficit was reduced and aid to ailing companies (previously justified as a way to preserve jobs) was halted.

The nature of the welfare state changed. Economic growth became the main priority in the Netherlands, too, at the expense of the link between wages and benefits, for example. Benefits were reformed; the emphasis shifted from providing income security via benefits to ensuring maximum participation in the labour market.

In the final quarter of the twentieth century, four further important developments took place in the welfare state, independently of the cuts. First, a process of individualization occurred (see chapter 9), meaning that care within the family was no longer taken for granted. Second, a pattern of rising expectations developed in medical care. Third, the cost of caring for the elderly and medical expenditure rose due to rising life expectancy (the ageing population). Fourth, large deficits in the government budget were no longer accepted (as a consequence of measures to combat inflation and European exchange rate policy). This necessitated stricter monitoring of social spending, which was again threatening to get out of hand. As a result, there seemed to be an almost permanent urgency to the budget cuts.

This problem complicated the negotiations between employers, employees and the trade unions, the latter retaining their importance as an official interlocutor in national consultative bodies, despite falling memberships. The consultations in the Netherlands nevertheless managed to achieve consensus on a number of occasions, usually based on a shared focus on the employment problem. In what later became known as the 'Wassenaar Agreement' (1982), for example, a policy of wage restraint was agreed in exchange for reduced working hours, in order to generate more jobs. This essentially came down to a redistribution of the available jobs and an active labour market policy by the government. The Wassenaar Agreement was followed by the 'New Course' agreement of 1993. The extensive rounds of consultations drew international praise in the 1990s because it resulted in a so-called Dutch employment miracle (see Chart 7.2), but a number of caveats should be added. The measures relating to labour relations, social security and labour market policy in the 1980s and 1990s created more jobs, but they were only possible thanks to the upturn in the global economy, successful European integration (both of which resulted in a growing export market), and the spectacular growth in house prices, which led to substantial growth in the assets of certain income groups. They also hinged on flexibilization of the labour force, resulting in a greater fall in the number of tenured full-time jobs than in other European countries.

THE 'EAST ASIAN MIRACLE' In the meantime, part of the non-Western world had pushed forward in the catch-up race with the rich West. The first countries to catch up were Japan and the 'Asian Tigers': Taiwan, South Korea, Hong Kong and Singapore.

The way in which the Japanese state managed, protected and financed the country's economic development is an example of catch-up growth with a major role for the government, consistent with Gerschenkron's model (see Text Box 7.2). Japan's modernization began with the Meiji restauration in 1868, when a new government came to power that was more open to imitating Western industrialization. Between 1880 and 1915, industrial production in Japan quadrupled and the production of textiles rose tenfold, no less.

On the eve of the Second World War, Japan's income per capita was still only a little higher than the Dutch equivalent in 1870, but the country grew rapidly in the post-war period (see Table 7.1). The economy was organized around large conglomerates of companies that were active in multiple sectors. Before the Second World War, these business groups consisted of *zaibatsu*: conglomerates in the hands of a single family. After 1945, the *zaibatsu* were dismantled by the

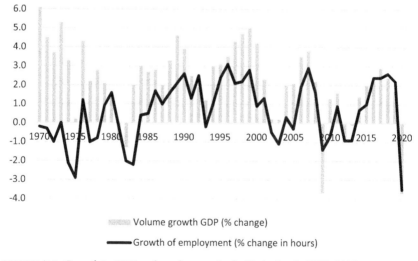

CHART 7.2 *Growth in GDP and employment in the Netherlands, 1970–2013.*
Source: CBS Statline.

allies. The individual companies did not disappear, but were regrouped into new conglomerates, organized around banks. These new industrial conglomerates were known as *keiretsu*. The emphasis was often on the vertical integration of commercial activities (from the raw materials to the end product).

In the early 1950s, the Japanese government set its sights on expanding the steel industry. This industry tripled between 1963 and 1970, thanks to strong growth in the domestic market and in exports. In particular after the first oil crisis in 1973, Japan was able to benefit from its modern, efficient and very competitive steel industry. In the 1970s, the Japanese government shifted its growth focus to advanced technology. Japan set the goal of competing with the market leader, the United States, especially in the semiconductor industry, which manufactured silicon chips with microscopically small electronic circuits that were etched onto silicon plates. To the annoyance and anger of the Americans, Japan succeeded in building up a large market share in this industry thanks to an aggressive, state-supported trade policy, which included keeping the Japanese yen artificially low in order to promote exports.

The Japanese system led to a kind of capitalist economy that was completely different from those in Western Europe or the United States, known as 'collective capitalism'. As implied by the term, in this model the individual is subordinate to the collective interest. Another name for the Japanese model is 'developmental state capitalism', which indicates that economic modernization serves the social and political ambitions of the state. Although Japan's social provisions are in the hands of the private sector, there is a high level of trust between businesses and the government.

The Japanese system did not converge with economies in the West, however. After 1985, the rising value of the yen meant that export-led growth (economic growth stimulated by exports) was no longer an option. At that point, a logical policy choice would have been to stimulate domestic consumption, open up the economy to imports from other countries, pursue deregulation and reduce the role of the state. With this strategy, Japan would have begun to resemble Europe and the United States much more closely. Japan chose a different approach, however, known as Japan's 'Asian strategy'. The government continued with its highly statist policy and focus on exports, while labour-intensive production was shifted to other Asian countries where wages were lower. As a result, Japan became more tightly integrated with other economies in the Asian region. Large sums were invested in neighbouring countries in East Asia and South-east Asia. There was a regional division of labour consisting of vertically organized production networks: Japan was responsible for management and design, while production took place in Malaysia or Indonesia, for example.

In 1993, the World Bank analysed the strong growth in East Asia and described it as the 'East Asian Miracle'. The macro-economic stability, investment in human capital (the educational level of the working population) and market-oriented economic policy were singled out for particular praise. The Asian financial crisis of 1997–8, which hit Thailand,

South Korea and Indonesia particularly hard, took the shine off this success; but in the following years, these economies recovered remarkably quickly.

THE COLLAPSE OF THE COMMUNIST BLOC AND RAPID GROWTH IN CHINA
The decades between 1950 and 1970 were also a time of growth in the Communist bloc. One structural problem, however, was that consumers were less well served under communism. It was not possible to plan the demand side effectively (ignoring or underestimating actual consumer demand), resulting in incorrect resource allocations and scarcity. Soviet citizens endured long waits to buy basic consumer goods such as telephones, refrigerators or cars. The technological gap with the West also widened. Computers were a rarity in management, for example, whereas computerization took off rapidly in Western firms. High-quality technology had to be imported, and exports from the Eastern bloc lacked competitiveness in the world market. This led to a growing balance of payments deficit in communist countries.

Until the 1970s, the Soviet Union had always assisted Eastern bloc economies that ran into difficulties, but the country became increasingly unable to provide aid due to its own growing debt. In addition, military spending remained high. As aid from the Soviet Union tailed off, various countries in the Eastern bloc gradually began to extricate themselves from the strict planned economy, a process that was accelerated by the revolutions of 1989 (see Chapter 8).

The transition from planned to market economies was not optimal, however, partly as a result of political instability. Property rights were not formulated clearly, for instance, allowing wily traders to make huge profits from selling collective firms. The fact that economies were often liberalized too rapidly created great uncertainty, meaning that many former Eastern bloc countries, including Poland, Bulgaria and Ukraine, went through difficult periods in the 1990s.

For much of the twentieth century, China was the world's other large communist bloc, alongside the Soviet Union. From 1949, this enormous country of more than 9.5 million km^2 was ruled by a Marxist-Leninist regime that kept a tight rein on the economy. We can identify several striking phases in China's economic development that illustrate the extent of the Communist Party's power. In the early 1950s, under party chairman Mao Zedong (1893–1976), local initiatives were still encouraged under the slogan 'Let a hundred flowers bloom'. In subsequent years, however, policy became increasingly centralist and dictatorial. In 1958, the Great Leap Forward began; an attempt by Mao to transform China into a modern, self-sufficient and collectivized economy, and make it a superpower. Independent farms were collectivized as 'people's communes', and farmers were encouraged to build steel furnaces on their land in order to smelt iron (despite China having very little iron ore). This policy disrupted the economy and resulted in famine. From 1966, 'social re-education' during the Cultural Revolution was likewise an example of centrally driven government intervention.

After Mao's death in 1976, market-oriented reforms were gradually introduced in China. Like other Asian countries, China copied certain aspects of Japan's success, such as keeping the exchange rate artificially low in order to stimulate exports, resulting in huge foreign reserves. Unlike Japan, though, China allowed foreign direct investment in the economy, which resulted in the presence of many Western companies. It was only in 2005–8 that China started to allow the renminbi (yuan) to appreciate relative to the dollar, but Chinese exports remained cheap. After China's accession to the WTO in 2001, Chinese products could not be deterred with trade barriers, either. The growth of China's economy from the late 1980s was nothing less than spectacular. As a result, China became the second largest economy in the world after the United States, based on purchasing power in 2007 (see Chart 7.3). If we look at income per capita of the population, we get a different picture: income per capita in China slowly increased to roughly match Brazil's level in 2006, but it is still far below that of Argentina, Russia and the OECD countries.

There are more reasons why China cannot be described as a 'second Japan' in the period between 1990 and 2005. Three differences in particular are striking. First, China was a dual economy, due to the massive differences between the dynamic Southern and Eastern coasts and the agrarian interior, which trailed behind. It is sometimes even described as an enclave economy,

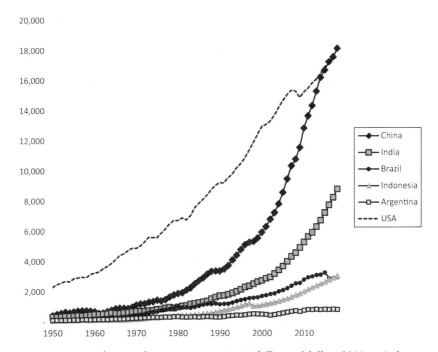

CHART 7.3 *GDP for several emerging economies, in billions of dollars, 2011 equivalents, based on purchasing power parity, 1950–2018.*
Source: Maddison Project Database, version 2020.

because the huge profits made the industrialized Special Economic Zones (such as the province of Guangdong's city of Shenzhen, which grew from being a fishing village into a city with over a million inhabitants) had very little impact on the standard of living in the vast interior, with its hundreds of millions of small farmers. Second, a large share of the exports was manufactured by subsidiaries of American, Japanese and Taiwanese multinationals. A large share of the profits flowed out of the country as a result, and only a small share ended up in the domestic economy in the form of wages and taxes. This is different from Japan, which was careful to keep production in Japanese hands. Third, a sizeable Chinese trade surplus was only able to emerge on the back of significant foreign demand; if this were to collapse, this would severely undermine China's status as an economic 'superpower'. This all changed with growing prosperity in the first decades of the twenty-first century, and domestic consumption accounted for an increasing share.

Due to higher wages in the cities, some production was moved to Vietnam, Bangladesh and India. Despite this, it is hard to imagine world trade without a considerable share of Chinese goods: in 2010, 70 per cent of all of the world's toys were manufactured in China, along with 60 per cent of bicycles and 55 per cent of all laptops.

Since 2000, Chinese foreign direct investment has increased enormously all over the world, particularly to countries in Africa and Latin America with large reserves of raw materials, but also in Europe. Since 2012, Chinese investments in Africa even exceeded that of the United States. This reflects the growing power of China in the world economy. With the 'One Belt, One Road' initiative that started in 2013 (the name refers to the ancient Silk Road), China began developing large-scale investment in infrastructure to further strengthen the trade with and investment flows to Eastern Europe, Africa and the Middle East. One of the main strategic reasons for the Chinese to expand internationally is to secure future access to resources such as oil, gas and minerals. China increases its political and economic influence over these countries as a result of their indebtedness.

A broader Asian initiative, in which China plays a leading role, is the Asian Infrastructure Investment Bank (AIIS) that was founded in Beijing in 2015. This multilateral development bank is sometimes viewed as an Asian alternative for the IMF and the World Bank. A number of European countries, among which the Netherlands, became a member of this organisation soon after its inception, signifying the shift away from a global economy dominated by the Western powers.

CONVERGENCE OR DIVERGENCE? If every country were to open its economy up to the free market, would this ultimately lead to a single, successful economic model? This would mean that industrialized economies would increasingly start to resemble one another; this is known as 'convergence'. In this case, not only income levels, but also economic institutions would converge. The opposite case, whereby we see widening differences, is known as 'divergence'.

In the period between c. 1980 and the credit crisis of 2008, economists and politicians often turned to the market to improve economic processes. In the Netherlands, for example, state-owned companies such as PTT were privatized, housing corporations and sickness insurance funds fell into private hands, and there was increasing reliance on the private sector in telecommunications, public transport and healthcare.

The idea that coordination in the economy would best be achieved by market forces was not only expressed in supply-side policy in the domestic market, but also in international policy. The term 'Washington Consensus', for example, is used to refer to the ideas in the 1990s that dominated institutions such as the World Bank and the IMF (which, together with the US Department of the Treasury, were at walking distance from one another in Washington), and that determined these institutions' approach to developing countries. These covered a series of policy priorities, such as fiscal discipline (eliminating budget deficits), cutting government subsidies and introducing market forces in interest rates, trade liberalization, privatization and deregulation. Especially after the Asian crisis of 1997–8, when the IMF forced several Southeast Asian countries to introduce reforms based on the Western model, there was significant criticism of these 'neoliberal' principles, and growing awareness that economies' different institutional characteristics also necessitated different, specific forms of policy. This insight also had key implications for development cooperation. Just as in Asia, economic growth in developing countries could not be stimulated by forcing countries unilaterally to resort to market forces.

Thus, we have not seen the emergence of a completely uniform institutional framework for countries' economies. The complex of rules, laws, preferences, traditions and customs emerges over time and is also culturally determined. Economies do not necessarily converge rapidly towards a single model in practice.

After the credit crisis of 2007–8, there was yet further criticism of far-reaching market deregulation. As we can see from Chart 7.2, the Netherlands suffered the consequences of the credit crisis (higher unemployment, less growth). Neoliberal market policy drew increasing criticism as a result.

Monetarist views, which were a vital ingredient of neoliberal policy and had been so characteristic of the period 1980–2007, also changed after the credit crisis. In the context of preventing deflation and the almost desperate stimulation of growth, the need for an ample money supply was reconsidered. To stabilize markets and stimulate economic growth, American and European central banks increased the money supply with enormous amounts of dollars and euros. Both the US Federal Reserve and the European Central Bank attempted to stimulate growth by adopting quantitative easing (a policy of providing cheap money by acquiring sovereign debt), as did the Japanese, British and many other central banks. In the wake of the financial crisis, from 2009 onwards, the European debt crisis created instability in financial markets, due to the high level of government debt in Southern European countries.

Between 2016 and 2017, for example, the ECB spent 60–80 billion euros per month on purchasing government bonds in the eurozone. In 2021, this trend was amplified when, faced with the Covid-19 crisis, many countries increased government intervention to support the private sector with loans. Remarkably, unlike in the 1970s and 1980s, inflation did not rise to unsustainable levels between 2008 and 2021.

As a result of neoliberal policy in many areas, from c. 1980 the Dutch economy became more liberal in many ways, but the institutional framework retained certain typical characteristics. In the twentieth century, the Netherlands characterized itself as a liberal country with strong corporatist structures. As a consequence of 'pillarization' (the term used to describe the socio-denominational separation of society), the consultations between different economic groups (entrepreneurs, trade unions, the government) were frequent and institutionalized in nature. Strikingly, this consultative culture ('polder model', 'platform economy'), with its coordinating mechanisms and relatively strong tendency to redistribute wealth, retained its position in an open economy that aspired to be globally competitive.

Remarkably, after the credit crisis and the subsequent eurocrisis, the Dutch government remained a steady supporter of fiscal discipline, despite being one of the EU countries with the lowest budget deficits and lowest levels of government debt. In 2012, even the IMF (formerly much in favour of balanced budgets) criticized the Netherlands for its austerity, but Dutch coalition governments continued to cut public expenditure. The Dutch

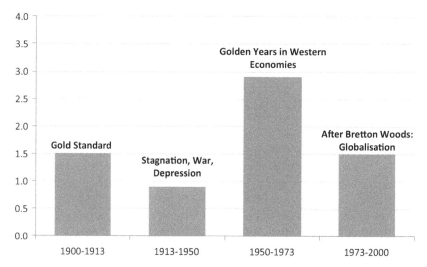

CHART 7.4 *Four periods of expansion. Global economic growth in percentages, 1900–2000.*
Source: IMF, Angus Maddison, Statistics and World Population, GDP.

welfare state, which had been so generous in the 1970s, thus retrenched its social entitlements considerably, while healthcare expenditure continued to rise. By 2020 the Dutch coordinated economy had become a much more liberal economy.

Summary

The world economy has undergone significant changes in the last 200 years. The nineteenth century was characterized by gradual internationalization and liberalization, resulting in a liberal era in which colonial empires traded around the world. The twentieth century began with prosperity and trust, and then experienced a period of stagnation and recession after 1914. After 1945, the richer part of the world enjoyed unprecedented growth, based on technology and rising productivity. The colonial empires were dismantled, but not all of the new states that emerged following decolonization were able to imitate the economic successes of the West (Chart 7.4).

Finally, let us return to the questions that we posed at the beginning of this chapter:

1. Globalization in the nineteenth century was mainly driven by the liberal trade policy pursued by Great Britain, the economic great power that dominated much of the world's economy. After the Second World War, the Bretton Woods Agreements gave an important boost to globalization. In the 1980s, the rise of the Internet made it possible for capital to flow rapidly from one part of the world to another. These developments involved both convergence and divergence. Convergence could be seen in economic policy, dominated first by Keynes and later by monetarism; in addition, most Western countries developed some kind of welfare state. Despite this, we also see signs of divergence. No single dominant type of economy emerged, although it was clear that the same economic forces were influential around the world (exchange rates, for example). Advanced economies adhered to different economic institutions, such as coordination systems or business networks. Moreover, for many years, Europe's Eastern bloc followed a relatively successful economic path, the drawbacks of which only clearly came to light in the final decades of the twentieth century.

2. The emergence of the European Union can be seen as a driving force of globalization; it ensured that the European countries could continue to participate in the world economy as an important bloc, while benefitting from the advantages of the competitive internal market.

3. In the early nineteenth century, the Netherlands had an advanced economy, which was a legacy of the Early Modern period. It lost its head start, however, when British industrialization gathered pace. The Dutch economy was characterized by a modern services sector

and modern agriculture. The country benefitted from its colonial possessions, especially those in the Dutch East Indies. However, it was slow to industrialize. In the second half of the twentieth century, the Netherlands retained its position as one of the most prosperous countries in the world; as a small, open economy, it benefitted significantly from European integration from the outset.

8

State formation, democratization and social care
Sociopolitical developments

LEO LUCASSEN

In Chapter 3, we saw how the constant competition between European states gave rise to a situation of almost constant warfare. In this permanent struggle for existence, the model of the territorial state (Prussia, France, Great Britain) proved better suited to the circumstances than, for example, the decentralized republican model of countries such as the Netherlands and Switzerland, or German and Italian city states. In the nineteenth century, this model was transformed into the nation state, which would likewise eventually demonstrate its superiority to a form of political organization that had dominated large parts of Europe (and also beyond) throughout much of history: namely, the imperial state, in which different ethnic groups were governed by a single ruler. The 'long' nineteenth century, which began with the French Revolution and ended with the First World War, saw the successive collapse of the Spanish, Ottoman and Austro-Hungarian empires. From the Second World War onwards, the colonial overseas empires that had been built up by European powers (Great Britain, France, the Netherlands, Portugal) and Japan were also disbanded. Nor did the Russian Empire, which had been transformed after 1920 into the Union of Soviet Socialist Republics, survive the twentieth century. Of all the old empires, it was only China that remained intact, despite a series of revolts and revolutions between 1850 and 1950. Finally, decolonization in Latin America, Africa and Asia led to the further dissemination of the nation state model.

State development took place along similar lines, in certain respects, but there were also considerable variations. The common factor was the fundamental change in the distribution of power within states, whereby the central state gathered more power and widened the scope of its tasks and powers. In the area of social policy, this could lead to far-reaching forms of intervention in people's personal lives in order to change their social behaviour (social engineering). On the other hand, national citizens formed all kinds of organizations to represent common interests, so as to influence state policy from below (civil society). The way and the degree to which citizens had a say in state governance varied significantly, however, as did the social policies that were followed.

State formation, democratization and social policy are the core themes of this chapter. We will focus on the following questions:

1. What were the most important consequences of the rise of the nation state for the relationship between the state and its citizens?
2. Under which conditions could democracies best develop?
3. Which factors determined the rise and nature of social policies, and what approach was taken in the Netherlands?

As elsewhere in this book, we will continually consider the interaction between developments in the Netherlands and the wider world.

8.1
Nation states, social engineering and international cooperation

After the Napoleonic Wars, European states were very different from how they had been in the Early Modern era. In *c.* 1800, the state formation process entered a new phase, which the historical sociologist Charles Tilly has called 'direct rule'. Typical features were an increase in the power of the central state and the unification of the legal and administrative system (see Text Box 8.1). After the fall of Napoleon and the Congress of Vienna (1814–15), power in European states increasingly shifted from the towns, churches, guilds and aristocracy to national governments. States became unitary states; the 'territorial consolidation' model now clearly prevailed (see Chapter 3). The position of the aristocracy weakened; one important step was the abolition of serfdom in Russia (1861) and parts of the Ottoman Empire, such as Wallachia, in 1856. Other institutions of the ancien régime, such as guilds, civic militias and other corporative unions, managed to persist for a little longer (certainly in Southern and Eastern Europe); but they, too, would eventually make way for more open and democratic associations, such as trade unions, chambers of commerce and government agencies.

The new model of the nation state that had developed in Western Europe spread to other parts of the world. The circulation of ideas through the veins of empire led to Atlantic revolutions, starting in North America in

1776. This process should not be interpreted as one of simple diffusion, however, as this longing for independence was fused with existing notions of resistance against oppression among subaltern populations in the New World, especially enslaved Africans in the Caribbean. Their quest for freedom and equality was accelerated by Atlantic networks of deserting soldiers, sailors, indentured servants and runaway slaves who met on board ships, in port cities and maroon communities. After the occupation of Spain by Napoleon's troops in 1808, the independence virus spread rapidly, thanks in part to the charismatic role played by Simón Bolívar, who was born in Caracas in 1783. After the independence of the former French slave island of Haiti in 1804, between 1810 (Mexico) and 1825 (Bolivia) almost every Latin American country broke away from the metropoles of Spain and Portugal, to continue as independent nation states.

The opposite occurred in Africa, when the continent was largely carved up by the imperialist European powers (France, Great Britain, Germany, Belgium, Italy and Portugal) at the Berlin Conference (1884–5). With the drawing of official borders, however, the colonization of large parts of Africa formed a blueprint for the independent nation states that would emerge on the continent in the 1950s and 1960s.

TEXT BOX 8.1 DIRECT AND INDIRECT RULE

In the Early Modern period, the European population was governed via all kinds of intermediary layers. In the Dutch Republic, many governmental tasks were carried out by the urban authorities, and they, in turn, relied on religious and guild organizations. The larger dynastic empires – composite monarchies, as the British historian John Elliott calls them – also included a number of countries and peoples who tended to be governed in an indirect way at the local, regional and even national level. The Spanish Habsburg Empire, for example, appointed a viceroy in Naples. Not only were there independent layers of governance between the central sovereign and the subjects, but much policy implementation was also left to semi-private entrepreneurs, most typically tax farmers and military entrepreneurs with mercenary armies. This is why the American sociologist Charles Tilly called this era the period of 'indirect rule'.

It was only in the course of the eighteenth century that a system of direct rule emerged: tax farmers were replaced by public officials who collected taxes, and a system of conscription slowly but surely emerged in the area of warfare. In this way, the central state increasingly assumed powers from the local and regional layers of governance. Direct rule would only truly break through in the nineteenth century, supported by nationalism. According to Max Weber, it was not until this time that bureaucratic rationalism started to typify the activities of the government.

The early-nineteenth-century transition from colonies to nation states in Latin America would not be imitated elsewhere until after the First World War. Starting in Europe with Irish independence (1922), this was followed in the 1930s by former British settler colonies such as South Africa, Canada, Australia and New Zealand, as well as the French and British mandates in the Middle East (such as Lebanon and Syria), which had previously formed part of the Ottoman Empire. Colonies such as India, the Dutch East Indies and a number of South-east Asian countries gained independence only after the Second World War. This was the prelude to a global domino movement. Between 1950 and 1970, as many as forty-three African countries became independent. The African wave was followed by a wave of independence in Oceania.

According to the British historian Chris Bayly, the desire to become independent can be seen as an outcome of the globalization of political ideas. Many nationalists were deeply inspired by European and American ideas about democracy and the right to the self-determination of peoples, such as those proclaimed by the American president Woodrow Wilson in 1918. These ideas spread via Western education in the colonies (such as Sukarno in Bandung and Lumumba in Kinshasa) and in the colonial metropole. Paris, London and Brussels functioned as hotbeds of anti-colonialism where many an important leader (from Jawaharlal Nehru and Gandhi to Hô Chí Minh) was formed. This process was not one of simple diffusion, either, but the result of an intense exchange of ideas through vibrant anti-colonial networks composed of migrants, both intellectuals and workers, from various parts of the empire, as well as native communists and socialists in cities such as Paris and London.

In the Netherlands these networks were less diverse, and tended to develop among Indonesian students at institutions of higher education in the Randstad region. One famous example is Mohammed Hatta (1902–80), who studied at the Rotterdam School of Commerce between 1921 and 1932, and was the driving force behind the nationalist newspaper *Indonesia Merdeka* (Free Indonesia). A similar development occurred among Surinamese (mainly Creole) students before, during and after the Second World War, when anti-colonialism had grown into a global movement.

STATISTICS AND SOCIAL ENGINEERING With the invention of the nation state, a new conception arose of the tasks and powers of the state, inspired by the Enlightenment ideals of rationality and equality. As observed by the American anthropologist James Scott, the state was increasingly responsible (and perceived as responsible) for improving the well-being of its inhabitants: their health, level of education, life span, productivity, morals and family life. At the same time, a process of homogenization took place in relation to language, education, law, infrastructure and culture. According to Scott, the well-being of the population was increasingly not only seen as a means for national power, but as an end in itself.

These new ideas about the role of the state would have far-reaching consequences. They lay at the root of what would later become the twentieth-century welfare state, in which the government harboured the express ambition of managing all kinds of political, economic and social developments. In order to be able to make these interventions in everyday life, also known as 'social engineering', the state – it was thought – had to penetrate to the core of society. According to Scott, the nineteenth-century nation state therefore had every interest in making society 'legible', as it were. Whereas Early Modern sovereigns and rulers had granted towns and the nobility a large degree of autonomy, public officials in the service of the nineteenth-century central state knew who the national citizens were, where they lived, what they were called, how old they were, their occupation and their gender; for only in this way could they raise taxes efficiently and call on young men to do military service – two crucial interests of the state.

In the course of the nineteenth century, the state also became interested in economic and social data on production, consumption, religion, occupations, demography, poor relief and criminality. Government statistics played a key role in helping to make society legible. As early as the eighteenth century, both the German cameralists (who focused on economic governance by the state) and French physiocrats (who saw nature as a primary source of prosperity) showed great interest in measuring and counting a whole range of things. It was thought that effective legislation could only be drawn up on the basis of empirical research.

In this way, in the nineteenth century, European states would chart out diverse social developments, based on ten-yearly censuses. The British reformer and politician James Phillips Kay compared statistics to the human nervous system. Just as our nerves immediately warn us if there is something wrong with our bodies, statistics could help the state to track down and fight social diseases. In his pamphlet on the moral and physical condition of the English working class of 1832, in which he described the troubling predicament of cotton workers in Manchester, Kay warned of the demoralizing influence of the large masses of Irish migrants. These backward and barbarian paupers were said to have become entirely accustomed to flagrant poverty, and their arrival in England would infect the mentality of English workers. As a consequence, they, too, would drink away their meagre wages in the pub and lose any desire for upwards mobility, instead of striving for more prosperity and a better life.

To use the language of computers, we can make a distinction between hardware and software in the formation of unitary states. The 'hardware' included tangible activities in the area of infrastructure (canals, roads, railways, ports), as well as the expanding bureaucracy and the establishment of a permanent population register (from *c.* 1850), a national education system, a national postal system, an army and police apparatus, and a uniform system of clock time.

Changes in the hardware also had consequences for the 'software' of society, or the hearts and minds of the population. This is illustrated by the American historian Eugen Weber in his book *Peasants into Frenchmen*. While at the beginning of the nineteenth century, French people from different parts of the country could hardly understand one another due to major differences in regional and sometimes local dialects, and there was hardly any shared national feeling, national identity was given a considerable boost in the course of the nineteenth century. In this process, a crucial role was played by the uniformization of education and the standardization of French, but equally by the introduction of national symbols, such as the flag and the national anthem. Moreover, the army, through the transition from mercenary armies to conscription (one of Napoleon's most spectacular innovations), worked like a national integration machine, bringing together young men from all over the country for years on end.

Boosted by the rise of national media (newspapers, later also radio), the nation became an 'imagined community' (see also Chapter 3). Citizens did not need to be personally acquainted in order to feel connected. These nationalistic feelings were fed at various levels, consciously and unconsciously, and mainly came to the surface during international conflicts and wars, when conscripts were expected to risk their lives for flag and fatherland (see also Text Box 8.2).

TEXT BOX 8.2 TYPES OF NATIONALISM

Following political scientists, social historians have identified different types of nationalism. One common type is ethnic nationalism, which defines the inhabitants of a nation on ethnic grounds: the 'people'. An individual's birth determines whether they belong to an ethnic group, and thus to the nation. The key sources of inspiration for this form of nationalism are to be found in Romanticism, mainly in the works of the German poet and philosopher Johann Gottfried von Herder. In civil or liberal nationalism, the state derives legitimacy from its 'contract' with the inhabitants of a certain territory. In this case, the individual has the choice to become a citizen and submit to the 'social contract'. Sources of inspiration can be found in the Enlightenment, mainly in the works of Jean-Jacques Rousseau, and in liberalism, including the ideas developed by John Stuart Mill. Although there are also other ways of distinguishing forms of nationalism (religious, cultural, ideological, corporative), these are the most important. Civic nationalism is most applicable in the Dutch case.

We talk of 'nationalism' when people in certain situations put national identity above other identities (family member, inhabitant of a region or town, member of a particular occupational group, young people, the elderly, men, women, supporter of a political party or religion, ethnic background). Nationalism can unite very diverse people and thereby have a positive effect on society, as in the case of sporting achievements or resistance to a foreign aggressor. It also has a darker side, though, which often reveals itself in times of war and international conflict. This can be expressed in the exclusion of foreigners and, in extreme cases, can even lead to genocide. Furthermore, nationalism can be mobilized in the event of domestic political, cultural, social or economic tensions. Groups that form a threat to the nation in the eyes of the majority, such as Jews, Roma, Catholics, Muslims, homosexuals, intellectuals or 'anti-social people' can be discriminated against, excluded and persecuted. The nationalist body of thought does not simply exist, however; it has to be invented ('invented tradition'), as argued by the British social historian Eric Hobsbawm. By this, he meant a body of implicit or explicit opinions and rituals intended to imprint values and norms that emphasized the continuity with the past. Education played an important role in the dissemination of such ideas. As well as geography, history education made an important contribution. National history, in particular, was used from primary school onwards to cultivate the idea of the nation, supported by life-sized visual material, especially by projecting the national discourse back in time in an anachronistic way.

The analyses by Eugen Weber and Eric Hobsbawm are very top-down, as though nationalism was a deliberate project by the central state to mould the population into a unified national mass. In practice, though, cultural regional differences and local particularism proved rather persistent. Take the example of Friesland in the Netherlands, or Limburg, where a large part of the population regarded everything and everyone from north of the rivers ('Hollenjer') with distrust, and where people felt closer to the Germans on the other side of the border, who spoke more or less the same dialect and with whom they shared Rhineland customs (such as carnival). Moreover, all kinds of other groups continued to exist, in addition to the national and regional ones. On the whole, religion and world view (Catholics, Jews, Protestants, socialists), class (workers, lower and upper middle class, intellectuals, the elite) and gender were significant rivalling identities (see Chapter 9). On the other hand, there were many who embraced the new idea of the nation with enthusiasm, certainly if it gave one additional status, as in the case of civil servants, the police, foresters, customs officials, soldiers or postal workers. It was precisely these occupations that provided the state with its human infrastructure in daily life (almost always a male one), right into the furthest reaches of the countryside.

SUPRANATIONAL TIES AND THE RETREAT OF THE NATION STATE After the First World War, states made their first serious attempts to achieve structural international cooperation, mainly in order to prevent war in future, but also to channel the flows of refugees and solve the problem of statelessness. The League of Nations, which was established in January 1919 as a result of the Treaty of Versailles, proved to be a weak instrument that was powerless to prevent a new world war. This initiative was nevertheless very important, because it marked the beginning of a long-term trend towards international cooperation, which would be taken up more powerfully by the United Nations after 1945. Although this organization also made a lacklustre impression, it ensured – together with other international organizations, such as UNESCO and African and Asian regional organizations – the emergence of a global awareness, with states increasingly seeing themselves as bound by international treaties, law and rules that limited national sovereignty.

After the war, similar forms of cooperation in Western Europe had far-reaching economic and political consequences, such as in the European Union, which grew out of the European Coal and Steel Community (ECSC), founded in 1951, becoming the European Economic Community (EEC) in 1958 (also see Text Box 8.3 and Chapter 7, Text Box 7.7). Although the Frenchman Jean Monnet is universally regarded as the father of the European Union, it is interesting to note that Dutch and Belgian politicians (such as Jan Willem Beyen and Paul-Henri Spaak) played a disproportionately significant

---

TEXT BOX 8.3 THE ORIGINS OF THE EUROPEAN UNION

- 1951 ECSC: Belgium, the Netherlands, Luxembourg, West Germany, France and Italy.
- 1957 EEC and Euratom, still 'the Six' of the ECSC.
- 1973 Accession of Great Britain, Ireland and Denmark.
- 1981 Greece becomes a member.
- 1986 Portugal and Spain join.
- 1990 German unification, bringing in the former East Germany.
- 1995 Sweden, Finland and Austria join.
- 2004 Accession of Poland, the Czech Republic, Hungary, Slovakia, Slovenia, Estonia, Latvia, Lithuania, Malta and Cyprus.
- 2007 Accession of Romania and Bulgaria.
- 2013 Accession of Croatia.
- 2020 Britain leaves EU.

role in the early years of European unification. These small states may have seen this as a way to extend their international influence and defend their national interests. This phenomenon can be observed in other supranational organizations, too, such as NATO, which was led by Dutchmen (Dirk Stikker and Joseph Luns) and a Belgian (Spaak) for no fewer than twenty years in the period between 1952 and 1984.Historically speaking, European unification is a unique phenomenon. Whereas they had frequently resorted to war or engaged in diplomacy in previous centuries, sovereign states now voluntarily relinquished part of their self-determination and autonomy in order to form a union. There is a lively debate about whether the EU was in essence an economic initiative (trade bloc) or a political initiative (guaranteeing peace). In their everyday lives, most people in the Netherlands mainly identify as Dutch (and as part of the Dutch nation state). Despite this, the EU is more than a vehicle for economic growth: it is very gradually assuming a more important role, with the European Parliament and the European Commission in Brussels as the most important organs.

In contrast to the original desires of some of the visionary founders of European cooperation, however, Europe is not yet a super-state with a common defence and foreign policy; for aside from being a supranational organ, the EU is also a form of cooperation in which the member states take collective decisions. The member states act as an intermediary for European guidelines that are always implemented at the national level. For now, then, the European Union is a union of member states, a kind of club, although the elitist quality of its decision-making has given it a negative image among European populations.

One should add that the erosion of national sovereignty in late-twentieth-century Europe was part of a wider tendency. A new, federal chapter seems to have begun in the history of European state formation, which, as Tilly has shown, was characterized from c. 1000 onwards as a gradual reduction in the number of states. As described in Chapter 7, blocs are also forming in other parts of the world, too, although these are often limited to economic cooperation.

STATE FORMATION IN THE NETHERLANDS AND THE DUTCH COLONIAL EMPIRE With the inauguration of Willem I, the son of the former stadholder Willem V, as 'sovereign ruler' in 1813, followed by his proclamation as king in 1815, the argument in favour of the unitary nation state was also settled in the Netherlands (see Text Box 8.4). The transition from the fragmented and decentralized system that had existed under the Republic to the unitary state began in the Batavian-French period (1795–1813). Typical of this 'unitarism' was the statement by the Speaker at the first meeting of the 'National Assembly' of the Batavian Republic (1795–1805) in 1796:

> Every member of this assembly is a true Representative of the whole people of the Netherlands, and should be regarded by each and every one as having lost all special provincial relations; such that the names of provinces or districts may no longer even be uttered here, now that the

interest of the whole people of the Netherlands must be the highest law for all, and all provincial interests have come to an end.

Unification also meant that all citizens were equal before the law, while the traditional special rights of all kinds of groups, communities and institutions were disbanded. Guilds and 'seignorial' rights were thus abolished, towns lost much of their independence, and the Jewish community lost its right to self-government and its own law (a decision that would be contested for decades by the community's leaders, the parnassim). In the nineteenth century, 'republican plurality', to cite the social historian Maarten Prak, would slowly but surely be transformed into 'democratic singularity'.
The unification of the Netherlands covered both the 'hardware' and the 'software' aspects of state formation. In this sense, the Netherlands was in step, to a great extent, with developments in other European nation states, such as France. In the Napoleonic era, the French model even had a very direct impact, as shown by the introduction of the land registry and the registry office, and the reform of the legal system, education and the tax system. The legacy of the Early Modern period did leave traces in some respects, though, as we shall see herein.

The 'hardware' included the construction of canals and maintenance of dikes, supervised by central government. During his time in Great Britain, Willem I had observed how canals could play a crucial role in industrial development, and no fewer than 500 km of canals would be built during the reign of the 'canals king'. A second driver of the Industrial Revolution was the railways. The first private railway line (between Haarlem and Amsterdam) was completed in the Netherlands in 1839. After this, the rail network would expand quickly, and would be nationalized from 1860. Finally, the state began to pay a role in the construction and renovation of roads, also under the supervision of the Department of Waterways and Public Works, which was formed in 1848 to replace its late-eighteenth-century predecessor.

The bureaucracy of the central state gradually penetrated the local level, and the bond with individual citizens gradually became stronger, partly because of the growing importance of national taxation. In addition, municipal finances were increasingly dependent on central government, certainly after Thorbecke's Municipalities Act of 1851. This was related to the expanding package of municipal duties. Education and poor relief were particularly costly, and municipalities received state subsidies for these; something we will consider in more detail below, in the section on social policy. National government spending expanded from around 1850 and would eventually assume phenomenal forms, especially in the twentieth century, as shown in table 8.1. Within national expenditure, we also see a striking shift from defence, which took up half the budget in 1850, to education, social affairs and public housing; this captures the transition from the liberal night-watchman state to the welfare state in a nutshell.

TEXT BOX 8.4 THE NORTH EXPLOITS THE SOUTH, 1815-30

Following a decision by the Congress of Vienna (1814–15), which wanted to strengthen the viability of European nation states, the Kingdom of the Netherlands was granted the Austrian Netherlands (later Belgium) in 1815. King Willem I was the most powerful ruler that the Netherlands had ever known, but he did not succeed in transforming the Southern and Northern Netherlands into a single national unit. Lying at the root of this were various discrepancies relating to ecclesiastical organization and education. In addition, the South felt discriminated against when it came to political representation.

Recent research has shown that a key reason for the discord lay in the economic-financial sphere. Willem I was fixated on reviving Amsterdam's traditional staple market, and the new canals were mainly oriented towards the ports of Holland. In his attempts to gain the confidence of the merchants and bankers of Holland, as they had the money to fund his ambitious industrial and colonial policies, the king paid too little attention to the interests of the South. The merger with the North meant that taxes had to be raised drastically in the South, so as to reach the same (high) level as in the North. Although the king established a fund to subsidize industry, and much of this money went to the South, the new, heavy taxation resulted in a net flow of funds from South to North, which only became larger over time. In 1816, the Southern Netherlands contributed 40 per cent of taxes; in 1829, 50 per cent. By contrast, only around 20 per cent of state expenditure flowed back to the South. The annual transfer of income from South to North is estimated to have been 17 million guilders in 1816 and 31.5 million in 1829; the latter is equivalent to 5-6 per cent of the gross domestic product of the Kingdom of the Netherlands. The Revolution of 1830, which resulted in the Secession, was the logical outcome of the discontent felt by the neighbours in the South, as well as the consequence of an enormous fiscal imbalance.

Another illustration of the influence of the nation state is the rapidly growing share of total government spending expressed as part of gross domestic product (GDP), that is, the value of all goods and services which the Netherlands produces each year (Table 8.2). Since the 1970s, we have spent around half of what we earn on goods and services that are allocated by the state in a democratic way, such as care, education, infrastructure and defence.

The legacy of the decentralized political system of the Early Modern period was most evident in the first half of the nineteenth century, when municipalities still had significant freedom to raise direct and indirect taxes (excises). The Municipalities Act of 1851 put a check on this, and fifteen

TABLE 8.1 *Central Government Spending in the Netherlands, Expressed in 1900 Guilder Value, in 1850, 1900 and 1960*

	1850	1900	1960
Total (× 1 million)	31	117	6177
Per capita of the population	10	23	117

Source: Knippenberg and De Pater, *Eenwording van Nederland*, 145.

TABLE 8.2 *Collective Expenditure by the Dutch State, as Percentage of GDP, 1815–2020*

1815	1850	1900	1950	1975	2000	2016	2018	2020
16	14	11	29	51	46	44	42	43

Source: Bos, *Nederlandse collectieve uitgaven*; CPB, macro-economische verkenningen 2020.

TABLE 8.3 *Municipal Expenditure in Guilders per Capita of the Population in the Netherlands, 1862–1907*

	Urban	**Rural**
1862	13.78	4.27
1907	46.27	10.81

Source: Knippenberg and De Pater, *Eenwording van Nederland*, 164.

years later, municipal excises were forbidden altogether. The Municipalities Act also marked the official end of the distinction between urban and rural government, although municipal autonomy was maintained in principle, and there were still major differences between towns and villages and between municipalities themselves. In the second half of the nineteenth century, for example, much more was spent per capita on urban-dwellers than on those living in the country, as shown in Table 8.3. It was not until after the First World War that these differences narrowed and the influence of central government grew considerably, certainly in relation to social policy.

As had previously happened in Great Britain, the growing influence of the central state was expressed in an increasing tendency to make society 'legible' with statistics and empirical social research. This drive for legibility would only really gather speed in the late nineteenth century. It led, for example, to the founding of the national statistics office (known today as Statistics Netherlands, established in 1899), and the rise of a range of state-funded, specialized planning agencies and research institutes – a development that was not reversed by the wave of deregulation that swept the Netherlands in the 1980s, although (semi) privatisation eroded their quality..

Growing uniformity also affected local customs, a well-known example being the fixing of clock time. Until the twentieth century, there were different time zones in the Netherlands, and the clock had pointed to different times for many years. Prompted mainly by the arrival of the railways, the decision was made in 1866 to use Amsterdam time. This was replaced by Greenwich time in 1892, but it was not until 1909 that it was the same time everywhere in the Netherlands. There are numerous other examples of increasing national uniformity, such as weights and measures, traffic rules and Standard Dutch.

In addition, attention was also paid to the 'software' of nation-building. As in other countries, the teaching of the nation's history, along with geography, played a key role. The nationalistic myth that the Dutch population had formed a homogenous cultural unit for centuries reached its zenith around 1900. It also covered the colonies and South Africa, which had been founded by 'the Dutch'.

The power of the Dutch unitary state grew overseas, too. Britain occupied a large number of Dutch colonial territories during the period of the French Revolutionary Wars, but this was followed by a restoration in 1814. Thereafter, the colonial empire underwent another significant expansion, especially in the Indonesian archipelago. This was accompanied by a long series of wars, culminating in the brutal subjugation of Aceh (North Sumatra) *c*. 1900. It was considered necessary to have a military presence in order to cream off the natural resources of the Dutch East Indies. Due to the size of its colonial 'possessions', the Netherlands could imagine itself a global player for a time.

The global expansion of power had various implications for the metropole. Aside from the economic consequences (see Chapter 7), a further outcome was that from the mid-nineteenth century, thousands of Dutch (mainly men, at first) came into contact with Asian cultures and Islam as soldiers in the Royal Dutch East-Indian Army (Koninklijk Nederlands Indisch Leger, KNIL), as public officials or as company employees. Until the First World War, aside from 70,000 immigrants, around 90,000 Dutch soldiers left for the East with the KNIL, which was founded in 1830 (see Figure 8.1). They commanded native soldiers there, including many Moluccans, who made up the majority of the KNIL. After the opening of the Suez Canal in 1869, migration to and from the Dutch East Indies rose sharply, peaking between the wars. As a consequence of this, the 'European' population of the East Indies rose from 15,000 in 1815 to 240,000 in 1930. In addition to working for the army and government, they were employed by Dutch companies extracting raw materials such as oil, sugar, rubber, tobacco, coffee, tea and quinine. Unlike in the Early Modern period, contact between the Dutch and Asians in the Indonesian archipelago was now much more intensive and prolonged, not least due to the higher mortality in the tropics, which led to the creation of many mixed Dutch-East Indian families, among other things.

FIGURE 8.1 *KNIL soldiers on patrol in the Dutch East Indies, c. 1935.*
© *Collection of the IISG, Amsterdam.*

The intervention in the West (Suriname and the Antilles) was overshadowed by that in Indonesia, but there, too, the colonial project had a global impact. For example, from 1853, around 2,500 Chinese moved there, as did 34,000 Hindustani contract labourers between 1873 and 1916. From 1890, they were joined by almost as many Javanese. When Suriname became independent, around 110,000 descendants of these East Indian labour migrants, known as Hindustanis, settled permanently in the Netherlands, particularly in The Hague, where they form around 10 per cent of the population.

Making the population in the Dutch East Indies 'legible' with government statistics went hand in hand with bringing the archipelago under direct rule in the late nineteenth century. This resulted in a broad census in 1905. One should add that these initiatives cannot be viewed in isolation from the Ethical Policy (since 1901), which aimed to improve the lot of the indigenous population, including through education and forms of political independence. Such a policy could only succeed if the state had enough detailed statistical data.

In practice, however, Little came of 'redeeming the debt of honour', especially for the inhabitants of Java. During the interwar period, this fed discontent among Indonesian nationalist intellectuals such as Mohammed Hatta and Sukarno. Their ideal of an independent Indonesia was (unintentionally) further stimulated by Dutch education, which brought them into contact with Western notions of self-determination and national sovereignty.

After the Japanese surrender in August 1945, Sukarno and his followers declared the Republic of Indonesia. Its rejection by the Dutch colonial powers provoked a mass armed nationalist resistance movement. The Netherlands responded by sending around 100,000 conscripts to the East Indies to fight what would later turn out to be the last Dutch colonial war (euphemistically described as 'police actions'), which cost the lives of 5,000 Dutch soldiers and as many as at least 100,000 Indonesians. All of the bloodshed proved to be futile, because under significant international pressure, especially from the United States, the Netherlands signed the independence declaration on 27 December 1949. This was followed by the large-scale migration of Dutch and Indo-Europeans to the Netherlands (300,000).

The scale and nature of Dutch decolonization in the East were similar to the developments in the British, French and Portuguese colonies, and in part, too, to the Japanese exodus from Korea and North-east China after the Second World War. In the West, there were parallels between the decolonization of Suriname and the Antilles and the developments in the French and American (Puerto Rico) overseas territories. Although they were granted greater autonomy, political ties were maintained for many years, meaning that people could migrate freely to the metropole. Finally, there were many similarities between the process of integrating repatriates from the East Indies and the French *pieds noir* from Algeria and repatriates from every corner of the British Empire.

8.2
Democratization and citizenship

Citizens in many states gained more say and national political participation rose sharply. 'Democratization' – in the sense of government of the people, by the people and for the people – slowly spread, although in very limited fashion in overseas empires, where natives were largely excluded. Typical features of a democracy are the presence of a representative body, universal suffrage, a plurality of political parties and the guaranteeing of basic rights, such as freedom of speech and freedom of association. An impression of the spread of general male and female suffrage in the West is given in Table 8.4.

Democratization did not occur without resistance, however. In a number of cases (such as in Germany, Italy, Portugal, Spain, Eastern Europe and Latin America), phases of democratization alternated with the rise of authoritarian or dictatorial regimes. Democratization was not (and is not) an irreversible process. There were also important differences in the ways in which citizens were granted participation (e.g. via a constituency voting

TABLE 8.4 *Introduction of Universal Suffrage in Western Countries, 1840–1920*

	Men	***Women***
United States*	c. 1840	1920
France	(1792) 1848	1944
Germany	1867	1919
New Zealand	1893	1893 (only active)
Australia**	1901	1902
Finland	1906	1906
Sweden	1911	1921
Denmark	1915	1915
The Netherlands	1917	1919 /1922
Great Britain	1918	1928
Belgium	1919	1948
Japan	1925	1945

* With the exception of African Americans (in northern states until 1865 and in southern states de facto between c. 1900 and 1965) and with the exception of the indigenous peoples (until 1940/47).
** Aboriginals did not get the vote de facto until c. 1962-7.

system or via proportional representation) and in the power of the central state relative to regional and local authorities. Although democracy in name has increasingly become the 'standard' form of government, in practice other variants remain. The citizens of Singapore, Myanmar, China and many Arab countries, for example, have much less say in the governance of their states, while in a number of countries, such as Malaysia, immigrants and their descendants are excluded from political participation on ethnic grounds.

DEMOCRATIZATION: PRECONDITIONS AND PATHS In general, democracy tended to thrive better in nation states than in empires, and to prove more sustainable in countries that had continuous economic growth than countries with stagnating economies. Nation-building and long-term economic growth did not automatically lead to democratization, though; more was needed. The American historical sociologist Barrington Moore has shown that the role played by a relatively large and powerful middle class was crucial for a sustainable form of democracy. The bourgeoisie often led the way in extracting concessions from the sovereign and limiting the power of the nobility, as happened in England during the Civil War and the seventeenth-century Glorious Revolution, and in France during the revolution of 1789. This also meant that the development of sustainable democracy was accompanied by a market-oriented economy and a certain level of urbanization. It had been the towns, after all, that had developed forms of autonomous communal governance at an early stage. In short, countries such as Great Britain, the Netherlands and Belgium formed a fertile seedbed for democracy (and these were also the countries that followed a 'capital-intensive' path of state formation at an early stage; see Chapter 3).

By contrast, in agrarian states such as Russia and China, landowners enjoyed a strong position and the buffer of a strong bourgeoisie was lacking. According to Barrington Moore, it is no coincidence that it was precisely these countries that experienced bloody revolutions and more dictatorial paths in the twentieth century. Something similar is true for many Latin American countries, where democracy, plagued by coups, usually proved fragile.

Recently, Moore's socio-historical approach has been supplemented by the economists Daron Acemoglu and James Robinson. Their rational choice theory assumes that people's behaviour can be explained by what they consider to be the costs and benefits of different options, and that every individual determines their own priorities. They argue that elites only share their power and wealth with more people when their position is threatened by 'collective action' by the less fortunate, in the form of riots, strikes, demonstrations, revolts or revolutions. Depending on the degree of protest, elites will resort to repression, concessions or, in extreme cases, create institutions that promote democratic development (parliament, an electoral system). The path that is chosen – repression or reform – depends on the associated costs. Elites that were dependent on land for their revenues, such as those in Russia and in many South American countries, were less quick to yield than elites in urbanized regions who relied on reliable wage labour, trade and financial transactions. Moreover, elites could lessen the threat of redistribution by gradually sharing power, given that the bourgeoisie had no interest in a radical levelling, either.

Great Britain is one example of the gradual path. Democratization was a long, sustained process; as early as the seventeenth century, the lower nobility, merchants and other groups of citizens gained access to power. From the late eighteenth century, the pressure from the less privileged grew. Industrialization brought growing social inequality and proletarianization, leading to violence against the owners of factories, landowners and large leasehold farmers (the Luddite movement in 1811–12, the Swing Riots in 1830–2), as well as mass demonstrations and strikes. The most notorious confrontation between reformers and the violent apparatus of the British state took place on 16 August 1819 at St. Peter Field, in the rapidly growing industrial city of Manchester. Around 60,000 people called for reform of the electoral system, so that cities with large populations (mostly workers) would gain equal representation in Parliament, and the sparsely populated countryside would no longer have an unfair advantage. Although the demonstration was orderly, rash charges by the police resulted in 11 dead and 400 wounded. As a result, this incident, which took place shortly after the Battle of Waterloo, went down in history as the 'Peterloo Massacre'. This was a new repertoire of collective action (see Text Box 3.2, Chapter 3).

The fight for the extension of suffrage and other reforms was given an important boost in 1838 by the Chartist movement, which was supported by skilled workers and the lower middle classes. In the same year, the Anti-Corn Law League was founded in Manchester by what was ostensibly an unlikely coalition of factory owners and workers, who wanted an end to import tariffs on grain. Whereas the latter movement achieved success with the abolition of the Corn Laws in 1846, the Chartists' achievements were less concrete. Nevertheless, the conservative leaders ultimately showed themselves amenable to the various forms of collective action, and passed a number of Reform Acts to increase the male electorate tenfold between 1832 and 1884. This would eventually result in universal male suffrage in 1918, and universal female suffrage ten years later.

In countries such as France and Germany, the path to democratization was filled with more revolutionary hurdles, as shown by the revolutions of 1789, 1848 and 1870, and the 1918 attempt to transform Germany into a communist soviet-style republic. Revolutionary situations would likewise emerge in 1989, this time in Eastern Europe, where citizens forced the undemocratic communist regimes to abdicate. With the exception of Romania, this happened everywhere in a peaceful way.

DEMOCRATIZATION IN THE NETHERLANDS In the Netherlands, where industrialization was slow and partial, collective action was more modest in nature for many years. Nevertheless, the revolutionary threat from below left its traces. A famous example is King Willem II's sudden volte-face in March 1848, in response to the revolutions that had broken out in France and Germany. Once Willem II had accepted the principle of constitutional monarchy, parliamentary democracy was established, largely shaped by the liberal politician Johan Rudolf Thorbecke. We should add that due to the use of census suffrage, political participation initially remained rather limited; just 11 per cent of males aged twenty-three and above were allowed to vote. The pool of enfranchised was extended slightly in 1887 and 1896. Universal male suffrage would not be introduced until 1917, however, and universal female suffrage in 1919.

The late nineteenth century saw the rise of more intense, mass collective action in the Netherlands, when an organized worker's movement came to fruition. An important role was reserved for the (mainly Jewish) Diamond Workers' Union, based on membership and structural contributions, which formed the model for modern socialist and Christian trade unions. In addition to mass demonstrations on 1 May from 1890 (at the instigation of the Second Socialist International) and petitioning the government, strikes were among the most important forms of collective action used to put pressure on governments. As shown in Table 8.5, the number of strikes rose sharply after 1890, the highpoint being the national railway strikes of January 1903, although Prime Minister Abraham Kuyper managed to break them in two months by banning strikes by railway officials. Most strikes were primarily aimed at improving the terms of employment, and reflected the growing power of the labour movement. It is no coincidence that the emergence of universal

TABLE 8.5 *Number of Strikes in the Netherlands by Decade, 1851–1940*

	Number of strikes
1851–60	21
1861–70	87
1871–80	111
1881–90	188
1891–1900	756
1901–10	1,603
1911–20	4,048
1921–30	2,411
1931–40	1,706

Source: Database of strikes in the Netherlands, IISG, Amsterdam.

suffrage coincided with the peak of strike activity in the Netherlands and the revolutionary threat in the wake of the Russian Revolution (1917).

THE PUBLIC SPHERE, CIVIL SOCIETY AND CITIZENSHIP The model of democracy that developed in Western countries is inseparable from the idea of individual citizenship, which comes with rights that are guaranteed by the state. This idea of civil rights and a contractual relationship between citizen and government was rooted in medieval municipal citizenship and, more generally, in the relationship between sovereign and subject that took shape in urban societies. Its contractual nature was expressed very clearly in the shifting power relations between sovereign and subjects in the Dutch Republic and England in the sixteenth and seventeenth centuries. The fact that new ideas about the relations between the state and its citizens then spread to wider circles from the late eighteenth century is related to the emergence of the 'public sphere' and the rapid growth of civil society.

By 'public sphere', the German philosopher and sociologist Jürgen Habermas meant a relatively autonomous space in which citizens could form opinions and organize for the purpose of diverse goals, political or otherwise, independently of the direct influence of the state, the market or the family (see Text Box 3.5). In public places such as coffee houses and cafes, citizens (initially well-to-do men, on the whole) discussed subjects that transcended local issues or private interests, such as the abolition of slavery, fiscal policy or the American Revolution.

This public sphere and the social movements that resulted from it are closely related to the development of civil society. Following the nineteenth-century thinker Alexis De Tocqueville, and more recently the American political scientist Robert Putnam, this term refers to the phenomenon whereby people with shared interests, values and aims voluntarily enter into forms of organization. In principle this happens, just as in the public sphere, outside the state, the market or the family, although these boundaries are often vague in practice. The concepts of civil society and the public sphere may overlap to some extent, but they are not identical. Civil society is much broader than the public sphere and covers all kinds of organizational initiatives by citizens that do not always result in public debate; it is also described as 'associative sociability'. Book clubs, for example, promoted a culture of literacy, but also, indirectly, 'public spirit', and thus the idea of forming part of a larger social whole. These organizations, Putnam argues, ensure that people outside family or neighbourhood networks gain more trust in one another, and thereby in society as a whole. Through connections within these organizations, known as 'social capital' (see also Text Box 3.4, Chapter 3), people gain more opportunities to exercise influence, including politically. Civil society is thus thought to have a positive effect on social cohesion and trust in democracy.

Recent studies on civil society emphasize that this phenomenon occurred across the whole of Europe, including Russia, and that clear phases can be distinguished within it. A first wave of club formation took place in the 1770s and 1780s under the influence of the Enlightenment, including the 'salons' in France, the chapters of the Maatschappij tot Nut van 't Algemeen ('society for public welfare') in the Netherlands, and the Freemasons in Great Britain (the first lodge was founded in 1717). The period between 1820 and 1848 was a golden age for voluntary organizations, especially in well-to-do (male) middle-class circles. These emphasized the ideal of social harmony and focused, among others things, on charity and the promotion of the economy and culture. From the 1860s, these organizations became less exclusive, and workers (and, in the United States, African Americans) also started to organize, especially around goals that would boost their respectability in the dominant middle classes, such as the temperance movement. Strikingly, in many countries these organizations took a strongly nationalist turn. In the Austro-Hungarian Empire, for example, citizens organized themselves along ethnic lines, such as organizations of Germans, Czechs and Hungarians.

The period between 1890 and 1914 can be described as a true 'club mania'. Almost every layer of the population founded associations to structure their activities, not least in the area of sport and culture. At the same time, this phase was characterized by increasing internationalization. For example, associations were founded to promote the spread of Esperanto, vegetarianism, and the fight against the trade in 'white slaves'. For many years, the government was suspicious of voluntary organizations, because they could threaten the established political order. In that respect, it is significant that freedom of association in countries such as France (1901) and Germany (1908) was achieved relatively late, compared to more liberal countries such as the United States (1787), Great Britain (1824) and the Netherlands (1848). Finally, educated colonial subjects in empires run by European powers also asserted their citizenship by joining ethnically mixed clubs and associations, which – as described by Lynn Lees with reference to Singapore in the early twentieth century – became part of a 'global public sphere'.

The Netherlands followed this international trend. Strikingly, from 1870 there was a split along religious and political lines, with the lower middle classes and skilled workers organizing within their own circles, separately from the dominant liberal movement. In the light of civil society, this phenomenon, which is known in the Netherlands as 'pillarization' (*verzuiling*), is less unique than is often thought. For example, the historian and geographer Hans Knippenberg has identified many parallels between religious identification and ethnicity, as Catholics, Jews and Protestants began to see each other as homogenous groups with associated mental and even physical characteristics. Thus, there were more parallels between pillarization and the emergence of ethnic group identities in other parts of the world (Austria-Hungary, the United States) than might first appear.

The growth of voluntary organizations does not always promote the development of democracy, however. Putnam makes a distinction between bonding and bridging social capital. Organizations of the latter type are much more effective in promoting democratization, because they bring people with very diverse backgrounds into contact with one other. By contrast, organizations that focus on linking the likeminded and that are only open to a specific ethnic community or occupational group mainly stimulate contact within their own circle. This could be useful in times of emancipation, but in the long term it could actually have an anti-democratic effect. Some voluntary organizations even had expressly anti-democratic aims and contributed actively to the destabilization of democratic regimes, such as veterans' associations (*Stahlhelm, Bund der Frontsoldaten*) and *Freikorpsen*, which sprang up in Germany after the First World War. Something similar applies to today's so-called libertarian movements in the United States, which argue for the abolition of the state, promote an extreme form of individual liberty (possession of firearms) and sometimes advocate the use of terror. Related to this is the recent rise of radical and extreme right parties that define 'the' people in exclusive ethnic or racial terms, in contrast to 'the' – treacherous – elite, immigrants, Muslims and minorities.

The rise of civil society was closely related to that of national citizenship. Whereas citizenship in the Early Modern period was still a rather exclusive, urban phenomenon, in the nineteenth century direct ties emerged between the nation state and its people, the nation's citizens. Initially, the rights linked to citizenship (such as the right to vote) were limited to the wealthy, male upper classes, but the circles of citizenship gradually widened. With the expanded role of the state in everyday life, the matter of who deserved full national citizenship and who did not became a topical political issue. Which social groups were excluded depended, among other things, on the desired level of internal cohesion of nation states and the power relations between political parties. If we limit ourselves to European states in the twentieth century, then we can roughly distinguish three types.

First, there were ethnically and religiously relatively homogenous states, such as in Scandinavia, where social differences were relatively small. From the 1930s, politics in these countries became dominated by social democratic regimes that attempted to build a welfare state. Groups that fitted less comfortably into this ideal, in the eyes of policymakers, such as 'antisocial people', Roma and sometimes homosexuals, were seen as parasites who had to be isolated or excluded. This could lead to the loss of civil rights, especially in countries where notions of social engineering and eugenic had caught on, such as in social democratic Sweden between 1930 and 1970, and some Swiss cantons. The consequences ranged from coercively taking children into care to forced sterilization, as happened in Scandinavia until long after the war.

The second type were those states, such as the Netherlands, France and the UK, that were much more divided socially, culturally or religiously, and where there was more of a balance of power between political parties. The groups at the bottom of society that were seen as 'unproductive' were subjected to attempts at reform, but these were less extreme and did not usually lead to the loss of civil rights.

The third type were dictatorial regimes, which removed all rights from 'internal enemies', marginalized them and often systematically massacred them. The most notorious example is the Nazi genocide of Jews and the Roma. In the Soviet Union the enemy was defined in social terms, which – under Stalin's rule – cost the lives of millions of 'class enemies', such as the kulaks (more prosperous farmers). After the Second World War, large-scale forms of extreme exclusion (and often genocide) such as these would be repeated in countries such as China during the Cultural Revolution and currently versus the Uyghurs in Xinjiang, Cambodia under the Khmer Rouge, Yugoslavia in the 1990s and during the Rwandan civil war in 1994.

The emphasis on national citizenship led to an increasing general tendency to keep immigrants (who were, after all, members of a different nation) apart from the rest. After the First World War, in particular, extensive bureaucratic systems were established to limit and regulate immigrants' access to a country's territory, labour market and full national citizenship (through naturalization). At the same time, however, the dominance of the nationality principle was curtailed by numerous international treaties and the influence of globalizing supranational organizations such as the International Labour Organization (ILO) and, from 1950, organizations that were formed as part of the United Nations to protect the rights of the stateless and refugees. Finally, the process of decolonization caused considerable migration by former subjects to the heart of the former empires, such as Great Britain, France, Portugal and the Netherlands.

COMPARING CHINA AND EUROPE For many years, the Western European model of democracy was used as a measure for the rest of the world. One of the best-known advocates of this vision was the German sociologist Max Weber, who saw the 'lack' of democracy and bourgeois society in China (and other Asian countries) as a deviation from the universal Western norm. Others, such as Karl Marx, were astonished by the absence of a capitalist system and the Chinese state's lack of interest in the world beyond the borders of the 'Middle Kingdom'. The American historian and sinologist Bin Wong has argued that the absence of a democratic system in China should not be seen as an expression of an unchanging and stagnating society that missed the modernization boat in the eighteenth century. Rather, we need to realize that states develop in different circumstances (economic, geopolitical, social, religious, cultural). The question is therefore less why certain developments did not occur in China, and more how we should understand the specific course taken by China.

The relationship between state and subject was quite different in China, partly due to the influence of Confucian philosophy (see Chapter 4). From early on, the Chinese identified much more with their state than Europeans, even if the emperor was a distant figure. For centuries, no independent or competing political entities (the nobility, church, urban corporations) developed separately from the state. Long before the nineteenth century, the state had already penetrated much more deeply into the pores of society than in Europe, and its highest ideal was to maintain social order and stability.

Notions of citizenship existed, but there was less competition between state and society. This does not mean that the Chinese imperial government functioned flawlessly – far from it – but in principle, the cause of problems was not sought in the state as such, but in the errors of individual public officials and administrators. When, during the nineteenth century, especially after the Taiping Rebellion (1851–64), which cost twenty million Chinese their lives, the central state collapsed and there was an increase in political anarchy – the result, among other things, of Western military pressure – more space emerged in towns for voluntary organizations. Their function was limited, however, and China remained a largely agrarian society until far into the twentieth century. Citizens were late to mobilize on a large scale, for example in student associations, professional organizations, or associations with a common place of origin (*tongxianghui*) forming a basis for connection. Even the nationalist leader and founder of the Chinese Republic, Sun Yat-sen (1866–1925), who was influenced by Western ideas, considered most associations to be a threat to the state and believed that, to the extent that they were unavoidable (such as trade unions), they should serve the state.

Under the communist regime, which was established in 1949, people built on the traditional model of broadly shared group feelings, a common fight for a social ideal on all levels, and the banning of opposition and conflicts. This model has come under pressure in recent decades, partly due to massive internal migration and the ensuing urbanization and growing social inequality. This has led to widespread strike activity, protests against environmental pollution and the suppression of free speech. Notwithstanding collective protests (such as the demonstrations on Tiananmen Square in 1989 and more recently in Hong Kong), burgeoning forms of civil society have yet seriously to threaten the power of the party.

8.3
Social policy and the rise of the welfare state

The notion that the central state should play a role in protecting its citizens against all kinds of social risks is a relatively recent one in Europe. It began with enlightened despots in German principalities in the later eighteenth century, who were susceptible to the view that the state should do more than raise taxes and wage war. The idea arose that the sovereign was responsible for the general welfare of his subjects. That idea was promoted, among others, by the German cameralists, who argued that the sovereign should not leave social care to towns, the church or the nobility, but should actively intervene themselves. Thinkers such as the Scottish economist Adam Smith (1723–90), known as the father of classical liberalism and the free market, likewise anticipated an interventionist role for the state, one that went much further than the night-watchman state that is often erroneously associated with him. Finally, French Enlightenment thinkers argued that the state should assume greater responsibility, especially for the poor and beggars. In these opinions, held by largely conservative thinkers, we can recognize a foreshadowing of the much more radical ideas of the French Revolution and utopian nineteenth-century thinkers such as Saint-Simon and the founders of communism and socialism, Karl Marx and Friedrich Engels, whose *Communist Manifesto* of 1848 and later works, such as *Das Kapital* (1867), would have an unprecedented impact.

The new vision of the relationship between the government and the people initially remained limited to scholars' studies and the libraries that collected their written outpourings. Even if they were sympathetic to these ideas, however, states were by no means able to realize the new aspirations. For example, the broad conception of state intervention, as propagated by the German *Policey* science of the eighteenth century, was quickly narrowed to the premise that although the state should assume more power, it was not responsible for solving social problems. The general welfare of the nation's citizens remained a recurring theme, but the priority was to guarantee the internal security of the state. This was accompanied by a strong emphasis on repression and control, especially of the poor, criminals, migrants and 'subversive' propagandists such as nationalists, and later communists and anarchists.

In this part of the chapter, we focus on the development of social policy in the late nineteenth and twentieth centuries. Social policy is conceived here as a centrally managed mix of measures intended to mitigate the risks of existence, such as poverty, unemployment, sickness and disability. We also pay attention to the response from the 'subjects' of this policy. Social policy is interpreted not so much as a triumphal march from less to more protection, or from less to more equality; instead, we investigate its diverse ideological motivations and the normative, sometimes frankly illiberal, nature of the social policy pursued. This was by no means a linear development that resulted in a modern, rational and just society.

How social policy was made, the effects it had, how these were valued and the responses it provoked differed according to the social group and period. On the whole, the upper classes had a much greater capacity to protect themselves against social and economic risks, such as unemployment and illness, and to impose their cultural values and norms on others. The latter was expressed, among other things, in patronizing social policy (the 'civilizing offensive', see Chapter 9) and various forms of social control. The 'subjects' of the policy were far from passive, however. They developed open or hidden forms of resistance or countercultures, and often organized

TEXT BOX 8.5 POLITICAL SYSTEM AND PROTEST. THE ENVIRONMENTAL MOVEMENT

The form that political parties or campaign groups take is dependent on the political system and whether there is space to criticize the government. In autocratically governed countries, the public sphere is small by definition. However, in Western countries there is also considerable variation in political culture. This is illustrated clearly with reference to the environmental movement. In the United States, environmental organizations pay lobbyists to influence members of Congress in Washington, because this has proved more effective than demonstrations. Environmental campaigners must therefore focus on raising money from wealthy sympathisers. The possibilities are also different in each state: campaign groups can sometimes force a referendum to hold back a nuclear power plant for example. More often, though, the American environmental movement starts legal proceedings, in order to use the courts to ensure that a factory sticks to the rules or that the mining industry stays within bounds. These legal proceedings are very expensive.

Japan is also a democracy, but the political scope in that country is limited, because the state is governed by a closed administrative elite. In the final decades of the twentieth century, however, environmental pollution became an urgent problem, with hundreds of fatalities and thousands of people suffering lifelong disabilities. Determined activists, who often have personal ties to the victims, are taking the lead in problem areas and do not rule out violence. It is difficult for them to convince politicians and public opinion that they are right.

In Europe, too, there are clear variations in political culture. The famous report to the Club of Rome, Limits to Growth (1972), stimulated the emergence of all kinds of environmental campaign groups and parties. In Great Britain, however, the constituency voting system meant that an environmental party could not get off the ground, because it could never achieve a majority in a single constituency. In Germany in 1980, all kinds of small groups merged into a single large party, the Greens. This party became an important player, and even participated in government, although its focus – the environment – was subsequently pushed into the background.

The Dutch electoral system encourages fragmentation and the country has a large, free public sphere, and there are thus all kinds of different parties and campaign groups. The movement that focuses on the conservation of nature (Natuurmonumenten, Vogelbescherming) dates from around 1900. In the late 1960s, though, new forms of protest arose, such as De Kleine Aarde, which advocated sustainable living, and various campaign groups that carried out hard-hitting campaigns against nuclear energy. There are no or hardly any legal proceedings and no paid lobbyists, as in the United States, and no hard deadlock between the government and campaigns, as in Japan. Instead, there is a mix of influencing public opinion by means of public-focused campaigns and demonstrations, and parties that use parliamentary influence to address the environmental problem. Just as in Germany, the environment has become somewhat of a background issue in the most important environmental party, Groenlinks.

Interestingly, there was a complete turnaround in Dutch policy in the 1970s. The year 1969 saw the introduction of the Pollution of Surface Waters Act, in 1972 the Air Pollution Act, in 1976 the Chemical Waste Act, in 1979 the Waste Act, and in 1981 there was an interim act on soil decontamination, a noise pollution act and a new Nuisance Act. In 1970, a Minister of Public Health and Environmental Hygiene was appointed for the first time, the name alone emphasizing that environmental policy was a governmental task. Attention shifted during this period: policymakers put less emphasis on the direct protection of human health, and more on the need to reach an ecological balance. The use of nuclear energy also remained limited in the Netherlands compared to other Western countries. For the most important executors of environmental policy, the Provincial States, environmental policy is hardly politicized, and almost all parties acknowledge the importance of having a high-quality living environment.

themselves in social movements focused on emancipation and equal rights (workers, women, homosexuals, the disabled).

Social policy can also provoke resistance from groups that believe that state interference is unwarranted, or object to what they see as extreme forms of equality, whether these are liberal movements calling for a greater role for the market, or movements that promote inequality and the exclusion of certain groups (e.g. Jews, women, intellectuals, Catholics, Muslims). In the 1930s, for example, the Nazis built what was an unprecedented welfare state for that time, but one that excluded political and 'racial' enemies. A more recent, much less extreme variant is that known as 'welfare chauvinism', which tends to restrict the benefits of the welfare state to the native population and exclude immigrants. Finally, social policy can provoke resistance because it is perceived as patronizing (a smoking ban in restaurants) or undesirable on political or religious grounds (compulsory vaccinations).

STATE RESPONSIBILITY FOR SOCIAL CARE The most typical change in social policy in the late nineteenth and twentieth centuries was what the Dutch sociologist Abram de Swaan called the 'statification of care arrangements'. The organization of services to cover all kinds of social risks was increasingly brought under the umbrella of the state. Viewed from a global historical perspective, this development was less pioneering than it might first appear. After all, the Chinese state had been concerned with the welfare of its inhabitants for centuries. As we saw in Chapters 2 and 4, for example, the central state built numerous storage depots for rice and grain in order to stabilize prices and prevent famine in times of scarcity. The Chinese state was also concerned with care at the level of the family, which was viewed as the core social unit. The *pater familias* played an important role in reproducing the social order desired by the state. The different households (*baojia*) within a family line were considered responsible for one another, both morally and materially.

The traces of this local, family-based system are still visible in the so-called *hukou* legislation that was introduced in the 1950s. For millennia, *hukous* (which could cover hundreds of households) had formed units for levying taxes, exercised social control, provided social care and controlled migration. They were primarily responsible for the population register. Although the system broke down in the final years of the Qing dynasty, the communists under Mao breathed new life into the *hukous* after 1949. This had particular consequences for rural migrants, who in the preceding years had moved temporarily in their hundreds of millions to work and live in cities, sometimes illegally. Although the state tolerated this migration, newcomers in cities (such as Beijing and Shanghai) were usually excluded from the local social care system, as they were officially covered by the *hukou* in their native village.

In Western countries, the centre of gravity of the care system shifted in the late nineteenth and twentieth centuries from the family, the local community, guilds, mutual societies and religious orders to the state. De Swaan explains this development with reference to the increasing identification of elites with 'the people'. Whereas solidarity with acquaintances and family originally prevailed, as society became more anonymous this was increasingly replaced by formal and bureaucratic regulations, resulting in the collective social insurance system of the welfare state. The elites benefitted directly from this, because the underclass was proving increasingly disruptive in the towns, as manifested in social unrest, criminality and infectious diseases. In order to prevent people from benefitting from social regulations without contributing to them ('free riders'), or to avoid shifting the problem to other cities or institutions, it was essential to have national legislation that obliged people to contribute to social insurance; and this is why the elite vision of the welfare state was the inevitable outcome.

In addition, political, economic, cultural and intellectual factors became increasingly intertwined on a global scale in the nineteenth and twentieth centuries. Following the revolutions in transport (steam ships, trains) and communication (telegraph, post, telephone) in the second half of the nineteenth century, international influence increased considerably. Not only did technical inventions and political systems start to resemble each other more closely, but a constant exchange also developed in the domain of social policy. The idea of cross-border 'modernity' thereby exercised great influence on thinkers, scientists and politicians, who strove for a reordering of society (see Text Box 8.6).

The widespread desire to participate in the 'modern' world brought about a convergence in social policy. The state became much more active in European countries, the United States, Japan, Latin America and European settler colonies overseas (such as Australia and New Zealand). Between 1890 and the First World War, numerous conferences were devoted to the new social policy. As a result, countries learned about initiatives across the border, and they sometimes literally copied social legislation from one another. Table 8.6 gives an impression of the spread of social legislation in Western countries since the late nineteenth century.

We should note that many of the social policy initiatives came from below; from cities, for example, where socialists and other reform-minded political parties had gained political power at the municipal level much earlier than in national governing bodies (such as in Amsterdam, with Socialist aldermen such as De Miranda and Wibaut) but also from the professionalization of

TABLE 8.6 *Introduction of Social Legislation in Various Countries, 1890–1965*

	Pensions	***Sickness Benefits Act***	**Unemployment**
New Zealand	1898		1930
France	1890[1]–1910	1893[3]	1958
Denmark	1891	1917	1907
Germany	1889	1884	1927
Japan	1941	1922	1947
United States	1935	1965	1935
Great Britain	1908	1911	1911
The Netherlands	1913/56[2]	1913/30[4]	1917[5]/49

[1] Only for miners and railway personnel.
[2] General Old Age Pensions Act, 1956.
[3] Only for the poor and via local and private channels.
[4] Passed in 1913, implemented in 1930.
[5] State contribution to trade unions' unemployment funds.

occupational groups such as doctors and social workers. One good example is that of middle-class and elite women who, as a result of the caring qualities that were attributed to them as women, and the fact that they were not admitted to other occupations, started to play a major role in implementing and designing social policy in many countries, from Argentina to the Netherlands. In doing so, they managed to augment their 'caring power' considerably.

Despite a certain convergence in social policy, large differences between countries remained. In the United States, for example, the fight against poverty was seen as disruption of the optimal functioning of the labour market, and recipients as people who lacked perseverance and inventiveness, or who were lazy and irresponsible. This principled distinction between the deserving and the undeserving poor led to much more stigmatization of the poor and unemployed in the United States than in Europe, even today. Welfare claimants are often seen as second-class citizens; poverty is framed as a consequence of irresponsible behaviour, and the poor are seen as bad citizens. That is why most American social programmes put more emphasis on the provision of food and clothing than money. In most European countries and settler colonies, by contrast, social policy was transformed in the 1930s into a social right and a means to distribute wealth, not primarily as a form of poor relief.

The best-known typology of welfare states is that developed by the Danish sociologist Gøsta Esping-Andersen, who categorized social policy on the basis of whether 'decommodification' had taken place. By 'decommodification', he meant that labour (and also workers) was seen less exclusively as a 'commodity' in the market. With the rise of wage labour, a labour market emerged in which workers supplied their labour and employers exercised demand for labour ('commodification'). In a fully liberalized labour market, workers – with the exception of the very poorest – only had recourse to their income from labour. Welfare states made people less dependent on income from wage labour and created provisions for mitigating the risks of existence (illness, unemployment, disability), so that a reasonable level of income would remain possible.

Esping-Andersen distinguished between 'liberal welfare states', such as the United States and Australia, where labour is mainly a commodity, and 'social democratic welfare states', such as Sweden, which have an extensive system of (generous) benefits that are much less stigmatized than in the liberal variant. Between the two are 'conservative corporatist welfare states' such as Germany, Belgium and Austria and, to a certain extent, the Netherlands and France, where benefits are admittedly a social right, but the state leaves negotiations to employers and employees, meaning that the benefits have a less egalitarian character. Moreover, private parties such as churches sometimes continue to play a subsidiary role in such contexts.

Esping-Andersen's typology is useful, but it should be applied flexibly. For example, there are sometimes major differences between countries that fall, strictly speaking, into the corporatist welfare category. Germany, for example, with its strongly authoritarian state tradition (Bismarck), is very different from Belgium or the Netherlands, where social policy emerged much more from below. In addition, it matters a great deal which period one is looking at. With the rise of national socialism in Germany and Austria in the 1930s, for example, a number of 'Bismarckian' characteristics, such as a minor role for the state in implementation and the performance principle (benefits dependent on the build-up of insurance contributions), were sidelined, and one of the first extensive welfare states was developed, albeit one that excluded groups such as Jews, homosexuals, Roma, the disabled and political opponents.

We should add that much of the social legislation in post-war European democracies proved to be 'colour blind', because it made no systematic distinction between nationals and foreigners. After all, foreigners in the labour market also paid contributions and built up social rights. Nor were provisions such as social security and pensions reserved for national citizens. Thus, while the nineteenth century saw the emergence of a clear distinction between national citizens and foreigners, and access to a country and its labour market was often subject to regulations, the borders of the welfare state remained quite porous. That was particularly evident when countries such as the Netherlands, Germany, Belgium and Sweden, in close collaboration with employers' organizations, started recruiting 'guest workers' in Southern Europe, and later in North Africa and Turkey. On the urging of the trade unions, which were concerned about unfair competition, guest workers were paid the same wages as native workers, ensuring their access to the social system. This allowed labour migrants who later became unemployed to claim from schemes that they had paid into for years, especially in relation to unemployment rights and incapacity for work. Together with residency status linked to length of stay, this resulted in large-scale family reunification and permanent settlement in Western Europe by Moroccans, Algerians and Turks.

THE WELFARE STATE AND WOMEN'S EMANCIPATION IN THE NETHERLANDS
The Netherlands is often mentioned in the same breath as Scandinavia, as a country with one of the most extensive care systems in the world, where the inhabitants are protected from cradle to grave from all kinds of risks, such as illness, disability, poverty and unemployment. Moreover, since the 1960s, the Netherlands has built a reputation for being a very egalitarian society that has used affordable and accessible education, progressive taxation and a plethora of subsidy schemes to redistribute wealth to a great extent.

What is often forgotten, in the process, is that these 'typically Dutch' characteristics are relatively new. The spectacular expansion of the welfare state dates from the 1960s, while the principle of non-discrimination in Article 1 of the Constitution did not come into force until 1983. Moreover, the specific development of Dutch society was the result of continuous interaction with the rest of the world. Thus, the rapid growth of the welfare state cannot be viewed in isolation from the global economic crisis of the 1930s, the social legislation introduced by the German occupying forces in the Second World War or the ideas of the British economist John Maynard Keynes on the state's role in stimulating the economy (see Chapter 7). The report on *Social Insurance and Allied Services* (1942) by Keynes's compatriot, the economist and politician William Henry Beveridge, also played an influential role. Finally, Article 1 of the Constitution was the very delayed implementation of the Universal Declaration of Human Rights by the United Nations (1948) and the European Convention on the Human Rights (1950), based on the former treaty.

Women's emancipation is likewise a recent phenomenon in the Netherlands. In the Early Modern period, Dutch women enjoyed considerable freedom compared to those in other countries (see Chapter 4), but they nevertheless faced frequent discrimination in public life. On the basis of their sex, for example, women were often forbidden from joining guilds or holding political office. This would change only slowly in the twentieth century. It was not until 1919, for example, that women (actively and passively) got the vote – partly thanks to the efforts of representatives of the first wave of feminism, such as Wilhelmina Drucker and Aletta Jacobs – and were thus viewed as full-fledged political citizens.

This weak position was closely related to the legal subordination of women to their husbands and the 'breadwinner principle' that dominated from the late nineteenth century, whereby it was thought that the breadwinner (almost invariably a man) should earn an income that allowed him to maintain a family. Until the 1950s, married women were seen as 'incapacitated' in legal terms, which meant that they needed the official permission of their spouse for all kinds of decisions (including larger purchases). It was not until 1976 that the dismissal of women on the grounds of pregnancy or marriage was banned. Furthermore, many women worked in low-wage sectors, and had few rights to benefits in the case of sickness or disability. Finally, the benefits that they did have a right to were systematically lower, due to the breadwinner principle.

It was not until the 1960s, with the rise of the international second feminist wave, that this sex discrimination would be denounced and dismantled, slowly but surely, by champions such as Joke Smit (1933–1981). In 1977, the government introduced an emancipation policy designed to eradicate the gap between women and men in areas such as education, work and care. One of the results was the abolition in 1985 of direct discrimination against women in social security, something that had been prescribed in international guidelines for some time. Moreover, from the 1990s, partly due to the rapid rise in female labour participation, more attention was paid to childcare – an issue that Scandinavian countries had started to address as early as the 1930s.

THE EARLY MODERN ROOTS OF THE 'DELAYED BANG' Although the Netherlands would overtake most countries at a rapid rate with the development of an extensive social safety net in the 1950s and 1960s, compared with other countries, the Dutch were late to introduce social legislation. This slow introduction, which De Swaan compared to a firework with 'a long fizzle and a delayed bang', was related to the unusually decentralized municipal and republican tradition, with its medieval roots (see Chapters 3 and 4). Existing social regulations at the municipal level remained strong, and churches and private organizations played an important role in social care until after the Second World War.

In the Netherlands, the Early Modern legacy contributed to the fact that the nation state left much to private initiative, such as poor relief, until far into the twentieth century. This was accompanied by the legacy of religious division and toleration of religious minorities, which distinguished the Dutch Republic and the Ottoman Empire (with its millet system) in the Early Modern period from mono-religious countries such as France (after 1685), Spain and most Scandinavian and German states. From the time of the Revolt in the late sixteenth century, the Netherlands became a country with two large religious denominations (Protestants and Catholics), plus a small Jewish community, while the Protestant community covered a whole range of sub-denominations, such as Calvinists, Lutherans, Remonstrants and Mennonites. From the Batavian-French period onwards, the state no longer made an official distinction between citizens on religious grounds. In practice, though, most church communities would retain a high degree of autonomy until far into the twentieth century, especially in the area of social policy.

Furthermore, since the Early Modern period, the Netherlands had distinguished itself economically and socially with its strong emphasis on commercial agriculture, services, small-scale industry and trade. The unique development of the Dutch economy explains the smaller size of the industrial working class, among other things. Moreover, in the nineteenth century, urbanization and geographical mobility were less fundamental processes than in neighbouring countries, as the Netherlands already had a high level of urbanization in the seventeenth century. The Netherlands had no cities that were bursting at the seams in the nineteenth century, such as Paris, Lyon, Manchester or Berlin, with the mass protests and revolutionary tensions that came with such conditions (Peterloo 1819, the revolutions of 1830 and 1848, the Commune revolt in Paris in 1870). Nor was there a moral panic in the Netherlands about *classes dangereuses*, as there was in Great Britain or France (think of Victor Hugo's *Les Miserables*). It is typical that the only evocative social literary work to be published in Dutch in the nineteenth century, Multatuli's *Max Havelaar*, was not about the Dutch proletariat, but about abuses in the colonies.

As a result of this specific background, the established classes and the Dutch state were under less revolutionary political pressure to give in to calls for democratization and state intervention in social and economic life.

Social policy, especially in relation to poor relief, therefore retained its local character for much longer. This position was also influenced by the ideology of the Maatschappij tot Nut van 't Algemeen (1784, 'the society for public welfare'), which, although it considered public welfare to be paramount, held on to the liberal principle of laissez-faire. The Poor Law of 1854, which made religious and private organizations responsible for poor relief, is a good example. Despite this, it would be incorrect to blame the liberals for the laissez-faire state. The liberal leader Thorbecke, for example, believed that a civilized state was obliged to ensure that its members did not perish from want, whereas confessional organizations were initially the fiercest opponents of state intervention.

DUTCH SOCIAL POLICY IN INTERNATIONAL PERSPECTIVE On this point, the Netherlands resembled Great Britain more closely than Germany. The Prussian state had recognized its responsibility for the poor as early as 1842. Chancellor Otto van Bismarck introduced a whole package of social laws in the 1880s (fearing the rise of socialism; see Table 8.6). Just as in Great Britain, the Dutch state held on to the ideology of laissez-faire for much longer. The first to introduce social policy were the liberals, at the end of the nineteenth century. Although the scope of the Liberal politician Sam van Houten's famous Child Protection Act (*Kinderwetje*, 1874), which banned children under the age of twelve from working in factories, was limited, it symbolized a turnaround in thinking about the role of the state.

Another similarity with Great Britain was that, compared to the German states and France, social movements were suppressed less rigorously by the police and army, and the geographical mobility of the proletariat was seen as less of a problem. A typical feature, in this respect, was the rather small size of the police service in the Netherlands and Great Britain, and the clear separation between the police and the army. Moreover, Dutch municipalities had much more influence over the local police force, and police services continue to have a strong local ethos even today (see table 8.7).

As we saw earlier in the section on democratization, it was not until the emergence of the socialist workers' movement in the second half of the nineteenth century that social policy moved up the political agenda, and there was a gradual realization that the state should play a role in this area. Somewhat later than in Great Britain (where the Education Act was passed in 1870), a number of social laws were introduced in short succession in the Netherlands from 1900: the Compulsory Education Act (1900), the Housing Act (1901), the Industrial Industries Insurance Act (1901), the Poor Law (1912), the Sickness Benefits Act (1913) and the Disability and Old Age Pensions Act (1913).

The socialist workers' movement was by no means the only group pressing for social legislation. Confessional political parties also became convinced that the state had a regulatory duty in this domain, albeit with civil society as an important partner. At the (Protestant) Christian Social

TABLE 8.7 *Typology of Police Services in European Countries*

	Great Britain and the Netherlands	**France**	**Germany**	**Italy**
Formal tasks	Few	Many	Many	Many
Informal tasks	Many	Some	Few	None
Political tasks	Very limited	Limited	Limited	Many
Structure	Decentralized	Centralized	Decentralized	Centralized
Accountability	Local-democratic	Central-bureaucratic	Local-bureaucratic	Central-bureaucratic
Training	Civilian	Military	Military	Military
Image	Reliable, approachable	Not trusted, unapproachable	Authoritarian, unapproachable	Feared, corrupt

Source: Bayley, 'The police and political development in Europe', 341.

Congress of 1891, their powerful political leader, Abraham Kuyper, blamed liberal capitalism for endangering the humanity of the worker, and therefore argued for an active approach to the 'social issue'. The papal encyclical *Rerum Novarum* ('Of revolutionary change') of the same year formed an important international source of inspiration for Catholics. In this letter, Pope Leo XIII argued that workers had a right to fair wages, and that the state and trade unions should show solidarity with the weak in society. The pope condemned both unbridled capitalism and socialism, and argued for cooperation between labour and capital in a corporatist framework. This important papal letter had a considerable influence on relations within the Netherlands, and partly lay at the root of the founding of Catholic trade unions and political parties, both of which would play an important role in the development of the Dutch welfare state.

As in other Western countries, there was also a clear relationship between the rise of democracy and the expansion of social policy in the Netherlands (see Figure 8.2). With the emergence of mass political movements, both socialist and confessional, the governing elite came under significant pressure to tackle the major social risks and social problems in the form of slums, infectious diseases, unemployment and poverty. Due to industrialization and the enormous population growth in Europe, not only towns and cities but also the problems that accompanied urbanization had grown spectacularly. The expansion of suffrage meant that the vote of the poor part of the population would weigh increasingly heavily.

FIGURE 8.2 *Dutch poster on women's suffrage and pension legislation, early twentieth century.*
© *Collection of the IISG, Amsterdam.*

Which parties managed to mobilize working- and middle-class voters, however, differed widely from country to country, as there was by no means a universal split along class lines. Due to the pillarization in the Netherlands, socialist parties only managed to appeal to a limited number of workers. When universal suffrage for men and women became a fact, the Social Democratic Workers' Party (Sociaal-Democratische Arbeiderspartij, SDAP) only managed to win 25 per cent of the votes in 1919. This was because many lower-class voters voted not on the basis of class affinity but in accordance with their religious convictions. A good example is Abraham Kuyper's Protestant Anti-Revolutionary Party (Anti-Revolutionaire Partij, ARP), which managed to unite many lower-class voters (see Figure 8.3), while the Roman Catholic State Party (Rooms-Katholieke Staatspartij) later enjoyed similar success with Catholics.

Due to the combined parliamentary influence of the socialist and confessional parties, as well as socially sympathetic liberals, between 1908 and 1913 the first insurance laws were introduced in the Netherlands (the Sickness Benefits Act and the Disability and Old Age Pensions Act). During the Great War, the negotiating position of the workers' movement was considerably strengthened, due to the scarcity of labour following mobilization and the precarious neutrality policy. Across the whole of Europe, the war functioned as a pressure cooker, in which the nineteenth-century laissez-faire policy began to dissolve. One good illustration of this in the Dutch case is the Unemployment Decree of 1917, whereby the state guaranteed that it would supplement unemployment benefits paid by trades unions, should they no longer be able to meet their obligations. With the Labour Act (1919), the working hours of adult men were limited for the first time and the eight-hour day was introduced (with the exception of agriculture and fishing). From now on, the working week would in principle not exceed forty-eight hours.

The definitive collapse of the laissez-faire state in the area of social policy came with the worldwide economic crisis of 1929 and the subsequent mass unemployment of the 1930s. In 1935 and 1936, for example, almost 18 per cent of the working population in the Netherlands was unemployed. The trauma caused by this crisis led to the breakthrough of an interventionist economic policy with a much larger role for the state. Essentially, many middle-class people realized that they, too, were now unable to shield themselves from the risk of unemployment. Whereas the cabinets led by Hendrick Colijn (1933–9) held fast to the classic liberal austerity policy, from 1939, when the SDAP entered government for the first time, Keynesian ideas would penetrate government circles. The cabinet may have also been more receptive to these ideas because, as a cabinet in exile in London, it had been strongly influenced by its host country. In 1941, for example, Churchill and Roosevelt agreed the Atlantic Charter, the provisions of which included freedom from want as a basic right. This principle was developed by William Beveridge in his famous report of 1942, mentioned earlier. After the war, a better social system would have to prevent extremist parties from rising once again.

> **TEXT BOX 8.6 MODERNITY AND MODERNIZATION**
>
> The period between 1880 and 1914 was full of optimism. All kinds of inventions developed in rapid succession: electricity, the telegraph, the telephone, film, the car, the aeroplane. A new idea made itself felt around the world: the idea of 'modernity'. Modernity is an ambiguous concept that is difficult to define; to be modern means wanting to 'move with the times'. People increasingly looked to what other (modern) people were doing, and adopted the elements that were successful. In the past, people had tended to look to the ancients and past golden ages as ideals (Antiquity, Confucius); 'Renaissance' means 'the rebirth of Antiquity', for example. The nineteenth-century sense of modernity was not entirely new: during the Enlightenment, thinkers had embraced the new and rejected the old. It was not until the later nineteenth century, however, that this feeling of progress, of progressiveness, took possession of large groups of people at every level. This was evident, among other things, from the way that people dressed: fashions changed increasingly quickly and stimulated consumerism. In the arts, people experimented with new, abstract forms.
>
> 'Modernization' was not confined to the Western world, by any means, as fashions in clothing also reached societies that had yet to industrialize. 'Modern' architecture spread across the whole world; boulevards, opera houses and large squares with statues and floral borders were built in the Ottoman Empire, too. New ideologies such as liberalism and socialism became established across the whole world. Science sought solutions to worldwide problems.
>
> 'Modernity' was also a core element in the social sciences. The idea of modernity permeated Max Weber's concepts of rationalization and disenchantment, and this subsequently shaped how twentieth-century social scientists and historians viewed the world. The sense of progress and progressiveness also provoked counter-movements from conservatives and fundamentalists, who wanted to preserve or revive the good aspects of the past; and the world became more politicized as result.

In the same period, ironically enough, it was the German occupying forces that made a start with building the modern welfare state, introducing the Child Benefit Act, among other things. Furthermore, with the Sickness Insurance Decree (1941), the Germans forced back private charity and emptied the trade unions' unemployment coffers. These decrees were not reversed after the war, and would become an integral part of the post-war social insurance system.

It would take some time to establish the new system. Although the Minister of Social Affairs, the social democrat Willem Drees, pushed through the Old Age Pensions (Emergency Provisions) Act in 1947, it was expressly meant to be temporary. Only ten years later – when Drees was in his third cabinet as prime

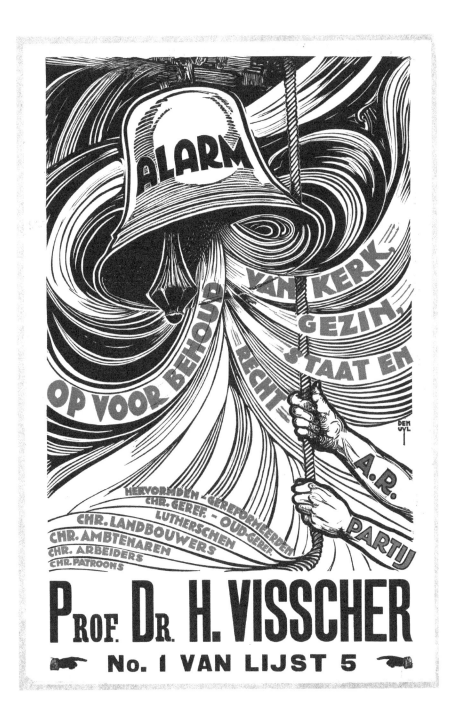

FIGURE 8.3 *The Anti-Revolutionary Party (Protestant conservatives) as the champion of church, state, family and law, 1929, for the elections in that year.*
© *Collection of the IISG, Amsterdam.*

minister – would this emergency act be replaced with the Old Age Pensions Act (AOW). In the tradition of the *Rerum Novarum*, Catholic politicians such as Marga Klompé (who in 1956 would become the first female minister of social work) would join the socialists in playing a prominent role. A general social safety net took some building, and it was not until 1 January 1965 that the Social Assistance Act was brought into force. The principle of insurance gradually shifted towards a general claim to 'care'.

The rapid growth of the social system was facilitated considerably by the favourable economic circumstances. Thanks to post-war economic growth, which particularly accelerated from 1960, the state had a larger budget than ever before. An additional windfall was the discovery of a large natural gas field near Slochteren (Groningen) in 1959. In the ensuing decades, many of the proceeds from this would be used to finance the new social security system.

The 'delayed bang' of the welfare state in the Netherlands in the 1960s can thus be explained by a combination of spectacular economic growth, progressive taxation and broad political support (both socialist and confessional). From the mid-1960s, the Dutch cradle-to-grave model of care grew to be one of the most generous in the whole of Europe. In 1980, social transfers amounted to 30 per cent of the gross national product, more than in most countries in Western Europe.

However, the extensive system of care that emerged in the Netherlands and neighbouring countries in the 1960s and 1970s soon came under pressure, when the oil crisis of 1973 brought the 'Golden years' of post-war economic growth to a definitive end. The changing course of economic policy (see also Chapter 7) led to major cuts, austerity in the welfare state and more space for the market. Compared to other countries, the reform of the Dutch social system proceeded in a relatively conflict-free fashion, thanks to close collaboration between the cabinet, employers and trade unions (symbolized in the 'Wassenaar Agreement' of 1982). Social transfers expressed as a percentage of gross national product fell from 30 per cent in 1980 to less than 20 per cent in 1990. The policies of the successive Lubbers cabinets in the 1980s forced a true break with the trend, with increasing emphasis on getting the unemployed back into paid work. Benefits were no longer taken for granted, partly as a result of the reform of disability legislation by liberal-social democratic coalition governments in the 1990s, which proved extremely sensitive in a political respect.

At the end of the twentieth century, the level of public expenditure in the Dutch welfare state resembled the Scandinavian model again, although the share of social spending in the government budget had decreased. In the first decade of the twenty-first century, government spending as a proportion of the gross national product remained high (more than 40 per cent, see able 8.2). But as a result of substantial cuts in social benefits, the proportion of social spending therein declined. In the new century the Dutch welfare provisions became substantially less generous than in the 1970s and 1980s.

Summary

At the end of this chapter, let us return to the three questions that were asked at the outset.

1. The most important consequences of the rise of the nation state were a shift in political power from the local to the national level; that the state had a growing need to collect systematic knowledge about the population, natural resources and the economy; and that the state increasingly influenced citizens' lives and wanted to protect them from various risks of existence. At the same time, this social engineering sometimes seriously curtailed people's freedom and fanned the flames of nationalism.

2. An important precondition for democratization was the formation of a public sphere and civil society. The urban middle classes or bourgeoisie played a crucial role in this. North-western Europe, which had urbanized at an early stage, had a clear head start in the process. Power-sharing with the rest of the population did not happen automatically, we should add, but was forced by the threat of revolution from below. By contrast, in societies such as China and Russia, where the power of urban and commercial elites had traditionally been weak, there was less space for civil society initiatives.

3. Particularly in the twentieth century, states assumed the task of providing a safety net for citizens to mitigate the risks of existence. The emergence of this social policy was partly related to the rise of the nation state and partly to democratization, as citizens began to demand more from the state via political parties. The best-known expression of this social policy was the welfare state, which reached its highpoint after 1945, especially in North-western Europe and European settler colonies overseas. Due to pillarization and the decentralized political structure (a legacy of the Early Modern period), the welfare state in the Netherlands emerged relatively late. This 'delayed bang', which saw close collaboration between socialists and confessionals, ensured that from the 1960s the Dutch welfare state became one of the most extensive in the world.

9

New opportunities, values and norms
Sociocultural developments

LEX HEERMA VAN VOSS

The nineteenth and twentieth centuries were a time of far-reaching social and cultural change. In part, this change went hand in hand with economic growth, state formation and democratization. It was thanks to economic growth, for example, that many more people were able to afford consumer goods in the course of the twentieth century. Democratization and the expanding role of the state led to the rise of the welfare state, among other things. This entailed a radical transformation in the key risks in a person's life, as well as in the way in which people attempted to mitigate these risks. The trend towards individualization was even clearer than in the past. More children survived, and the elderly were no longer dependent on their children for care. Social relations became more fluid, and education increasingly facilitated. In addition, people developed new forms of protest to ensure their voices were heard. Geographical mobility also increased: growing numbers of people saw more and more of the world. All of these changes in lifestyle were accompanied by changing world views. Religion played a less decisive role, especially in Northwestern Europe.

These new opportunities did not occur all over the world to the same extent, however; the risks of existence remained high in the non-industrialized world for many years, and in many cases could not be offset by growing prosperity or a welfare state. Thus, there was not only a Great Divergence in an economic respect, but also in a sociocultural respect; something that was reflected in different demographic patterns.

In this chapter, we will describe and compare the sociocultural developments in the period after 1800, and we will answer the following questions:

1. Which changes in demographic behaviour took place in the world, and why did the Netherlands deviate from key aspects of the new demographic pattern in North-western Europe for some time?
2. What were the overall changes in the social order and social mobility, and to what extent did the Netherlands follow these? Why was there a sharp rise in social mobility?
3. How did forms of disciplining and resistance change? Was the Netherlands a trend-follower or trendsetter in this respect?
4. Which key changes took place in people's lifestyles and world views, and how did the Netherlands relate to these trends?

9.1
Demographic changes and the risks of existence

THE FIRST DEMOGRAPHIC TRANSITION In Chapter 6, we described how the population of the West grew in the nineteenth century, and that this was followed by the growth of the global population in the twentieth century. The transformation from low or stagnating population growth to rapid population growth, which took place between *c.* 1750 and 1960, is known as the First Demographic Transition. We can identify four phases in this transition. In the initial phase, large numbers of children were born, but mortality rates remained high. The population did not grow (or hardly grew) in the long term, a situation that was characteristic of almost the whole world until *c.* 1800.

In the second phase, mortality fell, thanks to the improving nutritional situation. In North-western Europe, agrarian yields rose from around 1750 (see Chapter 2). As well as better nutrition, better public hygiene also led to fewer fatal illnesses. Household rubbish was collected, and sewers and water pipes were installed. Housing improved, allowing more families to benefit from daylight and clean air. Personal hygiene also improved. Within households, people increasingly became aware that a clean house, clean textiles and good food hygiene contributed to good health. It is often thought that better public health is the consequence of vaccinations and the discovery of new medicines to fight disease. These certainly played a role, but not until the twentieth century, when the most important fall in mortality had already been realized. It was better hygiene, in particular, that led to a fall in child mortality. As the growing cohort of children themselves had children later in life, the population grew rapidly.

When people realized that better living conditions were leading to much higher child survival rates, the birth rate also fell in phase three. As a result of

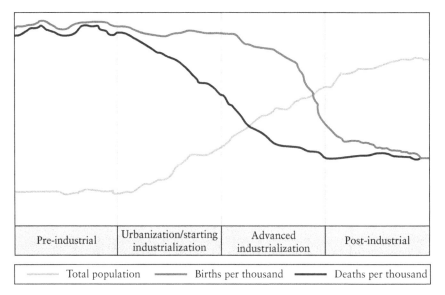

CHART 9.1 *Stages in the Demographic Transition*

increased productivity in the primary sector (see Chapter 7), a smaller share of the growing population lived in the countryside, and a larger share worked in industry and in the services sector in towns and cities. This led to greater demand for education. Children therefore attended school for longer, and it became more expensive to raise a family. Women also worked outside the home more often. Knowledge of birth control made it easier to limit the number of children.

Finally, in the fourth phase, both the birth rate and the mortality rate remained low, and population growth tailed off. As the number of young people stopped growing, the population experienced dejuvenation and ageing: the number of juveniles fell, while the share of the elderly in the population rose.

As mentioned earlier, the First Demographic Transition first took place in the West, where the second phase lasted a relatively long time. The rest of the world followed later. The countries that experienced the second phase in the twentieth century often saw rapid population growth. At present, in the early twenty-first century, much of sub-Saharan Africa is in phase two, large parts of Asia and Latin America are in phase three, and North America and Europe are in phase four.

On the whole, the Netherlands experienced the Demographic Transition in the same way as other European countries. Between 1800 and 2020, the Dutch population grew from two million to more than seventeen million. The first phase continued in the Netherlands for a large part of the nineteenth century, until *c.* 1870. The birth rate, which was above 35 (per 1,000 inhabitants), did not start to fall until *c.* 1880. The sharp peaks and falls in mortality until the 1870s are particularly striking, reflecting the impact of epidemics on the death rate. In the early nineteenth century, life expectancy at birth was still strongly determined by child mortality (see also Chapter 4); more than a quarter of all deaths involved children aged under a year, and half of all deaths involved juveniles under twenty. Due to the high infant and child mortality rate, in *c.* 1860 life expectancy was around 35 years, similar to the situation before 1800. The marital fertility rate (the number of children per marriage) was high. Population growth was kept in check by a limit on the number of marriages: many people remained unmarried because they could not afford to get married.

When the mortality rate began to fall from *c.* 1870, the Netherlands entered the second phase. Although the birth rate also fell, there was a considerable difference between the two, meaning that the Dutch population grew rapidly in the second and third phases. In most European countries, the fourth phase began around 1930, but in the Netherlands the high rate of growth continued until 1960. More and more Dutch people entered into permanent relationships in the course of their lives. In 1850, half of Dutch women aged between 20 and 44 were married; in 1971, the figure was almost 80 per cent. The birth rate fell when more children started to survive. The number of (live) births per 1,000 inhabitants fell from around 35 in the late nineteenth century, to just over 10 after 1980. The number of children could be managed thanks to the increasing use of birth control, especially the pill after 1962.

Even before the pill became available, though, the number of children per family fell in the first two generations of the twentieth century. An average number of 2.1 children per woman is needed to maintain the population size. Dutch women born in 1900 were still having 2.9 children, on average; women born in 1945, 2.0; and those born in 1960, 1.8. The mortality rate has remained stable since the 1950s. The birth rate has hardly fluctuated since the early 1970s, but dropped somewhat after 2000. The Netherlands has evidently entered the fourth phase. Life expectancy has risen sharply in the meantime. By 2020, it had increased to 83 years for women and 80 years for men.

The causes of death also underwent an important change over time. Whereas infectious diseases were still the most important cause of death in the nineteenth century (peaks and fluctuations in Chart 9.2 until 1890), in the late twentieth century people were more likely to die of ailments of old age and illnesses associated with affluence, such as cancer and heart disease. The chart also shows two exceptional peaks after 1900. In 1918–19, an epidemic of Spanish flu claimed many victims, and in 1940–5 there was an extreme mortality peak as a consequence of the Second World War. The latter peak was in fact greater than shown here, as the government's statistics agency registered those citizens who were deported to concentration camps abroad as having left the Netherlands, not as citizens who had died. In total, there were around 280,000 war fatalities in a population of nine million, most of them as a result of hostilities, hunger and death in captivity and concentration camps. A phenomenon on a scale incomparable to all of the other violent deeds that had taken place on Dutch soil in recent centuries was the transport and murder of the majority of the Jews in the Netherlands by the German occupying forces, resulting in the deaths of more than 100,000 people.

TEXT BOX 9.1 NATURAL DISASTERS AND THE FRAGILITY OF LIFE

A disaster is only a disaster if it affects large groups of people. In the case of many disasters that are categorized as natural disasters, it turns out that (ill-considered) government policy actually increased the vulnerability of large groups of people to such events. This vulnerability is usually greatest among the poorer groups in society: slum residents, landless farmers and ethnic minorities.

Take El Niño, for example, which is now recognized worldwide as a climatic effect that causes drought and, as a result, failed harvests. El Niño also occurred prior to the late eighteenth century, but it led to fewer fatalities. But this changed, for example, when greater numbers of farmers in British imperial India were pushed to live on the limit of subsistence. Monoculture (the cultivation of a single crop, such as rubber or coffee) limited their opportunities to earn a living; a poor harvest of a monoculture crop immediately spelled disaster. The introduction of market forces by the colonists did little to alleviate immediate needs. The result was mass famines and millions of deaths (estimates for 1876–9 alone suggest excess mortality of seven million in India). Opportunities for other forms of livelihood also shrank on other continents, too. In Tanzania, the German colonial regime undermined the position of the wealthier Tanzanian peasants, and in doing so destroyed the social networks that had maintained poor local peasants in times of failed harvests and famine. In South Africa, droughts led to a sharp decline in the already marginalized indigenous population, indirectly increasing the power of British famers.

The colonizers did try to take measures to counter natural disasters such as these. The British thought that better irrigation was the key to improving the standard of living in their colonies. However, the dams and dykes that the British engineers built on the Indus around 1900 actually increased the risks for the population. Indians were encouraged to go and live close to the banks of the river as a result, but these regions in particular were vulnerable to flooding. In the past, Indian rulers had dissuaded people from living too close to the river, but colonial engineers paid too little attention to existing indigenous knowledge. In Uganda, the British introduced a ban on hunting large game in the 1930s – a praiseworthy policy, from the perspective of maintaining biodiversity. But, unlike its Indian cousin, the African elephant cannot be tamed. Many Ugandan farmers therefore suffered the consequences of destructive elephant herds, which they were no longer allowed to hunt. The large numbers of these wild animals also led to the spread of the tsetse fly, which infects people and cattle with the dreaded sleeping sickness (the East African variant of sleeping sickness can be fatal within months). Although local people were aware of this symbiotic relationship, the colonists were heedless of it. The mortality level rose in the African population as a result, as a result of both sleeping sickness and reduced agricultural yields.

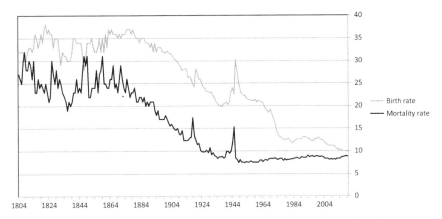

CHART 9.2 *Birth and mortality rates in the Netherlands (per thousand), 1804–2019.*
Source: CBS.

TABLE 9.1 *Population Development in the Netherlands, Belgium and Germany, 1800–2000*

	Absolute numbers (× 1,000)			Index numbers, 1800 = 100		
	Netherlands	**Belgium**	**Germany**	**Netherlands**	**Belgium**	**Germany**
1800	2,115	4,035	24,500	100	100	100
1850	3,057	4,413	33,746	145	109	138
1900	5,104	6,694	56,368	241	166	230
1950	9,925	8,512	69,200	469	211	282
2000	15,864	10,239	82,163	750	254	335

Source: Engelen, *Van 2 naar 16 miljoen mensen*, 13; Smits, Horling and Van Zanden, *Dutch GDP*, 109; http://www.populstat.info/Europe/belgiumc.htm; Wehler, *Deutsche Gesellschaftsgeschichte*.

As mentioned earlier, the second and third phases lasted longer in the Netherlands than in most other European countries. In Table 9.1, the Netherlands is compared to Belgium and Germany. In the nineteenth century, the Dutch population grew faster than the Belgian population. The Netherlands and Germany kept roughly the same pace in the nineteenth century, but the Dutch population continued to grow faster for longer, resulting in the strikingly high growth figures in the twentieth century.

How can the long-lasting population growth in the Netherlands be explained? This formed the subject of a long historical debate, in which

E. W. Hofstee emphasized traditions in agrarian regions, and F. van Heek considered the influence of religion. Theo Engelen and Hans Hillebrand have since shown that both factors played a role in the Netherlands. All groups started to have fewer children, but the number of children was always highest among Catholics, then among orthodox Protestants, then among non-orthodox Protestants, and lowest among non-believers. In addition, independently of religion, the number of children was always highest among agricultural workers and farmers, then among workers and then among employees and the liberal professions. The influence of religious differences was greater, however, than that of occupational differences. But how does this explain the differences between the Netherlands and other European countries? After all, many other countries certainly had high numbers of Catholic families and agrarian workers, too. One key factor was pillarization, which meant that different religious groups competed with one another in the Netherlands. As a result, each group maintained its own high standards, to show that it was just as respectable as the other social groups. This was why the 'old' norms prevailed for so long in the Netherlands, until the 1960s.

MIGRATION For many years, historians thought that most people in preindustrial times were tied to an agrarian community, and that they did not migrate; but in recent decades, historians of migration have revealed this assumption to be unfounded. After 1800, however, there was a clear difference between farmers and people who did not work (or who no longer worked) in agriculture. Farm workers often migrated for short periods, such as the harvest season, to places where agricultural work was available. Farmers and agricultural workers who wanted to work in farming moved to regions where agricultural land was easier to obtain, such as the United States, Canada and Australia. For those who could no longer find work in the countryside, sometimes due to agricultural mechanization, there remained the option of moving to the towns. Cities such as Paris, Milan, Prague and Barcelona, or the industrial cities of the Ruhr, grew with the flow of migrants from the nearby countryside, and later from more distant rural regions. There was (and is) all kinds of work to be found in industry and services in a city, but the risk of unemployment is also greater there. On a farm, there is always useful work for an extra pair of hands, and there is food for family members who are unemployed or who are too old or too sick to work. By contrast, someone in the town who is unable to work must appeal to family members or claim poor relief, or migrate to another city, possibly abroad, where there is more work. International migration flows were and are often fed by an earlier move from the countryside to the city.

Migration from the countryside to the towns also took place in the Netherlands; from Friesland to Amsterdam, for example, and from Brabant and Zeeland to Rotterdam. There was less and less demand for labour in the countryside, particularly after the agricultural depression of 1873–95 (see Chapter 7). Compared to neighbouring countries, however, the Netherlands never had many true industrial towns. There was industry in the towns and cities, of course; a city such as Leiden, the fifth largest city in the Netherlands in 1860, was dominated by the textiles industry for centuries. In the seventeenth and eighteenth centuries, however, Leiden's textile entrepreneurs had already moved part of their production to rural areas in the south of the country, where wages were lower. For the time being, the up-and-coming textiles factories in Tilburg and Twente had enough labour from the surrounding region.

A second reason why real factory towns remained relatively rare was the result of a deliberate control strategy by the Dutch elite. As the Netherlands was late to industrialize, people recognized its potential pitfalls, which were evident abroad: they included large working-class neighbourhoods with poor living conditions, which formed a seedbed for the workers' movement. Attempts were made to avoid such pitfalls. In Limburg, the state mines company (Staatsmijnen), a government-run enterprise, was responsible for much of the exploitation of the mines. In other countries, mining regions and militant trade unions were flashpoints for the socialist movement. In Limburg, however, the government worked with the Catholic Church to achieve reasonable working conditions. The state influenced the general wage level, and the housing associations were managed by the mines themselves or run on a Catholic basis.

As we saw in Chapter 6, after 1850 a flow of migration stepped up from Europe to the New World, prompted by rapid population growth and the agrarian crisis of the 1870s. The Netherlands participated in this migration, but only to a limited extent. A significant percentage of Dutch emigrants went not to the United States, but to the Dutch East Indies (see Chapter 8). Most migrants who crossed the Atlantic Ocean left for two reasons, religious and economic. Many were orthodox Protestants who felt that their religious lives in the Netherlands were limited by the dominance of the Dutch Reformed Church. Numerous farmers left for the United States, too, where they saw more opportunities to build up farming businesses. Often they came from Groningen, Friesland and Zeeland, where there were fewer and fewer jobs in the large-scale mechanized agricultural sector.

The overall picture of Dutch migration is shown in Chart 9.3. Between 1865 and 1960, migration from the Netherlands outweighed migration flows to the Netherlands. After the Second World War, Canada, Australia and New Zealand were popular destinations. Dutch post-war governments encouraged this outward flow, with the crisis of the 1930s in mind, because they feared structural unemployment (see also Text Box 9.2 and Chart 9.4). This prospect led to an active emigration policy, which continued until 1967.

Immigration to Europe also increased after the Second World War, in the form of postcolonial migrants, guest workers and refugees. The Netherlands shared the first flow with other former colonial powers in Europe, and the latter two with other wealthy and peaceful countries of North-western Europe.

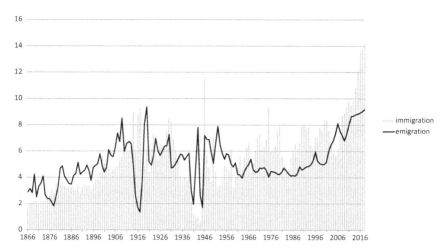

CHART 9.3 *Migration to and from the Netherlands (per thousand) 1866–2018.*
Source: CBS.

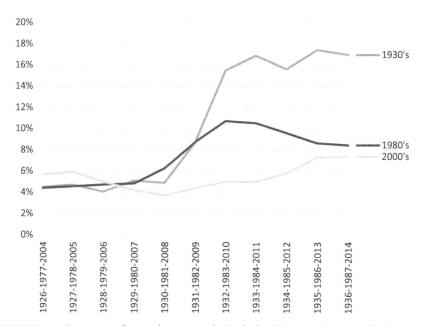

CHART 9.4 *Percentage of unemployment in the Netherlands during the crises of 1931, 1982 and 2009. The years when the greatest economic contraction occurred (1931, 1982 and 2009) are projected on one another on the horizontal axis. The chart shows the percentage of unemployment in the Netherlands in the five years before and after the three low-points.*
Source: CBS.

Decolonization and the dismantling of colonial relations led to the arrival of inhabitants from the former colonies in the European metropole. The first group of postcolonial immigrants (300,000) came from the former Dutch East Indies. This was followed by the Surinamese (100,000) after independence in 1975, consisting of people who had little confidence in the new state's political or economic future, and who thus made use of their right to come to the Netherlands before it expired. In the final decades of the twentieth century, immigration from the Dutch Antilles also began (see Text Box 9.3 and Chart 9.5).

TEXT BOX 9.2 UNEMPLOYMENT IN THE ECONOMIC CRISES OF 1931, 1982 AND 2009

The 1930s were the decade of the Great Depression, when unemployment rose to high levels. There were also serious global economic crises in the 1980s and again in 2008–9 (see Chart 9.4). In the crisis of the 1930s, the Netherlands fared worse than most other countries, whereas its performance was average in the 1980s and clearly better after 2008. Although the unemployed did not starve in the 1930s, the long-term jobless certainly suffered material deprivation. The level of prosperity in 1980 was three times higher than that in 1929. In the first place, of course, this meant that people had more reserves to fall back on. Between 1980 and 2008, the Netherlands experienced a long period in which wage rises remained limited; real wages did not rise as much as they had during the Golden Years of 1945–73. In many more families, however, both the man and the woman had jobs, meaning that double-income families were able to offset the unemployment of one breadwinner more easily.

In the 1930s, the Colijn governments tried to fight the crisis by allowing wages and prices to fall. Unemployment benefits – over which the government had more control than over wages – also fell. The unemployed were put to work in large employment-creation schemes, such as the building of roads, parks and sports complexes. They had to take part, or some of their benefits were docked. After the Second World War, there was a broad consensus that poor relief and employment-creation schemes such as these were degrading. The welfare state was subsequently built. During the crisis of the 1980s, the welfare state was fully functional: the unemployed could fall back on unemployment benefits, and there were also other, more attractive options. In the case of dismissal, employers and employees preferred to use disability or early retirement schemes, which were much more financially advantageous for those involved than unemployment regulations. This unintended use was countered in the decades after 1980. In 2008, the social safety net was far less substantial than it had been in 1982. More or less to the surprise of the policymakers, though, there was not a huge rise in unemployment in the Netherlands. The growing number of self-employed people, in particular, helped to absorb the blow. Although this group had less work, they were less likely to be reduced to full unemployment.

TEXT BOX 9.3 IMMIGRANTS IN THE NETHERLANDS AFTER THE SECOND WORLD WAR

The Dutch East Indians who immigrated in the 1950s underwent a rigorous assimilation programme. That their integration in areas such as education and the labour market subsequently went smoothly, however, was at least as much to do with the fact that they already spoke Dutch and settled at a time when the economy was booming. Moreover, the majority of them were already quite well educated. None of these factors applied, or they applied to a far lesser extent, to the unskilled guest workers from Turkey and Morocco who were recruited to cover temporary labour shortages in the metalworking, mining and textile industries. An extensive integration policy would not be introduced until the 1980s. Given their unfavourable starting position, the integration process proved to be very challenging, and was beset by major social problems (school dropout, criminality). The Surinamese had a slightly easier time, because they already spoke the language and some of them were better educated, but they also faced a fierce economic head-wind in the 1970s and 1980s.

The problems facing the children of immigrants were discussed more openly from the 1990s. The issue was given an extra dimension by concerns about radical Islam, especially after the attacks on the Twin Towers in New York in September 2001. Populist parties (the Pim Fortuyn List and later the Party for Freedom) drew a direct link between the integration problems and Islam, and urged drastic cuts in immigration, particularly from non-Western countries. Although the migration dynamic in neighbouring countries is similar and the scale of the integration problems in the Netherlands is by no means greater, since the 1990s a decidedly hard tone has been struck in the debate about Muslim immigrants in the Netherlands.

In the 1960s, Dutch industry recruited guest workers from Southern Europe, Turkey and Morocco, as did companies in Germany and other European countries. They were almost exclusively men. Three-quarters of the Spanish and two-thirds of the Italians who came to the Netherlands on this basis in the end returned to their countries of origin, while ten thousands of them settled for good. The situation was different for Turkish and Moroccan guest workers. Like the Southern European workers they also entered the Dutch welfare state and thus automatically built up social en residency rights. After the oil crisis of

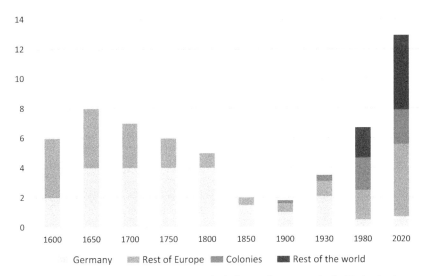

CHART 9.5 *Share of the total population of inhabitants born outside the Netherlands, 1600–2010 (percentages). The Early Modern period was characterized by continuous immigration from surrounding countries. In the nineteenth century the number of immigrants fell sharply, because industrialization in the Netherlands trailed behind that of neighbouring countries. The number of immigrants would not pick up again until the interwar period.*
Source: Jan Lucassen en Leo Lucassen, *Vijf eeuwen migratie: Een verhaal van winnaars en verliezers* (Amsterdam 2018); CBS Statline.

1973 the (centre-left) government decided to stop recruitment and close the borders. Different from Italians, who enjoyed freedom of movement by then, they realized that when they would return to their countries of origin, the door would close behind them. As a result they used the right, already realised after demands of Christian politicians around 1960, to bring their spouses and family over. This family reunification coincided with mass layoffs at the end of the 1970s and explains the rather unlucky timing of their settlement in the Netherlands, at the beginning of a long recession. For some of them their decision to stay was stimulated by the authoritarian and instable political regimes in Morocco and Turkey.

The third factor that led to increasing immigration was the political and social turmoil in certain parts of the world. From the second half of the 1980s, more refugees sought asylum in Western countries, including the Netherlands. They came both from Eastern Europe, where communism had collapsed, and from hot spots in the Third World. Moreover, as EU citizens, Eastern European labour migrants had free access to the Dutch labour market.

TABLE 9.2 *Immigrants and Their Descendants in the Netherlands, First and Second Generation, by Several Countries of Origin, in Thousands and as Percentage of the Population, 1972–2020*

Country of origin, or country of origin of one of the parents	1972	1980	1990	2000	2010	2020
Morocco	21	69	163	262	349	409
Turkey	30	112	203	309	383	417
Suriname	53	157	232	303	342	356
Netherlands Antilles and Aruba	22	40	76	107	138	166
Non-Western immigrants, total	162	475	865	1,409	1,858	2,392
As percentage of total Dutch population	1.2%	3.4%	5.8%	8.9%	11.3%	13.7%
Western migrants, total	1,062	1,141	1,221	1,367	1,501	1,829
Total immigrants	1,225	1,617	2,086	2,775	3,359	4,221
As percentage of total Dutch population	9.4%	11.5%	14.0%	17.5%	20.4%	24.4%

Source: CBS.

9.2
Social order and social mobility

THE OCCUPATIONAL STRUCTURE OF SOCIETY With industrialization, urbanization and migration, social mobility increased after 1800. This is evident from the changes that occurred in the occupational structure of society. In Table 9.3, this is compared in a number of countries. In Great Britain, the birthplace of the Industrial Revolution, agriculture, industry and the service sector were already roughly equally important employers in the first half of the nineteenth century. Employment in agriculture fell sharply in the nineteenth century.

In the first half of the twentieth century, Great Britain had a true industrial economy, with half of all employees working in industry. Industrialization in the Netherlands look place later than in Great Britain, and the consequences were less radical. A steep fall in agricultural employment would not occur until the twentieth century. As we saw in Chapter 7, in the nineteenth century the United States was much more of an agrarian nation, but the services sector and

TABLE 9.3 *Employment by Sector in the Netherlands (NL), Great Britain (GB), the United States (US), Finland (FI) and Indonesia (IN), in Percentages, 1800–2000*

	Agriculture and fishing					**Industry**					**Services and trade**				
	NL	GB	US	FI	IN	NL	GB	US	FI	IN	NL	GB	US	FI	IN
1800	43	36		82		26	30		4		31	34		14	
1850	40	21	72	71		31	41	12	10		29	38	16	19	
1900	34	9	38	52	73	33	46	30	11	5	33	44	32	37	22
1925	20	8	24	67	68	39	51	33	14	11	41	41	43	20	21
1950	19	5	12	46	72	35	53	35	28	6	46	42	53	26	22
1975	9	3	4	15	66	32	39	31	35	9	59	58	65	50	25
2000	4	2	3	6	48	18	25	23	27	19	77	73	74	66	40

Sources: GB 1800–1950: Thompson (ed.), *Cambridge Social History of Britain, vol. 2*, 133; NL: Smits, Horlings and Van Zanden, *Dutch GNP*; US, FI, IN 1800–1950: Mitchell, *International Historical Statistics*; 1975, 2000: ILO Laborsta Internet; D. Marks, *Accounting for Services. The Economic Development of the Indonesian Service Sector, ca. 1900–2000*.

industry developed rapidly there, too. In the late twentieth century, these three countries strongly resembled one another, with a services sector employing three quarters of the working population, industry employing a quarter to a fifth, and agriculture just a few per cent. Finland and Indonesia are also included in the table as examples of countries that, in Europe and internationally, followed a much more common pattern than industrial economies such as Great Britain, the Netherlands and the United States. In both countries, agriculture continued to be the most important employer for much longer: in Finland, until the mid-twentieth century; in Indonesia, until even later.

SOCIAL CLASS In addition to the occupational structure, there was also a transformation in the way in which social positions were claimed and granted in society. The 'estate-based society', in which one's social position was mainly determined by one's father's birth and status, changed into a 'class-based society', in which one's place in society was dependent on how one related to the means of production. The class of owners possessed means of production and employed others to work for them; the class of workers did not possess means of production, and had to sell their labour for wages in order to earn a living. It is not possible to draw a sharp distinction between estate- and class-based societies in every context and in all periods, of course; the nobility, for example, also owned means of production (land), and employed tenants or agricultural labourers to work for them. But the influence of the nobility waned in a class-based society, while directors and managers in industry and trade became more powerful.

Although estate and class are thus different categories, in both situations, social status could be read from a series of outward manifestations, such as how one spoke and one's clothing. A gentleman or lady wore a hat, a worker wore a cap and a working-class woman wore a shawl. Depending on their class, women were 'ladies' ('dames', the inscription on the toilet door in first-class train carriages) or 'women' ('vrouwen', the inscription in second-class carriages). People cut back on other important expenditure in order to keep up the appearances expected by their class, such as having net curtains in the windows. Recourse to poor relief was accompanied by a loss of status. Orphans wore special clothes to show that they were cared for by the orphanage, and the poor sat in special places in church.

For the upper classes, indications of one's class also included the retention of staff: a kitchen maid, a chamber maid to answer the door and clean, a third maid to do the shopping and sometimes also a nursery maid, gardener or chauffeur. A house and many staff showed how important its residents were, something that the American sociologist Thorstein Veblen (1857–1929) called 'conspicuous consumption'. In *c.* 1900, one needed at least two servants if one wanted to be included among the better circles. Occupations on the margins of the lower and upper middle classes – teachers, ministers or minor public officials – usually had to get by with one servant. Staff were necessary to give the master and mistress of the house the space they needed to meet their social obligations: the working days of elite men were often pleasantly short, leaving enough time to meet acquaintances at the gentleman's club, for example. In the 1920s and 1930s, however, it became increasingly difficult to find domestic staff. Growing freedom and better wages for what was now widely available work in factories and offices were evidently a greater draw. After 1950, employing domestic staff for whole days was an exception, although many people still employed a 'domestic help' for a few hours a week.

As a result, an important indicator of upper-class status disappeared; instead, one's occupation and level of education became increasingly important as a way of positioning oneself in society. For their research on social mobility between the generations, in the 1950s the Dutch sociologists F. van Heek and J. J. N. van Tulder developed a classification of occupations. A sample of Dutch people was asked how much prestige they attached to certain occupations. The advantage of this classification was that it brought together occupations from different economic areas in a single social layer (see Table 9.4).

The table shows that there was a significant expansion in occupations in groups I and II, which required a high level of education. In the course of the century, the group of skilled and unskilled workers declined sharply. As more jobs were added higher up the ladder and jobs disappeared from the bottom, there was a net rise in social mobility between the generations.

TABLE 9.4 *Male Working Population of the Netherlands, Based on Social Categories Devised by Van Tulder, 1899–1992*

		1899	**1919**	**1954**	**1977**	**1992**
i	Senior civil servants, directors of large companies, professionals	4.7	1.4	2.8	7.1	13.7
ii	Senior employees, high-ranking officials, large farmers, mid-ranking technicians		5.9	8.4	20.0	23.7
iii	Middle classes; mid-ranking officials, farmers and employees	46.1	19.3	19.5	13.3	11.6
iv	Lower middle classes and farmers, skilled workers, low-ranking civil servants		31.6	34.0	35.7	33.9
v	Skilled labourers, lower-ranking officials	39.0	31.8	27.9	19.8	14.5
vi	Unskilled labourers	10.2	10.0	7.5	4.1	2.5

Source: Mandemakers, 'De sociale structuur', 199.

SOCIAL INEQUALITY In Chapter 7, we addressed the economist Simon Kuznets's definition of economic growth. Kuznets also thought that there was a link between economic development and social inequality. In countries with a low level of economic development, incomes and assets are distributed rather equally. When the economy grows, some people obtain more capital and become richer, while the workers become poorer. When the average income rises, there is thus an initial increase in inequality. After some time, however, workers gain political influence. Incomes are distributed more equitably because taxes are raised on high incomes and inheritance, and the poorest groups receive insurance and benefits from the welfare state. Moreover, further economic growth also requires an increasingly large group of well-educated employees. They receive better wages, but the relative value of a good education (the skill premium; see also Chapter 2) falls, because an increasing number of people are educated. After some time, then, as the average income rises higher, income inequality falls again. The graph representing this development is known as the Kuznets curve. It has the shape of an upside-down U, as shown in Chart 9.6.

Historians have long debated the question of whether the Kuznets curve applied to Great Britain during the Industrial Revolution. It is

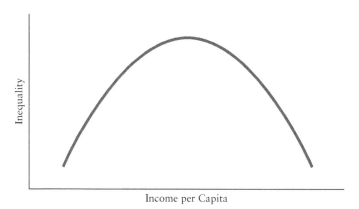

CHART 9.6 *The Kuznets curve.*

clear that in the long term, the purchasing power of ordinary British people improved, but what was the situation for industrial workers? The 'pessimists' in the debate based their arguments on accounts by nineteenth-century authors, who painted a sombre picture of the living and working conditions of British workers. 'Optimists' such as Nicholas Crafts, Peter Lindert and Jeffrey Williamson used figures to show that real wages rose. In the end, it mainly comes down to the question of when things started to improve. Research has shown that the lowest incomes grew very little between 1760 and 1820, and the standard of living of the ordinary population did not improve substantially until after 1820. If we take unemployment into account, which was a frequent phenomenon, as well as the unhealthy living conditions in the industrial towns, then an optimistic interpretation would be misplaced. In any case, income inequality rose in Great Britain during the first decades of the Industrial Revolution.

In the Netherlands, the rise of modern industry and the acceleration of economic growth started around 1860. Among those in the better occupations, the best educated did indeed earn much more, but lower down the social ladder the opposite occurred, and the skill premium for these groups fell. In 1850, unskilled construction workers earned around 60 per cent of the salary of a skilled worker, but in the construction boom of 1850–80, this rose to around 80 per cent. Thus, taken as a whole, social inequality did not rise sharply. The fact that the Netherlands did not follow the Kuznets curve in the initial phase of modern economic growth can be explained by the gradual nature of the growth.

In the twentieth century, inequality did fall, as predicted by Kuznets. Before the First World War, there was still quite a sizeable group of people in the Netherlands with a substantial income from capital. In the upper classes, income from labour was often not the most important source of income; a gentleman should not be dependent on his labour. This group shrank, as a result of higher and higher income tax. Inequality fell rapidly in the period between 1916 and 1923, when unemployment schemes were created during the First World War and new social legislation was introduced. A further fall took place between 1955 and 1980, when the trade unions managed to achieve pay rises for the lowest-paid and the welfare state expanded.

In Table 9.5, we see that inequality in the Netherlands in the second half of the twentieth century was much lower than in the United States, where the trade union movement was weaker and the free market economy was much more dominant. Inequality in the Netherlands did rise again from the 1980s, as it did in many Western countries. That phenomenon was related to the far-reaching transformation in socio-economic policy that took place in the 1980s, including the retrenchment of the welfare state (see Chapters 7 and 8).

In recent decades, social inequality in China has outstripped that in the United States. Under Mao (1949–76), there was little inequality in China, but also little economic growth, just as Kuznets had predicted. Although its Gini Coefficient was similar to that of the Netherlands, there was a high level of poverty; there were simply very few wealthy people in China. With gradual liberalization from 1978, incomes rose across China. The very worst poverty disappeared, but because the incomes of a relatively small group of city-dwellers (mainly managers of the new companies) rose rapidly, inequality continued to rise (see also Chapter 7).

TABLE 9.5 *Income Inequality in the Netherlands and the United States (after Taxation), Measured Using the Gini Coefficient, 1800–2019. The Gini Coefficient is a measure: a coefficient of 0 means perfect equality (everyone has an equal amount); a coefficient of 100 means maximal inequality (one person has everything and the rest have nothing).*

	The Netherlands	**United States**
c. 1800	c. 52-54	44
1914/1915	50	45
1977	23	41
1990	26	43
2000	26	46
2019	29	48

Sources: Van Zanden and Soltow, *Income and wealth inequality*; Van den Brakel-Hofmans, 'Ongelijkheid van inkomens'; US Census Bureau; CBS; http://eml.berkeley.edu/~webfac/cromer/e211_f12/LindertWilliamson.pdf.

SOCIAL GROUPS IN DECLINE: THE ARISTOCRACY, FARMERS AND THE TRADITIONAL MIDDLE-CLASS Increasing social mobility particularly eroded the position of the aristocracy, a group that enjoyed its final heyday in the 'long nineteenth century' (until the First World War). The aristocracy was one of the most active groups in society in international terms. Aristocratic families spoke foreign languages (especially French), crossed national borders with ease, and were over-represented in the diplomatic corps and colonial administration. But the political structure changed, the de facto power of the monarch declined, and the aristocratic network lost political and social influence as a result. They continued to have considerable influence in some countries, such as Germany, where the Junkers owned most of the cultivable land in East Prussia and also held key commercial positions; and in Great Britain, where the peerage dominated the House of Lords until late in the twentieth century.

In the Netherlands in the nineteenth century, the aristocracy and the families that had previously dominated municipal governance (the patriciate) still formed the top layer in society. Until the First World War, they provided the majority of the members of the House of Representatives (see Chart 9.7). After 1870, industrialization brought new, non-aristocratic families to power in the financial and governing elite; and after the First World War in particular, there was more political representation for other layers in society.

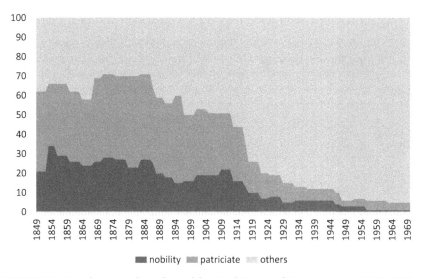

CHART 9.7 *Social origins of members of the Dutch House of Representatives, 1849–1967.*
Source: J.Th.J. van den Berg, *De toegang tot het Binnenhof. De maatschappelijke herkomst van Tweede-Kamerleden tussen 1849 en 1970*, Weesp 1983, 47-49.

In addition to the aristocracy, farmers also came under pressure. In Table 9.3, we saw that the share of agricultural jobs fell in Western European countries. Although there was not an immediate drop in the number of farms, the number of agricultural workers and smallholders did decline. This trend was also evident in the Netherlands. The large farms on clay soil in the coastal provinces, where agriculture was pursued by a small number of wealthy farmers with many servants and maids, were forced to employ fewer staff. It was increasingly easy for workers to find employment in industry, and industrial wages were high by agricultural standards. On the sandy soil, by contrast, where many small farms were based, it was the smallest farms that disappeared. The net effect was a levelling: both on the coastal clay and on the sandy ground, the medium-sized family business became the norm among farmers (also see Chapter 7). These family farms found support in the recently founded cooperatives. In the Netherlands, the first purchasing cooperative, known as 'Welbegrepen Eigenbelang', was founded in Aardenburg in 1877. The collaboration with cooperatives allowed farmers to cut out the middleman when obtaining credit (the Boerenleenbank or farmers' credit bank), raw materials (seeds, artificial fertilizer, the Boerenbond or farmers' union) or processing products (sugar refineries, potato flour-processing plants, dairy factories). This strengthened the viability of the farming business.

In the twentieth century, mechanization and growing efficiency, as well as cheap imports of agricultural products, were responsible for a sharp fall in the number of farming businesses. Resentment grew among farmers, largely prompted by increasing government intervention, and was expressed among other things by the founding of the Farmers' Party (Boerenpartij, 1959–81). Compared to countries such as Germany and France, however, where a much greater share of the population had worked in agriculture in the nineteenth century, and where the decline in the twentieth century was sharper, Dutch farmers were a weaker conservative force. The agrarian sector was also a major political player in Scandinavia. Coalitions of agrarian parties and social democrats came to power in Denmark (1933), Sweden (1933) and Norway (1935), pursuing a programme of support for the agricultural sector and social insurance for workers. This coalition also shaped the broad nature of the welfare states that emerged in these countries.

Aside from the aristocracy and the farmers, a third group lost influence: the traditional middle class of craftsmen and shopkeepers. They were a true middle class, in the sense that they had some property (a business, tools, trading stock), but their lives were dominated by physical labour. Industrialization threatened craftsmen, because more and more skilled work was gradually replaced by the products of mass and mechanized factory labour. Ready-to-wear clothing replaced the made-to-measure garments produced by tailors: first for underwear, then outerwear for women and children, and finally men's suits and overcoats (see Figure 9.1). Made-to-measure clothing became a luxury product for a small upper class. In a similar way, pottery, furniture, food, homes, tools and vehicles were also increasingly made in standard series in factories, and less and less likely to be commissioned by a particular client. Small, specialized shops were increasingly pushed aside by chain stores, and later by supermarkets. The craftsman felt the competition from cheap mass production, the shopkeeper from shops where customers no longer received specialized and personal attention, but were instead drawn by price.

In the nineteenth century, governments in Europe were generally somewhat reticent with regard to economic affairs. The twentieth century saw the introduction of regulations on the treatment of staff, opening times and the quality of products, however, and these rules also applied to medium-sized businesses. The traditional middle class saw increasing state regulation as undue interference that put limits on their personal relations with customers and staff, and made it even more difficult to compete with large outfits. All in all, the freedom and the pride of this class came under pressure.

Democratization, bureaucratization, statification, industrialization and upscaling thus put pressure on the aristocracy, the farmers and tradespeople. Understandably, they sometimes harked back to their class traditions in their attempts to resist the political status quo. Right-wing nationalist political parties, which were also critical of democratization and economic and political liberalism, held particular appeal. This explicitly happened in the Netherlands, for example, with the National Socialist Movement (NSB) in the 1930s. Members of the aristocracy were strikingly well represented in national socialist and fascist movements. After 1945, national socialist ideas were discredited, but resistance to modernization by the state continued to appeal to these classes, as shown by the aforementioned Farmers' Party.

EMERGING SOCIAL GROUPS: ENTREPRENEURS, THE NEW MIDDLE CLASS AND WORKERS Compared to the waning prospects of the aristocracy, farmers and the traditional middle class, new groups emerged and/or became more influential as a result of industrialization: industrial entrepreneurs, factory workers and the salaried middle class. Among the entrepreneurs, it was mainly self-employed entrepreneurs, such as factory owners, whose numbers grew in the nineteenth century; in the course of the twentieth century, the number of salaried entrepreneurs (managers) gradually grew.

Workers were the second group to become more important, especially in Great Britain. In that country, industrialization led to the emergence of a large industrial working class, most of whom lived close to factories and mines. A rather uniform working-class culture emerged. The typical industrial worker lived with other workers in a working-class street and a working-class neighbourhood. The shop and the pub on the corner, the working men's club, the cooperative shop and the trade union were the

FIGURE 9.1 *Sale notice from the 1920s. As ready-to-wear is cheaper than made-to-measure, many more people were able to follow fashion. This meant, though, that there was unsold stock left at the end of the season, giving rise to a new phenomenon: the sale.*
© *Collection of the IISG, Amsterdam.*

cornerstones of British working-class culture, although there were variations according to the region or sector. They were often quite indifferent to the Church of England, an attitude they shared with workers in other countries with an established church.

Other industrializing countries followed this general pattern; each, of course, with its own emphasis. In a number of countries, including the Netherlands, Belgium, Germany, Austria and Switzerland, separate Catholic working-class cultures, and also Protestant ones in some of these countries, began to organize from the 1890s. In all of these countries, the socialist labour federation was the largest. Confessional labour federations tended not to mobilize more than 20 per cent of trade union members. In countries such as Germany and Great Britain, where the socialists put less emphasis on anti-clericalism, the confessional trade unions remained small. Only in Belgium and the Netherlands was this figure much higher.

The Netherlands, with its pillars of Catholics and orthodox and non-orthodox Protestants, was a clear example of a country with a religiously divided working class. Socialist trade unions and workers' parties – the most important being the Social Democratic Workers' Party (SDAP), founded in 1894 – were anti-clerical, like elsewhere, although they were officially neutral on religious issues. Within the churches, there were calls to keep workers for the church by founding their own organizations. This led to the creation of numerous organizations that aimed to bind Christians to their faith. Three large labour federations eventually emerged in the Netherlands: the socialist

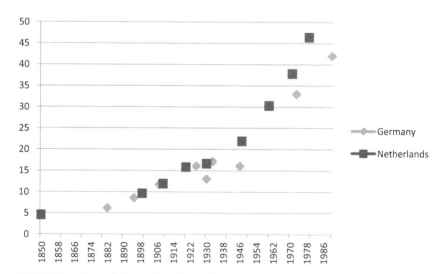

CHART 9.8 *Share of white-collar jobs in the working population, Germany and the Netherlands, 1850–1986.*
Sources: Wehler, *Deutsche Gesellschaftsgeschichte V*, 146; Wijmans, *Beeld en betekenis*, 79, 85-86, 142–143, 215.

Confederation of Trade Unions (NVV, 1906), the Protestant Christian National Trade Union Federation (CNV, 1909) and a Catholic labour federation (1909), known from 1925 as the Roman Catholic Workers' Union (RKWV). This was consistent with the Dutch pattern of 'pillarization': all kinds of social institutions and media, including schools, hospitals, foundations, care homes, poor relief, newspapers and broadcasting services, were organized or partly organized along denominational lines (see also Chapter 8).

As a result, workers could join confessional labour organizations without experiencing any conflict with the anti-clerical nature of a socialist organization. It meant that within one's own 'pillar', workers' interests were recognized and workers could join a trade union without sacrificing respect within their pillar. This was important, for example, if the workers needed poor relief from the church, or were dependent on fellow believers as employers and clients. The existence of confessional trade organizations also lowered the threshold for organization. In the Netherlands, but also in other countries, Protestant and Catholic organizations had relatively high membership rates among women, agricultural workers, employees with office jobs, and also among government and uniformed personnel, such as police officers and soldiers. These groups might not have been so well-organized if confessional alternatives had not existed. The ideology of confessional labour organizations included a principled preference for negotiation, as opposed to fighting out conflicts with employers. The socialist NVV unions likewise believed that it was first necessary to try to strike an agreement with the employers in peaceful dialogue. Confessional labour organizations tended to make less radical demands than socialist ones, and they were more willing to end a strike once it had begun.

The working class thus expanded in all Western countries, including the Netherlands, and the workers' movement developed a strong apparatus in the first half of the twentieth century, which could exercise considerable influence on policy. This influence promoted the emergence of the welfare state (see Chapters 7 and 8). With the further development of the economy after the 1960s, however, the classical working class shrank again, and blue collars were replaced with white ones.

We thereby come to the third group that became more important: the salaried middle classes. They held a whole range of jobs, with typical positions including office jobs for larger companies, business services (banks, for example) and jobs in the expanding government apparatus. In the nineteenth century and for much of the twentieth century, these wage-dependent office workers wore white shirts with collars, and are thus known as 'white-collar workers'. White-collar office workers had a very different status and working conditions from their blue-collar colleagues in the factories. In Germany, for example, factory and office personnel rarely married. In terms of salary, white-collar workers tended to be better off, but this was not always the case; a skilled worker could sometimes earn more than someone who worked in an office.

The social status of the new middle class, positioned between management and blue-collar workers, could be precarious, but they were less likely to be sympathetic to the radical right than the traditional middle class – probably because there was no old class-based tradition to hark back to. This was a group that grew rapidly in size in industrial economies, as shown for Germany and the Netherlands in Chart 9.8. As there is quite a lot of uncertainty about how to define this group, particularly in the early period, the figures are subject to debate. That is not the case for the overall trend, however: from a small share of the working population in the second half of the nineteenth century, the new middle class became the largest group in the working population.

As shown by the chart, the development in the Netherlands mirrored that in Germany. In 1850, for example, Amsterdam had around 1,500 office workers. In 1920, there were 40,000, although the city itself was only three times larger. Office work was initially done by men, and office workers' organizations did their best to keep it that way; but from around 1920, women were on the rise in the office.

The rapid expansion of office work was a consequence of the changing nature of production, in which planning and supervision played increasingly large roles. Greater and more far-reaching mechanization meant there was less need for workers, something that was also due to the shift of manufacturing to low-wage economies after 1970. The expansion of the services sector created additional office jobs. This also applied, for example, to the large transport sector in the Netherlands.

The rising middle classes developed their own bourgeois culture. Whereas factory workers in the early twentieth century wore caps, and workers in mid-century Manchester wore a particular style of corduroy trousers, the salaried middle classes wore suits and hats. A similar distinction was made in the household, where it was considered proper to eat at a laid table. For these workers, it was taken for granted that one participated in 'bourgeois' culture: attending lectures, concerts and plays. Germans used the term *Bildungsbürgertum* to describe the practitioners of intellectual occupations, such as lecturers, doctors, engineers, artists or lawyers. For these people, education and culture were considered to be more important than income.

EDUCATION AND MOBILITY The rising level of education played a critical role in the transformation of the occupational structure and the rise of the new middle class. In Europe, the nineteenth century was the century when it was established that the whole population should be able to read and write. In *c*. 1920, this was the case for the bulk of the male population and a large part of the female population in Europe. Countries in North-western Europe, where the Little Divergence had occurred, had a long tradition of high levels of literacy (see Chapter 4); but in the early twentieth century, the gap closed rapidly across the whole of Europe.

In the Netherlands around 1860, slightly more than 80 per cent of boys aged between six and twelve attended primary school, and 75 per cent of girls. The remaining children were not entirely deprived of education, but many of them did not complete six years at school. By around 1900, these figures had risen to 92 per cent of boys and 90 per cent of girls. Compulsory education was introduced in the same year, and all children aged between six and twelve had to attend primary school.

In the developed West, the twentieth century was marked by the expansion of secondary education. Progress was also made in higher education. Table 9.6 shows that in this respect, the Netherlands was in step with most neighbouring countries, and also other industrializing countries such as Russia and Japan. The United States clearly led this development. Turkey trailed behind all of these countries, something that was still the case in the early twenty-first century.

In the twentieth century, the Netherlands saw steady growth in educational participation. Compulsory education was extended stepwise until a pupil's sixteenth year. The number of children in secondary education rose from 8,000 in 1880 to 200,000 in 1965. In the second half of the twentieth century, the range of education expanded rapidly. The growth of tertiary education was related to the need for a highly developed knowledge society, and a higher level of education was one of the conditions for upwards social mobility. It was increasingly common for children in the Netherlands to rise slightly higher on the social ladder than their parents, on average. Despite this, it was still possible to slip down, too. All in all, Dutch society gradually became more open and social mobility rose.

TABLE 9.6 *Percentage of 20- to 24-Year-Olds in Higher Education, 1910–2005*

	1910	1950	1960	1970	1980	1990	1995	2005
The Netherlands	1	8	13	20	29	40	49	59
Belgium	1	3	9	18	26	40	54	62
West Germany	1	4	6	14	26	34	44	
France	1	4	7	16	25	40	51	55
Great Britain	1	3	9	14	19	30	50	59
United States	3	17	21	31	56	75	81	82
Russia (Soviet Union)			11	25	52	52	43	72
Japan			9	17	31	30		55
Turkey			3	6	5	13	18	32

Sources: Kaelble, *Sozialgeschichte Europas*, 392; UNESCO.

FIGURE 9.2 *Women's labour in agriculture, 1898: Reed-cutting. Due to the 'male breadwinner model', paid work by women became increasingly uncommon, but women and children continued to work longer in the agricultural sector.*
© Collection of the IISG, Amsterdam.

Most countries developed in the same direction: the level of education increased while the influence of one's parents' occupations declined. Individual ability thus started to play a greater role. The pace of the shift was different in different countries, however. In the United States, Australia and Canada, the influence of a father's occupation on his children had already been very modest around 1920. At that time, the Netherlands, like Latin America, was still one of the countries where the influence of one's father's occupation was greatest. When it came to openness in choosing an occupation, the Netherlands would not catch up with the United States until 1980.

WOMEN AND WORK What did growing social mobility mean for women's participation in the labour market? As we saw in Chapter 4, a family norm developed in most Western countries whereby the man was expected to earn an income for the whole family, while the woman ideally did no paid work outside the home, but instead focused on the household. In the academic debate, this is known as the 'male breadwinner model'. This model applied, for example, to the middle class and the upper layer of the working class in Great Britain, the United States and in the Netherlands.

How can we explain the emergence of this norm? In the first place, it was advantageous to have a caring adult – in practice, a woman – at home. Medical science was still unable to cure many diseases; the great age of synthetic medicines would not arrive until the twentieth century. In the nineteenth century, however, people were aware that hygiene, light and fresh air reduced the chance of contagion, and mortality rates dropped around the world. This was due, in the first place, to a fall in infant and child mortality, thanks to improved nutrition, but also thanks to better care from mothers. Moreover, the housewife could run a well-ordered household and help to bring the children up in a virtuous way. Women's wages also tended to be low, and the contribution to the family income made by a woman working outside the home was not always substantial. That of children who still lived at home quickly became more important. Thus, in the nineteenth century, the existing model of the pious mother who stayed at home for her children, in contrast to the male breadwinner who was active in public space, became dominant.

Table 9.7 shows how this norm took root in Belgium, the Netherlands and Great Britain, based on female labour participation. In Great Britain, the lowest level was reached before the First World War, but in the Netherlands and Belgium, rates of participation continued to fall until 1950–60. In 1960, female labour participation was already much higher in countries such as Great Britain, Denmark, Sweden, Germany and France. This was followed by a clear rise in female labour participation in all of the countries. The Netherlands initially trailed far behind the neighbouring countries in this respect, but achieved a comparable level around 2000, becoming one of the countries with the highest levels of female labour force participation in the early twenty-first century.

TABLE 9.7 *Women in the Labour Market in Europe and the United States, as a Percentage of All Women, 1850–1960, and of Women aged 15–64, 1960–2019*

	The Netherlands	Belgium	Great Britain	Germany	France	Sweden	Denmark
1850	24	38	30				25
1870	(1859) 18	36	28		24	29	25
1890	15	29	27	25	33	28	26
1910	18	25	26	30	39	28	30
1930	19	24	27	34	37	29	34
1950	20	19	30	31	30	29	30
1960	16	20	32	33	28	33	30
1960	26	36	49	49	47	51	44
1980	36	47	58	53	54	74	72
2000	65	57	69	64	62	76	75
2019	77	65	74	75	68	81	76

Sources: Pott-Buter, *Facts and Fairy Tales*, 21 and 28; ILO, Laborsta, World Bank.

It is striking that the Netherlands embraced the breadwinner model so strongly between the mid-nineteenth century and late twentieth century. This can partly be explained by pillarization. The idea that a married woman belonged at home, not in the labour market, was strongest among orthodox Protestants and in the Catholic pillar; but this norm was also promoted by other groups, including the socialists. In practice, the pillars competed for the moral high ground, meaning that this idea became very influential.

The result was that until around 1970, married women in the Netherlands rarely worked outside the home. This was in striking contrast to Sweden, for example, where shortages in the labour market in the early twentieth century resulted in many married women resorting to paid work. Swedish society reoriented to facilitate this, and provided good childcare facilities. In the Netherlands, it was customary for the government and some private sector actors not to employ married women, and to dismiss women when they got married. It was not until 1956 that a tiny majority in the House of Representatives passed a motion stating that 'barring evidence of wrongdoing, it is not for the State to prohibit the labour of married women.'

At the same time, of course, the table also shows that women did do paid work in practice. Working in service was the largest category. For some women, this was a job for life, but this was not the case for most: women tended to serve in the period between finishing primary school and getting married. More than half of working-class women, and a significant share of women from the social layers above, worked as maidservants for a few years. The occupation of maidservant was seen as a respectable job. Factories, with their masses of male and female workers, were considered morally suspect workplaces. When more jobs for women emerged in industry and in offices, however, with more leisure time and adequate pay, fewer and fewer women wanted to do domestic work. In the 1920s and 1930s, the decline in the number of Dutch servants was partly absorbed by women from Germany, but after 1945, the number of servants fell rapidly.

After 1970, as the table shows, Dutch women sought refuge in the labour market relatively often, albeit mainly part-time. By the early twenty-first century, Dutch women had caught up completely. They valued the personal development and independence brought by paid employment. It became the norm for Dutch families to count on the additional earnings of a second partner working outside the home.

9.3
Disciplining and counter-movements

As explained in Chapter 8, in the Western world the state evolved from being a 'night watchman state' into a 'welfare state'. One of the clearest forms of government intervention involved the use of violence: vengeance, honour killings and taking the law into one's own hands were prohibited; criminals were tracked down by the government's police force and tried by the judiciary; and warfare was exclusively a matter for state armies. In the Early Modern period, it had been customary to make a cautionary example of criminals by physically punishing them before a mass audience (floggings or brandings, for example), or, in the case of serious crimes, executing them. In the late eighteenth century, this practice encountered increasing resistance, while the number of death sentences simultaneously fell. The growing aversion to violence (or at least overt violence) is consistent with Norbert Elias' description of the development in Europe of a growing disciplining of people's emotional lives, the suppression of overt physical aggression, and the monopolization of violence by the state (see also Chapters 3 and 4).

This development was also evident in the Netherlands. The execution of Joannes Nathan on Maastricht's market square in 1860 was the last execution to be held in public, and ten years later the death penalty would be abolished altogether. The Netherlands was a forerunner in this respect. Most Western European countries would not abolish the death penalty until the twentieth century (Sweden in 1921, West Germany in 1949), and many did so only well into the second half of the century (Great Britain in 1969, France in 1981 and Belgium in 1995).

Beyond Europe, however, different norms held sway. In the colonies in the East and West, coercion and violence by Westerners against non-Westerners were the norm, and this was increasingly legitimized on racist grounds (see Text Box 9.4). In Suriname, slavery was not abolished until 1863. The demand for labour was subsequently met by contract workers from Indonesia and India. In order to cover their transport costs, they had to sign long-running employment contracts, from which they could only release themselves with many years of labour. If they wanted to stop work before then, they exposed themselves to criminal prosecution. Suriname became an ethnically diverse society as a result, with communities originating from America, Africa, Europe and Asia. In Indonesia, the 'Coolie Ordinance' of 1880 included the so-called penal sanction, which gave plantation owners almost unlimited power over the workers on their plantations. Workers could be subjected to corporal punishment for 'laziness', for example.

With the exception of Germany and Italy, the 1930s saw a trend in Western Europe towards punishing offences with fines and suspended prison sentences. The average duration of prison sentences fell. When it came to penal reform, the Netherlands emerged from the late 1940s as a 'model country' (*gidsland*): a country that provided a moral example to the world. Although there was no fall in criminality and reoffending rates even rose, there was an increasing focus on rehabilitation. Open institutions were given an enthusiastic reception. Thus, long before the progressive and permissive 1960s and 1970s, the incarceration rate fell drastically, reaching an international low of fewer than 19 inmates per 100,000 inhabitants in 1975. Even when a more repressive wind began to blow in the 1980s, the incarceration rate remained relatively low. The trend would not be reversed until the early twenty-first century, when Dutch judges briefly ranked among the strictest in Europe, after which the trend was reversed again (see Table 9.8). Compared to states such as Russia and the United States, however, the incarceration rate in Northwestern Europe remained relatively low.

PERMISSIBLE AND IMPERMISSIBLE BEHAVIOUR In the nineteenth century and for much of the twentieth century, people in the West believed their civilization to be the measure for others. Western countries assumed a civilizing mission in the countries they colonized, and used this to justify colonization. But civilization could also be an objective at home. Nations increasingly saw themselves as engaged in a struggle with others for survival. Military conscription was not only a means to replenish armies, for example, but was also an excellent opportunity to give a country's young men physical and moral training; and the same was true for compulsory primary education. Public morals were also a matter of concern.

TABLE 9.8 *Number of Prisoners per 100,000 Inhabitants in Several European Countries and the United States, 1950–2018*

	1950	1965	1975	1980	1985	1992	1998	2004	2010	2018
The Netherlands	66	25	19	23	33	49	85	123	92	63
Sweden	50	c.70	50	55	52	63	60	81	74	63
Germany		c.100	80	91	95	71	96	98	85	77
France		c.70	50	66	78	84	86	92	99	114
US	109	108		138	330	505	600	685	731	639

Source: Huls et al., *Criminaliteit en rechtshandhaving*; Human Development Reports 2007/2008; O'Brien, 'The prison on the Continent: Europe', 197; Kuhn, 'Incarceration rates'; World Prison Brief.

The policy on prostitution is a good illustration of this development. In the Early Modern period, governments had opposed prostitution on the grounds that it was contrary to God's word. In the nineteenth century, there was a change in perspective. At that time, many European states were more concerned about the risk of transmitting venereal disease, and began to regulate prostitution to facilitate some form of medical supervision. In this way, and often in partnership with civil society organizations, the government also began to regulate other forms of undesirable behaviour, such as alcohol consumption, gambling and visits to fairs. Pure opposition gave way to a policy of partial suppression and partial toleration.

The mid-nineteenth century saw the rise of the active propagation of certain norms and values, which were paraded as Christian or civic. Charitable associations and institutions tried to civilize the Dutch people with all kinds of initiatives, ranging from the promotion of frugality to the cultivation of plants. Civic culture also had to become accessible for the working classes. In the late nineteenth century, adult education institutions (*volksuniversiteiten*) were established in a number of places, and special concerts and exhibitions were organized for workers at low rates. Often, however, the organizers of such activities had to conclude that while they had been successful, they had appealed to middle-class people, rather than workers: students, clerks and housewives, who did not have much money to spend.

The disciplining of sexuality intensified in the early twentieth century, under the influence of a Christian campaign. In 1911, the Dutch government banned all brothels and advertising for contraceptives. Homosexuality was suppressed more actively, and sexual contact between adult men and youths aged under twenty-one was criminalized (the age of consent for heterosexual

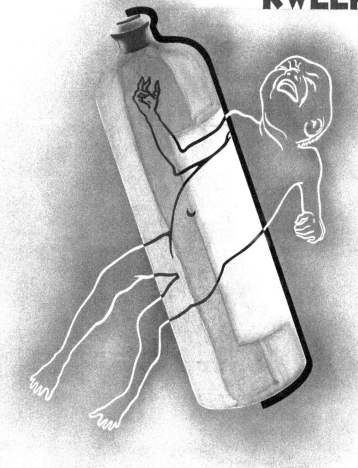

FIGURE 9.3 *Campaigning poster against alcohol abuse. Design by Henri Pieck, c. 1932.*
© *Collection of the IISG, Amsterdam.*

TEXT BOX 9.4 RACISM, A TENACIOUS NINETEENTH-CENTURY DOCTRINE

Around 1800, the word 'race' was mainly used in a biological sense, as an objective scientific concept. By the end of the nineteenth century, however, 'race' had acquired new, cultural connotations, and was used to legitimize existing differences, such as the oppression of black people by white people. This legitimization of cultural or historical inequality based on a belief in the immutability of alleged group characteristics (phenotypical, religious, social) is known as 'racism'.

In addition to differences between white and black people, Europeans also perceived increasing differences between white people themselves. Romanticism spurred a search for the typical characteristics of a nation's 'people', giving rise to notions of the 'Finnish' or 'German' races. Darwin's *Origin of Species* provided a scientific framework for these debates. A different scientific framework had its origins in linguistics, where researchers identified similarities in Indo-Germanic or Indo-Iranian languages. That distinction would later provide racists with a basis for pitting Indo-Iranian peoples against Semitic peoples (including Jews). The Western doctrine of race also reached China and India. In Confucianism, the degree of refinement was determined by race, and in Hinduism, one's degree of purity depended on one's race.

Racism was also an instrument in immigration policy. In the United States, biological racial differences were used to restrict immigration from Asia (Chinese Exclusion Act 1882) and Europe (Quota Acts 1917–24). Australia went even further with an official White Australia policy, which remained in place until the 1960s. In the colonial empires, the ruling powers, including the Dutch, used ethnic differences to uphold the existing order.

Ideas about race thus influenced all kinds of domains in the final decades of the nineteenth century. Social scientists such as Emile Durkheim and Max Weber, however, were diametrically opposed to the trend of the day; they perceived no essential differences between races, only historical differences. Racism proved especially lethal when it became a state ideology, as happened in Nazi Germany.

Although the Holocaust discredited race as a useful concept and racism as an ideology, and decolonized states used the United Nations (1945) in the 1950s and 1960s to reject racism, its legacy remained tenacious. In South Africa, Apartheid was officially installed in 1948 (and lingered on until the 1990s), and in large parts of the United States racist segregation and miscegenation laws were abolished only after a violent struggle during the civil rights era, starting with the 'Montgomery Bus Boycott' in 1955. Institutional racism, however, did not disappear in the

> United States. The life chances of African Americans are far below those of the white population, and discrimination, racial profiling and police brutality are endemic. Whether the more recent Black Lives Matter social movement will change this pattern remains to be seen, not least because 'white supremacist' ideologies have been voiced more openly in the last decade. Although less deeply rooted (due to the lack of a domestic history of slavery), institutional racism is also a feature of Dutch society, as shown by the persistent discrimination against immigrants and their descendants, both from the former colonies and those from Islamic countries (who face Islamophobia).

contact was sixteen). In the mid-twentieth century, the Netherlands was an exceptionally strait-laced country, with very low extra- and premarital birth rates, for example, both compared to other periods and to other countries (see Table 9.9).

COUNTER-MOVEMENTS The display of power by the state and the attempts by the church, associations and the state to impose certain norms also met with resistance. In Europe, the labour movement – the rise and key activities of which were covered in Chapter 8 – was the most important counter-movement from below. As shown by a comparison of data on strikes (Table 8.5), Dutch workers were not extremely militant in this regard. In that sense, the Netherlands was – and is – typical of a group of countries in North-western Europe where there was a marked tendency towards employer–employee consultations in the twentieth century. Only when the consultations between employers and employees failed could a strike go ahead. Such strikes therefore involved many workers and often lasted a long time. In South-western Europe, it was more common for a (short) strike to start a conflict, and only then would negotiations begin. However, the Dutch tradition of moderate strikes and the power of confessional organizations did not mean that there were no major conflicts between employers and employees.

For example, there were a number of strikes in the textile industry in Twente. The textile industry was subject to tough international competition, which encouraged employers to introduce new machines, increase the workload and reduce wages. Textile workers resisted these changes with strikes, and the relations between the two sides quickly hardened. In the event of a strike, all of the workers were locked out and no one was paid. As the factories were so large, thousands or tens of thousands of workers were involved. The conflicts would often last for months, such as in January-June 1902, October 1923-June 1924 and November 1931-April 1932.

FIGURE 9.4 *Provos promoting the 'White bike' bicycle-sharing scheme, 19 March 1966.*
© *IISG, Amsterdam, photo and copyright Koen Wessing.*

Another counter-movement was the movement for sexual reform. The morality campaigns of the nineteenth and early twentieth centuries had given rise to prudishness. Information about sexuality was taboo and difficult to obtain. In some countries, including the Netherlands after 1911, selling contraceptives was banned. Activists campaigned for the distribution of contraceptives and for practical information about sexuality. The Neo-Malthusian Society (1881), which later became the Netherlands Association for Sexual Reform, established a network of volunteers selling contraceptives, among other things. The movement advocated the acceptance of sexuality as a human need and source of pleasure. From this standpoint, they were champions of sexual education, the widespread availability of contraceptives and the acceptance of homosexuality.

In the 1930s, homosexuals launched a cautious emancipation movement. From the 1950s, in particular, they were clearly less intimidated by the police, and gay emancipation broke through a decade later. In 1971, the special age limit for homosexual relations was dropped from legislation. In 2001, the Netherlands even became the first country in the world to legalize same-sex marriage.

The breakthrough of the gay rights movement is just one of the ways in which traditional authority was eroded in Dutch society from the 1960s onward. Counter-movements could now draw on much broader support. The 'happenings' of the Provo movement drew a lot of media attention; completely new 'repertoires' of action developed (cf. Chapter 3, Text Box 3.2, Text Box 9.5 and Figure 9.4). Around 1970, the universities were democratized; before then, professors had been all-powerful in their institutes. The repression of brothels was once again replaced with regulation. In hospitals, psychiatric institutions and in doctor–patient relations, the authority of the white coats ebbed away. The same was true for the clergy, politicians, the police and judges.

The family changed, in the words of Abram de Swaan, from being a 'household of authority' to being a 'household of negotiation'. Husbands had had legally sanctioned authority over their wives: they determined where the family would settle, and had the final say – on paper, at least – over major expenses and important upbringing decisions. Parents had determined what teenagers and young adults living at home were allowed to do, how late they had to be home, the music they listened to, their clothes and hairstyles, and how far they went in their sexual relations. From the 1960s, spouses and children dismantled this patriarchal power. In doing so, women were in a stronger position than their mothers, because they were more likely to have an education and income, were able to divorce and could fall back on welfare payments. In a single generation, children gained enormous independence from their parents.

9.4
Lifestyles, worldviews and the Netherlands as a 'model country'

THE SECOND DEMOGRAPHIC TRANSITION From the 1960s, there was another shift in the demographic pattern. This change, which would influence marriage and reproduction in all Western developed countries, is known as the Second Demographic Transition. Marriage became less important; many people married later, or not at all. Alternative forms of cohabitation developed, particularly cohabitation without marriage. The birth rate fell and families became smaller. Due to the growing importance of education, children remained financially dependent on their parents for longer. When they started earning, they no longer had to contribute to the family income, but went and lived independently. The number of divorces rose.

The traditional marriage vow, 'until death do us part', had a literal meaning in the nineteenth century, with its low life expectancy. When a marriage was dissolved in 1850, this was almost always due to the death of a spouse. Marriage, family and kinship were also intended to cover people against social risks. Children from single-parent families had considerably worse life-chances than children who grew up with both parents. Unmarried mothers and their children were shunned. If one of the two parents died, from the common puerperal fever or due to high mortality in general, young children's life-chances deteriorated. Families without a mother quickly fell apart, and widowers with young children therefore tended to remarry quickly. Parents expected their children to care for them in their old age.

In the second half of the twentieth century, welfare payments reduced the urgency of the marital vow to remain faithful until the end, and long life-expectancy made it harder to keep. Those who no longer loved their partners increasingly opted for divorce. Until far into the twentieth century, divorce was almost exclusively an upper-class phenomenon. In the Netherlands, divorce was made easier by the introduction of the welfare safety net in 1965, and likewise by the liberalization of legislation in 1971, which also permitted divorce in the case of 'permanent marital breakdown'. When a marriage ended in 2000, in 44 per cent of cases this was due to the death of the husband, in 19 per cent of cases due to the death of the wife, and in 37 per cent of cases due to divorce. This latter figure was even lower than it would otherwise have been because from the 1970s, more and more couples lived together but did not marry. As a result, not all relationships and break-ups were reflected in the marriage statistics. The fact that cohabiting without getting married became more common after 1970 is one of the signs that searching for a partner was now less bound by social conventions, leaving more room for romance. A new phase of independent young adulthood emerged, in which young people experimented with love and sex for much longer than they had done in the early twentieth century.

TEXT BOX 9.5 THE GENERATION OF THE 1960S

Historical swings mean that one generation of young adults can have different experiences from the next, meaning that one generation will develop a different perspective on life from the next. In the years after 1945, a generation of adults grew up across the world that had lived through the crisis and war, and had to work hard on the reconstruction. In the 1960s, a generation came of age that had been born after the war. In Western countries, their parents' lives had kept improving. They took growing prosperity for granted, and pursued different goals in life.

From the late 1950s, a culture spread from the United States and England that was focused explicitly on young people. Music was an important element of this culture: rock and roll and beat were popular with young people the world over, but dismissed by older generations as 'noise'. Young people also used clothing and behaviour to distinguish themselves from the previous generation's way of life. The protest rapidly became political. In the United States, the civil rights movement fought discrimination against African Americans. In Montgomery (Alabama) in 1955–6, African Americans boycotted municipal buses because they were forced to sit at the back. In Greensboro in North Carolina in 1960, African American students organized a sit-in to protest against segregated lunch facilities. From 1963, there were protests against the war in Vietnam, mainly by students. Students demanded that their universities democratize; in Berkeley in 1964–5, they called for the right to discuss politics (the Free Speech Movement). In 1968 students occupied their universities, from the Sorbonne in Paris to Columbia University in New York. Women, psychiatric patients, homosexuals: every group that felt discriminated against followed the pattern of protesting against the authorities.

This global movement did not pass the Netherlands by. Between 1965 and 1967, the Provo action group carried out 'happenings' in many Dutch cities (see Figure 9.4). Their alternative forms of protest caught the authorities off guard; the student Koosje Koster was arrested and mistreated for handing out currants in the street, for example. The Provos won much publicity in this way. In April 1969, the Catholic University in Tilburg was occupied, followed in May by the Maagdenhuis, the administrative centre of the University of Amsterdam. Partly inspired by the fact that the men there acted as spokespeople and women made the sandwiches, the feminist campaign group Dolle Mina was founded. Dolle Mina had a good instinct for publicity-grabbing campaigns, too, such as when they interrupted a gynaecologists' conference in 1970 with the slogan 'Boss of my own belly' written on their naked stomachs, in support of abortion rights.

The proportion of births that took place within marriage fell compared to the past. Traditionally, religious and civic morals had proscribed women from having sexual relations or children before or outside marriage. Given the unreliability of birth control, until 1960 extramarital births gave a good indication of the degree of premarital and extramarital (heterosexual) sexual intercourse. Migration to the city and work outside the home were seen as risk factors: they took young women beyond the circle of the family, leaving the latter less able to protect their chastity. The risks were significant, as men tended to marry late: around 1900, the average age of marriage was twenty-seven for men and twenty-five for women. Premarital sex was relatively common; 30–50 per cent of first children were conceived before marriage. Despite this, there were few extramarital births (see Table 9.9): parents usually married before the birth of their child. These social norms were upheld by the family, church, employer, neighbourhood or village. Pillarization, whereby different religious denominations vied with one another to uphold moral standards, reinforced this tendency.

Until 1960, the extramarital birth rate in the Netherlands was clearly lower than that in other North-western European countries; in 1960, it was level with that of Greece, a country governed by the strong patriarchal norm that women should enter into marriage as virgins. But with the Second Demographic Transition, this picture changed radically. Alternative forms of households

TABLE 9.9 *Percentage of Extramarital Births in Several European Countries, 1870–2019*

	First Demographic Transition				*Second Demographic Transition*				
	1870	*1900*	*1930*	*1960*	*1980*	*1990*	*2000*	*2010*	*2019*
The Netherlands	3.5	2.5	1.8	1.3	4.1	11.4	24.9	44.3	52.4
England and Wales	5.5	4.0	4.5	5.8	11.5	27.9	39.5	46.9	48.2 (2017)
France	7.3	8.8	7.9	5.9	11.4	30.1	43.6	55.0	61.0
Sweden	10.0	11.3	16.4	11.3	39.7	47.0	55.3	54.2	54.5
Denmark	11.2	9.9	10.5	7.7	33.2	46.4	44.6	47.3	54.1
Italy	5.6	5.9	5.2	2.3	4.3	6.5	9.2	21.8	35.4
Spain	4.5	4.7	6.5	2.4	3.9	9.6	17.7	35.5	48.4
Portugal	11.4	11.2	15.2	9.9	9.2	14.7	22.2	41.3	56.8
Greece	1.3	1.3	1.3	1.3	1.5	2.2	4.0	7.3	12.4

Source: Public Thirty-year file of the Princeton European Fertility Project, Office of Population Research, Princeton; US Census Bureau; Eurostat.

developed, particularly cohabitation out of wedlock. As a result of these developments, the number of single-parent families grew. In the 2010s, a new European norm emerged in which just half of children were born in wedlock, with Greece and Italy moving in the same direction, albeit more slowly.

The Second Demographic Transition can be explained by a series of interconnected changes: women's emancipation, the sexual revolution, the rejection of traditional authority and the waning influence of the church. In the United States, for example, African Americans demanded their civil rights from the 1950s, and that model had a contagious effect on many other groups. Increasingly, people opted to make individual choices that differed from traditional practices.

ETHICAL ISSUES From the 1970s, the term *gidsland* or 'model country', which portrayed the Netherlands as extremely progressive on a number of ethical issues, became an important part of the Dutch self-image. The typically Dutch focus on the rehabilitation of criminals was mentioned earlier. Another issue was *abortus provocatus*, the artificial termination of a pregnancy. For centuries, it had been used as a form of birth control. If one could afford it, one could go to a private clinic, but for less money, illegal back-street abortionists carried out risky procedures. Feminists campaigned for women to have control over their own bodies: 'boss of my own belly', as the activist group Dolle Mina put it. From 1971, the Dutch government tolerated clinics that openly offered abortions to women who wanted to terminate a pregnancy. Abortion was eventually regulated by law in the early 1980s.

In the area of prostitution, from the 1970s policy was increasingly left to municipal administrators, resulting in a patchwork approach. From 2000 onwards, influenced by the women's movement, this was followed by attempts to find a solution to the issue by recognizing sex work as legitimate work. Running a brothel was decriminalized as a result. This formal recognition did not reduce the stigma attached to prostitution, however. A very different policy was followed in Sweden, where from 1999 onwards the clients were prosecuted and prostitutes were left alone.

The Netherlands also took a pioneering ethical approach to the issue of euthanasia. Although it had become technically possible to keep the seriously ill, who were usually elderly, alive for a very long time, many saw such an existence as undignified. They wanted doctors to be allowed to help them to end their lives. Euthanasia became a topic of social debate in the Netherlands from 1969, and led to dozens of discussion papers and test cases. What had become a broad social consensus was codified in 2001. If a patient is experiencing unbearable and incurable suffering, and if they have voluntarily and deliberately asked for euthanasia, then under certain conditions the doctor is allowed to grant their request.

Table 9.10 gives an overview of the legalization of a number of pressing ethical issues. Most countries have long had prohibitions in place; few countries use legalization. Prohibition does not automatically lead to

TABLE 9.10 *Legalization of Pressing Ethical Issues in a Number of Countries, 1920–2020*

	Abortion	**Euthanasia**	**Prostitution**	**Gay marriage**
Netherlands	1971–81	1985–2002	2000	2001
Belgium	1990	2002		2003
(West) Germany	1974–76	2014–20	2002	2017
Sweden	1974	2010		2009
Great Britain	1967			2013–20
France	1975			2013
Italy	1978			
United States	1973			2015
Russia	1920, 1955			

prosecutions, however. Most countries choose to leave a ban in the statute book, but to tolerate the practice to a greater or lesser extent. Until around 1970, the Netherlands was such a country. Euthanasia is a case in point: it had been prohibited since 1886, but this prohibition was neither checked in practice by the judiciary nor criticized by society. What is striking about the Dutch position is the desire to tackle issues with legislation, if possible. The argument that the lack of statutory regulation creates too much legal uncertainty for those involved evidently weighs more heavily in the Netherlands than in other countries.

Of a different nature is the extension of marriage to homosexuals, which has been included in the table for comparison. This is a less complex issue in an ethical sense, as there is no difficult delineation of boundaries. In 1911, and also in 1950, homosexuality was still an issue in the Netherlands that fell into the category of 'immoral acts'. Today, homosexuality is largely accepted in the Netherlands. Xenophobic political movements have even made tolerance of homosexuality a test of a person's acceptance of Dutch culture. In countries where religion holds more sway over politics than in the Netherlands, same-sex marriage has encountered much more resistance.

CONSUMPTION PATTERNS Increasing individual freedom of choice was also reflected in consumer behaviour. From the late nineteenth century, a mass consumer culture arose, initially in the Western world. The impetus came from rising prosperity among the working classes and increasing leisure time, which created space for consumption. Technological developments facilitated many new products, from cars to radios and MP3 players. People were increasingly able to choose from all kinds of brands, and from products that had been made in distant countries.

Back in the nineteenth century, most people still had very limited leisure time, because workers had long working days and little to spend. Recreation was limited to visits to cafes and the annual fair. A twelve to thirteen-hour working day was the norm. The development towards more commercial leisure activities began in the nineteenth century in the United States and Great Britain, where people had more purchasing power and where various industries, under pressure from workers, had already introduced a shorter working day. In the Netherlands, a mass consumer culture developed from 1910, with the introduction of the eight-hour day (1919), the rise of the free weekend, new leisure pursuits such as football and the cinema, and somewhat later, also holidays and radio. External cultural influences (sports such as football, dance crazes such as the foxtrot and swing, music such as jazz and pop, films and television series) had a major influence on how people spent their free time. The internationalization of leisure culture can be seen as the predominant trend of the twentieth century.

People from all social classes had more possessions, and there was an increase in factory-made goods and branded products compared to the unbranded products made by local craftsmen. The rise of department stores and chain stores and the relative decline in retail trade and home sales were related to this development. The first massive department stores in the United States mainly targeted female consumers. There was a sharp rise in the amount of living space per capita, home ownership and DIY activities, particularly in the second half of the twentieth century.

In addition to their inherent utility, the new products also had novel symbolic qualities. Consuming the right products was modern and young, ethical and environmentally friendly, or hip and cool. All these changes did mean, though, that the individualization of consumption was limited, to the extent that people increasingly adopted particular consumption patterns and styles: some groups had their own specific hairstyles or dress codes. The advertising industry responded deftly to these connections by identifying and targeting different types of consumers.

Table 9.11 gives an overview of the ownership of consumer durables in different industrialized countries. It is clear that the Netherlands moved with the other North-western European countries, all of which trailed significantly behind the United States. Within North-western Europe, the Dutch consumer remained relatively frugal until 1960, but was thriving by the end of the twentieth century.

Technological development and purchasing power led to constant innovation in the media: the twentieth century saw the successive rise of newspapers and magazines with mass readerships, and of the cinema, radio, television and the Internet. Mass media had a growing reach, and in some cases even became global. With the growth in prosperity, around 1930 the average family had a newspaper subscription. Local and denominational

TABLE 9.11 *Ownership of Consumer Durables in Industrialized Countries per 1,000 Inhabitants, 1937–2010*

	Radios			Televisions			
	1938	**1950**	**1960**	**1960**	**1975**	**1989**	**2003**
The Netherlands	129	195	272	69	259	485	499
Belgium	135	179	289	68	252	447	455
France	114	165	241	41	235	402	559
Sweden	196	307	367	156	354	471	513
Denmark	178	283	332	119	289	282	579
Great Britain	182	244	289	211	315	434	512
West Germany	172	180	287	83	305	506	623
East Germany		190	323	60		413	
Portugal	11	27	95	5	66	176	317
United States	315	590		289[a]	571	814	755
Russia		61	205	22	217	323	418

	Cars							PCs	
	1937	**1950**	**1960**	**1975**	**1989**	**2002**	**2010**	**1990**	**2006**
The Netherlands	11	14	45	254	362	477	528	94	854
Belgium	17	32	82	267	335	520	559	88	377
France	48	37	121	290	340	576	578[b]	71	575
Sweden	21	36	160	336	369	500	520	105	836
Denmark	27	28	89	289	282	430	480	115	696
Great Britain	40	46	105	249	366	515	519	109	758
West Germany	16	13	81	289	412	586	572[b]	82	606
East Germany	16		18	110	234				
Portugal	4	7	18	84	159		548	26	133
United States	197	266	347	495	589	812	797[b]	215	762
Russia				30	58		293[b]	3	122

a =1965; b =2014
Source: Therborn, *European Modernity*, 141-143; Dargay, Gately and Sommer, 'Vehicle ownership'; World Bank; Übergizmo, 'Computer ownership'.

newspapers were superseded by what were de facto increasingly national papers. In the Netherlands, a pillarized national radio and TV system was established in the 1920s and 1930s. From the 1960s, this system faced competition from foreign radio and television broadcasters. For some decades, the pillarized Dutch broadcasting service attempted to hold its ground, but commercial and foreign television gradually broke through.

WORLD RELIGIONS, SECULARIZATION AND VISIONS OF THE WORLD The nineteenth century was an extremely devout century in many respects. Secularization advanced, but only in a few circumscribed domains. The sciences and some political and social movements liberated themselves from religious dogmas. Religion continued to shape most people's worldviews in the nineteenth century, however; it remained of importance for political policy and ethical norms and values, and played a significant role in birth, marriage and death.

Christianity was propagated actively across the world by Western colonizers, via delegations and missionary work. The other world religions – Islam, Hinduism, Buddhism and Confucianism – responded by defining their own doctrines more precisely, so as to arm themselves more effectively against the competition. After the Meiji Revolution in Japan, Shintoism, until then a rather vague and localized cult, was given the status of a state religion. Hinduism, Buddhism and Confucianism had never been centralized religions – in fact, Confucianism had only consisted of a set of rules on how to behave – but now people set about canonizing ancient texts that were made into religious dogma. Under this disciplining force of established religions, the local, 'Little Traditions' were suppressed (see Chapter 4). All of the world religions defined their identities more clearly and became more spiritual, hierarchical, uniform and bureaucratic. Religious laws were recorded – sometimes at the request of the colonizers, who wanted to uphold order with the aid of local (non-Christian) religious frameworks.

At the same time, new philosophical and scientific insights gave rise to doubts about the message of the Bible and the Koran in the Christian and Islamic world. Darwin's theory of evolution provoked heated discussions about the creation of the world. The principle of natural selection undermined the image of an almighty God. Historical source criticism promoted a less literal reading of the Bible. In Islam, intellectuals such as Sayyid Ahmad Khan from India and Muhammad Abduh from Egypt promoted reason as the foundation for critical thinking about the Koran. In a remarkably free discussion about culture, they challenged taboos on the traditional subordination of women, for example. In 1876, freedom of religion was established by law in the Ottoman Empire. These modernizing tendencies provoked a reaction from orthodox believers, who wanted to uphold the literal interpretation. In the Netherlands, for example, this resulted in orthodox Protestants seceding from the Dutch Reformed Church (1834, 1886). In Turkey, orthodox Islamists opposed the secularization of the state, but would lose the argument due to the revolution by the ultra-secular Young Turks between 1908 and 1923 (when Ataturk emerged as the great leader).

Social scientists had by now become convinced that organized religion would eventually succumb to the challenge from scientific reason, a belief that was reinforced by the flourishing of the sciences in the late nineteenth century (see Text Box 9.6). Westerners could now explain the world so well that it was no longer necessary to appeal to a Supreme Being. Indeed, this did happen in Western Europe, where the importance of the church waned and atheism became socially acceptable. Churches also adapted to the new age. The Second Vatican Council (1962–5), for example, created room for the democratization of the Catholic Church and permitted the use of the vernacular in the liturgy. But the social acceptance of 'non-believers' did not immediately bring an end to people's belief in a 'higher being'. Recent research shows that convinced atheists remain a minority in the European population – around one-fifth, if one includes spiritual movements such as the New Age movement as religious. In the rest of the world, including the United States, the importance of the established religions remains undiminished (see Table 9.12). From the end of the twentieth century, more orthodox currents gained strength in many of the established churches, be it Islam in Iran or Turkey, or the Dutch Catholic Church.

The Netherlands followed the Western European pattern, if somewhat belatedly. In the nineteenth century, the Netherlands was still a very religious society. In the twentieth century, this high level of piety was maintained for many years, mainly under the influence of pillarization. The confessional pillars disintegrated rapidly after 1970, leaving important institutional remnants behind them, such as the formally pillarized character of schools, hospitals and

TABLE 9.12 *Faith and Churchgoing in Different Countries, 1947–2014*

	Believes in God							**Attends at least one church service per week**				
	1947	1968	1975	1981	1990	2001	2010/ 2014	1970	1981	1990	2001	2010/ 2014
The Netherlands	80	79		64	61	58	48	41	26	20	14	11
(W) Germany			81	72	68	63	69	63	29	19	18	16	10
France	66	73	72	59	57	56		23	13	13	10[b]	7[c]
Great Britain		77	76	73	72	61		16[a]	9	13	4	17[d]
Sweden	80	60		52	38	46	41		6	4	7	4
US	94	98	94	96	93	94	88		43	44	46	33
Brazil	96				98	99	98					50

a = 1973; b = 1998; c = 2006; d = 2005
Sources: Norris & Inglehart, *Sacred and Secular*; World Values Survey.

the media. At the same time, there was rapid secularization (see Table 9.12). Due to falling church attendance, churches were less able than in the past to play a role in disciplining society and forcing compliance with imposed rules, and this was replaced with the increasing internalization of social norms.

> ### TEXT BOX 9.6 SCIENCE AND SOCIETY IN THE NINETEENTH AND TWENTIETH CENTURIES
>
> From the late nineteenth century, science was practised on a much greater scale than in the past. The era of 'big science' began. There was increasing investment in laboratories and equipment, more and more scientific practitioners were active, and increasing numbers of scientific publications were published. In 1910, there were around 8,000 physicists and chemists in Germany and Great Britain combined. Eighty years later, there were around five million researchers working across the world in the natural and technical sciences, one million of whom were based in the United States, and just over one million in Europe as a whole. From the 1930s, partly due to the immigration of top researchers from Europe and Asia, the United States became the global centre of scientific practice.
>
> The practice of science became increasingly dependent on investment from government and business; and government and business, in turn, made much more use of scientific knowledge. From the time of the Second Industrial Revolution (see Chapter 7), manufacturing technology and science became more and more interwoven. Scientific developments facilitated the rise of whole new industries, such as the manufacturing of electrical equipment, the generation of nuclear power, the pharmaceuticals industry, ICT and biotechnology. Thanks to their scientific knowledge, states could radically expand their military capacity, for example by developing guided weapons or building advanced aircraft. The government could also draw on knowledge from the arts and social sciences. Economics and public administration supplied instruments for social engineering. Anthropology, linguistics and history provided useful knowledge for colonial rule and the formation of national identity (see Chapter 8).
>
> Scientific developments not only made it possible for people to produce more, live longer and kill on a massive scale, but they also put existing visions of the world to the test. The universe turned out to be much older and vaster than anyone had thought. The smallest particles in nature did not obey the rules of classical physics. The Bible was analysed as a product of complex historical developments. People and animals turned out to have more in common than had traditionally been assumed. Individuals also proved to be far less autonomous and reasonable creatures than they had often imagined themselves; their behaviour and character were also determined, to a great extent, by genes, circumstances and history.

The Netherlands was at the forefront of some of these new developments for a while. Indeed, Dutch science was held in such high international regard in the late nineteenth and early twentieth centuries (as shown, among other things, by the relatively large number of Dutch scientists awarded Nobel prizes) that historians refer to a 'Second Golden Age'. At that time, international recognition for the achievements of Dutch physicists, chemists, astronomers, biologists and linguists formed (and continues to form) a source of national pride, and provided extra ammunition for the arsenal of nationalism. The flourishing of Dutch science was no coincidence. The introduction of a new type of secondary school in 1863, the HBS (hogereburgerschool or high school) and the modernization of the universities in 1876, which took place under liberal governments, gave a boost to scientific specialization and ensured the creation of many more facilities for research in the natural sciences.

Summary

Finally, let us summarize the answers to the questions posed at the beginning of this chapter.

1. From around 1800, the demographic pattern that had existed for centuries underwent important changes. In the West, mortality rates started to fall, meaning that the population began to grow at a rapid rate. After a few decades, this was followed by a fall in the birth rate. This intermediary phase of low mortality rates and high birth rates lasted much longer in the Netherlands than in other Western countries, meaning that the Dutch population grew faster than elsewhere. As the social pillars competed with one other for the moral high ground, pillarization stimulated the formation of large, stable families. The Netherlands also underwent the Second Demographic Transition in the second half of the twentieth century, a phase when people married increasingly later or not at all, and the birth rate also fell.
2. There was a decline in the significance of the aristocracy, the farmers and the traditional middle class in the social order. Industrial workers, and subsequently blue- and then white-collar workers, began to play an increasingly important role. Offices also provided more employment for female workers. Compared to other countries, social mobility in the Netherlands was modest, but the Netherlands caught up in the course of the twentieth century. As in many other Western countries, social mobility was supported by the

strong expansion of education. Female labour force participation increased quickly after 1990, when the Netherlands abandoned its traditionally low rate of female labour participation.

3. When it came to disciplining, state intervention grew strongly in every area. The government increasingly determined what was permissible. Private organizations also played an active role in civilizing the citizenry, often in the context of pillarization. In the nineteenth century, the Netherlands was a follower of this trend. In the early twentieth century, Dutch society became increasingly straitlaced, with stricter regulation of sexuality than in other Western countries. There were relatively few strikes in the Netherlands, but those that were held were at least as intensive and protracted as elsewhere. The unusual forms of protest ('happenings') adopted by the counter-movement of the 1960s temporarily made the Netherlands a trendsetter.

4. From the late nineteenth century, there was a transformation in consumer behaviour in the Western world, facilitated by growing prosperity, leisure time and technology. Globalization stimulated the spread of mass consumer culture. The world's religions strengthened their organizational bases in the nineteenth century. Secularization was initially limited to a few domains, such as science, but it would continue to take root in Western Europe in the course of the twentieth century. Beyond Western Europe, however, there was hardly any secularization. In quite a short period, the Netherlands went from being an extremely Christian and moral country to being a relatively irreligious country, and a frontrunner in debating ethical issues.

10

Conclusion to Part II

In the preceding chapters, we have seen how fundamental changes took place in the nineteenth and twentieth centuries in relation to how the basic problems of income, power and the risks of existence were tackled. The contours of these changes were sketched out in the introduction to part II. To conclude, we draw a comparison between Europe and other parts of the world, and we look in more detail at the role that the Netherlands played in these great changes. What exactly was the Great Divergence? When and in what respects did the gap close? Which interactions between economic, sociopolitical, sociocultural and mental factors can we identify? And to what extent was the Netherlands a 'plaything' or a 'key player' in these global developments?

If there was ever a time when Europe made its mark on the development of the world, it was the 'long' nineteenth century, which lasted from the French Revolution to the First World War. This was the age when the Great Divergence became fully established in all kinds of areas (economic, sociopolitical, sociocultural). The European share of the world's population grew to unprecedented levels, large numbers of Europeans emigrated overseas and rapidly expanding European settler colonies were established all over the world. This enormous population expansion was related to the beginning of the Demographic Transition (falling mortality but high birth rates), in which Europe – and especially Western Europe – was ahead of the rest of the world. North-western Europe was the first region in the world to experience sustained economic growth; it was where modern industry developed, the majority of the working population worked outside agriculture, and more than half of the population lived in towns. The Little Divergence, which had emerged in the seventeenth century, would continue long into the twentieth century. For many years, the average standard of living in North-western Europe was much higher than anywhere else in the world (with the exception of the United States). Empires with a European metropole covered a large part of the globe, and European countries had the largest share in world trade.

Together with the United States and some settler colonies, West European countries were also pioneers of democratization. The Atlantic revolutions spread ideas of freedom and equality across the world, and these would later become anchored in the United Nations. European countries were leaders in the modernization of social policy, such as the 'statification of welfare arrangements', the creation of the nation state, the growth of science, the development of technology, the secularization of society and the design of all kinds of new ideas and ideologies, ranging from liberalism, socialism, Christian democracy and human rights to nationalism, communism, fascism and racism. On all these points, a Great Divergence opened up between Europe, then still seen as the heart of the West, and non-Western parts of the world, such as China, India, Southeast Asia, the Middle East and Africa. The leading thinkers on the origins of the great divide were also Europeans: Adam Smith, Robert Malthus, Karl Marx and Max Weber.

The gap began to close after 1920, and within Europe, the Little Divergence between the North-west and the rest became less significant. Europe's overall demographic share fell sharply, both due to the slowing of population growth in Europe itself and due to the enormous growth in other parts of the world. In an economic respect, considerable changes took place in the 'short' twentieth century, which lasted from the First World War to the fall of the Berlin Wall (1989). The world economy was divided into three blocs: the Western countries, now led by the United States, which enjoyed long-lasting growth in prosperity and technological progress; a communist bloc, which followed its own economic and political model; and a very diverse group of developing countries (the 'Third World'), which were used to supply raw materials and as an export market for Western industrial products, and generally had much lower levels of prosperity and less technological development.

The First and Second World Wars proved highly disruptive for Europe and brought an end to its ascendancy in an economic, political and moral respect. In the decades that followed, the world became more differentiated; economic, sociopolitical and sociocultural changes no longer followed the path taken by 'the' West. Globalization showed both convergent and divergent tendencies. On the one hand, the communist economies disappeared almost completely as a separate category after 1989, while on the other hand, an unprecedented economic dynamic emerged in some parts of the former Third World. Around the year 2000, the world beyond the original group of industrialized countries (North America, Europe and Japan) was home to various newly industrializing and/or rapidly growing economic regions in the northern and southern hemispheres: China, India, Brazil, Mexico, Australia and South Korea. The part of the world that experienced the least growth was Africa.

A lessening of economic differences did not mean that the world was converging towards a single type of market economy, however: diverse kinds of capitalism continued to exist alongside one another. This pattern was also visible in other aspects of social development. Non-European countries followed European examples to a certain extent when it came to the formation of nation states, democratization or the development of a public sphere, but often interpreted them in different ways. China's state-led economy did not appear to preclude a booming market economy. When it came to secularization, however, the influence of the European model remained. Numerous non-European countries, including the United States, became more religious rather than less. Europe also lost its scientific and technological hegemony, and the leading thinkers on global processes increasingly came from North America, not the Old World: Charles Tilly, William McNeill, Immanuel Wallerstein.

These developments frequently showed how economic, social, political and cultural factors could influence one another. Colonial oppression by Western countries was supported by their industrial power bases and defended with nationalist and racist arguments. The growing prosperity of the industrialized world facilitated the rise of the welfare state, which helped to absorb and mitigate the risks of existence. With the formation of the European Union, economic motives tended to dominate. Now that European unification is further advanced, there is more need than ever to define Europe politically and culturally, too; an urgent search is underway for a European identity. By ensuring that those at the bottom of society also had a reasonable standard of living, the democratization process gained a broad base. Growing prosperity also brought new threats, however, such as global warming and environmental pollution. The question is whether the 'rest' of the world can match the economic level of the West without this leading to a drastic worsening of living conditions and environmental destruction, and thus a considerably higher level of existential risk.

To what extent was the Netherlands a 'plaything' or a 'key player' in the global changes after 1800? The course of the world economy was clearly changed by the Great Divergence. After all, the Netherlands had been a key player and leader in various areas in the Early Modern period. The Netherlands played a leading role in the Little Divergence, characterized by the high average income per capita of the population, breaking through the Malthusian ceiling at an early stage, a flexible and free labour market, a small share of the working population in agriculture, efficient state finances, strong civilian control over military institutions, an important diplomatic role in the European state system, a broad public sphere, a high level of literacy, a radical version of the Enlightenment that brought radical ideas, the early development of the nuclear family with considerable scope to choose one's own partner, to name a few salient characteristics.

From the Great Divergence onwards, however, the Netherlands largely became a follower of trends. Compared to other Western European countries, the Netherlands industrialized relatively late; in the industrialization process, it was more of a follower than a pioneer. Innovations could be introduced on a larger scale only after the institutional framework had been adjusted.

Like Great Britain, the Netherlands had a relatively open economy after 1850. As a result, the country could also participate fully in the wave of globalization that lasted until the First World War. The Dutch share in world trade and capital exports was relatively large, thanks in part to its sizeable colonial possessions. After the Second World War, the Netherlands, which had industrialized at a rapid rate in the meantime, could profit significantly from renewed globalization and growing economic cooperation within Europe. As a co-initiator of the cooperation, it also exercised considerable influence at this early stage.

When it came to the transition to the nation state, the Netherlands was more of a follower than a leader. The formation of a national unitary state was possible only with French intervention and the Congress of Vienna. In the later nineteenth century and early twentieth century, nationalist ideas had less chance to penetrate pillarized Dutch society for a time, because attachment to one's own pillar was sometimes a higher priority than enthusiastic commitment to the nation state. The Netherlands was not a key player in the democratization process, either. However, the unique legacy of the Early Modern period – especially the presence of a decentralized negotiation structure, the general lack of feudal influences and the traditionally strong position of civil society, thanks to the broad public sphere – helped the transition to a democratic form of government to take place in a relatively smooth and conflict-free fashion.

When it came to the development of social policy, the Netherlands followed its own path to a certain extent, which left a considerable amount of space for civil society. It would be some time before the Netherlands had a state-led model, such as that introduced by Bismarck in Germany. To an important extent, the specific path taken by the Netherlands was contingent on specific historical circumstances. The industrial proletariat in the Netherlands was smaller than that in countries such as Germany or France, which partly explains the less radical and less massive nature of Dutch social movements. Moreover, for many years, it was an essential characteristic of the Netherlands that denominational differences were institutionalized in the state, to a high degree. Partly due to this 'pillarization', the established class in the Netherlands experienced less revolutionary political pressure from below to give in to calls for democratization and state intervention in social and economic life. Social policy, especially poor relief, could retain its local, laissez-faire character for many years to come, and was also partly outsourced to the 'pillars'. The old laissez-faire ideology would not collapse until the major economic crisis of the 1930s. The trauma caused by this crisis led to a more interventionist policy, in which the state intervened much more actively in the economy and assumed a greater role in providing facilities to mitigate and limit the risks of existence. By the 1950s and 1960s, the Dutch welfare state had become one of the most comprehensive in the world.

The greatest variations were evident in sociocultural development, where the Netherlands moved from one extreme to another. Between the mid-nineteenth century and the 1960s, the Netherlands remained a thoroughly churchgoing and religious society. It was an exceptionally 'strait-laced' country at that time; unlike in many other Western countries, for example, very few Dutch children were born outside of or before marriage. On the whole, birth rates remained high for a longer period. As a result, the population continued to grow in the Netherlands for longer than elsewhere in Western Europe. Moreover, the Netherlands experienced a considerable wave of emigration after the Second World War; from the 1960s, this was followed by growing immigration from overseas and from countries in the Mediterranean. The Netherlands also took its own path where it came to the role of women in the labour market. While a relatively large number of married women had engaged in paid work in the eighteenth century, the male breadwinner model prevailed in the nineteenth century. Pillarization helped to anchor this model further in the Netherlands.

From the 1960s, there was a rather sudden turnaround. For a time, the Netherlands even became a kind of trendsetter in the Western world. There was rapid growth in secularity, to the extent that the Netherlands became an outspoken example of an almost irreligious civil society. Birth control became a standard part of life. On moral and ethical issues such as drugs policy, euthanasia and abortion, the Netherlands followed a liberal path. In the labour market, female participation grew sharply, with the Netherlands distinguishing itself from the 1980s onwards by its large proportion of part-time workers. In many respects, however, the trends that began in the 1960s appear to have come to an end in the early twenty-first century. The role of the Netherlands as a cultural pioneer ('model country') may be over.

Early-twenty-first-century globalization led to a sharpening of the risks of existence. A deep economic crisis, environmental disasters, looming disruption of the climate, threatening epidemics and growing numbers of refugees trying to escape far-reaching political-military conflicts were clear consequences of this. Solving problems such as these requires international cooperation, yet a common response in recent years has been to protect the familiar and, increasingly, to emphasize national identity. In many countries, this tendency has been further reinforced by the crumbling of the welfare state, which makes it especially difficult to mitigate the risks of existence.

This reflex has also been evident in the Netherlands. More than in other countries, here this development forms a break with the past. After all, for many years, the Netherlands had a very strong system of social provision, it had no virulent nationalism and it welcomed dissenters. This relatively high degree of open-mindedness was not only fed by the tradition of tolerance from the Early Modern period but also maintained by the strong social embedding of church institutions in the era of pillarization. With increasing individualization at the end of the twentieth century, all kinds of existing institutions, including the churches, lost their ability to discipline society and their major influence over norms and values. Within a short period, for many Dutch people traditional 'mental constructions' lost much of their significance as points of reference. This recent development perfectly captures something that we have repeatedly tried to demonstrate in this book on the social and economic history of the last thousand years: how changes in income, power, risks and mental constructions, and the interactions between them, can have a far-reaching impact on the daily lives of ordinary people.

RECOMMENDED LITERATURE

A more extensive literature list for each chapter is available on the website (https://www.bloomsburyonlineresources.com/the-world-and-the-netherlands)

Abu-Lughod, Janet L., *Before European hegemony. The world system A.D. 1250–1350* (Oxford, 1989).
Adams, Julia, Elisabeth S. Clemens & Ann Shola Orloff, *Remaking modernity. Politics, history, and sociology* (Durham and London, 2005).
Altena, Bert & Dick van Lente, *Vrijheid en rede. Geschiedenis van westerse samenlevingen 1750–1989* (Hilversum, 2003).
Anderson, Benedict, *Imagined communities. Reflections on the origin and spread of nationalism* (London, 1991²).
Anderson, Perry, *Lineages of the absolutist state* (London, 1979²).
Aston, T.H. & C.E.H. Philpin (eds), *The Brenner debate. Agrarian class structure and economic development in pre-industrial Europe* (Cambridge, 1987).
Bank, Jan & Maarten van Buuren, *Dutch culture in a European perspective 3: 1900. The age of a bourgeois culture* (London, 2004).
Barkey, Karen, *Empire of difference. The Ottomans in comparative perspective* (Cambridge, 2008).
Bartlett, Robert, *The making of Europe. Conquest, colonization and cultural change 950–1350* (London, 1993).
Bavel, Bas van, *Manors and markets. Economy and society in the low countries* (Oxford, 2010).
Bavel, Bas van, *The invisible hand. How market economies have emerged and declined since AD 500* (Oxford, 2016).
Bayly, C.A., *The birth of the modern world 1780–1914* (Oxford, 2004).
Berkel, Klaas van & Leonie de Goei (eds), *The international relevance of Dutch history*. Special issue of Bijdragen en Mededelingen betreffende de Geschiedenis der Nederlanden/The Low Countries History Review, 125, no. 2–3 (2010).
Bieleman, Jan, *Boeren in Nederland. Geschiedenis van de landbouw 1500–2000* (Amsterdam, 2008).
Bin Wong, Roy, *China transformed. Historical change and the limits of European experience* (Ithaca, 1997).
Blockmans, Wim, *Metropolen aan de Noordzee. De geschiedenis van Nederland 1100–1650* (Amsterdam, 2010).
Blockmans, Wim & Peter Hoppenbrouwers, *Eeuwen des onderscheids. Een geschiedenis van middeleeuws Europa* (Amsterdam, 2002).

Blum, Jerome, *The end of the old order in rural Europe* (Princeton, 1978).
Boomgaard, Peter & Marjolein 't Hart (eds), *Globalization, environmental change, and social history* (Cambridge, 2010).
Bourdieu, Pierre, *Distinction. A social critique of the judgement of taste* (Abingdon, 2010, first published 1984).
Braudel, Fernand, *Civilization & capitalism 15th–18th century*, 3 volumes (New York, 1981–84).
Burke, Peter, *Popular culture in early modern Europe* (New York, 1978).
Burke, Peter, *History and social theory* (Oxford, 1992).
Burke, Peter, *The European Renaissance. Centres and peripheries* (Oxford, 1998).
Burke, Peter, *A social history of knowledge*, 2 volumes (Cambridge, 2000–2012).
Burleigh, Michael, *Earthly powers. Religion and politics in Europe from the enlightenment to the great war* (London, 2006).
Cain, P.J. & A.G. Hopkins, *British imperialism*, 2 volumes (London, 1993).
Chandler, Alfred, *Scale and scope. The dynamics of industrial capitalism* (Cambridge, MA, 1994).
Chaudhuri, K.N., *Trade and civilisation in the Indian Ocean. An economic history from the rise of Islam to 1750* (Cambridge, 1985).
Clark, Gregory, *A farewell to alms. A brief economic history of the world* (Princeton, 2007).
Clark, Peter (ed.), *The Oxford handbook of cities in world history* (Oxford, 2013).
Cohen, Floris, *How modern science came into the world. Four civilisations, one 17th century breakthrough* (Amsterdam, 2012).
Crafts, Nicholas & Gianni Toniolo (eds), *Economic growth in Europe since 1945* (Cambridge, 1996).
Crosby, Alfred W., *Ecological imperialism. The biological expansion of Europe, 900–1900* (Cambridge, 1986).
Darwin, John, *After tamerlane. The global history of empire* (London, 2007).
Davids, Karel, *The rise and decline of Dutch technological leadership. Technology, economy and culture in the Netherlands*, 2 volumes (Leiden, 2008).
Davids, Karel & Jan Lucassen (eds), *A miracle mirrored. The Dutch republic in European perspective* (Cambridge, 2010²).
Deursen, A.Th. van, *Plain lives in a golden age. Popular culture, religion and society in seventeenth-century Holland* (Cambridge, 1991).
Diamond, Jared, *Guns, germs and steel. A short history of everybody for the last 13,000 years* (London, 1997).
Eichengreen, Barry, *The European economy since 1945. Coordinated capitalism and beyond* (Princeton, 2008).
Eijnatten, Joris van & Fred van Lieburg, *Nederlandse religiegeschiedenis* (Hilversum, 2005).
Elias, Norbert, *The civilizing process: Sociogenetic and psychogenetic investigations*, 2nd edition (Hoboken, 2000).
Elliott, John, *Empires of the Atlantic world. Britain and Spain in America 1492–1830* (New Haven, 2006).
Engelen, Theo, *Van 2 naar 16 miljoen. Demografie van Nederland, 1800–nu* (Amsterdam, 2009).
Esping-Andersen, Gøsta, *The three worlds of welfare capitalism* (Cambridge, 1990).

Fahrmeir, Andreas, *Citizenship. The rise and fall of a modern concept* (New Haven, 2007).
Ferguson, Niall, *The cash nexus. Money and power in the modern world 1700–2000* (London, 2001).
Ferguson, Niall, *The ascent of money. A financial history of the world* (London, 2008).
Fernández-Armesto, Felipe, *Civilizations* (London, 2000).
Foreman-Peck, James, *A history of the world economy. International economic relations since 1850* (Brighton, 1995).
Foucault, Michel, *Discipline and Punish. The birth of the prison* (New York, 1995).
Frank, André Gunder, *ReOrient. Global economy in the Asian age* (Berkeley, 1998).
Frijhoff, Willem & Marijke Spies, *Dutch culture in a European perspective 1: 1650. Hard-won unity* (London, 2004).
Gerwen, Jacques van & Marco H.D. van Leeuwen, *Zoeken naar zekerheid. Risico's, preventie, verzekeringen en andere zekerheidsregelingen in Nederland 1500–2000*, 4 volumes (The Hague and Amsterdam, 2000).
Goebel, Michael, *Anti-Imperial metropolis. Interwar Paris and the seeds of third world nationalism* (Cambridge, 2015).
Goldgar, Anne, *Impolite learning. Conduct and community in the Republic of Letters 1680–1750* (New Haven, 1995).
Goldstone, Jack A., *Revolution and rebellion in the early modern world* (Berkeley, 1991).
Gordon, Robert J., *The rise and fall of American growth. The U.S. standard of living since the civil war* (Princeton, 2016).
Grove, Richard, *Green imperialism. Colonial expansion, tropical islands Edens and the origins of environmentalism, 1600–1860* (Cambridge, 1994).
Gruzinski, Serge, *Les quatre parties du monde. Histoire d'une mondialisation* (Paris, 2004).
Habermas, Jürgen, *Strukturwandel der Öffentlichkeit. Untersuchungen zur einer Kategorie der bürgerlichen Gesellschaft* (Darmstadt and Neuwied, 1968³).
Hart, Marjolein 't, *The making of a bourgeois state. War, politics and finance during the Dutch Revolt* (Manchester, 1993).
Hatcher, John & Mark Bailey, *Modelling the middle ages. The history and theory of England's economic development* (Oxford, 2001).
Headrick, Daniel, *The tools of empire. Technology and European imperialism in the nineteenth century* (New York, 1981).
Headrick, Daniel, *The tentacles of progress. Technology transfer in the age of imperialism, 1850–1940* (New York, 1988).
Heerma van Voss, Lex, Jan De Maeyer & Patrick Pasture (eds), *Between cross and class. Christian labour in Europe 1840–2000* (Bern, 2005).
Heijden, Manon van der, *Huwelijk in Holland. Stedelijke rechtspraak en kerkelijke tucht 1550–1700* (Amsterdam, 1998).
Held, David et al., *Global transformations: Politics, economics and culture* (Stanford, 1999).
Hemerijck, Anton & Jelle Visser, 'Change and immobility: Three decades of policy adjustment in the Netherlands and Belgium', in M. Ferrera & M. Rhodes (eds), *Recasting European welfare states* (London, 2000), 229–256.
Hobsbawm, Eric, *Age of extremes. The short twentieth century* (London, 1994).
Hobsbawm, Eric & Terence Ranger (eds), *The invention of tradition* (London, 1983).

Hohenberg, Paul & Lynn Hollen Lees, *The making of urban Europe 1000–1994* (Cambridge, MA, 1995).
Hollifield, James F., *Immigrants, markets, and states: The political economy of post-war Europe* (Cambridge, MA, 1992).
Hopkins, A.G. (ed.), *Globalization in world history* (London, 2002).
Inalcik, Halil & Donald Quataert (eds), *An economic and social history of the Ottoman Empire*, 2 volumes. (Cambridge, 1997²).
Inikori, Joseph E., *Africans and the industrial revolution in England* (Cambridge, 2002).
Israel, Jonathan I., *Dutch primacy in world trade 1585–1740* (Oxford, 1989).
Israel, Jonathan I., *The Dutch Republic. Its rise, greatness and fall 1477–1806* (Oxford, 1995).
Jacob, Margaret C. & Wijnand W. Mijnhardt (eds), *The Dutch Republic in the eighteenth century. Decline, enlightenment, and revolution* (Ithaca, 1992).
Jones, Eric, *The European miracle. Environments, economies and geopolitics in the history of Europe and Asia* (Cambridge, 2003³).
Joyce, Patrick, *The rule of freedom: Liberalism and the modern city* (London, 2003).
Judt, Tony, *Postwar. A history of Europe since 1945* (London, 2005).
Kaelble, Hartmut, *Sozialgeschichte Europas. 1945 bis zur Gegenwart* (Munich, 2007).
Kaplan, Benjamin J., *Religious conflict and the practice of toleration in early modern Europe* (Cambridge, MA, 2007).
Katznelson, Ira & Aristide Zolberg (eds), *Working-class formation. Nineteenth-century patterns in Western Europe and the United States* (Princeton, 1986).
Kennedy, Paul, *The rise and fall of the great powers. Economic change and military conflict from 1500 to 2000* (New York, 1987).
Kloek, Els, *Vrouw des huizes. Een cultuur-geschiedenis van de Hollandse huisvrouw* (Amsterdam, 2009).
Kloek, Joost & Wijnand W. Mijnhardt, *Dutch culture in a European perspective 2: 1800. Blueprints for a national community* (London, 2004).
Knippenberg, Hans & Ben de Pater, *De eenwording van Nederland: schaalvergroting en integratie sinds 1800* (Nijmegen, 1988).
Kuran, Timur, *The long divergence: How Islamic law held back the middle east* (Princeton, 2010).
Landes, David S., *The unbound prometheus. Technological change and industrial development form 1750 to the present* (Cambridge, 1969).
Landes, David S., *The wealth and poverty of nations* (London, 1998).
Landes, David S., Joel Mokyr & William J. Baumol (eds), *The invention of enterprise. Entrepreneurship from ancient mesopotamia to modern times* (Princeton, 2010).
Lechner, Frank J., *The Netherlands. Globalization and national identity* (New York and London, 2006).
Lees, Andrew & Lynn Hollen Lees, *Cities and the making of modern Europe, 1750–1914* (Cambridge, 2007).
Lees, Lynn Hollen, *Planting Empire, cultivating subjects: British Malaya, 1786–1941* (Cambridge, 2018).
Lindert, Peter, *Growing public. Social spending and economic growth since the eighteenth century* (Cambridge, 2004).

Livi-Bacci, Massimo, *A concise history of world population* (Oxford, 2001³).
Lucassen, Jan, *Migrant labour in Europe 1600–1900. The drift to the North Sea* (London, 1987).
Lucassen, Leo, *The immigrant threat: The integration of old and new migrants in Western Europe since 1850* (Urbana and Chicago, 2005).
Lucassen, Leo & Jan Lucassen, *Winnaars en verliezers. Een nuchtere balans van vijf eeuwen immigratie* (Amsterdam, 2011).
MacCulloch, Diarmaid, *Reformation. Europe's house divided 1490–1700* (London, 2003).
Maddison, Angus, *The world economy. A millennial perspective* (Paris, 2001).
Malanima, Paolo, *Pre-modern economy. One thousand years (10th–19th centuries)* (Leiden, 2009).
Manning, Patrick, *Migration in world history* (New York, 2005).
Mayer, Arno J., *The persistence of the old regime. Europe to the great war* (London, 1981).
McNeill, John, *Something new under the sun. An environmental history of the twentieth century* (London, 2000).
McNeill, William, *Plagues and peoples* (Oxford, 1976).
McNeill, William & John McNeill, *The human web. A bird's eye view of world history* (New York and London, 2003).
Middelaar, Luuk van, *The passage to Europe. How a Continent became a Union* (New Haven, 2020).
Mitterauer, Michael, *Warum Europa? Mittel- alterliche Grundlagen eines Sonderwegs* (Munich, 2003).
Mokyr, Joel, *The lever of riches. Technological creativity and economic progress* (Oxford, 1990).
Mokyr, Joel, *The enlightened economy. An economic history of Britain 1700–1850* (Princeton, 2010).
Moore Jr., Barrington, *Social origins of dictatorship and democracy. Lord and peasant in the making of the modern world* (Harmondsworth, 1967²).
Muchembled, Robert, *L'invention de l'homme moderne'. Culture et sensibilités en France du XVe au XVIIIe siècle* (Paris, 1994).
North, Douglass C., *Institutions, institutional change and economic performance* (Cambridge, 1990).
Ogilvie, Sheilagh, *The European guilds. An economic analysis* (Princeton, 2019).
O'Rourke, Kevin H. & Jeffrey G. Williamson, *Globalization and history. The evolution of a nineteenth century Atlantic economy* (Cambridge, MA and London, 1999).
Osterhammel, Jürgen, *The transformation of the world. A global history of the nineteenth century* (Princeton, 2014).
Osterhammel, Jürgen & Niels P. Petersson, *Globalization. A short history* (Princeton and Oxford, 2005).
Parthasarathi, Prasannan, *Why Europe grew rich and Asia did not. Global economic divergence, 1600–1850* (Cambridge, 2011).
Persson, Karl Gunnar, *An economic history of Europe. Knowledge, institutions and growth, 600 to the present* (Cambridge, 2010).
Pomeranz, Kenneth, *The great divergence. China, Europe and the making of the modern world economy* (Princeton, 2000).

Pounds, N.J.G., *A historical geography of Europe* (Cambridge, 1990).
Prak, Maarten, *Citizens without nations: Urban citizenship in Europe and the world, C.1000–1789* (Cambridge, 2018).
Prak, Maarten, *The Dutch Republic in the seventeenth century* (Cambridge, 2022).
Putnam, Robert D., *Bowling alone. The collapse and revival of American community* (New York, 2000).
Radkau, Joachim, *Nature and power. A global history of the environment* (Cambridge, 2008).
Rediker, M., T. Chakraborty, et al. (eds) *A global history of runaways. Workers, mobility and capitalism, 1600–1850* (Berkeley, 2019).
Reid, Anthony, *Southeast Asia in the age of commerce, 1450–1680*, 2 volumes (New Haven, 1988–1993).
Richards, John F., *The unending frontier. An environmental history of the early modern world* (Berkeley, 2003).
Rooy, Piet de, *Republiek van rivaliteiten. Nederland sinds 1813* (Amsterdam, 2002).
Rowe, William T., *China's last empire. The great Qing* (Cambridge, 2009).
Roy, Tirthankar, *An economic history of early modern India* (London, 2013).
Roy, Tirthankar and Giorgio Riello (eds.), *Global economic history* (London, 2019).
Said, Edward W., *Orientalism. Western conceptions of the orient* (London, 1978).
Scheidel, Walter, *The great leveler. Violence and the history of inequality from the stone age to the twenty-first century* (Princeton, 2017).
Schot, Johan, Harry Lintsen and Arie Rip (eds), *Technology and the making of the Netherlands. The age of contested modernization, 1890–1970* (Cambridge, MA, 2010).
Schuyt, Kees & Ed Taverne, *Dutch culture in a European perspective 4: 1950. Prosperity and welfare* (London, 2004).
Scott, James C., *Seeing like a state: How certain schemes to improve the human condition have failed* (New Haven, 1998).
Shapin, Steven, *The scientific revolution* (Chicago, 1996).
Skocpol, Theda, *States and social revolutions. A comparative analysis of France, Russia and China* (Cambridge, 1979).
Sluyterman, Keetie E., *Kerende kansen. Het Nederlandse bedrijfsleven in de twintigste eeuw* (Amsterdam, 2003).
Spence, Jonathan D., *The search for modern China* (New York, 1990).
Spierenburg, Pieter, *De verbroken betovering. Mentaliteitsgeschiedenis van pre-industrieel Europa* (Hilversum, 1990).
Stuurman, Siep, *The invention of humanity. Equality and cultural difference in world history* (Cambridge Mass, 2021).
Swaan, Abram de, *In care of the state. Health care, education and welfare in Europe and America Oxford, 1988* (Amsterdam, 1989).
Taylor, Charles, *A secular age* (Cambridge, MA, 2007).
Thomas, Keith, *Religion and the decline of magic. Studies in popular beliefs in sixteenth- and seventeenth-century England* (Harmondsworth, 1971).
Thompson, E.P., *The making of the English working class* (Harmondsworth, 1968²).
Tilly, Charles, *Big structures, large processes, huge comparisons* (New York, 1984).

Tilly, Charles, *Coercion, capital and European states, AD 990–1992* (Cambridge, 1990).
Tilly, Charles, *European revolutions, 1492–1992* (Oxford, 1993).
Tilly, Charles, *Contention and democracy in Europe, 1650–2000* (Cambridge, 2004).
Touwen, Jeroen, *Extremes in the archipelago: Trade and economic development in the Outer Islands of Indonesia 1900–1942* (Leiden, 2001).
Vanhaute, Eric, *World history. An introduction* (Abingdon, 2012).
Ven, G.P. van de (ed.), *Leefbaar laagland. Geschiedenis van de waterbeheersing en landaanwinning in Nederland* (Utrecht, 2003).
Vries, Jan de, *European urbanization 1500–1800* (London, 1984).
Vries, Jan de, *The industrious revolution. Consumer behaviour and the household economy, 1650 to the present* (Cambridge, 2008).
Vries, Jan de and Ad van der Woude, *The first modern economy. Success, failure, and perseverance of the Dutch economy, 1500–1815* (Cambridge, 1997).
Vries, Peer, *Escaping poverty. The origins of modern economic growth* (Göttingen, 2013).
Wacquant, Loïc, *Urban outcasts: A comparative sociology of advanced marginality* (Cambridge, 2008).
Wallerstein, Immanuel, *The modern world-system*, 3 volumes (New York, 1974–1989).
Weatherford, Jack, *Genghis Khan and the making of the modern world* (New York, 2004).
Weber, Eugen, *Peasants into Frenchmen. The modernization of rural France, 1870–1914* (Stanford, 1976).
Weber, Max, *Wirtschaft und Gesellschaft* (Tübingen, 1925).
Wee, Herman van der, *De gebroken welvaartscirkel* (Leiden, 1983²).
Wehler, Hans-Ulrich, *Deutsche Gesellschaftsgeschichte*, 5 volumes (Munich, 1987–2008).
Wesseling, H.L., *Divide and rule. The partition of Africa, 1880–1914* (Westport and London, 1996).
Wielinga, Friso, *Nederland in de twintigste eeuw* (Amsterdam, 2009).
Wolf, Eric R., *Europe and the people without history* (Berkeley, 1982).
Wrigley, E.A., *Continuity, chance and change. The character of the industrial revolution in England* (Cambridge, 1988).
Zanden, Jan Luiten van, *Een klein land in de 20ste eeuw. Economische geschiedenis van Nederland 1914–1995* (Utrecht, 1997).
Zanden, Jan Luiten van, *The long road to the industrial revolution. The European economy in a global perspective, 1000/1800* (Leiden, 2009).
Zanden, Jan Luiten van and Arthur van Riel, *The strictures of inheritance. The Dutch economy in the nineteenth century* (Princeton, 2004).
Zanden, Jan Luiten van and Pim de Zwart, *The origins of globalization. World trade in the making of globalization, 1500–1800* (Cambridge, 2018).

INDEX

Abbasidian empire 22
Abduh, Mohammed 292
Aboriginals 160, 222
Abortion 286, 288–289, 301
Abu-Lughod, Janet 18
Académie Royale des Sciences 136
Acapulco 17
Aceh War 177, 219
Acemoglu, Daron 223
Acid rain 188
Adams, Julia 92
Aden 51
Aeroplane 98, 244
Africa 6–8, 13–14, 17, 20–22, 47, 54, 136, 153–155, 157, 160, 209, 250, 278, 298; *see also* East Africa; North Africa; South Africa
African Americans 222, 227, 282, 284, 288
Ageing society 197, 250
Agrarian capitalism 33–34, 59
Agrarian depression 174
Agricultural policy 193
Agriculture 16, 25–27, 30, 43–45, 57, 59, 63, 71, 102, 107, 119, 122, 166–167, 169–170, 174, 187, 190, 206, 239, 243, 254, 260–261, 267, 274, 297, 299
AIDS 284
Air pollution 188, 233
Alabama 284
Alba, Duke of 80–81, 87
Alcohol 162, 279
Algeria 184, 221, 237
America 6, 13–14, 17, 22, 30, 38, 54–57, 60, 62, 65, 68–69, 79, 85, 90, 94, 102, 113, 136, 142, 153–154, 160, 166–167, 174, 181, 192, 195, 278; *see also* Central America; Latin America; North America; South America; Spanish America
American Civil War 54, 166
American Revolution 103, 107, 226
American War of Independence 103
Americanization 7
Amsterdam 32, 46, 48, 50, 56, 90, 92–93, 105, 120–121, 128, 134, 137, 139, 149, 155, 177, 194, 210, 217, 219, 235, 254, 272, 284
Ancien Régime 208
Anderson, Benedict 106
Anglican Church 93; *see also* Church of England
Anhui 28
Animal husbandry 45, 174
Animals 17, 22, 64, 133, 136, 160, 252, 295
Anthropology 2, 132, 294
Antilles 221, 257, 260
Anti-Revolutionary Party (ARP) 243
Antwerp 46, 56, 79, 80, 143
AOW (Old Age Pensions Act) 235, 240, 243–244, 246
Arabic 22, 54, 68–69, 96
Argentina 157, 169, 201, 236
Ariès, Philippe 114
Aristotle 22, 135–136
Armenians 36
Army 54, 76, 80, 83–88, 91–93, 102, 121, 147, 219, 240; *see also* Soldiers
Arnhem 190
Art 136, 138, 244, 294
Artists 272
ASEAN 192
Associations 35, 40–41, 90, 95, 118, 120, 123, 127, 162, 194, 208, 227–228, 230, 255, 279, 281
Astronomers 135, 295
Asylum seekers 259
Atatürk, Kemal 293
Atlantic Charter 243
Atlantic Ocean 17, 21, 50–55, 157, 255
Atlantic revolutions 96, 102, 105, 107, 208
Augsburg; *see* Peace of Augsburg
Australia 7, 55, 128, 157, 160–161, 222, 235–236, 255, 275, 281, 298
Austria 104, 191, 214, 236–237, 270; *see also* Austria-Hungary
Austria-Hungary 13–15, 106, 227
Austrian Netherlands 217; *see also* Southern Netherlands
Authoritarian regimes 222, 237, 259
Aztecs 69, 96

INDEX

Baghdad 15, 22
Balance of payments 174–175, 185, 190, 197, 200
Balance of Powers 77, 92, 149, 228
Balkans, the 68
Baltic coast 6, 36; *see also* Baltic region
Baltic region 32, 35, 44–45, 80
Banda Islands 101
Bandung 200
Bangladesh 14, 164, 202
Bank of England 84
Banks 168, 170, 173–174, 179–180, 183, 196, 199, 203, 252, 271
Baptists 54, 83, 120, 123–124; *see also* Dissenters
Barbados 97
Barcelona 254
Batavia 51
Batavian-French period 91, 215, 239
Bavaria 8
Beer 44, 47, 78, 143
Beggars 125, 128, 231; *see also* Poor
Beijing 74, 110–111, 155, 234
Bekker, Balthasar 134
Belgium 8, 13, 30, 65, 106, 109, 154–155, 161, 176, 180–181, 191–192, 194, 209, 214, 217, 222, 236–237, 253, 270, 273, 275–276, 278, 289, 291; *see also* Austrian Netherlands; Southern Netherlands
Benelux, the 192
Berkeley 284
Berlin 155, 239
Berlin Conference 209
Berlin Wall 298
Beveridge, William Henry 238, 243
Beyen, Jan Willem 214
Bible 126, 138, 292, 295
Bildungsbürgertum 272
Bin Wong, Roy 118, 229
Biotechnology 294
Birmingham 188
Birth, extramarital 287
Birth control 250–251, 287–288, 301
Birth rate 26–27, 29, 162, 249–251, 253, 281, 286–287, 295, 297, 301
Bismarck, Otto von 237, 240, 300
Black Death 16, 29, 55, 78, 113; *see also* Plague
Blue-collar workers 271
Bolívar, Simón 209
Bolivia 209
Bombay; *see* Mumbai
Borneo 172
Bosch, Johannes van den 177

Botany Bay 160
Bourdieu, Pierre 88, 90
Bourgeois 229, 272
Brabant 46, 74, 254
Bratislava 188
Brazil 8, 54, 157, 169, 201, 293, 298
Breadwinner model; *see* Male Breadwinner Model
Brenner, Robert 33–34, 59
Bretton Woods system 184–187, 205
Brielle 74, 81
Bruges 17, 78, 81
Brussels 210, 215
Buddhism 135, 292
Budget deficit 183, 194, 196–197, 203–204
Buenos Aires 169
Bukhara 17
Bulgaria 200, 214
Bureaucracy 67, 72, 74, 92, 118, 193, 212, 216
Bureaucratization 23, 72, 92, 268
Burgher 89, 121; *see also* Citizen
Burgundy 8, 79
Burke, Peter 140
Byzantine Empire 68, 135

Cairo 17
Calcutta 155
Calicut 17, 51
Caliph 68–69
Calvinists 5, 81, 91, 93, 106, 121, 123, 125–127, 134, 239; *see also* Reformed Church, Dutch
Cambay 17
Cambodia 184, 229
Cambridge 114
Cameralists 211, 230
Canada 157, 161, 173, 188, 219, 254–255
Canals 60, 65, 98, 176–177, 211, 216–217
Canton 15, 51, 96
Cape of Good Hope 17, 20, 101–102
Capellen tot den Pol, Johan Derk van der 105
Capital 6, 17, 35, 38, 43, 46, 50, 58, 88, 90, 98–99, 148, 156–157, 194, 205, 241, 263–264, 300
Capital flows 1, 181, 185
Capital goods 168, 170, 178, 184
Capital holdings 52, 73, 121
Capital market 41, 48
Capital productivity 167
Capital-intensive model 74, 76, 78, 221
Capitalism 38, 59, 65, 73, 184, 199, 241, 298; *see also* Agrarian capitalism; Industrial capitalism; Merchant capitalism

Car   187–188, 200, 244, 278, 289, 291
Caracas   209
Caravans   20, 96
Care, medical   35, 192
Care, social   118, 121, 123–125, 142, 147, 207, 231, 234, 239
Care arrangements   123, 149, 234
Caribbean, the   8, 22, 38, 97, 209
Carnegie, Andrew   160
Cartel   171
Castile   41, 99
Catalonia   6
Catch-up growth   178, 198
Cathars   126
Catholic Church   59, 69, 113, 126, 128, 132, 143, 169, 255, 293
Catholics   55, 83, 90, 93, 106, 123, 125, 137, 213, 227, 232, 239, 243, 254, 270
Celebes   177
Celibate   110
Census   13, 89, 211, 225
Central America   7, 104
Central Asia   17, 22, 29, 54, 157, 179
Central Europe   55–56, 59, 66, 133
Centralization   23, 38, 79, 145
Centrally planned economy   179, 184; *see also* Five-year plan
Ceylon   51; *see also* Sri Lanka
Champagne   35
Chandler, Alfred   170
Charity   123–125, 132, 227, 244
Charivari   127
Charles the Bold   79
Charles V   79, 84–85, 125
Chartists   224
Chemical industry   47, 167, 170–171, 178, 196
Chen Hongmou   132
Child benefit   244
Child Protection Act   240
China   5–6, 8, 15–17, 22–23, 29–30, 32, 35, 37–38, 40–41, 51, 54, 57–58, 64, 66, 71, 73, 76, 92, 94–96, 107–110, 117–118, 131–132, 135, 137, 139, 143, 147, 154–155, 157, 163, 178, 192, 200–202, 207, 223, 229–230, 265, 281, 298
Chocolate   142–143
Cholera   160
Christian Democracy   298; *see also* Confessional parties
Christianity   20, 22, 93, 113, 292
Church of England   270; *see also* Anglican Church
Churchill, Winston   243

Citizen   105, 120, 136, 212, 226; *see also* Burgher
Citizenship   89, 104, 118, 120–121, 140, 226–230
City state   46, 67
City walls   23; *see also* Fortifications
Civic guard   80–81, 88
Civil rights   226, 228–229, 282, 284, 288
Civil society   162, 208, 226–228, 230, 240, 247, 300–301
Civilization   136, 278
Class   26, 34, 103, 106, 117–119, 162, 166–167, 179, 211, 213, 223, 227, 229, 236, 243, 266–268, 270–271, 277, 279, 285, 295, 300
Class conflicts   26, 33
Class-based society   261, 272
Clergy   67, 72, 78, 133, 140, 147, 162, 284
Cleves   134
Climate   16, 27, 30, 71, 73, 97, 155, 301
Clocks   140
Club of Rome   155
Coal   48, 60, 63–64, 166, 168, 174, 188, 192, 196, 204
Cocoa   22, 47, 55
Coen, Jan Pietersz   101
Coercion-intensive model   74, 76
Coffee   22, 47, 55, 60, 65, 142–143, 173, 177, 219, 226, 252
Coffee house   95, 226
Cold War   1, 194
Colijn, Hendrik   181, 234, 257
Collective action   81, 223–225
Collective bargaining   179
Colonial government   252
Colonies   6, 23, 36, 53–54, 62, 67, 96–99, 101–103, 105, 107, 127, 157, 161, 173, 184, 189, 210, 219, 221, 235–236, 247, 252, 256–257, 278, 297–298
Colonists   16, 96, 98–99, 101–103, 105, 166, 169, 252
Colonization   16, 29, 34, 68, 77, 96–99, 101, 107, 128, 169, 174, 189, 209, 270
Columbus, Christopher   97
Commercialization   26, 35–38, 45, 59, 65–66, 113, 118–119, 131, 148
Communal land   41
Commune (Paris)   239
Communication   38, 64, 98–99, 103, 157, 185, 197, 235
Communist   7, 161, 179, 184, 200, 224, 230–231, 298
Community   39, 52–53, 106, 108–109, 117–118, 120, 127, 132–133, 135, 137,

140, 143, 147, 184, 212, 216, 228, 234, 239, 254
Compagnie des Indes   101
Composite monarchy   209
Concentration camp   251
Confessional parties   243
Confucianism   135, 281, 292
Congress of Vienna   77, 106, 208, 217, 300
Conservatives   224, 231, 244–245, 267
Conspicuous consumption   262
Constantinople   15; *see also* Istanbul
Constitution   79, 80, 93–94, 103, 177, 237–238
Construction workers   55–56, 264
Consumer revolution   142
Consumers   60, 130, 171, 196, 200, 290
Consumption   30, 113, 130, 133, 142, 155, 162, 170, 183, 189, 199, 202, 211, 262, 279, 289–290
Continental System   167
Contract   43, 71–72, 101, 117, 189, 212, 221, 278
Convergence   6, 164, 202, 205, 235–236
Cooperatives   164, 174, 287
Copernicus, Nicolaus   135
Copra   177
Corn Law   224, 273
Corporation   41, 120, 171
Corporatism   120
Coryate, Thomas   140
Cottage industry   36–38, 63, 130
Cotton   22, 35, 37, 47, 55, 57, 60, 63–64, 143, 166, 169, 173, 211
Counter-Reformation   93
Countryside   23, 25, 33–37, 46, 48, 78, 85, 110–111, 114, 118, 120–121, 131, 140, 143, 174, 181, 203, 224, 250, 254
Court   79, 85, 92, 118, 126, 131, 148
Crafts, Nicholas   264
Craftsmen   40, 47, 64, 73, 112, 120, 147, 267, 290
Credit   7, 35, 37, 170, 174, 196, 203–204, 267
Criminals   128–129, 142, 231, 277, 288
Cultivation System   177
Cultural capital   90
Cultural Revolution   200, 229
Currency   4, 29, 79, 174–175, 181, 185, 192–193; *see also* Money
Cyprus   214
Czech Republic   32, 214

Dairy   36, 108, 174, 267; *see also* Milk
Dance   290

Darwin, Charles   281–282
Death penalty   277
Decentralization   85
Decolonization   173, 184, 205, 207, 221, 229, 256
Deforestation   97, 155
Delfshaven   105
Delft   89
Delhi   68, 74
Demand side   182, 200
Democratization   5, 161–162, 208, 222–224, 228, 239–240, 247–248, 268, 293, 298–300
Demographic transition   162, 249–250, 286–288, 295, 297
Demonstrations   81, 223–225, 230, 232–233
Dependencia school   189
Depression   121, 157, 162, 174, 179–180, 204, 254, 257
Deregulation   199, 203, 218
Devaluation   79
Development cooperation   187, 203
Dialect   212–213
Diamond, Jared   71, 225
Dickson, Peter   84
Dictatorial regimes   222, 229
Direct rule   208–209, 221
Disabled   23, 52, 123, 194, 232, 237
Disaster   23, 160, 191, 252
Disciplining   3, 126–128, 131, 143, 162, 249, 277, 279, 292, 294, 296
Disease   26, 29, 109, 111–112, 249, 251, 279
Disenchantment   244
Dissenters   93–94, 102, 169, 301
Division of labour   35, 37, 43, 199
Divorce   116, 162, 284–285
Doctors, medical   236, 272, 288
Domain   33, 34, 97
Domain state   72
Domestic staff   262; *see also* Servants
Donetsk   188
Doorn, J.A.A. van   178
Dordrecht   83
Drainage   45, 59; *see also* Polders; Reclamation
Drees, Willem   244
Drucker, Wilhelmina   238
Dual economy   201
Duel   131
Dürer, Albrecht   142
Durkheim, Emile   282
Dutch disease   196
Dutch East Indies   177–178, 206, 210, 219, 221, 255; *see also* Indonesia

Dykes   30, 45, 252
Dysentery   111–112

East Africa   20, 35, 69
East Asia   17, 68, 108, 110–111, 143, 145, 199
East India Company (VOC)   47, 50, 92, 101, 137
Eastern bloc   200, 205
Eastern Europe   30, 53, 118–119, 179, 202, 208, 222, 224, 259
Ecclesiastical institutions   131, 147
Economic growth   3, 5, 25, 34–35, 39, 43, 47, 62, 65, 85, 147, 155, 161, 163–164, 168–170, 176, 178, 183–184, 188–189, 191–197, 199, 203–204, 215, 223, 246, 248, 263–265, 297
Edo   15, 32; *see also* Tokyo
Education   35, 50, 59–60, 65, 90, 92, 104, 132, 137, 139, 148–149, 162, 175, 177–178, 189, 200, 210, 212–213, 216–217, 221, 237–238, 240, 246, 248, 262–263, 272–273, 275, 278–279, 284–285, 296
Egypt   292
Eighty Year's War, the   85
El Niño   252
Elbe   16, 29, 34, 53, 119, 167
Elderly   123, 161, 194, 197, 213, 248, 250, 288; *see also* Old age
Electrical industry   161, 171, 178
Electricity   178, 196, 244
Electronics   199
Elias, Norbert   72, 131, 140, 177
Elite   67, 90–92, 96, 103, 107, 113, 118, 134–135, 142–144, 162, 218, 222, 232, 234, 241, 255, 262, 266
Elite culture   140; *see also* Great Tradition
Elizabeth I   125
Elliott, John   209
Elzas-Lotharingen   168
Emancipation   6, 53, 113, 116, 228, 238, 284, 288
Emigration   29, 157, 255–256, 301
Employees   51, 53, 55, 164, 192, 194, 197, 219, 236, 257, 260, 263, 271, 281, 282; *see also* Workers
Employers   53, 159, 161, 281, 287; *see also* Entrepreneurs
Employment   47, 87, 120, 181, 191, 193, 195–198, 225, 257, 260–261, 270, 278, 295
Enclosure movement   59
Energy   48, 60, 63–64, 189, 196, 233
Engelen, Theo   254

Engels, Friedrich   231
Engineers   178, 252, 272
England   13–15, 21–23, 30, 32–33, 35, 41, 43, 50–51, 55–63, 72, 76, 83, 88, 93, 95, 110–111, 115–117, 119, 121, 125, 127–128, 130, 134, 138–139, 142, 145, 160, 173, 211, 223, 226, 284; *see also* Great Britain
English Civil War   223
Enkhuizen   81
Enlightenment   54, 65, 94, 103, 137, 144, 161, 210, 212, 227, 231, 244, 299
Entrepreneurs   41, 50, 64, 87, 97, 167–168, 175–176, 195, 204, 209, 255, 268
Environment   9–10, 45–46, 148, 155, 188, 233
Environmental awareness   97
Environmental effects   97
Environmental movement   232
Environmental policy   233
Epidemics   29, 55, 133, 160, 250, 301; *see also* Black Death; Disease
Equality   5, 54, 95, 104–105, 107, 161, 206, 209–210, 231–232, 265, 298
Erasmus, Desiderius   125
Erosion   16, 23, 80, 97, 215
Esperanto   227
Esping-Andersen, Gøsta   236
Estate-based society   261
Estates   10, 16, 34, 41, 59, 72–73, 78, 80, 83, 88, 94, 107, 131, 162
Estonia   214
Ethical issues   288, 296, 301
Ethical Policy   178, 221
Etiquette book   131, 140
Eucalyptus   160
Eurasia   16, 22, 58–59, 68–69, 71–74, 94, 96, 106–107, 109, 111, 121, 145
Euratom   214
Europe; *see* Central Europe; Eastern Europe; North-western Europe; Western Europe
European Commission   193, 215
European Economic Community (EEC)   190–191, 194, 214
European Monetary System (EMS)   185
European Parliament   215
European Union (EU)   1, 13, 161, 164, 187, 192, 205, 214–215, 299
Euthanasia   288–289, 301
Exchange rate   175, 181, 184–185, 196–197, 201
Excises   84, 123, 217–218
Execution   101, 133–134, 142, 277

INDEX

Expenditure, government   195–196
Experimental physics   60, 64
Experimentation   24, 133, 136, 144, 147
Export   50, 52, 59–60, 69, 101, 156, 167–169, 174, 176–177, 181, 187, 193, 196, 198–199, 298
Export duties   177
Export-led growth   199
Expulsion   29, 126, 128
Extended family   114, 118

Factory   63, 130, 224, 232, 255, 267–268, 271–272, 290
Factory owners   224, 268; *see also* Entrepreneurs
Faith   81, 83, 102, 126, 133–134, 137, 270, 293; *see also* Religion
Family   24, 33–34, 56, 58, 59, 80, 92, 108, 109, 113–114, 116–118, 122–125, 130, 143, 162, 170, 178, 197–198, 210, 213, 226, 234, 237–238, 250–251, 254, 259, 275, 286–287, 290, 299
Family business   39, 168, 175, 267
Famine   26–27, 109, 112, 121, 125, 200, 234, 252
Farm credit bank   174
Farmers   33, 37, 45–46, 59, 102, 111, 119, 148, 167, 173–174, 179, 181, 193, 200, 202, 229, 244, 252, 254–255, 263, 266–268, 295
Farmers' Party   267
Fascism   184, 268, 298; *see also* Nazis
Federal Reserve System   182, 196, 204
Feminists   238, 284, 288
Fertilizer   174, 267
Feudal mode of production   33
Feudalism   16, 161
Film   157, 244, 290
Financial Revolution   84, 87
Financial services   48, 191
Finland   194, 214, 261
First World War   156–157, 160, 162, 174–175, 177–180, 207, 210, 214, 218, 228–229, 235, 264–266, 275, 297–298, 300
Fish   44, 113, 116, 188
Fishing   43–45, 148, 177, 202, 243, 261
Five-year plan   179
Flanders   6, 23, 35, 37, 40, 44, 46, 70–72, 81, 139, 148, 166
Flax   36–37, 45, 64
Floods   112, 133
Florence   41
Food prices   16, 27, 29, 160, 177

Food supply   29–30, 32, 121, 193
Forced labour   22–23, 53, 125, 161
Forest   97, 169
Fortifications   82, 99
Fossil fuels   155, 160, 188
Foucault, Michel   130
Fourth Anglo-Dutch War   104
France   6, 8, 13–15, 21, 27, 32, 34, 36–37, 44–45, 47, 50, 54, 60, 62, 65–66, 72, 74, 76, 83–84, 89, 92, 94, 97, 99, 101, 105, 109, 111, 118, 126, 128, 138–139, 152–154, 166, 174, 181, 184, 191–194, 207, 209, 214, 216, 222–225, 227–229, 235–236, 239–241, 267, 273, 275–276, 278–279, 289, 291, 293
Free riders   234
Free trade   32, 35, 171, 184, 187
Freedom of association   222, 227
Freedom of speech   94–95, 107, 147, 222
Freemasons   227
Fremdzwang   131, 140
French Revolution   94, 103–106, 207, 231, 297
Friedman, Milton   183
Friesland   78–79, 83, 213, 254–255
Fundamentalists   244

Galilei, Galileo   136
Gandhi, Mahatma   210
Ganges   71
Garrisons   85, 87
Gas (natural)   186, 246
Gay   284; *see also* Homosexuals
Gelderland   78–79, 81, 134
Gender   166, 211, 213
General Agreement on Tariffs and Trade (GATT)   184, 187, 192–193
Genghis Khan   17, 68
Genoa   17, 39
Genocide   101, 213, 229
Geography   2, 9, 213, 219
Germany   6, 8, 13, 15, 32, 36, 44, 48, 109, 111, 116, 119, 128, 134, 139, 142, 153–154, 161, 163, 166–168, 170, 174–176, 181, 188, 192–194, 209, 214, 222, 224–225, 227–228, 232–233, 235–237, 240–241, 253, 258–259, 266, 270–272, 275–279, 282, 289, 291, 293–294, 300; *see also* Bavaria; Prussia; Saxony
Gerschenkron, Alexander   170
Ghana   8, 69
Ghent   78, 81
Gilded Age   166
Gini coefficient   265

Globalization 1–2, 6–7, 9, 17, 20–21, 96, 98, 101, 105, 107, 132, 143, 156–157, 160, 164, 173, 179, 187, 192, 205, 210, 296, 298, 300–301
Glorious Revolution 84, 223
Goa 51
Gold Standard 174–175, 180–183, 185, 204
Golden Age 23, 43, 46, 50, 87, 295
Golden Years 191, 195, 204, 246, 257
Good governance 189
Government finances 177
Government spending 183, 185, 195–196, 216–218, 246
Grain 22, 27, 30, 32, 35, 45, 57–59, 62, 80, 89, 119, 121, 124, 167, 169, 173, 224, 234
Grand Tour 138
Great Britain 24, 26, 44, 47, 54, 58–60, 62, 64–66, 88–89, 92, 96, 98–99, 102–105, 109, 128, 153–154, 163–168, 170, 173–176, 179–181, 188, 191, 194–196, 205, 207, 209, 214, 216, 218, 222–224, 227, 229, 232–235, 239–241, 260–261, 264, 266, 268, 270, 275–276, 278, 289, 291, 293–294, 300; *see also* England; Ireland; Scotland; Wales
Great Divergence 6–7, 9, 13, 25–26, 56–58, 66, 145, 149, 153, 162–163, 248, 297–299
Great Lakes 188
Great Leap Forward 200
Great Mughal 68–69, 74, 89
Great Privilege 79
Great Society 185
Great Tradition, the 132, 133, 135, 140; *see also* Elite Culture
Greece 188, 194, 214, 287–288
Greenhouse effect 188
Greensboro 284
Greenwich 219
Groningen 79, 134, 196, 246, 255
Gross domestic (national) product 48, 191, 194, 217; *see also* National income
Grove, Richard 97
Guangdong 202
Guest workers 237, 255, 258; *see also* Migrants
Guilds 10, 40, 50, 55, 78–80, 88–89, 95, 120, 123, 127, 140, 143, 148, 161, 208–209, 216, 234, 238
Gujarat 17, 51
Gutenberg, Johann 138
Guyana 8

Haarlem 104, 128, 216
Habermas, Jürgen 94–95, 226

Habsburg 46, 209
Hacienda 169
Haiti 104, 209
Haitian Revolution 104
Hajnal, John 109–110
Hamburg 124
Hanseatic League 6, 36, 44, 69
Hatta, Mohammed 210, 221
Heek, F. van 254, 262
Heemskerck, Maarten van 142
Hemp 36, 45
Henry VIII 93
Herder, Johann Gottfried von 212
Herring fishery 47
High school (Hogereburgerschool, HBS) 295
Hillebrand, Hans 254
Hinduism 281, 292
Hindustan 221
Hô Chí Minh 210
Hobsbawm, Eric 213
Hofstee, E.W. 254
Holidays 56, 132, 290
Holy Roman Empire 69, 81
Homestead Act 167
Homosexuals 10, 218, 228, 232, 237, 284, 286, 289
Hong Kong 198, 230
Hormuz 51
Horses 22, 45
Horticulture 45, 174, 179, 196
Hospitals 123, 130, 271, 284, 293
Household 52–53, 56, 59, 114, 117, 130, 143, 193, 249, 272, 275, 284
Houten, Sam van 240
Huai River 29
Hugo, Victor 239
Huguenots 60, 83, 93
Hukou 234
Human capital 40, 50, 59, 64, 66, 199
Human rights 238, 298; *see also* Freedom of association; Freedom of speech
Hungary 32, 214
Huydecoper, Johan 90
Huygens, Christiaan 136
Hygiene 112, 233, 249, 275

Iberian Peninsula 6, 17, 30, 44
Iconoclastic fury 80, 81, 91
ICT 197, 294
Identity 4, 105, 120, 132, 136, 162, 212–213, 295, 299, 301
Ideology 9, 65, 77, 132, 240, 271, 282, 300
Immigration 110, 157, 255–259, 281, 286, 301

INDEX

Imperialism 5, 97, 173
Impoldering 48; *see also* Drainage; Reclamation
Import 60, 103, 171, 173, 181, 187, 190
Import duties and tariffs 171, 173–174, 177, 181, 187, 224
Import quotas 181
Import substitution 189
Incapacity for work 237; *see also* Disabled
Incas 69, 96
Income 3–7, 9, 13, 23, 25, 33, 37, 45, 52, 56, 59–60, 99, 110, 112, 118, 120, 130, 134, 145, 147, 160, 163, 173, 197–198, 236, 238, 257, 263–265, 272, 275, 284–285, 297, 302; *see also* National income
Income, levelling of 162
Income inequality 96, 160, 263–265
Income per capita 23, 25, 43–44, 57, 62–63, 163–164, 201, 264, 299
Indentured labour 53, 55, 65, 209
India 8, 14, 17, 22, 37, 51, 57–58, 66, 71, 73, 76, 96, 98, 154–155, 157, 162, 166, 173, 184, 187, 189, 201–202, 210, 272, 278, 281, 292, 298
Indian Ocean 21–22, 36, 51
Indians 136, 167, 252, 258
Indirect rule 209
Individualization 113–114, 116, 118, 142–144, 147, 197, 248, 290, 301
Indonesia 8, 184, 199–201, 210, 221, 261, 278; *see also* Dutch East Indies
Indus 71, 252
Industrial capitalism 65
Industrial Enlightenment 65
Industrial products 36, 60, 167, 171, 174, 187, 298
Industrial Revolution 6, 23, 25–26, 56–58, 62–63, 65–66, 81, 145, 163, 167–168, 178, 216, 260, 263–264, 294
Industrialization 5, 6, 23, 36–37, 56, 62, 130, 160–164, 166–168, 170, 174–177, 179, 187–188, 198, 205, 224, 241, 250, 259–260, 266–268, 299
Industrious revolution 56, 59–60, 63, 130
Industry 36–37, 43–48, 60, 62–64, 80, 130, 140, 160, 166–171, 173–179, 181, 184, 187, 189–191, 196, 199, 217, 232, 239, 250, 254–255, 258, 260–261, 264, 267, 277, 282, 290, 294, 297
Inequality (social) 55, 90, 114, 160, 162, 173, 185, 224, 230, 232, 263–265, 281
Infant industry 171
Infanticide 110, 143
Inflation 29, 183, 191, 195–197, 204

Information 17, 39, 41, 50, 69, 121, 136, 139, 189, 284
Infrastructure 60, 65, 78, 123, 136, 167, 173, 176–177, 189–190, 193, 202, 210–211, 213, 217
Inheritance 113, 116–117, 132, 143, 263, 281
Inikori, Joseph 60
Innovation 35, 41, 50, 167, 170, 173, 175–176, 178–179, 290
Inquisition 79, 83, 126–128
Institutions 3, 4, 10, 26, 39–41, 46, 59, 65–66, 69, 88–89, 123–128, 130–132, 147–149, 169, 189, 202–203, 205, 208, 210, 216, 223, 234, 271, 278–279, 284, 299, 301
Insurance 173–174, 203, 234, 237–238, 240, 243–244, 246, 263, 267
Intellectuals 210, 213, 233, 292
Interest level; *see* Interest rate
Interest rate 37, 41, 58, 80, 84, 89, 203
International Labour Organization (ILO) 229
International Monetary Fund (IMF) 184–185, 202–204
Internet 1, 205
Invented tradition 213
Investments 101, 168, 170–171, 174, 177, 202
Iran 17, 68, 293
Iraq 17
Ireland 13, 27, 194, 214
Iron 63–64, 168, 200
Irrigation 30, 178, 252
Islam 20, 22, 219, 258, 292–293
Islamic world 6, 8, 17, 22, 37, 292
Israel 195
Istanbul 15, 32
Italy 6, 8, 13–15, 23, 32, 40, 44, 117, 128, 134, 138–139, 142, 153, 181, 192, 194, 209, 214, 222, 241, 278, 287–289

Jacobs, Aletta 238
Japan 5, 7, 15, 37, 40, 51, 54, 57, 110–111, 154–155, 160, 164–166, 187–188, 190, 192, 198–199, 201–202, 207, 220, 232–233, 235, 273, 292, 298
Java 97, 189, 221
Jews 55, 93, 102, 120, 123–124, 126, 137, 213, 227, 229, 233, 237, 251, 281
Johnson, Lyndon 185
Johnson, Simon 189
Joyous Entry 74
Junkers 119, 167, 266

Katowice 199
Kay, James Phillips 211
Kent 121
Keynes, John Maynard 183–184, 205, 238
Keynesianism 182
Khan, Sayyid Ahmad 292
Khoikhoi 102
Kin 41, 120
Kindleberger, Charles 181
Kinshasa 210
Klompé, Marga 246
Knippenberg, Hans 227
Knowledge 6, 17, 60, 64, 69, 90, 112, 132, 136–139, 166, 247, 250, 252, 273, 294
Kobe 188
Koch, Robert 112
Konfessionalisierung 93–94, 123, 127
Koran 292
Korea (South) 137, 188, 198, 200, 221, 298
Koster, Koosje 286
Kublai Khan 69
Kuyper, Abraham 225, 241
Kuznets, Simon 163–164, 263–265
Kuznets curve 263–264

Labour conflicts 81; see also Strikes
Labour costs 50, 195
Labour demand 236, 254, 278
Labour market 40, 55, 113, 120, 161, 192, 195, 197–198, 229, 236–237, 258–259, 275–277, 299, 301
Labour movement 162, 225, 282
Labour participation 116, 147, 238, 275, 296
Labour productivity 167
Labour relations 38, 52–53, 55, 113, 116, 130, 198
Lagos 155
Laissez faire 171, 240, 243, 300
Land registry 216
Landowners 16, 33–34, 54, 59–60, 64, 85, 118–119, 140, 223–224
Laos 184
Latin America 40, 154–155, 160, 167, 169, 207, 210, 222, 235, 250, 275
Latin schools 138
Latvia 214
Lawyers 140, 171, 272
League of Nations 77, 214
Lebanon 210
Leiden 117, 123, 128, 136, 255
Leisure 277, 289, 290, 296
Lenin, Vladimir 179
Leo XIII 241
León 123

Leprosy 112
Liaoning 110–111
Liberalism 212, 231, 244, 268, 298
Life expectancy 110–111, 143, 162, 197, 251, 285
Limburg 213, 255
Limited company 168
Lindert, Peter 264
Linen 47
Linguistics 281, 294
Literacy 50, 59, 102, 139, 144, 226, 292, 299
Lithuania 214
Little Divergence 6–7, 145, 147, 272, 297–299
Little Ice Age 16
Little Tradition, the 132, 140; see also Popular culture
Liverpool 173
Loans 37–38, 41, 48, 52, 76, 80, 84–85, 89, 121, 123, 168, 170, 174, 181, 187, 190, 204
London 15, 32, 56, 110–111, 128, 136, 149, 155, 157, 174, 210
Los Angeles 188
Louis I, Count of Flanders 81
Louis XIV 118
Lourens, Piet 120
L'Ouverture, Toussaint 104
Low-wage economies 197, 272
Lubbers, Ruud 197, 246
Lucassen, Jan 120
Luddite movement 224
Lumumba, Patrice 210
Luns, Joseph 215
Lutherans 83, 123–124, 127, 239
Luxembourg 67, 106, 192, 194, 214
Lyon 239

Maastricht 192, 194, 277
Maatschappij tot Nut van 't Algemeen 106, 227, 240
Macedonia 67
Machine-building 167
Madrid 32, 61
Magalhães, Fernão de 17
Maghribis 39
Magic 111, 132–135, 139, 144; see also Sorcery
Magna Carta 72
Magnitogorsk 188
Mainz 138
Maize 22, 30
Malacca 17, 51
Malaysia 184, 199, 223

INDEX

Male breadwinner model 275, 301
Malta 214
Malthus, Thomas Robert 26, 62, 64, 109, 298
Malthusian 26, 33, 45, 59, 64, 109, 148, 160, 188, 284, 299
Managers 170, 261, 265, 268
Manchester 211, 224, 239, 272
Manchuria 31, 157
Manorial system 16, 33, 46; see also Feudalism
Mao Zedong 200–201, 234, 265
Marital fertility 109, 143, 251
Market economy 38, 184, 194, 265, 298–299
Market equilibrium 195
Market forces 53, 203, 252
Marriage 10, 26, 29, 69, 109–117, 126–127, 132, 140, 143, 147, 162, 238, 251, 284–289, 292, 301
Marrons 102
Marshall Aid 190–191
Marx, Karl 33, 229, 231, 298; see also Marxist
Marxist 26, 33–34, 200; see also Communist; Socialist
Mass media 290
Matelief, Cornelis 98
Mauritius 97
Maurits, stadholder 87, 91
Maximilian of Austria 81
Mayan Empire 69
McKeown, Adam 157
McNeill, John 155
McNeill, William 299
Measles 22; see also Disease
Meat 36, 113, 143, 169, 171
Mechanization 62, 64, 173, 181, 254, 267, 272
Medical 35, 112, 134–135, 197, 275, 279
Medicine 104, 111, 139, 249, 275
Mediterranean 6, 22, 36, 39, 47, 68, 123, 157, 301
Meiji 198, 292
Men 10, 50, 54, 72, 106, 109–110, 113–116, 127, 130–131, 138–139, 142, 147, 211–213, 219, 222, 226, 238, 243, 251, 258, 262, 272, 278–279, 286–287
Mennonites 83, 239
Mental constructions 4–5, 9–10, 133, 147, 302; see also World view
Mentality 169, 176, 211
Mercantilism 62
Merchant capitalism 38, 41, 62, 65

Merchants 35–39, 44, 47–48, 62, 69, 73, 78–80, 92–93, 99, 121, 147–148, 217, 224
Merger 194, 217
Mesta 41
Methodists 54; see also Dissenters
Mexico 17, 54, 69, 155, 169, 209, 298
Michels, Robert 88
Middle classes 105, 113, 118–120, 131, 138, 162, 213, 223–224, 227, 236, 243, 247, 262–263, 266–268, 271–272, 275, 279, 295
Middle East 8, 15, 17, 20–21, 40–41, 71, 202, 210, 298
Midlands 188
Migrants 10, 44, 48, 90, 93, 123, 137, 148, 156–157, 166, 210–211, 221, 231, 234, 237, 254–255, 259–260
Migration 5, 7, 10, 16, 21, 29, 44, 46, 48, 110–113, 148, 156–157, 169, 188, 219, 221, 229–230, 234, 254–260, 281, 287, 294, 301
Migration ratio 21, 39, 156
Milan 139, 254
Military service 211
Milk 113, 174, 193; see also Dairy
Mill, John Stuart 212
Mineral-based energy economy 64
Mines 17, 22, 168, 196, 255, 268
Ming dynasty 29, 118, 131
Minimum prices 193
Minimum wage 194
Mining 102, 168, 173, 191, 232, 255, 258
Miranda, De 235
Mission, missionaries 22, 99, 278, 292
Mobile telephone 1
Model country 278, 285, 288, 301
Modern economy 52, 189
Modernity 5–6, 244, 253
Modernization 5–6, 167–170, 179, 198–199, 229, 244, 268, 295, 298
Mokyr, Joel 64
Moluccas 51, 101, 177
Monetarism 205
Money 29, 35, 37, 41, 56, 73–76, 83–84, 87, 89–90, 96, 168, 181–185, 195–196, 203, 217, 232, 236, 279, 288
Monnet, Jean 194, 214
Monopoly 51, 72, 99, 131, 171
Montgomery 282, 286
Montpellier 124
Moore, Barrington 223
Moral economy 89, 91; see also Norms
Morality 132, 136, 284
More, Thomas 125

Morgan, J.P.   166
Moriscos   93
Mortality   3, 16, 22, 26–29, 110–114, 162, 219, 249–253, 275, 285, 294–297
Muchembled, Robert   133
Multatuli   239
Mumbai   155
Municipal administration   125
Municipal elite   67; *see also* Bourgeois
Municipal privileges   74, 78–79, 105
Municipalities   104, 216–218, 240
Münster   83
Music   127, 157, 284, 286, 290
Muslims   93, 99, 137, 213, 228, 232
Mutinies   85–87
Mwanamutapa Empire   69
Myanmar   223

Naples   209
Napoleon Bonaparte   54, 104, 149, 167, 208–209, 212, 216
Napoleonic period   104, 149, 208, 216
Nation state   106, 116, 130, 161–162, 176, 207–211, 214–215, 217, 228, 239, 247, 298, 300
National Assembly   104, 215
National income   125, 163, 177–178, 190–191, 195; *see also* Gross domestic product
Nationalism   103, 105–106, 209, 212–213, 247, 295, 298, 301
Nationality   161
Nazis   161, 229, 282
Nehru, Jawaharlal   184, 210
Neighbourhoods   116, 120, 123, 125, 127, 226, 268, 287
New Age   149, 293
New Deal   127, 182
New Netherlands   106
New York   155, 173, 180, 258, 286
New Zealand   157, 160, 210, 222, 235, 255
Newspapers   105, 139, 212, 271, 290, 292, 294–95
Newton, Isaac   136
Night watchman state   171, 216, 231, 277
Nine Years' War   77
Nixon, Richard   185
Nobel prizes   295
Nobility   46, 67, 69, 72, 78, 80, 85, 89, 92, 103, 114, 118–119, 161–162, 211, 223–224, 230–231, 261, 266
Norms (social)   4, 39, 71, 107, 126–127, 131–132, 213, 231, 254, 278–280, 287, 292, 294, 301

North, Douglass   39
North Africa   20, 36, 39, 237
North America   7, 16, 55, 102, 169, 192, 208, 250, 298–299
North Carolina   286
North Sea region   6
North-western Europe   6, 8, 10, 30, 36, 38, 48, 55–59, 114, 120, 128, 145–147, 191, 247–249, 255, 272, 281, 287, 290, 297
Norway   188, 267
Nuclear family   24, 58, 117, 299
Numeracy   50, 59
Nutrition   113, 249, 275

Occupational   35, 43–44, 55, 120, 213, 228, 236, 254, 260–261, 272
Oceania   154, 160, 210; *see also* Australia
Office work(ers)   271–272
Oil crisis   195–196, 199, 246, 258
Old age   3, 106, 112, 240, 243–246, 251, 285; *see also* Elderly
Oldenbarnevelt, Johan van   91
Oligarchy, oligarchization   78, 88, 92, 104–105, 149
Opera   244
Opium   96, 101
Opportunity hoarding   90
Organic economy   64
Organization of Petroleum Exporting Countries (OPEC)   195
Orphanage, orphans   123, 262
Osaka   188
Ostsiedlung   119
Ottoman Empire   20, 29, 54, 57, 68, 71, 73, 94–96, 107, 208, 210, 239, 244, 292
Overijssel   79, 91, 105
Oxford   128

Pacific Ocean   17
Paintings   143
Pakistan   14, 154
Pamphlet   105, 211
Paper industry   47, 60
Paper money   37
Paris   15, 54, 56, 136, 155, 169, 190, 194, 210, 239, 254, 286
Parish   120, 139
Parliament   54, 60, 76, 88, 89, 215, 223–224
Pasteur, Louis   112
Patents   41, 50, 60, 64
Pathogens   17, 22
Patriarchal system   114, 117, 127, 284, 287
Patriciate   226

Patrimonial   72, 92
Patriot Movement   104–105, 107
Peace of Augsburg   77
Peace of Rijswijk   77
Peace of Utrecht   77
Peace of Westphalia   77
Peasant model   36, 46
Peasant revolt   76
Peat   44–45, 48, 64, 130, 148, 176
Peatlands   45–46, 148
Pepper   51, 143
Persians   36
Peru   17, 69, 169
Peterloo   224, 239
Petition (*rekest*)   89
Petroleum   171–173, 195
Pharmaceutical industry   294
Philip II   79
Philip the Good   79
Physics   60, 64, 135–136, 295
Physiocrats   211
Pillarization   204, 227, 243, 247, 254, 271, 276, 287, 293, 295–296, 300–301
Plague   22, 29, 55, 111–112, 123; *see also* Epidemics
Plantations   22, 38, 55, 60, 96–98, 101–102, 173, 278
Plants   17, 22, 133, 136, 160, 167, 279
Plassey, Battle of (1757)   96
Plockhoy, Pieter Cornelis   94
Poivre, Pierre   97
Poland   13, 32, 34, 139, 154, 181, 188, 200, 214
Polder model   78, 204
Polders   78; *see also* Drainage; Reclamation
Police   212–213, 221, 224, 240–241, 271, 277, 282, 284
Political culture   74, 88–89, 92–93, 102, 232
Political participation   88–89, 222–223, 225
Political parties   222, 228, 232, 235, 240–241, 247, 268
Political system   68–69, 71, 74, 87, 103, 217, 232
Pollution   155, 188, 230, 232–233, 239
Pomeranz, Kenneth   7
Poor, the   37, 89, 121, 124–125, 128, 140, 231, 236, 240–241, 262
Poor Law   125, 128, 240
Poor relief   10, 121, 123–126, 128, 147, 211, 216, 236, 239–240, 254, 257, 262, 271, 300
Pope   93, 241
Popular culture   140; *see also* Little Tradition
Popular sovereignty   94

Population growth   5, 16, 26, 29, 36, 71, 110, 143, 164, 174, 191, 241, 249–251, 253, 255, 298
Population pressure   110, 178
Population register   212, 234; *see also* Registry office
Population size   13, 26, 29, 251
Populist   258
Porcelain   20, 47, 143
Portugal   13, 76, 99, 101, 127, 188, 194, 207, 209, 214, 222, 229, 287, 291
Positive check   26, 29, 109
Postal service   60
Potatoes   22, 30, 113, 142
Pottery   47, 60, 143, 268
Poverty   3, 62, 117, 121, 123, 128, 174, 185, 191, 211, 231, 236–237, 241, 265
Power   2–5, 9–10, 13, 16, 23, 32–34, 45–48, 51–54, 60, 62–64, 67–74, 77–81, 85–98, 101–107, 113, 118–119, 127–128, 131, 145, 147–149, 153, 157, 160–165, 172, 176–183, 189–190, 192, 196, 198, 200–203, 205, 207–208, 211, 219, 223–226, 228, 230–233, 235–236, 247, 252, 264, 266–267, 278, 282, 284, 290, 294, 297, 299, 302
Prague   254
Prak, Maarten   120, 216
Preventive check   26, 29, 109–110
Price level   55, 165
Price regulation   32, 165
Price revolution   29
Printing technology   137, 144
Prison   128, 278–279; *see also* Reformatories; Workhouse
Private sphere   130, 132
Privatization   203
Privileges   73–74, 78–79, 103, 105, 119, 147, 149
Production, means of   33, 90, 194, 261
Production, mode of   33, 38
Productivity   6, 16, 30, 33, 35, 37, 43, 46, 48, 50, 52, 57, 59–65, 72, 135, 148, 164, 169, 175–179, 193, 197, 205–210, 250
Progress   40, 175, 244, 273, 298; *see also* Modernity
Proletariat   118, 133, 143, 162, 239–240, 300
Property relations   34, 38, 147–148
Property rights   39–40, 43, 126, 200
Prosperity   7, 23, 25, 35, 38, 43, 47, 57, 132, 160, 163, 165, 171, 176, 178, 193, 202, 205, 211, 248, 257, 286, 289–290, 296, 298–299
Prostitute   128, 288

Protectionism   50, 181, 287
Proto-industry   38; *see also* Cottage industry
Provo movement   284
Prussia   50, 62, 89, 92, 94, 105, 207, 266
Psychiatric patients   284, 286
Ptolemy   22
Public church   55, 123, 125; *see also* Reformed Church, Dutch
Public officials   121, 140, 209, 211, 219, 230, 262
Public sphere   23, 94–95, 102, 105, 107, 147, 149, 226–227, 233, 247, 299–300
Public transport   203
Publishers   94
Puerperal fever   285; *see also* Disease
Purchasing power   164–165, 177, 181, 183, 201, 264, 290
Purmerend   74
Putnam, Robert   90, 226–227
Putting-out system   36; *see also* Cottage-industry

Qing dynasty   29, 121, 131, 137, 234
Quakers   54; *see also* Dissenters
Quinine   219

Racism   281–282, 298
Radio   212, 290, 292
Railways   65, 98, 166–169, 173, 176, 211, 216, 219
Randstad   155, 210
Rapeseed   36, 45
Rational choice theory   223
Rationalization   5, 108, 135–137, 170, 244; *see also* Reason
Raw materials   36, 48, 64–65, 155, 168, 199, 202, 219, 267, 298
Reading culture   139
Reading revolution   139
Reagan, Ronald   196
Real estate   52, 90
Reason   6, 24, 135–136, 144, 147, 161, 292–293; *see also* Rationalization
Reciprocity   71, 187
Reclamation   46, 48, 148; *see also* Peatlands; Polders
Reconciliation   124
Reform Acts   224
Reformation   40, 56, 59, 71, 79, 93, 116, 123, 134, 147
Reformatories   128; *see also* Prison
Reformed Church, Dutch   56, 255, 292
Refrigerator   178, 200

Refugees   83, 93, 149, 214, 229, 255, 259, 301
Regents   89, 114, 121, 140; *see also* Municipal elite
Registry office   216; *see also* Population register
Religion   2, 77, 79, 93–94, 99, 106, 108, 211, 213, 248, 254, 289, 292–293; *see also* Faith; Reformation; separate religions
Remonstrants   123, 139; *see also* Dissenters
Renaissance   244
Reparations   124, 181
Repertoires of collective action   80–81, 103, 107, 224
Retail trade   142, 290
Reversal of fortune   189
Revolt (Dutch)   23, 46, 56, 79–81, 83, 85, 88, 92, 104, 106, 123, 126, 239
Revolutionary situations   89, 91–92, 224
Revolutions (socio-political)   2, 68, 77, 80, 95–96, 102, 104–107, 137, 200, 207–208, 223–225, 235, 239, 298
Rhineland   6, 213
Ribbon mill   48–49
Rice   35, 57, 113, 234
Riots and revolts   76, 78, 81, 88–89, 91, 207, 223–224; *see also* Revolutionary situations; Revolutions
Risks of life   110–112, 114, 147, 212, 243, 254, 287, 299
Robinson, James   189, 223
Rockefeller, John D.   166
Roma   213, 228–229, 237
Roman Empire   69, 81
Romance (love)   285
Romania   154, 214, 224
Rome   155, 192, 195, 232, 265
Roosevelt, Franklin D.   243
Rostow, Walt W.   62, 187
Rotterdam   105, 155, 190, 210, 254
Rousseau, Jean-Jacques   94, 212
Royal mechanism   72
Royal Society (London)   136
Rubber   60, 171, 173, 177, 219, 252
Ruhr   168, 188, 254
Rural estates   34
Rural industry   36; *see also* Cottage-industry
Russia   5, 13–15, 32, 50, 62, 71, 76, 89, 106, 134, 153–154, 157, 170, 173, 179, 188, 201, 208, 223, 226, 247, 273, 278, 289, 291; *see also* Soviet Union
Russian Revolution   226
Rwanda   229

INDEX

Sahara   20, 250
Saint-Simon, Claude Henri de   231
Salon (French, during Enlightenment)   95
Samarkand   17
São Paulo   155
Saxony   37, 119
Scaliger, Joseph   136
Scandinavia   13, 32, 36, 48, 109, 128, 139, 188, 195, 228, 237, 267
Schonen (Sweden)   35
School dropout   258
Science   2, 22, 137, 231, 244, 275, 294–296, 298
Scientific Revolution   65, 135
Scotland   13–15, 62, 116, 139
Scott, James   210–211
Seasonal labour   112
Second Golden Age   295
Second Industrial Revolution   167–168, 178, 294
Second Vatican Council   293
Secularization   133, 292, 294, 296, 298–299
Seed-sowing factor   30
Selbstzwang   131, 140
Self-determination   6, 210, 215, 221
Self-sufficiency   36, 45, 148
Serfdom   33, 46, 53–54, 65, 148, 161, 208
Servants   58, 81, 114, 121, 137, 209, 213, 262–263, 267, 277
Service sector   43, 260–261
Settler colony   102, 161, 210, 235–236, 247, 297–298
Seven Years' War   103
Sewerage   111
Sewing machine   171
Sexuality   131–132, 136, 162, 279, 284, 296
Shanghai   155, 234
Shares   50, 81
Shintoism   292
Shipbuilding   45, 87, 96, 175, 177, 191, 197
Shipping   44, 47, 50, 62, 99, 148, 174
Shopkeeper   112, 120, 143, 267
Shorter, Edward   114
Siberia   157
Sickness insurance   3, 120, 133, 140, 203, 231, 235, 238, 240, 243–244
Silk   35, 37, 47, 51, 57, 60, 96, 202
Silver   17, 29, 51, 57–58, 85, 169
Simons, Menno   83
Singapore   198, 223, 227
Skill premium   58–59, 262–264
Slave labour   54, 102
Slave trade   20–21, 47, 51, 54, 60, 98, 136–137

Slavery   51, 53–54, 65, 161, 166, 226, 278, 282
Sleeping sickness   252; *see also* Diseases
Slochteren   246
Slovakia   32, 214
Slovenia   214
Smallholder   119, 167, 267; *see also* Peasant model
Smallpox   22, 111–112; *see also* Diseases
Smit, Joke   238
Smith, Adam   35, 62, 231, 298
Smithian   26, 34–36
Social capital   88, 90, 226, 228
Social care   118, 121, 123–125, 143, 147, 207, 231, 234, 239
Social control   3, 116, 126–128, 131, 231, 234; *see also* Disciplining
Social engineering   208, 210–211, 228, 247, 294
Social mobility   162, 249, 260, 262, 266, 273, 275, 295
Social policy   162, 208, 216, 218, 230–243, 247, 298, 300
Social problem   231, 241, 258
Social science   9, 244, 294
Social security   120, 183, 195–196, 198, 237–238, 246
Social structure   80, 120
Socialist   161, 179, 207, 225, 235, 240–243, 246, 255, 268, 270–271
Societies   3, 5, 10, 20, 23, 27, 34, 43, 53, 55, 76, 94, 106, 109–110, 113, 116, 121–122, 136, 147, 155, 160, 226, 234, 244, 247, 261
Soldiers   84–85, 87, 104, 107, 209, 213, 219, 221, 271
Song dynasty   8, 17, 23, 38, 139
Sorcery   111, 132, 134–135; *see also* Magic
South Africa   8, 51, 102, 160, 181, 210, 219, 252
South America   55, 98, 136, 142, 167, 169, 192
Southern Netherlands   8, 13–15, 32, 44, 55, 78–79, 83, 128, 217; *see also* Austrian Netherlands; Belgium
Sovereign   39, 46, 50, 67, 72, 74, 85, 88, 91–92, 94, 203, 209, 215, 223, 226, 230
Sovereignty   77, 94, 103, 106, 214–215, 221
Soviet Union   154, 161, 184, 200, 229, 273; *see also* Russia
Spaak, Paul-Henri   214–215
Spain   8, 13–15, 21–22, 32, 41, 44, 54, 76, 79, 91, 93, 96, 99, 101, 106, 127, 134, 153, 194, 209, 214, 222, 239, 287

324   INDEX

Spanish America   29; *see also* Latin America
Spanish flu   160, 251; *see also* Disease
Specialization   26, 35–38, 45–46, 65, 118, 121, 131, 142, 174, 179, 295
Specialization model   36, 46
Spices   47, 57, 101–102, 142–143; *see also* Pepper
Spinning Jenny   63
Spinning wheel   37, 63
Spinoza, Baruch de   137
Sri Lanka   8
St. Helena   97
St. Vincent   97
Stadholder   77, 83, 85, 91–92, 104, 215
Stadholderless period   91
Stagflation   196
Stalin, Joseph   179, 229
Standard of living   10, 43, 55, 66, 89, 147, 174, 202, 252, 264, 297, 299
Staple market   50, 149, 217
State finances   299; *see also* Government finances; State loans
State formation   3, 5, 9–10, 39, 67–68, 71–74, 76, 78–79, 84–85, 105–106, 147–148, 161, 176, 207–208, 215–216, 223, 248
State loans   84; *see also* Loans
State mines   255
State system   77, 106, 149, 299
States General   50–51, 76, 79, 85, 88–89, 91, 103, 106; *see also* National assembly; Parliament
Statistics   112, 204, 210–211, 218, 221, 251, 285
Steam engine   63–64
Steam train   98; *see also* Railways
Steamship   98, 167, 173
Steel industry   168, 199
Stikker, Dirk   215
Stock exchange   50
Stock market crash   7
Stone, Lawrence   114
Strikes   81, 222–226, 230, 271, 282, 296
Subsidies   62, 124–125, 177, 193, 195, 203, 216
Subsistence crisis   27
Suez Canal   219
Suffrage   102–103, 222, 224–226, 241–243
Sugar   22, 38, 47, 55, 60, 97, 142–143, 173, 175, 177, 219, 267
Sukarno   210, 221
Sultan   68–69, 74
Sumatra   51, 177, 219
Sun Yat-sen   230
Supply side   183, 196–197, 203

Suriname   8, 101–102, 221, 260, 278
Swaan, Abram de   234, 239, 284
Sweden   35, 50, 62, 117, 154, 188, 194, 214, 222, 228, 236–237, 267, 275–277, 279, 287–289, 291, 293
Swing Riots   24
Switzerland   12, 32, 37, 154, 181, 207, 270
Sworn community   40
Sydney   160
Symbolic capital   90
Syria   210

Tabriz   17
Taiping revolt   230
Taiwan   198
Take-off   62, 189
Tang dynasty   135
Tanzania   252
Taoism   135
Tax burden   50, 85, 195
Tax farmers   54, 84, 209
Tax monopoly   72
Tax riot   81, 91
Tax state   72
Tax system   76, 84, 93, 103, 216
Taxation   73, 79, 84, 103–104, 125, 216–217, 237, 246, 265; *see also* Excises
Te Brake, Wayne   91
Tea   20, 22, 47, 57, 103, 112, 142–143, 173, 177, 219
Technology   25, 39, 71, 76, 137, 144, 170, 176, 178, 185, 188, 193, 199, 200, 205, 294, 296, 298
Telecommunications   203; *see also* Telegraph; Telephone
Telegraph   235, 244
Telephone   200
Television   290
Temperance movement   227
Tenants (tenant farmers)   33, 261
Terms of employment   225
Textile industry   80, 166, 168, 177, 189, 282; *see also* Cotton; Silk; Wool
Thailand   199
Thatcher, Margaret   196–197
Third World   7, 160, 259, 298
Thomas, Keith   133
Thompson, E.P.   89
Thorbecke, Johan Rudolf   177, 216, 225, 240
Tiananmen Square   230
Tilburg   86, 255, 286
Tilly, Charles   2, 74, 76, 81, 208, 209, 215, 299
Timber   97, 167

Time zone 19
Tinbergen, Jan 178
Tobacco 20, 38, 47, 55, 60, 171, 173, 177, 219
Tobago 97
Tocqueville, Alexis de 226
Tokyo 15, 32, 155
Toledo 123
Tolerance, toleration 68, 93–94, 102, 107, 137, 289, 301
Toulouse 123
Tourism 157, 160
Toynbee, Arnold 162
Tracy, James 84
Trade 85, 96, 98–99, 101, 107, 116, 136–137, 139, 142, 147–148, 155–156, 163–164, 171–181, 184–187, 192–208, 215, 224–225, 227, 230, 235, 237, 239, 242–246, 255, 261, 265, 268, 270–271, 290, 297, 300
Trade bloc 192, 215
Trade networks 22, 35, 37, 44, 51, 72, 96
Trade Union 192, 194, 196–197, 204, 208, 225, 230, 237, 241, 244, 246, 255, 265, 268, 270–271
Trading company 51
Trading post 36, 51, 96, 98–99, 102, 173
Traditions 3, 69, 102, 135, 142, 203, 254, 268, 292
Training 40–41, 50, 148, 241, 278; *see also* Education
Tramping 125, 128
Transaction costs 39, 41, 50, 62, 79, 147, 175, 185
Transatlantic migration 157
Transport 17, 21, 34–37, 44–45, 51, 54, 60, 65, 157, 167–169, 173–174, 176, 203, 235, 251, 272, 278
Travel journals 114, 142
Treaty of Maastricht 192, 194
Treaty of Versailles 77, 181, 214
Tribute 32, 53–54
Trier 123
Trieste 58, 109
Trust 171, 177, 184, 199, 205, 226
Tulder, J.N.N. van 262
Turkey 40, 237, 258–260, 273, 292–293
Twente 282
Typewriters 171
Typhus 111; *see also* Disease

Uganda 252
Ukraine 17
Unemployment 3, 17, 80, 112, 123, 180–183, 192, 195–197, 203, 231, 235–237, 241–244, 254–257, 264–265
UNESCO 214
Union of Utrecht 93
Unitary state 208, 211, 215, 219, 300
United States 5, 8, 54, 65, 149, 154–155, 157, 160–164, 166–171, 173, 175–193, 195–196, 199, 201, 221–222, 227–228, 232–233, 235–236, 254–261, 265, 273, 275, 278–279, 281–282, 286–291, 293–294, 297–299
University 72, 90, 114, 136, 178, 286
Unmarried 106, 109–110, 117, 143, 251, 285
Upscaling 171, 192, 268
Urbanization 2, 5, 14–16, 45, 57, 72, 119, 121, 128, 147–148, 154, 171, 223, 230, 239, 241, 250, 260
USSR 179; *see also* Soviet Union
Utopian 231
Utrecht 46, 77–78, 93, 134

Vanderbilt, Cornelius 166
Vassal 16, 69, 71–72
Veblen, Thorstein 262
Vegetarianism 227
Venereal disease 279
Venezuela 8, 104
Venice 17, 41, 127, 139
Vesalius, Andreas 112, 135
Vespucci, Amerigo 136
Veteran associations 228
Vietnam 54, 184–185, 202, 286
Village community 123, 131, 133
Violence 72, 83, 124, 131, 224, 232, 277–278
Vitoria, Francisco de 136
Vives, Juan Luis 125
Vlissingen 81
Volcker, Paul 196
Vries, Jan de 36, 43, 56, 125

Wage labour 23, 34, 53, 55, 113, 118, 130, 162, 224, 236
Wage labourers 53, 55, 66, 81, 112, 120, 140, 145; *see also* Workers
Wage restraint 197
Wage-price spiral 195
Wages 53, 55–58, 62, 64, 120, 130, 142, 173, 177, 181, 192, 194–197, 199, 202, 211, 237, 241, 255, 257, 261–264, 267, 275, 282
Walcheren 190
Wales 125, 287

Wallachia   208
Wallerstein, Immanuel   38, 101, 299
War   2–3, 23, 29, 50, 54, 67, 73–78, 80, 84–88, 96, 103–107, 112, 114, 125, 147, 156–157, 160–164, 166, 168, 174–181, 184–187, 190–191, 193–198, 204–205, 207, 210, 213–215, 218–219, 221, 223, 228–230, 235, 237–239, 243–246, 251, 255, 257–258, 264–266, 275, 286, 297–301
War of the Spanish Succession   77
Warehouses   121
Warwick   123
Washing machine   178
Washington   203, 232
Washington Consensus   203
Wassenaar Agreement   197, 246
Water frame   63
Water power   60, 63
Waterloo   224
Watt, James   64
Weber, Eugen   212–213
Weber, Max   72, 92, 108, 209, 229, 281, 298
Welfare state   161, 183, 194–195, 197, 205, 211, 216, 228, 230, 233–234, 237, 241, 244, 246–248, 257–258, 263, 265, 271, 277, 299–301
West India Company (WIC)   50, 137
West Indies   55, 61
Western Europe   5–8, 10, 20, 24, 30, 36–38, 41, 48, 53, 55–59, 66, 108–111, 114–121, 127–128, 130–131, 134–135, 137, 139, 143, 145–147, 161, 174, 179, 190–191, 199, 208, 214, 229, 237, 246–249, 255, 267, 272, 277–278, 282, 287, 290, 293, 296–297, 299, 301; *see also* North-western Europe
Western hemisphere   8, 47–48
Westphalian state system   77, 106
Wetsverzetting (change of legislature)   92
Weyer, Johan de   134
Whaling   47
White, Harry Dexter   184
White collar workers   270–271, 295
Wibaut, Floor   235
Widowers   117
Widows   116–117
Willem I, King   176, 215–217
Willem II, King   225
Willem II, Stadholder   91
Willem III, King-Stadholder   77
Willem V, Stadholder   104–105, 215
William of Orange, Stadholder   81, 83, 87, 93
Williamson, Jeffrey   155, 264
Wilson, Woodrow   210
Windmills and wind power   45, 48, 176

Wine   89
Witch hunts   135
Witches   133–135; *see also* Sorcery
Witt, Johan de   77
Women   10, 50, 55–56, 109–110, 113–117, 120, 125, 127, 130, 134, 137, 142, 147–148, 157, 177, 213, 222, 233, 236, 238, 239, 243, 250–251, 262, 267, 271–277, 284, 286–288, 292, 301
Women's emancipation   237–238, 288
Women's suffrage   242
Wood   37, 64, 97, 129
Wool   35, 37, 41, 60, 64, 169
Workers   40, 46, 52–53, 55–56, 59, 81, 87, 96, 112, 140, 162, 169, 171, 210–211, 213, 224–226, 236–237, 240–241, 243, 254–255, 258, 260–264, 267, 270–272, 278–281, 290, 295, 301; *see also* Labourers
Workers' movement   240, 243, 255, 271
Workhouse   128; *see also* Reformatories
Working class   78, 166, 211, 239, 255, 262, 268, 270–271, 275, 277
Working hours   140, 197, 243
Working population   193, 199, 243, 261–263, 272, 297, 299
Working-class culture   255, 262, 268, 270, 277
World Bank, the   184, 187, 189, 199, 202–203, 276, 291
World economy   38–39, 179–180, 190, 192, 202, 205, 298–299
World religion   292
World view   4, 132–135, 139, 149, 213
World War   156–157, 160–162, 164, 174–175, 177–180, 184–185, 190, 193–194, 198, 205, 207, 210, 214, 218–219, 221, 228–229, 235, 238–239, 251, 255, 257–258, 264–266, 297–298, 300–301
World wide web   157; *see also* Internet
Woude, Ad van der   43, 125
Wrigley, E.A.   64

Yangzi Delta   30, 32, 37, 57–58, 145
Yellow fever   104, 112
Yom Kippur War   195
Yorkshire   37
Young Turks   54, 293
Yuan dynasty   29, 201
Yunnan   132

Zaanstreek   50
Zaiton   17, 51
Zanden, Jan Luiten van   43
Zeeland   44, 46, 79, 83–85, 93, 254–255
Zollverein   168

The World and the Netherlands

The World and the Netherlands

A Global History from a Dutch Perspective

Edited by
Marjolein 't Hart, Manon van der Heijden
and Karel Davids

BLOOMSBURY ACADEMIC
LONDON • NEW YORK • OXFORD • NEW DELHI • SYDNEY

BLOOMSBURY ACADEMIC
Bloomsbury Publishing Plc
50 Bedford Square, London, WC1B 3DP, UK
1385 Broadway, New York, NY 10018, USA
29 Earlsfort Terrace, Dublin 2, Ireland

BLOOMSBURY, BLOOMSBURY ACADEMIC and the Diana logo are trademarks of
Bloomsbury Publishing Plc

First published in Great Britain 2023

Copyright © Marjolein 't Hart, Manon van der Heijden and Karel Davids, 2023

Marjolein 't Hart, Manon van der Heijden and Karel Davids have asserted their right under the Copyright, Designs and Patents Act, 1988, to be identified as Editor of this work.

Translated by Vivien Collingwood. English language translation © Vivien Collingwood, 2023.

Cover image: Dutch East India Company in Amsterdam showing warehouses and shipyard. Hand-colored woodcut. (© Alamy Stock Photo)

The publisher gratefully acknowledges the support of the Dutch Foundation for Literature.

Nederlands letterenfonds
dutch foundation for literature

All rights reserved. No part of this publication may be reproduced or transmitted in any form or by any means, electronic or mechanical, including photocopying, recording, or any information storage or retrieval system, without prior permission in writing from the publishers.

Bloomsbury Publishing Plc does not have any control over, or responsibility for, any third-party websites referred to or in this book. All internet addresses given in this book were correct at the time of going to press. The author and publisher regret any inconvenience caused if addresses have changed or sites have ceased to exist, but can accept no responsibility for any such changes.

Every effort has been made to trace copyright holders and to obtain their permissions for the use of copyright material. The publisher apologizes for any errors or omissions and would be grateful if notified of any corrections that should be incorporated in future reprints or editions of this book.

A catalogue record for this book is available from the British Library.

A catalog record for this book is available from the Library of Congress.

ISBN: HB: 978-1-3501-9193-8
PB: 978-1-3501-9192-1
ePDF: 978-1-3501-9194-5
eBook: 978-1-3501-9195-2

Typeset by Deanta Global Publishing Services, Chennai, India
Printed and bound in Great Britain

To find out more about our authors and books visit www.bloomsbury.com and sign up for our newsletters.

CONTENTS

List of text boxes, maps, tables, charts, and figures viii

About the authors xiii

Preface xv

Introduction 1
0.1 *'How ordinary people lived the big changes'* 2
0.2 *Basic problems* 3
0.3 *Changes, phasing and demarcation in time and space* 5
0.4 *The structure of the book* 9

PART I
Before the Great Divergence, *c.* 1000–*c.* 1800

1   Introduction to Part I 13
1.1 *Population development and the natural environment* 13
1.2 *Long-distance connections* 16
1.3 *The three basic problems: Contours of change* 23

2   Growth and economic development before the Great Divergence 25
    KAREL DAVIDS

2.1 *Economic development in the world* 26
2.2 *The rise of the Dutch economy* 43
2.3 *Labour relations and income distribution* 52
2.4 *Industrialization and the Great Divergence* 56
    Summary 65

3   The struggle for power: Sociopolitical developments 67
    MARJOLEIN 'T HART

3.1 *International political relations and state formation* 68
3.2 *State formation in the Netherlands* 78
3.3 *Participation and political culture* 88
3.4 *Overseas colonization and the Atlantic revolutions* 96
     Summary 106

4   The tension between the community and the individual: Social-cultural developments 108
    MANON VAN DER HEIJDEN

4.1 *Patterns of marriage and family formation* 109
4.2 *Social order, social care and disciplining* 118
4.3 *A changing world view and the growth of the private sphere* 132
     Summary 143

5   Conclusion to Part I 145

PART II
After the Great Divergence, *c.* 1800–present day

6   Introduction to Part II 153

6.1 *Population development and the natural environment* 153
6.2 *Long-distance connections* 155
6.3 *The three basic problems: Contours of change* 160

7   Expansion, stagnation and globalization: Economic developments 163
    JEROEN TOUWEN

7.1 *Industrialization and the growth in world trade before the First World War* 164
7.2 *Conflict and stagnation, 1914–1945* 178
7.3 *Institutional renewal and economic growth after 1945* 184
7.4 *Changing priorities and new players, 1973–2010* 195
     Summary 205

8	State formation, democratization and social care: Sociopolitical developments 207
LEO LUCASSEN	
8.1	*Nation states, social engineering and international cooperation* 208	
8.2	*Democratization and citizenship* 222	
8.3	*Social policy and the rise of the welfare state* 230
Summary 247	
9	New opportunities, values and norms: Sociocultural developments 248
LEX HEERMA VAN VOSS	
9.1	*Demographic changes and the risks of existence* 249	
9.2	*Social order and social mobility* 260	
9.3	*Disciplining and counter-movements* 277	
9.4	*Lifestyles, worldviews and the Netherlands as a 'model country'* 285
Summary 295	
10	Conclusion to Part II 297	

Recommended literature 303

Index 310

LIST OF TEXT BOXES, MAPS, TABLES, CHARTS, AND FIGURES

Text box 2.1　　Guilds in the world 40
Text box 2.2　　The VOC in Asia 51
Text box 2.3　　The abolition of the slave trade and slavery 54
Text box 3.1　　The European state system, based on the sovereignty of nation states 77
Text box 3.2　　Repertoires of collective action 81
Text box 3.3　　The Financial Revolution 84
Text box 3.4　　Economic, social and cultural capital 90
Text box 3.5　　Habermas's theory of the public sphere 95
Text box 3.6　　Colonialism and environmental awareness 97
Text box 3.7　　Three phases in the colonization from Europe 98
Text box 3.8　　The Patriot Movement, 1785–87 105
Text box 4.1　　Risks of existence in the pre-industrial period 112
Text box 4.2　　Neighbourhood organizations 116
Text box 4.3　　Peace and reconciliation 124
Text box 4.4　　Charivari, social control from below 127
Text box 4.5　　The transition from family economy to family consumer economy 130
Text box 7.1　　Latin America, stunted growth 169
Text box 7.2　　Gerschenkron and catch-up growth 170
Text box 7.3　　The Gold Standard 175
Text box 7.4　　Keynesians and monetarists 183
Text box 7.5　　Exchange rates after the Gold Standard 185
Text box 7.6　　Economic growth and the environmental problem 188
Text box 7.7　　Milestones in European cooperation 194
Text box 8.1　　Direct and indirect rule 209
Text box 8.2　　Types of nationalism 212
Text box 8.3　　The origins of the European Union 214
Text box 8.4　　The North exploits the South, 1815–30 217
Text box 8.5　　Political system and protest. The environmental movement 232
Text box 8.6　　Modernity and modernization 244

LIST OF TEXT BOXES, MAPS, TABLES, CHARTS, AND FIGURES

Text box 9.1   Natural disasters and the fragility of life 252
Text box 9.2   Unemployment in the economic crises of 1931, 1982 and 2009 257
Text box 9.3   Immigrants in the Netherlands after the Second World War 258
Text box 9.4   Racism, a tenacious nineteenth-century doctrine 281
Text box 9.5   The generation of the 1960s 286
Text box 9.6   Science and society in the nineteenth and twentieth centuries 294

Map 0.1   Map of the Netherlands, c. 2020 xviii
Map 1.1   Long-distance trade networks in the thirteenth century by the historical sociologist Janet Abu-Lughod 18
Map 2.1   China in the late Qing Empire 31
Map 2.2   The Atlantic World in the Early Modern period 61
Map 3.1   Towns in Europe, early sixteenth century 75
Map 3.2   The Dutch Republic, in *c.* 1650 86
Map 5.1   The most important towns in Europe, early nineteenth century 146
Map 6.1   The British world empire in *c.* 1900 158

Table 1.1   Estimated Population Trends in Different Parts of the World, 1000–1800 14
Table 1.2   Estimated Population Trends in Various European Countries, 1300–1800 14
Table 1.3   Urbanization in Various European Countries, 1300–1800 15
Table 1.4   Estimated Growth in Intercontinental Overseas Trade to and from Europe, 1500–1900 20
Table 1.5   The African Slave Trade, 1500–1900 21
Table 1.6   Cross-border Migration by Europeans, 1500–1850 21
Table 2.1   Average Harvest Yield per Seed for Sowing in Europe, 1300–1800 32
Table 2.2   Corvée Labour and Wage Labour on Rural Estates in Korczyn (Poland), 1533–1660 34
Table 2.3   The Occupational Structure of Holland/the Netherlands by Sector, in Percentages, Compared to Several Other European Countries, 1500–1800 44
Table 2.4   Estimated Income per Capita of the Population in the Netherlands, Compared with Several Other European Countries, 1500–1820 44
Table 2.5   Overseas Imports to the Netherlands, Great Britain and France, *c.* 1770 47
Table 2.6   Development of Imports to the Netherlands from Asia and the Western Hemisphere by Value, 1640–1780 48
Table 2.7   Estimated Value of Capital Holdings in Holland, in Millions of Guilders, 1650 and 1790 52
Table 2.8   Taxonomy of Labour Relations 53
Table 2.9   Real Daily Wages of Unskilled Construction Workers in European Towns, 1500–1850 56

Table 2.10	Real Daily Wages of Unskilled Labourers in India and the Yangzi Delta (China), Compared with Southern England, 1550–1850 58
Table 2.11	Estimate of Average Annual Growth in Income per Capita in England, 1700–1870 63
Table 2.12	Cost of Spinning a Pound of Raw Cotton Yarn, in 1784 Prices, England, 1760–1830 63
Table 3.1	Revolutionary Situations in the Netherlands, 1500–1800 91
Table 4.1	Average Age of Marriage of Women in Western Europe, Late Eighteenth Century 109
Table 4.2	Life Expectancy in Western Europe and East Asia until the Nineteenth Century 111
Table 4.3	Heads of Households in Leiden, and Poverty, 1622 117
Table 4.4	Social Stratification of the Population of Saxony, 1550 and 1750 119
Table 4.5	Estimated Production of Manuscripts and Printed Books in Europe, 1000–1800 138
Table 6.1	Population Trends in Europe and Different Parts of the World, 1700–2000 154
Table 6.2	Estimated Growth in Intercontinental Overseas Trade to and from Europe, 1700–1992 156
Table 6.3	Foreign Investment as a Percentage of Total World Production, 1870–1995 156
Table 7.1	Gross Domestic Product per Capita, 1820–2010 165
Table 7.2	Total Length of Railway Track per Country, 1850–1910 166
Table 7.3	World Energy Consumption, 1800–1990 189
Table 7.4	Economic Growth in North-western Europe, 1890–1992 191
Table 8.1	Central Government Spending in the Netherlands in 1850, 1900 and 1960 218
Table 8.2	Collective Expenditure by the Dutch State, as Percentage of GDP, 1815–2020 218
Table 8.3	Municipal Expenditure in Guilders per Capita of the Population in the Netherlands, 1862–1907 218
Table 8.4	Introduction of Universal Suffrage in Western Countries, 1840–1920 222
Table 8.5	Number of Strikes in the Netherlands by Decade, 1851–1940 225
Table 8.6	Introduction of Social Legislation in Various Countries, 1890–1965 235
Table 8.7	Typology of Police Services in European Countries 241
Table 9.1	Population Development in the Netherlands, Belgium and Germany, 1800–2000 253
Table 9.2	Immigrants and Their Descendants in the Netherlands, 1972–2020 260
Table 9.3	Employment by Sector in the Netherlands, Great Britain, the United States, Finland and Indonesia, 1800–2000 261
Table 9.4	Male Working Population of the Netherlands, 1899–1992 263

LIST OF TEXT BOXES, MAPS, TABLES, CHARTS, AND FIGURES xi

Table 9.5	Income Inequality in the Netherlands and the United States, 1800–2019 265
Table 9.6	Percentage of 20- to 24-year-olds in Higher Education, 1910–2005 273
Table 9.7	Women in the Labour Market in Europe and the United States, 1850–2019 276
Table 9.8	Number of Prisoners per 100,000 Inhabitants in Several European Countries, 1950–2018 279
Table 9.9	Percentage of Extramarital Births in Several European Countries, 1870–2019 287
Table 9.10	Legalization of Pressing Ethical Issues in a Number of Countries, 1920–2020 289
Table 9.11	Ownership of Consumer Durables in Industrialized Countries per 1,000 Inhabitants, 1937–2010 291
Table 9.12	Faith and Churchgoing in Different Countries, 1947–2014 293
Chart 2.1	The subsistence crisis in Amiens, 1693–4 27
Chart 3.1	The rise of towns in Central Europe, 1150–1950 73
Chart 7.1	The development of unemployment in the Netherlands and its most important trading partners, 1929–39 180
Chart 7.2	Growth in GDP and employment in the Netherlands, 1970–2013 198
Chart 7.3	GDP for several emerging economies, 1950–2018 201
Chart 7.4	Four periods of economic growth, 1900–2000 204
Chart 9.1	Stages in the Demographic Transition 250
Chart 9.2	Birth and mortality rates in the Netherlands (per thousand), 1804–2019 253
Chart 9.3	Migration to and from the Netherlands (per thousand) 1866–2018 256
Chart 9.4	Percentage of unemployment in the Netherlands during the crises of 1931, 1982 and 2009 256
Chart 9.5	Share of the total population of inhabitants born outside the Netherlands, 1600–2010 259
Chart 9.6	The Kuznets curve 264
Chart 9.7	Social origins of members of the Dutch House of Representatives, 1849–1967 266
Chart 9.8	Share of white-collar jobs in the working population, Germany and the Netherlands, 1850–1986 270
Figure 0.1	The relationships between the three basic problems in history 4
Figure 0.2	The relationships between the three basic problems in history and mental constructions 4
Figure 2.1	The pillar of the Holy Trinity in Olomouc (Czech Republic), erected to commemorate the end of a plague in 1715 28

LIST OF TEXT BOXES, MAPS, TABLES, CHARTS, AND FIGURES

Figure 2.2	Amsterdam price-list from January 1686, showing goods prices by type and/or origin 42
Figure 2.3	Ribbon mill depicted on the stamp of the Haarlem-based businessman Cornelis van den Brie, eighteenth century 49
Figure 3.1	*Riddarhuset* in Stockholm, Nobility Chamber of the Swedish Parliament, seventeenth century 70
Figure 3.2	Rioters plunder the house belonging to the tax collector on the Singel canal in Amsterdam, 1748 82
Figure 3.3	Fort Galle, Dutch East India settlement on the South-Western coast of Sri Lanka 100
Figure 4.1	Portrait of the *Dordtse Vierling* (quadruplets, including Elizabeth who died directly after birth), 1621 115
Figure 4.2	A granary with a fence and veranda in a Chinese village at the time of the Song dynasty 122
Figure 4.3	Rasp house (prison for young male criminals) in Amsterdam in the seventeenth century 129
Figure 4.4	Caricature of wig fashions in England in the late eighteenth century 141
Figure 7.1	Political cartoon on the power of Standard Oil from 1904 172
Figure 7.2	Kindleberger's spiral 182
Figure 7.3	The Mount Washington Hotel in Bretton Woods, New Hampshire 186
Figure 8.1	Dutch East Indies Army on patrol, *c.* 1935 220
Figure 8.2	Dutch poster on suffrage and pension legislation, early twentieth century 242
Figure 8.3	The Anti-Revolutionary Party as the champion of church, state, family and law, 1929 245
Figure 9.1	Advertisement poster from the 1920s 269
Figure 9.2	Women's labour in agriculture, 1898 274
Figure 9.3	Campaigning poster against alcohol abuse, 1932 280
Figure 9.4	Provos promoting the 'White bike' bicycle-sharing scheme, 1966 283

ABOUT THE AUTHORS

Karel Davids is Professor Emeritus of Economic and Social History at the Vrije Universiteit Amsterdam. His research interests are global history, maritime history and the history of knowledge, in particular the history of early modern technology. His publications in English include *The Rise and Decline of Dutch Technological Leadership. Technology, Economy and Culture in the Netherlands, 1350-1800* (2008), *Religion, Technology, and the Great and Little Divergences: China and Europe compared, c.700-1800* (2013), *Global Ocean of Knowledge, 1660-1860. Globalization and Maritime Knowledge in the Atlantic World* (2020) and (co-edited with Jan Lucassen) *A Miracle Mirrored. The Dutch Republic in European Perspective* (1995). See also https:// https://research.vu.nl/en/persons/ca-davids.

Marjolein 't Hart is Professor Emeritus of the History of State Formation in a Global Context at the Vrije Universiteit Amsterdam and research fellow at Huygens Institute for the History of the Netherlands (Amsterdam). Her research focuses on the history of and resistance to political power formation, war and economics, environmental history, urban networks and the role of money. 't Hart is the author of, among others, *The Making of a Bourgeois State. War, Politics and Finance during the Dutch Revolt* (1993) and *The Dutch Wars of Independence. Warfare and Commerce in the Netherlands, 1570–1680* (2014), and the co-author of *Globalization, Environmental Change, and Social History* (2010). See also https://research.vu.nl/en/persons/marjolein-t-hart.

Lex Heerma van Voss is research fellow at the International Institute of Social History in Amsterdam and Professor Emeritus of the History of Social Security at Utrecht University. He conducts research on the international comparative history of occupations in the period between 1600 and 2000, and on the North Sea coasts. He is the author of *De doodsklok van den goeden ouden tijd. De achturendag in de jaren twintig* (1994) and co-editor of two volumes *Wereldgeschiedenis van Nederland* (2018, 2022), *The Ashgate Companion to the history of Textile Workers, 1650–2000* (2010) and *Selling Sex in the City, Prostitution in World Cities, 1600 to the Present* (2017). See also https://iisg.amsterdam/en/about/staff/lex-heerma-van-voss.

Manon van der Heijden is Professor of Urban History at Leiden University. She specializes in the field of social history in the Early Modern period. She is the author of *Civic Duty. Public Services in the Early Modern Low Countries* (2012), *Women and Crime in Early Modern Holland* (2016) and co-editor of *The Uses of Justice in Global Perspective, 1600-1900* (2019) and *Women's Criminality in Europe, 1600-1914* (2020). See also https://www.universiteitleiden.nl/en/staffmembers/manon-van-der-heijden.

Leo Lucassen is Director of the International Institute of Social History in Amsterdam and Professor of Global Labour and Migration History at Leiden University. He specializes in migration history, urban history and sociopolitical developments in modern states. Among his publications are: *The Immigrant Threat. The Integration of Old and New Migrants in Western Europe since 1850* (2005); co-editor of *Globalising Migration History. The Eurasian Experience (16th-21st Centuries)* (2014); co-editor of *The Encyclopedia of Migration and Minorities in Europe. From the 17th Century to the Present* (2011); and co-editor of *Borders and Mobility Control in and between Empires and Nation-States* (2022). See also https://iisg.amsterdam/nl/about/staff/leo-lucassen.

Jeroen Touwen is Associate Professor of Economic and Social History at Leiden University. He wrote his doctoral thesis on the economic history of colonial Indonesia, and is now researching the economic history of the Netherlands in international comparative perspective. His publications include: *Extremes in the Archipelago. Trade and Economic Development in the Outer Islands of Indonesia, 1900–1942* (2001) and *Coordination in Transition. The Netherlands and the World Economy, 1950–2010* (2014). See also https://www.universiteitleiden.nl/en/staffmembers/jeroen-touwen.

Preface

Several years ago, we conceived a plan to write a new textbook on social and economic history. The aim was to produce a book that would give university and college students, as well as other interested readers, a concise, up-to-date overview of the current state of knowledge in this field. We would pay the requisite attention to Dutch history, of course, but always in relation to developments in other parts of the world, both within Europe and beyond, while embedded in academic theory. We bear in mind the wise words of the American baseball star 'Yogi' Berra: 'In theory there is no difference between theory and practice. In practice there is.' Drawing on the latest research, the textbook would cover a long period: a thousand years, no less. After all, when viewed from the perspective of global history and current Dutch historiography, the developments that took place before 1500 are just as important as those that occurred after 1500 or 1750. The new textbook would also reveal as many connections as possible between economic, social, political and cultural-mental developments.

The result of our enterprise, which began in 2007, is this book: *The World and the Netherlands: A Global History from a Dutch Perspective*. As the reader will immediately see from the table of contents, the book consists of two parts, each containing three chapters, an introduction and a conclusion. The first part covers the period from *c.* 1000 CE until what is known as the 'Great Divergence' between Europe and Asia in *c.* 1800. The second part covers the period between the Great Divergence and the early twenty-first century. The structure of the book is explained in the general introduction. In each chapter, in addition to the running text – which is supported by tables, charts, maps and figures – the reader will find several text boxes that highlight particular topics in more detail. These can be read in relation to the surrounding text or separately. The book concludes with a list of recommended literature and an index. There is also a supporting website (https://www.bloomsburyonlineresources.com/the-world-and-the-netherlands), where readers will find a glossary, questions about the material, files that delve into major debates and issues in the field, and an extended bibliography for each chapter.

The book is the outcome of a collaborative process between six authors, each of whom was responsible for one of the main chapters. Karel Davids wrote Chapter 2, Marjolein 't Hart Chapter 3, Manon van der Heijden Chapter 4, Jeroen Touwen Chapter 7, Leo Lucassen Chapter 8 and Lex Heerma van Voss Chapter 9. The introduction and Chapters 1, 5, 6 and 10 were written by Karel Davids and Marjolein 't Hart. Marjolein, Manon and Karel were responsible for the coordination and final editing of the book.

While writing the book, the authors frequently discussed and commented on each other's chapters. We also received helpful and inspiring feedback from the following participants in a workshop held at Columbia University, New York, in June 2010, where we presented our ideas for this textbook: Julia Adams, Carolyn Arena, Laura Cruz, Philip Gorski, Evan Haefeli, Martha Howell, Ira Katznelson, Wim Klooster, Richard Lachmann, Anne McCants, Steven Pincus, Ariel Rubin, Margaret Schotte, Pamela Smith, Carl Strikwerda, Wayne te Brake and Carl Wennerlind. In addition, helpful suggestions came from numerous colleagues, among whom are Ariadne Schmidt, Marlou Schrover and Anton Schuurman. All chapters received a thorough update for the English edition.

We are also grateful for the enthusiasm and expertise of the Bloomsbury team that made the publication of *The World and the Netherlands* possible, with Rhodri Mogford and Laura Reeves in Editorial, Emma Tranter in Production, and Joseph Kreuser and Wei Ming Kam in Marketing. In the first, and Dutch edition, we received inestimable support from Eva Wijenbergh, Juliette Geers, Aranka van der Borgh, Geert van der Meulen and other staff at Uitgeverij Boom. Vivienne Collingwood did an excellent job in translating the text into English. Her kind, proactive attitude helped us solve numerous problems regarding terminology.

On behalf of the authors,
Marjolein 't Hart, Manon van der Heijden and Karel Davids
August 2022

MAP 0.1 *Map of the Netherlands*, c. 2020.
Source: Wikimedia Commons, public domain.

Introduction

This is a textbook on economic and social history that examines the connections between developments in the world and the Netherlands between *c.* 1000 CE and the early twenty-first century. It is a new type of textbook; we aim to go beyond the old national frameworks, present Dutch history in the context of global history and take account of recent historiography.

Since the end of the Cold War (1989), the rapid expansion of the European Union and increasing globalization – as shown by the explosive growth of international capital flows, the breathtaking rise of the Internet and the phenomenal spread of mobile phone technologies, for example – it has seemed harder to achieve a clear view of the world. The 'state of the world' can no longer be summed up on a Sunday-afternoon radio talk show, as it used to be. As the connections with the outside world become denser and more complex, there is a growing need in the Netherlands and in other countries to profile ourselves more as groups, regions or nations. Increasing unpredictability has been met with loud calls for the protection of people's 'identities'.

Historiography, by contrast, has shown the opposite trend. More and more historians are moving away from the relatively closed circle of national historiography and towards the more open, spacious sphere of what is now known as 'global history', 'world history' or 'transnational history', where the traditional dividing lines between nations, epochs and sub-disciplines are gradually fading. Likewise, historians who focus on the history of a single country in a single period are increasingly examining the interconnections between their 'own' research field and the outside world, and paying more attention to comparisons.

The changes that have occurred in the world and in the Netherlands, and the relations between them, are the focus of this book. We are guided by the following questions: What are the similarities or differences between developments in the Netherlands and other countries, to what extent has Dutch history been influenced by other countries, and how far has the Netherlands influenced developments elsewhere? At certain points, the history of the Netherlands diverged remarkably from developments in the West and the rest of the world, and at times the Netherlands clearly influenced what happened in other parts of the globe. But we shall also see that the Netherlands often took paths that had been taken by other countries, too. Connections and comparisons such as these will be traced over the following chapters.

0.1
'How ordinary people lived the big changes'

In this book, we approach developments in the world and the Netherlands from the perspective of economic and social history. To quote the American historian and sociologist Charles Tilly, the objective of this approach is to describe and analyse 'how ordinary people lived the big changes'. We will therefore consider both major, fundamental changes in history, and the ways in which ordinary people experienced and reacted to them. What exactly did large-scale changes such as industrialization, globalization or the rise and fall of states involve, and why did they happen? How did these changes affect the lives of ordinary people? How did people try to respond to these developments, and how did they attempt to shape them? These are the questions that drive economic and social historians. When answering them, they tend to focus on the *collective* aspects of human existence: they examine how people form groups (or are grouped), how they act collectively, their shared experiences and opinions, how groups of people differ (or want to differ) from one another and how they enter into conflicts or make agreements with other groups. Groups can be formed on the basis of all kinds of criteria: well-being, lifestyle, power, occupation, generation, religion, sex, origin and so forth; and combinations of criteria are also possible.

A further characteristic of the economic and social historian's approach to the past is the attention paid to both the long and the short term. Economic and social history does not focus primarily on a particular event or period, but on developments. The duration of these developments can range from a few years to a number of decades or even several centuries, meaning that the traditional dividing lines between periods (the Middle Ages, the modern age, the post-war period) become less significant. Taking a long-term perspective is not only important because changes often occur very gradually, but also because events that might appear to have happened very rapidly, such as revolutions, may have roots that stretch far back into the past, and because something that started to happen a very long time ago may still resonate today. Urbanization in the Late Middle Ages and the Early Modern period, the growth of long-distance trade and the division between the Northern and the Southern Low Countries all have left their mark on present-day Dutch society.

Economic and social historians take a problem-oriented approach. They focus on specific, clearly defined historical problems that they attempt to solve in a systematic way. This is often done by using a combination of description, analysis and comparison, making frequent use of quantitative data and insights and methods from related disciplines, including sociology, economics, anthropology, geography and political science. A work of economic and social history – such as this textbook – will usually contain descriptive sections as well as tables, charts and theoretical argumentation based on social-scientific concepts. In this way, economic and social historians work at the interface between the humanities and the social and behavioural sciences.

0.2
Basic problems

Like many other textbooks on social and economic history, this book takes a problem-oriented approach. We describe and analyse the developments in the Netherlands and the rest of the world with reference to several basic problems. These are the general problems encountered by human societies; problems that people have wrestled with over the ages, regardless of time or place. These basic problems can be summarized under the headings 'income', 'power' and 'risks', and each covers a number of aspects.

a. *Income:* the problem of acquiring and distributing income. This covers questions such as: How is the economy structured? How many goods and services are produced? How is this linked to technological developments? How is wealth distributed? How could we describe the patterns of consumption? Which groups influence the acquisition and distribution of income, and in what ways?

b. *Power:* the problem of forming and distributing power. This includes questions such as: How is access to power regulated? Which groups are excluded from this? Which groups influence the degree and forms of disciplining and social control? Which groups determine frameworks of social cohesion? How does state formation work?

c. *Risks of existence:* the problem of the fragility of existence. Here we address questions such as: How are people, individually or collectively, able to manage or limit the risks of existence (illness, disability, old age, mortality, unemployment, poverty, disasters, war, etc.)? What measures can they take, or which institutions or organizations can they form to do this? To what extent are access to and the quality of facilities equal for all kinds of groups?

These three basic problems are linked, of course, because there are interchanges between them. Political power can magnify the risks of existence, for example, as in the case of war; but the government can also ensure that risks are managed more effectively or reduced, and economic growth can increase the scope for taking social measures to fight sickness and unemployment, and so forth. The interactions between these influences are shown in the following diagram (Figure 0.1).

This diagram is incomplete, however. When dealing with any problem, people's actions are shaped by their customs, traditions, ideas, convictions or beliefs. These, in turn, are shaped by their options with regard to the distribution of income and power, and the nature and extent of the risks of

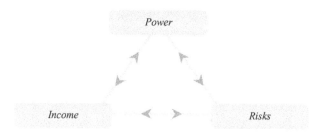

FIGURE 0.1 *The relationships between the three basic problems in history.*
© Karel Davids and Marjolein 't Hart.

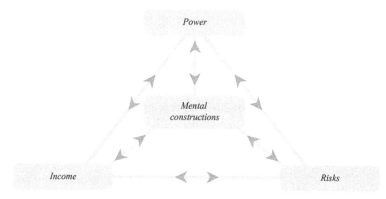

FIGURE 0.2 *The relationships between the three basic problems in history and mental constructions.*
© Karel Davids and Marjolein 't Hart.

existence. At the same time, ideas and beliefs also shape the development of wealth, power relations or social arrangements, institutions and organizations. These actions are guided by what we shall describe in this book as 'mental constructions'. In Figure 0.2 they form a separate component. As shown in the diagram, mental constructions both shape the three problem fields and are in turn influenced by the circumstances in these problem fields.

It is no accident that mental constructions lie at the heart of the diagram. Views on identity, justice or honourable behaviour, for example, cannot be separated into economic, sociocultural or sociopolitical spheres. Likewise, the economy only functions thanks to the existence of specific norms and values, such as confidence in the currency, opinions on what constitutes a fair wage or consumer preferences for certain products or services: e-books rather than paper books, designer suits rather than ready-to-wear clothing, eating out rather than microwave dinners. Moreover, mental constructions function as a connecting link: if the distribution of income is perceived as being unfair, this can have an effect on power relations and motivate people to act within sociocultural networks. The same views (e.g. in the religious sphere) can regulate access to power and institutions providing social support. A world view that presents the Netherlands as part of 'the' West or as belonging to 'the' Calvinist stronghold has far-reaching consequences for all kinds of areas, not least the political-military field. The fact that mental constructions have been placed at the heart of Figure 0.2 does not mean that they form the most important element of this book, but we shall return to them frequently in the description and analysis.

0.3
Changes, phasing and demarcation in time and space

The basic problems of income, power and risks are a constant in human society, but they can be tackled in different ways. The solutions to these problems can change over time as a result of long-term, fundamental processes, such as population growth, urbanization, increasing long-distance migration, industrialization, growth in international trade, democratization, religious reform, rationalization, state formation and nation-building, imperialism or European unification.

Researchers usually classify major changes in recent centuries under the heading of 'modernization'. Until recently, 'modernization theory' had many proponents. This theory asserts that the transformation of a 'traditional' society into an industrialized society always follows a standard pattern; that this standard pattern consists of a complex of mutually dependent changes in the demographic, economic, institutional, social and cultural spheres; and that the outcome of the transformation is roughly the same in all highly developed countries. These days, few still hold this view. Although today's societies are still regularly described as 'modern' (and the period between 1500 and 1800 is commonly referred to as 'Early Modern'), 'modernization' as an overarching concept has become obsolete in scholarship. That is because it is overly suggestive of a one-dimensional, linear course of development; as though everything used to be traditional and under developed, and that all societies will eventually reach the same 'endpoint'.

Historical research shows, though, that societies in the past were *different*, above all else, and that the path to today's societies could (and can) be taken in different ways, with different consequences for different social groups. Outcomes can vary by region. Modern societies in Western Europe may be different from those in the United States, Russia, Japan or China, but it is not possible to say which is the most 'modern'. In any case, Western European societies can no longer be seen as a general yardstick. It is better to conceive of modernity as a programme of core values pursued by certain groups, than as a description of a historical situation or historical process. These core values include 'economic growth', 'equality', 'individual freedom', 'self-determination', 'emancipation', 'mobility', or 'primacy of reason', for example, but the emphasis of the programme can differ by group, time or place. 'Modernity' is thus a plural, programmatic concept, and it is in that sense that it will be used in this book.

Another general concept that frequently appears in this book is that of 'globalization'. Globalization refers to the expansion and intensification of relationships between people on a global scale. In addition to economic facets, these relationships also have cultural, social, political or ecological aspects. Globalization need not mean that everywhere in the world increasingly resembles everywhere else; as well as homogenization or convergence, there are also trends towards divergence. Indeed, divergence can occur precisely because countries are becoming more closely intertwined: industrialization in the metropole, for example, may go hand in hand with de-industrialization in the colonies. Although globalization is therefore a rather amorphous concept, it is nevertheless a useful tool for describing certain large-scale changes that have occurred over the past millennium.

The timing, nature, causes and consequences of globalization between 1000 CE and the present day are the subject of a lively debate between historians and social scientists. Aspects of this debate will be addressed later in this book. Here it is sufficient to say that globalization, like modernization, has not followed a single, fixed pattern. Globalization did not begin in the late twentieth century, but much earlier, and the expansion and intensification of global connections took place in waves, with various ups and downs. Before the sixteenth century, in any case, Europe occupied a decentralized, even rather peripheral, place in the web of global connections; and within Europe, the Northern Netherlands played only a marginal role until the Late Middle Ages. Until that time, the most important interchanges in the world were situated in China and the Islamic world. Within Europe between 1200 and 1500, the economic centres were located in Northern and Central Italy, Southern Germany/Rhineland, Flanders/Northern France, Catalonia and the Hanseatic cities along the Baltic Sea.

From the late fifteenth century, various movements emerged that would radically change this pattern. A process of transoceanic expansion began from the Iberian Peninsula, aided by Italian knowledge and capital, leading to new connections with Africa, the Americas and Asia. Within Europe from the late sixteenth century, the economic centre of gravity shifted from the Mediterranean towards the Atlantic coast and the North Sea region, giving North-western Europe a head start in productivity and income. This development is also known as the 'Little Divergence'; 'little' in comparison to the 'Great Divergence.' In the eighteenth century, Britain emerged as a new economic centre that, as the cradle of the Industrial Revolution, contributed to the sharply growing gap in wealth that emerged between North-western Europe and Asia after 1800: the Great Divergence.